Wine

for
dummies®
A Wiley Brand

Wine

7th Edition

by Ed McCarthy
Certified Wine Educator

and

Mary Ewing-Mulligan
Master of Wine

A Wiley Brand

Wine For Dummies®, 7th Edition

Published by: **John Wiley & Sons, Inc.,** 111 River Street, Hoboken, NJ 07030-5774, www.wiley.com

Copyright © 2019 by John Wiley & Sons, Inc., Hoboken, New Jersey

Published simultaneously in Canada

No part of this publication may be reproduced, stored in a retrieval system or transmitted in any form or by any means, electronic, mechanical, photocopying, recording, scanning or otherwise, except as permitted under Sections 107 or 108 of the 1976 United States Copyright Act, without the prior written permission of the Publisher. Requests to the Publisher for permission should be addressed to the Permissions Department, John Wiley & Sons, Inc., 111 River Street, Hoboken, NJ 07030, (201) 748-6011, fax (201) 748-6008, or online at http://www.wiley.com/go/permissions.

Trademarks: Wiley, For Dummies, the Dummies Man logo, Dummies.com, Making Everything Easier, and related trade dress are trademarks or registered trademarks of John Wiley & Sons, Inc., and may not be used without written permission. All other trademarks are the property of their respective owners. John Wiley & Sons, Inc., is not associated with any product or vendor mentioned in this book.

For general information on our other products and services, please contact our Customer Care Department within the U.S. at 877-762-2974, outside the U.S. at 317-572-3993, or fax 317-572-4002. For technical support, please visit https://hub.wiley.com/community/support/dummies.

Wiley publishes in a variety of print and electronic formats and by print-on-demand. Some material included with standard print versions of this book may not be included in e-books or in print-on-demand. If this book refers to media such as a CD or DVD that is not included in the version you purchased, you may download this material at http://booksupport.wiley.com. For more information about Wiley products, visit www.wiley.com.

Library of Congress Control Number: 2018955849

ISBN 978-1-119-51273-8 (pbk); ISBN 978-1-119-51276-9 (ebk); ISBN 978-1-119-51270-7 (ebk)

Manufactured in the United States of America

C10005012_100418

Contents at a Glance

Table of Contents

Introduction

We love the amazing variety of wines in the world, and we love the way wine brings people together at the table. We want you and everyone else to enjoy wine too — regardless of your experience or your budget.

We will be the first to admit that the trappings of wine — the ceremony, the fancy language, the paraphernalia — don't make it easy for regular people to enjoy wine. You have to know strange names of grape varieties and foreign wine regions. You have to figure out whether to buy a $20 wine or an $8 wine that seem to be pretty much the same thing. You usually even need a special tool to open the bottle when you get it home — although screwcaps are being used more and more for many wines.

All the complications surrounding wine will not go away easily because wine is a very rich and complex field. But you don't have to let the complications stand in your way. With the right attitude and a little understanding of what wine is, you can begin to buy and enjoy wine. And if, like us, you decide that wine is fascinating, you can find out more and turn it into a rewarding hobby.

We hate to think that wine, which has brought so much pleasure into our lives, could be the source of anxiety for anyone. We want to help you feel more comfortable around wine. Some knowledge of wine, gleaned from the pages of this book and from our shared experiences, will go a long way toward increasing your comfort level around wine.

Ironically, what will *really* make you feel comfortable about wine is accepting the fact that you'll never know it all — and that you've got plenty of company. You see, after you really get a handle on wine, you discover that *no one* knows everything there is to know about wine. There's just too much information, and it's always changing. And when you know that, you can just relax and enjoy the stuff.

About This Book

Because wine is always changing, we have written a seventh edition of *Wine For Dummies*. We have added some new countries and regions, have updated prices, and updated information on the latest vintage years. If you already have a previous edition, you might be wondering whether you need this book. We believe that you do. We wrote the first edition of *Wine For Dummies* in 1995, and the world of wine has changed tremendously since then. It has even changed a lot since our sixth edition in 2016:

>> The wine world has an exciting new face thanks to the communities of wine lovers who share opinions, chat, and blog on Internet sites, and these voices are shaping new trends. New styles of popular wine are emerging, and a whole new approach to food and wine pairing has taken root.

>> The wines of South America have come on strong, and they offer some of the best values around. We've ramped up our coverage of Chile and Argentina to give you the inside track on these explosive wine regions.

>> Hungary, Croatia, and Slovenia have recently become a more important part of the wine world. We have added them to the 7th Edition.

>> English sparkling wines have become an important part of the sparkling wine world, even challenging Champagne.They are now in our 7th Edition.

>> Dozens of California wineries have opened, a few have gone out of business, many have improved, and a few have slipped. Our recommendations reflect all these changes.

>> Remember those prices we listed for wines worth trying in our earlier editions? Well, big surprise: Just about all those prices have increased. But we point out some bargains, especially in Parts 3, 4, and 5.

>> Several new vintages have occurred; we give you the lowdown on them throughout the book, and especially in our vintage chart in Appendix C.

We wrote this book to be an easy-to-use reference. You don't have to read it from cover to cover for it to make sense and be useful to you. Simply turn to the section that interests you and dig in. Note that sidebars, which are shaded boxes of text, consist of information that's interesting but not necessarily critical to your understanding of the topic.

Also, when this book was printed, some web addresses may have needed to break across two lines of text. If that happened, rest assured that we haven't put in any extra characters (such as hyphens) to indicate the break. So, when using one of these web addresses, just type in exactly what you see in this book, pretending that the line break doesn't exist.

Foolish Assumptions

We assume that you picked up this book for one of several reasons:

>> You know very little about wine but have a strong desire to find out more.

>> You do know something about wine, more than most people, but you want to understand it better, from the ground up.

>> You're already very knowledgeable but realize that you can always discover more.

We also assume that you don't have a lot of ego invested in wine — or maybe you do, and you're buying this book "for a friend." And we assume (correctly, we hope) that you are someone who doesn't appreciate a lot of mumbo jumbo and jargonistic language about wine — that you're someone who wants straight talk instead.

Icons Used in This Book

The pictures in the margins of this book are called *icons*, and they point out different types of information.

REAL DEAL

A bargain's not a bargain unless you really like the outfit, as they say. To our tastes, the wines we mark with this icon are bargains because we like them, we believe them to be of good quality, and their price is low compared to other wines of similar type, style, or quality. You can also interpret this logo as a badge of genuineness, as in "This Chablis is the real deal."

REMEMBER

Some issues in wine are so fundamental that they bear repeating. Just so you don't think that we repeated ourselves without realizing it, we mark the repetitions with this symbol.

TECHNICAL STUFF

This odd little guy is a bit like the 2-year-old who constantly insists on knowing "Why, Mommy, why?" But he knows that you may not have the same level of curiosity that he has. Where you see him, feel free to skip over the technical information that follows. Wine will still taste just as delicious.

TIP

Advice and information that will make you a wiser wine drinker or buyer is marked by this bull's-eye so that you won't miss it.

There's very little you can do in the course of moderate wine consumption that can land you in jail — but you could spoil an expensive bottle and sink into a deep depression over your loss. This symbol warns you about common pitfalls.

Unfortunately, some of the finest, most intriguing, most delicious wines are made in very small quantities. Usually, those wines cost more than wines made in large quantities — but that's not the only problem; the real frustration is that those wines have very limited distribution, and you can't always get your hands on a bottle even if you're willing to pay the price. We mark such wines with this icon, and hope that your search proves fruitful.

Beyond the Book

As if all the great information in this book weren't enough, you can go beyond the book for even more! Check out this book's online Cheat Sheet for a quick guide to wine pronunciation, tips on how to buy wine with confidence, and more. Just go to www.dummies.com and search for this book's title.

Where to Go from Here

We recommend that you go to Chapter 1 and start reading there. But if you don't have time because you're about to head out to a fancy restaurant, then begin at Chapter 7. If you already have bottle in hand, wine in glass, and want to know more about what you're about to sip, turn to Chapter 4 to decode the words on the label, and then consult the index to find the regional section that corresponds to your wine, to read about the wines of that area. Or — because so many wines today are named after grape varieties — start with Chapter 3, which explains the major grape varieties for wine.

In other words, start wherever you wish, closer to the beginning if you're a novice and closer to the middle if you know something about wine already. On the journey of wine appreciation, *you* get to decide how far to go and how quickly — and you get to choose the route to get there. The final destination is pleasure.

1
Getting Started with Wine

IN THIS PART . . .

Gain some basic wine knowledge to get you started on your wine-loving journey.

Find out the techniques involved in tasting wine.

Become familiar with the different varieties of grapes and the wines they make.

Understand how to read wine names and labels.

Take a sneak peek at the process of winemaking.

Chapter **1**

Wine 101

We know plenty of people who enjoy drinking wine but don't know much about it. (Been there, done that ourselves.) Knowing a lot of information about wine definitely isn't a prerequisite to enjoying it. But familiarity with certain aspects of wine can make choosing wines a lot easier, enhance your enjoyment of wine, and increase your comfort level. You can master as much or as little as you like. The journey begins here.

How Wine Happens

Wine is essentially just fermented fruit juice. The recipe for turning fruit into wine goes something like this:

1. Pick a large quantity of ripe grapes from grapevines.

You could substitute raspberries or any other fruit, but 99.9 percent of all the wine in the world is made from grapes, because grapes make the best wines.

2. Put the grapes into a clean container that doesn't leak.

3. Crush the grapes somehow to release their juice.

Once upon a time, feet performed this step.

4. Wait.

In its most basic form, winemaking is that simple. After the grapes are crushed, *yeasts* (tiny one-celled organisms that exist naturally in the vineyard and, therefore, on the grapes) come into contact with the sugar in the grapes' juice and gradually convert that sugar into alcohol. Yeasts also produce carbon dioxide, which evaporates into the air. When the yeasts are done working, your grape juice is wine. The sugar that was in the juice is no longer there — alcohol is present instead. (The riper and sweeter the grapes, the more alcohol the wine will have.) This process is called *fermentation*.

Fermentation is a totally natural process that doesn't require man's participation at all, except to put the grapes into a container and release the juice from the grapes. Fermentation occurs in fresh apple cider left too long in your refrigerator, without any help from you. We read that even milk, which contains a different sort of sugar than grapes do, develops a small amount of alcohol if left on the kitchen table all day long.

Speaking of milk, Louis Pasteur is the man credited with discovering fermentation in the 19th century. That's discovering, not inventing. Some of those apples in the Garden of Eden probably fermented long before Pasteur came along. (Well, we don't think it could have been much of an Eden without wine!)

Now if every winemaker actually made wine in as crude a manner as we just described, we'd be drinking some pretty rough stuff that would hardly inspire us to write a book about wine. But today's winemakers have a bag of tricks as big as a sumo wrestler's appetite, which is one reason no two wines ever taste exactly the same.

>> The men and women who make wine can control the type of container they use for the fermentation process (stainless steel and oak are the two main materials) as well as the size of the container and the temperature of the juice during fermentation — and every one of these choices can make a real difference in the taste of the wine.

>> After fermentation, winemakers can choose how long to let the wine *mature* (a stage when the wine sort of gets its act together) and in what kind of container. Fermentation can last three days or three months, and the wine can then mature for a couple of weeks or a couple of years or anything in between. (If you have trouble making decisions, don't ever become a winemaker.)

REMEMBER

Obviously, one of the biggest factors in making one wine different from the next is the nature of the raw material, the grape juice. Besides the fact that riper, sweeter grapes make a more alcoholic wine, different *varieties* of grapes (Chardonnay, Cabernet Sauvignon, or Merlot, for example) make different wines. Grapes are the main ingredient in wine, and everything the winemaker does, he does to the particular grape juice he has. Chapter 3 covers specific grapes and the kinds of wine they make.

THE 411 ON SULFITES

Sulfur dioxide, a compound formed from sulfur and oxygen, occurs naturally during fermentation in very small quantities. Winemakers add it, too. Sulfur dioxide is to wine what aspirin and vitamin E are to humans — a wonder drug that cures all sorts of afflictions and prevents others. Sulfur dioxide is antibacterial, preventing the wine from turning to vinegar. It inhibits yeasts, preventing sugar that has remained in a wine (if any) from fermenting in the bottle. It's an antioxidant, keeping the wine fresh and untainted by the demon oxygen. Despite these magical properties, winemakers try to use as little sulfur dioxide as possible because many of them share a belief that the less you add to wine, the better (just as many people prefer to ingest as little medication as possible).

Most wine labels in the United States carry the phrase *Contains Sulfites* (meaning sulfur dioxide) because of a law enacted to protect the extremely tiny percentage of the population who are very sensitive to sulfites. That law requires that any wine containing more than 10 parts per million of sulfites carry the *Contains Sulfites* phrase on its label. Considering that about 10 to 20 parts per million of sulfites occur naturally in wine, that covers just about every wine.

Ironically, winemakers today need to rely on sulfur dioxide less than ever before because winery hygiene is so advanced, and sulfur dioxide use is probably at an all-time low.

Actual sulfite levels in wine range from about 30 to 150 parts per million (about the same as in dried apricots); the legal max in the United States is 350. White dessert wines have the most sulfur — followed by medium-sweet white wines and sweet rosé (pink) wines — because those types of wine need the most protection. Dry white wines generally have less, and dry reds have the least.

Of course, grapes don't grow in a void. Where they grow — the soil and climate of each wine region, as well as the traditions and goals of the people who grow the grapes and make the wine — affects the nature of the ripe grapes and the taste of the wine made from those grapes. That's why so much of the information about wine revolves around the countries and regions where wine is made. In Parts 3 and 4, we cover all the world's major wine regions and their wines.

What Color Is Your Appetite?

Your inner child will be happy to know that when it comes to wine, it's okay to like some colors more than others. You can't get away with saying "I don't like green food!" much beyond your sixth birthday, but you can express a general preference for white, red, or pink wine for all your adult years.

(Not exactly) white wine

Whoever coined the term *white wine* must have been colorblind. All you have to do is look at it to see that it's not white; it's yellow (sometimes barely yellow, sometimes a deeper yellow). But we've all gotten used to the expression by now, so *white wine* it is.

White wine is wine without any red color (or pink color, which is in the red family). Yellow wines, golden wines, and wines that are as pale as water are all white wines.

Wine becomes white wine in one of two ways: First, white wine can be made from white grapes — which, by the way, aren't white. (Did you see that one coming?) *White* grapes are greenish, greenish yellow, golden yellow, or sometimes even pinkish yellow. Basically, white grapes include all the grape types that aren't dark red or dark bluish. If you make a wine from white grapes, it's a white wine.

The second way a wine can become white is a little more complicated. The process involves using red grapes — but only the *juice* of red grapes, not the grape skins. The juice of almost all red grapes has no red pigmentation — only the skins do — therefore, a wine made with only the juice of red grapes can be a white wine. In practice, though, very few white wines come from red grapes. (Champagne is one exception; Chapter 15 addresses the use of red grapes to make Champagne.)

TECHNICAL STUFF

In case you're wondering, the skins are removed from the grapes either by pressing large quantities of grapes so that the skins break and the pulpy juice flows out — sort of like squeezing the pulp out of grapes, the way kids do — or by crushing the grapes in a machine that has rollers to break the skins so that the juice can drain away.

You can drink white wine anytime you like, but typically, people drink white wine in certain situations:

>> Most people drink white wines without food or with *lighter foods,* such as fish, poultry, or vegetables. Chapter 9 covers the dynamics of pairing wines with food and has suggestions of foods to eat with white wine.

>> White wines are often considered *apéritif* wines, meaning that people consume them before dinner, in place of cocktails, or at parties. (If you ask the officials who busy themselves defining such things, an apéritif wine is a wine that has flavors added to it, as vermouth does. But unless you're in the business of writing wine labels for a living, don't worry about that. In common parlance, an apéritif wine is just what we said.)

>> A lot of people like to drink white wines when the weather is hot because they're more refreshing than red wines, and they're usually drunk chilled (the wines, not the people).

WHITE WINE STYLES: THERE'S NO SUCH THING AS PLAIN WHITE WINE

White wines fall into four general taste categories, not counting sparkling wine or the really sweet white wine that you drink with dessert (see Chapters 15 and 16 for more on each of those). If the words we use to describe these taste categories sound weird, take heart — they're all explained in Chapter 2. We also explain the styles in plentiful detail in our book *Wine Style: Using Your Senses to Explore and Enjoy Wine* (Wiley). Here are our four broad categories:

- **Fresh, unoaked whites:** These wines are crisp and light, with no sweetness and no oaky character. (Turn to Chapter 3 for the lowdown on oak.) Most Italian white wines, like Soave and Pinot Grigio, and some French whites, like Sancerre and some Chablis, fall into this category.

- **Earthy whites:** These wines are dry, fuller-bodied, unoaked or lightly oaked, with a lot of earthy character. Some French wines, such as Mâcon or whites from the Côtes du Rhône region (covered in Chapter 10), have this taste profile.

- **Aromatic whites:** These wines are characterized by intense aromas and flavors that come from their particular grape variety, whether they're *off-dry* (that is, not bone-dry) or dry. Examples include a lot of German wines and wines from flavorful grape varieties, such as Riesling or Viognier and, in some cases, Sauvignon Blanc.

- **Rich, oaky whites:** These wines are dry or fairly dry and full-bodied with pronounced oaky character. Most Chardonnays and some French wines — like many of those from the Burgundy region of France — fall into this group.

TIP

We serve white wines cool, but not ice cold. Sometimes, restaurants serve white wines too cold, and we actually have to wait a while for the wine to warm up before we drink it. If you like your wine cold, fine; but try drinking your favorite white wine a little less cold sometime, and we bet you'll discover it has more flavor that way. In Chapter 8, we recommend specific serving temperatures for various types of wine.

Red, red wine

In this case, the name is correct. Red wines really are red. They can be purple red, ruby red, or garnet, but they're red.

Red wines are made from grapes that are red or bluish in color. So guess what wine people call these grapes? Black grapes! We suppose that's because black is the opposite of white.

POPULAR WHITE WINES

These types of white wine are available almost everywhere in the United States. We describe these wines in Parts 3 and 4.

- **Chardonnay:** Can come from California, Australia, France, or almost any other place

- **Pinot Grigio** or **Pinot Gris:** Can come from Italy, France, Oregon, California, and other places

- **Prosecco:** Comes from Italy (and it's a bubbly wine)

- **Riesling:** Can come from Germany, California, New York, Washington, France, Austria, Australia, and other places

- **Sauvignon Blanc:** Can come from California, France, New Zealand, South Africa, Italy, and other places

- **Soave:** Comes from Italy

The most obvious difference between red wine and white wine is color. The red color occurs when the colorless juice of red grapes stays in contact with the dark grape skins during fermentation and absorbs the skins' color. Along with color, the grape skins give the wine *tannin*, a substance that's an important part of the way a red wine tastes. (See Chapter 2 for more about tannin.) The presence of tannin in red wines is actually the key taste difference between red wines and white wines.

Red wines vary quite a lot in style — partly because winemakers have so many ways of adjusting their red winemaking to achieve the kind of wine they want. For example, if winemakers leave the grape juice in contact with the skins for a long time, the wine becomes more *tannic* (firmer in the mouth, like strong tea; tannic wines can make you pucker). If winemakers drain the juice off the skins sooner, the wine is softer and less tannic. And heating the crushed grapes can extract color without much tannin.

TIP

Traditionally, people have consumed red wine as part of a meal or with accompanying food rather than as a drink on its own, but plenty of red wines today are made to taste delicious even without food.

Thanks to the wide range of red wine styles, you can find red wines to go with just about every type of food and every occasion when you want to drink wine. The one exception is times when you want to drink a wine with bubbles: Although bubbly red wines do exist, most bubbly wines are white or pink. In Chapter 9, we give you some tips on matching red wine with food.

One sure way to spoil the fun in drinking most red wines is to drink them too cold. Those tannins can taste really bitter when the wine is cold — just as in a cold glass of very strong tea. On the other hand, way too many restaurants serve red wines too warm. (Where do they store them? Next to the oven?) If the bottle — or the glass of wine — feels cool to your hand, that's a good temperature. For more about serving wine at the right temperature, see Chapter 8.

Rosé wines

Rosé wine is the name that wine people give to pinkish wine. These wines are made from red grapes, but they don't end up red because the grape juice stays in contact with the red skins for just a short time — only a few hours, compared to days or weeks for red wines. Because this *skin contact* (the period when the juice and the skins intermingle) is brief, rosé wines also absorb very little tannin from the skins. Therefore, you can chill these wines and drink them as you'd drink white wines.

Rosé wines are not only lighter in color than red wines, but they are also lighter in body (they feel less heavy in your mouth; Chapter 2 explains body and other taste characteristics of wine). They have a fascinating range of color, from pale orange to deep pink, depending on the grape variety that they come from. Some rosé wines are actually labeled "White [red grape name]" — "White" Zinfandel is the most common — as a marketing gimmick.

The rosé wines that call themselves *white* are fairly sweet; they are sometimes referred to as *blush* wines, although that term rarely appears on the label. Wines labeled *rosé* can be sweetish, too, but some wonderful rosés from Europe, including Champagne (and quite a few from the United States) are *dry* (not sweet). The popularity of rosé wines has varied over the years, but in the decade of the 20-teens, it is at an all-time high (about five times as popular in the U.S. now, compared to 30 years ago). Even hard-core wine lovers are discovering what a pleasure — not to mention what a versatile food partner — a good rosé wine can be.

Choosing your color

Your choice of a white wine, red wine, or pink wine will vary with the season, the occasion, and the type of food you're eating (not to mention your personal taste). Choosing a color usually is the starting point for selecting a specific wine in a wine shop or in a restaurant. As we explain in Chapters 6 and 7, most stores and most restaurant wine lists arrange wines by color before making other distinctions, such as grape varieties, wine regions, or taste categories.

Certain foods can straddle the line between white wine and red wine compatibility — grilled salmon, for example, can be delicious with either a rich white wine or a fruity red. But your personal preference for red, white, or rosé wine will often be your first consideration in pairing food with wine.

RED WINE STYLES: THERE'S NO SUCH THING AS PLAIN RED WINE, EITHER

Here are four red wine styles:

- *Soft, fruity reds* have a lot of fruitiness and fairly little tannin (like Beaujolais Nouveau wine from France, some Pinot Noir wines from California, and many under-$15 U.S. wines).

- *Mild-mannered reds* are medium-bodied with subtle flavors that are savory more than fruity (like less expensive wines from Bordeaux, France, and some inexpensive Italian reds).

- *Spicy reds* are flavorful, generally fruity wines with spicy accents and some tannin (such as some Malbecs from Argentina and Dolcettos from Italy).

- *Powerful reds* are full-bodied and tannic (such as the most expensive California Cabernets; Barolo, from Italy; Priorat, from Spain; the most expensive Australian reds; and lots of other expensive reds).

POPULAR RED WINES

You find descriptions and explanations of these popular and widely available red wines all through this book.

- **Barbera:** Comes from Italy, but can also come from other countries
- **Beaujolais:** Comes from France
- **Bordeaux:** Comes from France
- **Cabernet Sauvignon:** Can come from California, Australia, France, Chile, and other places
- **Chianti:** Comes from Italy
- **Côtes du Rhône:** Comes from France
- **Malbec:** Comes from Argentina, France, Chile and other places
- **Merlot:** Can come from California, France, Washington, New York, Chile, and other places
- **Pinot Noir:** Can come from California, France, Oregon, New Zealand, and other places
- **Zinfandel:** Usually comes from California

FIVE OCCASIONS TO DRINK ROSÉ

Here are some of our favorite reasons to drink pink:

1. When she's having fish and he's having meat (or vice versa)
2. When a red wine just seems too heavy
3. On the patio or deck on warm, sunny days
4. To wean a son/daughter, mate, friend (yourself?) off cola
5. When serving ham (hot or cold) or other pork dishes

RED WINE SENSITIVITIES

Some people complain that they can't drink red wines without getting a headache or feeling ill. Usually, they blame the sulfites in the wine. We're not doctors or scientists, but we can tell you that red wines contain far less sulfur than white wines. That's because the tannin in red wines acts as a preservative, making sulfur dioxide less necessary. Red wines do contain numerous substances derived from the grape skins that could be the culprits. Whatever the source of the discomfort, it's probably not sulfites.

Pairing food and wine is one of the most fun aspects of wine, because the possible combinations are almost limitless. (We get you started with the pairing principles and a few specific suggestions in Chapter 9.) Best of all, your personal taste rules!

Other Ways of Categorizing Wine

We sometimes play a game with our friends: We ask them, "Which wine would you want to have with you if you were stranded on a desert island?" In other words, which type of wine could you drink for the rest of your life without getting tired of it? Our own answer is always Champagne, with a capital *C* (more on the capitalization later in this section).

In a way, Champagne is an odd choice because, as much as we love Champagne, we don't drink it *every day* under normal circumstances. We welcome guests with it, we celebrate with it after our team wins a Sunday football game, and we toast our cats with it on their birthdays. We don't need much of an excuse to drink Champagne, but it's not the type of wine we drink every night.

What we drink every night is regular wine — red, white, or rosé — without bubbles. These wines have various names. In the United States, they're called *table* wines, and in Europe, they're called *light* wines. Sometimes, we refer to them as *still* wines, because they don't have bubbles moving around in them.

In the following sections, we explain the differences among three categories of wines: table wines, dessert wines, and sparkling wines.

Table wine

Table wine, or light wine, is fermented grape juice whose alcohol content falls within a certain range. Furthermore, table wine isn't bubbly. (Some table wines have a very slight carbonation but not enough to disqualify them as table wines.) According to U.S. standards of identity, table wines may have an alcohol content no higher than 14 percent; in Europe, light wine must contain from 8.5 percent to 14 percent alcohol by volume (with a few exceptions). So unless a wine has more than 14 percent alcohol or has bubbles, it's a table wine or a light wine in the eyes of the law.

The regulation-makers didn't get the number 14 by drawing it from a hat. Historically, most wines contained less than 14 percent alcohol — either because the juice didn't have enough sugar to attain a higher alcohol level or because the alcohol killed the yeasts when it reached 14 percent, halting the fermentation. That number, therefore, became the legal borderline between wines that have no alcohol added to them (table wines) and wines that might have alcohol added to them (dessert or fortified wines; see the next section).

TECHNICAL STUFF

But today, the historical phenomenon of 14 percent alcohol as the natural limit of fermentation is, well, history. Many grapes now grow in warm climates where they become so ripe and have so much natural sugar that their juice attains more than 14 percent alcohol when fermented. The use of gonzo yeast strains that continue working even when the alcohol exceeds 14 percent is another factor. Most red Zinfandels, Cabernets, and Chardonnays from California — and many red wines from almost everywhere — now have 14.5 or even 15 to 16 percent alcohol. While U.S. government definitions have not changed, the U.S. tax code has recognized the new reality by raising to 16 percent the upper limit for a wine to be taxed at the table-wine rate of excise tax, which is lower than for a higher-alcohol dessert wine. (Read about dessert wines in the next section.)

REMEMBER

Here's our own, real-world definition of table wines: They're the normal, non-bubbly wines that most people drink most of the time.

HOW TO (SORT OF) LEARN THE ALCOHOL CONTENT OF A WINE

Regulations require wineries to state a wine's alcohol percentage on the label (again, with some minor exceptions). It can be expressed in degrees, like 12.5 degrees, or as a percentage, like 12.5 percent. If a wine carries the words *Table Wine* on its label in the United States but not the alcohol percentage, it should have less than 14 percent alcohol by law.

But for wines sold within the United States — whether the wine is American or imported — there's a big catch. The labels are allowed to lie. U.S. regulations give wineries a 1.5 percent leeway in the accuracy of the stated alcohol level. If the label states *12.5 percent,* the actual alcohol level can be as high as 14 percent or as low as 11 percent. For wines with a stated alcohol level above 14 percent, the leeway is just 1 percent; a wine with a stated alcohol content of 14.5 percent, can legally fall within the 13.5 to 15.5 range.

Many winemakers have told us that wineries (their competitors, surely!) routinely understate the alcohol content of their wines. When you read a wine's label, bear in mind that the number you see is not necessarily what you get.

Dessert wine

Some wines have more than 14 percent alcohol because the winemaker added alcohol during or after the fermentation. That's an unusual way of making wine, but certain parts of the world, like the Sherry region in Spain and the Port region in Portugal, have made quite a specialty of it. We discuss those wines in Chapter 16.

Dessert wine is the legal U.S. terminology for such wines, even if they're not necessarily sweet and not necessarily consumed after dinner or with dessert. (Dry Sherry is categorized as a dessert wine, for example, but it's dry, and we drink it before dinner.) In Europe, this category of wines is called *liqueur wines,* which carries that same unfortunate connotation of sweetness.

We prefer the term *fortified,* which suggests that the wine has been strengthened with additional alcohol. But until we get elected to run things, the term will have to be *dessert wine* or *liqueur wine.*

Sparkling wine (and a highly personal spelling lesson)

Sparkling wines are wines that contain carbon dioxide bubbles. Carbon dioxide gas is a natural byproduct of fermentation, and winemakers sometimes decide to trap it in the wine. Just about every country that makes wine also makes sparkling wine. In Chapter 15, we discuss how sparkling wine is made and describe the major sparkling wines of the world.

In the United States, Canada, and Europe, *sparkling wine* is the official name for the category of wines with bubbles. Isn't it nice when everyone agrees?

Champagne (with a capital *C*) is the most famous sparkling wine — and probably the most famous *wine,* for that matter. Champagne is a specific type of sparkling wine (made from certain grape varieties and produced in a certain way) that comes from a region in France called Champagne. It is the undisputed Grand Champion of Bubblies.

Unfortunately for the people of Champagne, France, their wine is so famous that the name *champagne* has been borrowed again and again by producers elsewhere, until the word has become synonymous in people's minds with practically the whole category of sparkling wines. For example, until a recent agreement between the United States and the European Union (E.U.), U.S. winemakers could legally call any sparkling wine *champagne* — even with a capital *C*, if they wanted — as long as the carbonation was not added artificially. Even now, those U.S. wineries that were already using that name may continue to do so. (They do have to add a qualifying geographic term such as *American* or *Californian* before the word *Champagne*.)

For the French, limiting the use of the name *champagne* to the wines of the Champagne region is a *cause célèbre.* E.U. regulations not only prevent any other E.U. country from calling its sparkling wines *champagne* but also prohibit the use of terms that even *suggest* the word *champagne,* such as fine print on the label saying that a wine was made by using the "Champagne method." What's more, bottles of sparkling wine from countries outside the European Union that use the word *champagne* on the label are banned from sale in Europe. The French are that serious about Champagne.

To us, this seems perfectly fair. You'll never catch us using the word *champagne* as a generic term for wine with bubbles. We have too much respect for the people and the traditions of Champagne, France, where the best sparkling wines in the world are made. That's why we stress the capital *C* when we say Champagne. *Those* are the wines we want on our desert island, not just any sparkling wine from anywhere that calls itself champagne.

TIP

When someone tries to impress you by serving a wine labeled "champagne" that's not French, don't fall for it. Nearly all the respectable sparkling wine companies in the United States refuse to name their wines champagne, out of respect for their French counterparts. (Of course, many of California's top sparkling wine companies are actually owned by the French — so it's no surprise that *they* won't call their wines champagne — but many other companies won't use the term, either.)

Chapter **2**

A Matter of Personal Taste (Buds)

We know they're out there — the cynics who are saying, right about now, "Hey, I already know how to taste. I do it every day. All that wine-tasting humbug is just another way of making wine complicated."

And you know, in a way, those cynics are right. Anyone who can taste coffee or a cheeseburger can taste wine. All you need are a nose, taste buds, and a brain. Unless you're like our friend who lost his sense of smell from the chemicals he used every day as a cosmetology teacher, you, too, have all it takes to taste wine properly.

You also have all it takes to speak Mandarin; of course, having the ability to do something is different from knowing how to do it and applying that know-how in everyday life. In this chapter, we show you how (how to taste wine, that is — you're on your own for the Mandarin).

The Special Technique for Tasting Wine

You drink beverages every day, tasting them as they pass through your mouth. But when it comes to wine, drinking and tasting are not synonymous. Wine is much more complex than other beverages: There's more going on in a mouthful of wine. For example, most wines have a lot of different (and subtle) flavors, all at the same time, and they give you multiple simultaneous sensations, such as softness and sharpness together.

If you just drink wine by gulping it down the way you do soda, you miss a lot of what you paid for. But if you *taste* wine, you can discover its nuances. In fact, the more slowly and attentively you taste wine, the more interesting it tastes.

REMEMBER

And with that, we have the two fundamental rules of wine tasting:

1. Slow down.
2. Pay attention.

The process of tasting a wine — of systematically experiencing all the wine's attributes — has three steps, which we discuss in the following sections. The first two steps don't actually involve your mouth at all: First, you look at the wine, and then you smell it. Finally, you get to sip it.

Savoring a wine's appearance

We enjoy looking at the wine in our glass, noticing how brilliant it is and the way it reflects the light, trying to decide precisely which shade of red it is and whether it will stain the tablecloth permanently if we tilt the glass too far.

TIP

To observe a wine's appearance, tilt a (no more than half-full) glass away from you and look at the color of the wine against a white background, such as the tablecloth or a piece of paper (a colored background distorts the color of the wine). Notice how dark or how pale the wine is and what color it is. Also notice whether the wine is cloudy, clear, or brilliant. (Most wines are clear. Some *unfiltered* wines — Chapter 5 explains filtering — can be less than brilliant but shouldn't be cloudy.) Eventually, you'll begin to notice patterns, such as deeper color in younger red wines and older white wines.

If you have time, at this point you can also swirl the wine around in your glass (see the following section) and observe the way the wine runs back down the inside of the glass. Some wines form *legs* or *tears* that flow slowly down. Once upon a time, these legs were interpreted as the sure sign of a rich, high-quality wine. Today, we know that a wine's legs are a complicated phenomenon having to do with the surface tension of the wine and the evaporation rate of the wine's alcohol. If you're a physicist, feel free to show off your expertise and enlighten your fellow tasters — but otherwise, don't bother drawing conclusions from the legs.

The nose knows

After you observe a wine's appearance, you get to the really fun part of tasting wine: swirling and sniffing. This is the stage when you can let your imagination run wild, and no one will ever dare to contradict you. If you say that a wine smells like wild strawberries to you, how can anyone prove that it doesn't?

Before we explain the smelling ritual, and the tasting technique that goes along with it (described in the next section), we want to assure you that (a) you don't have to apply this procedure to every single wine you drink; (b) you won't look foolish doing it, at least in the eyes of other wine lovers (we can't speak for the rest of the human population); and (c) it's a great trick at parties to avoid talking with someone you don't like.

WARNING

To get the most out of your sniffing, swirl the wine in the glass first. But don't even *think* about swirling your wine if your glass is more than half full.

Keep your glass on the table and rotate it three or four times so that the wine swirls around inside the glass and mixes with air. Then quickly bring the glass to your nose. Stick your nose into the airspace of the glass and smell the wine. Free-associate. Is the aroma fruity, woodsy, fresh, cooked, intense, mild? Your nose tires quickly, but it recovers quickly, too. Wait just a moment and try again. Listen to your friends' comments and try to find the same things they find in the smell.

As you swirl, the aromas in the wine vaporize so that you can smell them. Wine has so many *aromatic compounds* that whatever you find in the smell of a wine is probably not merely a figment of your imagination.

The point behind this whole ritual of swirling and sniffing is that what you smell should be pleasurable to you, maybe even fascinating, and that you should have fun in the process. But what if you notice a smell that you don't like? Hang around wine geeks for a while, and you'll start to hear words like *petrol, sweaty saddle, burnt match,* and *asparagus* used to describe the aromas of some wines. "Yuck!" you say? Of course you do! Fortunately, the wines that exhibit such smells are not the wines you'll be drinking for the most part — at least not unless you really catch the wine bug. And when you do catch the wine bug, you might discover that those aromas, in the right wine, can really be a kick. Even if you don't come to enjoy those smells (some of us do, honest!), you'll appreciate them as typical characteristics of certain regions or grapes.

WARNING

Wine can also have bad smells that nobody will try to defend. It doesn't happen often, but it does happen, because wine is a natural, agricultural product with a will of its own. Often, when a wine is seriously flawed, it shows immediately in the nose of the wine. Wine judges have a term for such wines. They call them *DNPIM — Do Not Put in Mouth*. Not that you'll get ill, but why subject your taste buds to the same abuse that your nose just took? Sometimes a bad cork is to blame, and sometimes the problem lies with some issue in the winemaking or even the storage of the wine. Just rack it up to experience and open a different bottle.

REMEMBER

When it comes to smelling wine, many people are concerned that they aren't able to detect as many aromas as they think they should. Smelling wine is really just a matter of practice and attention. If you start to pay more attention to smells in your normal activities, you'll get better at smelling wine.

The mouth action

After you've looked at the wine and smelled it, you're finally allowed to taste it. This is the stage when grown men and women sit around and make strange faces, gurgling the wine and sloshing it around in their mouths with looks of intense concentration in their eyes. You can make an enemy for life if you distract a wine taster just at the moment when he's focusing all his energy on the last few drops of a special wine.

TIPS FOR SMELLING WINE

Try these techniques for getting more out of wine when you sniff:

- Be bold. Stick your nose right into the airspace of the glass where the aromas are captured.

- Don't wear a strong scent; it will compete with the smell of the wine.

- Don't knock yourself out smelling a wine when strong food aromas are present. The meat you smell in the wine could really be a stew cooking on the stove.

- Become a smeller. Smell every ingredient when you cook, everything you eat, the fresh fruits and vegetables you buy at the supermarket, even the smells of your environment — like leather, wet earth, fresh road tar, grass, flowers, your wet dog, shoe polish, and your medicine cabinet. Stuff your mental database with smells so you'll have aroma memories at your disposal when you need to draw on them.

- Try different techniques of sniffing. Some people like to take short, quick "rabbit sniffs," while others like to inhale a deep whiff of the wine's smell. Keeping your mouth open a bit while you inhale can help you perceive aromas. (Some people even hold one nostril closed and smell with the other, but we think that's a bit kinky.)

Here's the procedure to follow:

1. **Take a medium-sized sip of wine.**

2. **Hold the wine in your mouth, purse your lips, and draw in some air across your tongue, over the wine.**

   (Be utterly careful not to choke or dribble, or everyone will strongly suspect that you're not a wine expert.)

3. **Swish the wine around in your mouth as if you're chewing it.**

4. **Swallow the wine.**

The whole process should take several seconds, depending on how much you are concentrating on the wine. (Wondering what to concentrate on? The next two sections tell you, along with the section "Parlez-Vous Winespeak?" later in this chapter.)

Feeling the tastes

Taste buds on the tongue can register various sensations, which are known as the *basic tastes* — sweetness, sourness, saltiness, bitterness, and umami, a savory characteristic. Of these tastes, sweetness, sourness, and bitterness are those most commonly found in wine. By moving the wine around in your mouth, you give it a chance to hit all your taste buds so that you don't miss anything in the wine (even if sourness and bitterness sound like things you wouldn't mind missing).

WINES HAVE NOSES — AND PALATES, TOO

With poetic license typical of wine tasters, someone once dubbed the smell of a wine its *nose* — and the expression took hold. If someone says that a wine has a huge nose, he means that the wine has a very strong aroma. If he says that he detects lemon *in the nose* or *on the nose,* he means that the wine smells something like lemons.

In fact, most wine tasters rarely use the word *smell* to describe how a wine smells because the word *smell* (like the word *odor*) seems pejorative. Wine tasters talk about the wine's nose or aroma. Sometimes they use the word *bouquet,* although that word is falling out of fashion.

Just as a wine taster might use the term *nose* for the smell of a wine, he might use the word *palate* in referring to the taste of a wine. A wine's palate is the overall impression the wine gives in your mouth, or any isolated aspect of the wine's taste — as in, "This wine has a harmonious palate," or "The palate of this wine is a bit acidic." When a wine taster says that he finds raspberries *on the palate,* he means that the wine has the flavor of raspberries.

As you swish the wine around in your mouth, you're also buying time. Your brain needs a few seconds to figure out what the tongue is tasting and make some sense of it. Any sweetness in the wine often registers in your brain first; *acidity* (which, by the way, is known to normal people as *sourness*) and bitterness register subsequently. While your brain is working out the relative impressions of sweetness, acidity, and bitterness, you can be thinking about how the wine feels in your mouth — whether it's heavy, light, smooth, rough, and so on.

Tasting the smells

Until you cut your nose in on the action, all you can taste in the wine are those three sensations of sweetness, acidity, and bitterness and a general impression of weight and texture. Where have all the wild strawberries gone?

They're still there in the wine, right next to the chocolate and plums. But to be perfectly correct about it, these flavors are actually *aromas* that you taste, not through tongue contact, but by inhaling them up an interior nasal passage in the back of your mouth called the *retronasal passage* (see Figure 2-1). When you draw in air across the wine in your mouth, you're vaporizing the aromas just as you did when you swirled the wine in your glass. There's a method to this madness.

TEN AROMAS (OR FLAVORS) ASSOCIATED WITH WINE

The following are some of the most common aromas you can find in wine:

- Fruits of all sorts
- Herbs
- Flowers
- Earth
- Grass
- Tobacco
- Butterscotch
- Toast
- Vanilla
- Coffee, mocha, or chocolate

FIGURE 2-1:
Wine flavors are actually aromas that vaporize in your mouth; you perceive them through the rear nasal passage.

Retronasal passage

Nasal cavity

Nasal passage

After you go through all this rigmarole, it's time to reach a conclusion: Do you like what you tasted? The possible answers are yes, no, an indifferent shrug of the shoulders, or "I'm not sure, let me take another taste," which means that you have serious wine-nerd potential.

Parlez-Vous Winespeak?

Now we have to confess that there is one step between knowing how to taste wine and always drinking wine that you like. And it's a doozy. That step is putting taste into words. You wouldn't have to bother with this detail if only you could always choose your wines the way that customers choose cheese in a gourmet shop. ("Can I try that one? No, I don't like it; let me taste the one next to it. Good. I'll take half a pound.")

"Like/Don't like" is a no-brainer when you have the wine in your mouth. But most of the time, you have to buy the stuff without tasting it first. So unless you want to drink the same wine for the rest of your life, you're going to have to decide what you like or don't like in a wine and communicate that to another person who can steer you toward another wine you'll like.

There are two hurdles here: Finding the words to describe what you like or don't like and then getting the other person to understand what you mean. Naturally, it helps if everyone speaks the same language.

Unfortunately, Winespeak is a dialect with an undisciplined and sometimes poetic vocabulary whose definitions change all the time, depending on who's speaking. In case you really want to get into this wine thing, we treat you to some sophisticated wine language in Chapters 5 and 19. In the following sections, we provide a few basic words and concepts to get you started.

Deconstructing a wine's taste

The tastes of a wine reveal themselves sequentially as the tongue detects them and your brain registers them. We recommend that you follow the natural sequence we describe in the next sections when you try to put words to what you're tasting.

Sweetness

As soon as you put the wine into your mouth, you can usually notice sweetness or the lack of it. In Winespeak, *dry* is the opposite of sweet. Classify the wine you're tasting as either *dry, off-dry* (in other words, slightly sweet), or *sweet.*

Acidity

All wine contains acid (mainly *tartaric acid,* which exists in grapes), but some wines are more acidic than others. Acidity is a key taste factor in white wines more than in reds. For white wines, acidity is the backbone of the wine's taste (it gives the wine firmness in your mouth). White wines with a high amount of acidity feel *crisp,* and those without enough acidity feel *flabby.*

IS IT SWEETNESS OR FRUITINESS?

Beginning wine tasters sometimes describe dry wines as sweet because they confuse fruitiness with sweetness. Here's the difference:

- A wine is *fruity* when it has distinct aromas and flavors of fruit. You smell the fruitiness with your nose; in your mouth, you "smell" it through your retronasal passage (see the earlier section "Tasting the smells").

- Sweetness, on the other hand, is a tactile impression on your tongue. When in doubt, try holding your nose when you taste the wine; if the wine really is sweet, you'll be able to taste the sweetness despite the fact that you can't smell the fruitiness.

TOUCHY-FEELY

Softness and firmness are actually *textural impressions* a wine gives you as you taste it. Just as your mouth feels temperature in a liquid, it also feels texture. Some wines literally *feel* soft and smooth as they move through your mouth, while others feel hard, rough, edgy, or coarse. In white wines, acid is usually responsible for impressions of hardness or firmness (or crispness); in red wines, tannin is usually responsible. Low levels of either substance can make a wine feel pleasantly soft — or *too* soft, depending on the wine and your taste preferences. Unfermented sugar also contributes to an impression of softness, and alcohol can, too. But very high alcohol — which is fairly common in wines these days — can give a wine an edge of hardness. Initially, it's enough to notice a wine's texture, without figuring out what factor is creating that sensation.

You generally perceive acidity in the middle of your mouth — what wine-tasters call the *mid-palate*. How much you salivate after tasting a wine can be a clue to its acidity level, because high acidity triggers saliva production. You can also sense the consequences of acidity (or the lack of it) in the overall style of the wine — whether it's a tart little number or a soft and generous sort, for example. Classify the wine you're tasting as *crisp*, *soft*, or *Pillsbury Doughboy*.

Tannin

Tannin is a substance that exists naturally in the skins, seeds (or *pips*), and stems of grapes. Because red wines are fermented with their grape skins and pips, and because red grape varieties are generally higher in tannin than white varieties, tannin levels are far higher in red wines than in white wines. Aging wine in new oak barrels can also contribute tannin to wines, both reds and whites.

Have you ever taken a sip of a red wine and rapidly experienced a drying-out feeling in your mouth, as if something had blotted up all your saliva? That's tannin.

To generalize a bit, tannin is to a red wine what acidity is to a white: a backbone. Tannins alone can taste bitter, but some wine tannins are less bitter than others. Also, other elements of the wine, such as sweetness, can mask the perception of bitterness (see the section "Balance," later in this chapter). You sense tannin — as bitterness or as firmness or richness of texture — mainly in the rear of your mouth, on the inside of your cheeks, and on your gums. Depending on the amount and nature of its tannin, you can describe a red wine as *astringent*, *firm*, or *soft*.

TIP

IS IT ACID OR TANNIN?

Red wines have acid as well as tannin, and distinguishing between the two as you taste a wine can be a real challenge. When you're not sure whether you're perceiving mainly tannin or acid, pay attention to how your mouth feels *after* you swallow the wine. Acid makes you salivate (saliva is alkaline, and it flows to neutralize the acid). Tannin leaves your mouth dry.

Body

A wine's body is an impression you get from the whole of the wine — not a basic taste that registers on your tongue. It's the impression of the weight and size of the wine in your mouth, which is usually attributable mainly to a wine's alcohol. We say *impression* because, obviously, one ounce of any wine will occupy exactly the same space in your mouth and weigh the same as one ounce of any other wine. But some wines *seem* fuller, bigger, or heavier in the mouth than others. Think about the wine's fullness and weight as you taste it. Imagine that your tongue is a tiny scale and judge how much the wine is weighing it down. Classify the wine as *light-bodied, medium-bodied,* or *full-bodied.*

The flavor dimension

Wines have flavors (uh, we mean *mouth aromas*), but wines don't come in a specific flavor. Although you may enjoy the suggestion of chocolate in a red wine that you're tasting, you wouldn't want to go to a wine store and ask for a chocolaty wine, unless you don't mind the idea of people holding their hands over their mouths and trying not to laugh at you.

TIP

Instead, you should refer to *families of flavors* in wine. You have your *fruity wines* (the ones that make you think of all sorts of fruit when you smell them or taste them), your *earthy wines* (these flavors make you think of minerals and rocks, walks in the forest, turning the earth in your garden, dry leaves, and so on), your *spicy wines* (cinnamon, cloves, black pepper, or Indian spices, for example), your *herbal wines* (mint, grass, hay, rosemary, and so on), and so on, and so on. So many flavors exist in wines that we could go on and on (and we often do!), but you get the picture, don't you? (By the way, chocolate-like flavors would fall into the family of nuts or kernels, along with flavors of coffee and of nuts themselves.)

If you like a wine and want to try another wine that's similar but different (and it will always be different, we guarantee you), one method is to decide what families of flavors in the wine you like and mention that to the person selling you your next bottle. In Parts 3, 4, and 5, you find wines that fit these specific flavors.

Another aspect of flavor that's very important to consider is a wine's *flavor intensity* — how much flavor the wine has, regardless of what those flavors are. Some wines are as flavorful as a chili cheese dog, while others have flavors as subtle as ungarnished fillet of sole. Flavor intensity is a major factor in pairing wine with food, as you can read in Chapter 9, and it's also an issue in determining how much a wine appeals to you.

The Quality Issue

Did you notice, by any chance, that nowhere among the terms we use to describe wines in the previous section are the words *great, very good,* or *good?* Instead of worrying about crisp wines, earthy wines, and medium-bodied wines, wouldn't it just be easier to walk into a wine shop and say, "Give me a very good wine for dinner tonight"? Isn't *quality* the ultimate issue — or at least, quality within your price range, also known as *value?*

In fact, a good deal of wine marketing revolves around the notion of quality, except in the case of the least expensive wines. Wine producers constantly brag about the quality ratings that their wines receive from critics, because a high rating — implying high quality — translates into increased sales.

REMEMBER

However, quality wines come in all colors, all degrees of sweetness and dryness, and all flavor profiles. Just because a wine is high quality doesn't mean that you'll actually enjoy it, any more than a three-star rating means that you'll love a particular restaurant. Personal taste is simply more relevant than quality in choosing a wine.

Degrees of quality do exist among wines. But a wine's quality is not absolute: How great a wine is or isn't depends on who's doing the judging.

The instruments that measure the quality of a wine are a human being's nose, mouth, and brain, and because everyone is different, everyone has a different opinion on how good a wine is. The combined opinion of a group of trained, experienced tasters (also known as wine experts) is usually considered a reliable judgment of a wine's quality. (Turn to Chapter 19 for more about expert opinion.)

In the following sections, we explore what makes a good wine good and what makes a poor wine inferior.

TASTE IS PERSONAL

Literally! The perception of the basic tastes on the tongue varies from one person to the next. Research has proven that some people have more taste buds than others, and are, therefore, more sensitive to characteristics such as sourness or bitterness in food and beverages. The most sensitive tasters are called, somewhat misleadingly, *supertasters* — not because they're more expert, but because they perceive sensations such as bitterness more acutely. If you find diet sodas very bitter, or if you need to add a lot of sugar to your coffee to make it palatable, you might fall into this category — and you, therefore, might find many red wines unpleasant, even if other people consider them great.

What's a good wine?

A good wine is, above all, a wine that you like enough to drink, because the whole purpose of a wine is to give pleasure to those who drink it. After that, how good a wine is depends on how it measures up to a set of (more or less) agreed-upon standards of performance established by experienced, trained experts. These standards involve mysterious concepts like *balance, length, depth, complexity, finish,* and *trueness to type* (*typicity* in Winespeak), which we explain in the following sections. None of these concepts is objectively measurable, by the way.

Balance

The three words *sweetness, acidity,* and *tannin,* which we talk about in the "Parlez-Vous Winespeak?" section earlier in this chapter, represent three of the major *components* (parts) of wine. The fourth is *alcohol.* Besides being one of the reasons we often want to drink a glass of wine in the first place, alcohol is an important player in wine quality.

Balance is the relationship of these four components to one another. A wine is balanced when nothing sticks out, such as harsh tannin or too much sweetness, as you taste the wine. Most wines are balanced to most people. But if you have any pet peeves about food — if you really hate anything tart, for example, or if you never eat sweets — you might perceive some wines to be unbalanced. If you perceive them to be unbalanced, then they are unbalanced for you. (Professional tasters know their own idiosyncrasies and adjust for them when they judge wine.)

REMEMBER

Tannin and acidity are *hardening elements* in a wine (they make a wine taste firmer and less giving in the mouth), while alcohol and sugar (if any) are *softening elements.* The balance of a wine is the interrelationship of the hard and the soft aspects of a wine — and a key indicator of quality.

BALANCE IN ACTION

TIP

To experience the principle of taste-balance firsthand, try this: Make a very strong cup of black tea and chill it. When you sip it, the cold tea will taste bitter, because it's very tannic. Now add lemon juice; the tea will taste astringent (constricting the pores in your mouth), because the acid of the lemon and the tannin of the tea are accentuating each other. Now add a lot of sugar to the tea. The sweetness should counterbalance the acid-tannin impact, and the tea will taste softer and more agreeable than it did before.

Length

When we call wines *long* or *short*, we're not referring to the size of the bottle or how quickly we empty it. *Length* describes a wine that gives an impression of going all the way on the palate — you can taste it across the full length of your tongue — rather than stopping short halfway through your tasting of it. Many wines today are very *upfront* on the palate — they make a big impression as soon as you taste them, but they don't go the distance in your mouth. In other words, they're *short*. Length is increasingly used also to describe a wine with a long after-taste. (See the section, "Finish," just ahead.) Length in the mouth can more precisely be called *palate length*, to avoid confusion. Long palate length is a sure sign of high quality.

Depth

Depth is another subjective, unmeasurable attribute of a high-quality wine. We say a wine has *depth* when it seems to have a dimension of verticality — that is, it doesn't taste flat and one-dimensional in your mouth. A "flat" wine can never be great.

Complexity

Nothing is wrong with a simple, straightforward wine, especially if you enjoy it. But a wine that keeps revealing different things about itself, always showing you a new flavor or impression — a wine that has *complexity* — is usually considered better quality. Generally, experts use the term *complexity* specifically to indicate that a wine has a multiplicity of aromas and flavors; some people use the term it in a more holistic (but less precise) sense, to refer to the total impression a wine gives you, but this use is becoming uncommon.

Finish

The impression a wine leaves in the back of your mouth and in your throat after you swallow it is its *finish* or *aftertaste*. In a good wine, you can still perceive the wine's flavors, such as fruitiness or spiciness, at that point. The more enduring the positive flavor perception is, the *longer* the finish is. Some wines may finish *hot*, because of high alcohol, or *bitter*, because of tannin — both shortcomings. Or a wine may have nothing much at all to say for itself after you swallow, which tells you that it is probably not a great wine.

Typicity

In order to judge whether a wine is true to its type, you have to know how that type of wine is supposed to taste. So you have to know the textbook characteristics of wines made from the major grape varieties and wines of the world's classic wine regions. (For example, the Cabernet Sauvignon grape typically has an aroma and flavor of black currants, and the French white wine called Pouilly-Fumé typically has a slight gunflint aroma.) Turn to Chapter 3 and Parts 3, 4, and 5 for all those details.

What's a bad wine?

TIP

Strangely enough, the right to declare a wine *good* because you like it doesn't carry with it the right to call a wine *bad* just because you don't. In this game, you get to make your own rules, but you don't get to force other people to live by them.

The fact is that very few bad wines exist in the world today. And many of the wines we could call *bad* are actually just bad *bottles* of wine — unlucky bottles that were handled badly so that the good wine inside them got ruined.

WARNING

Here are some characteristics that everyone agrees indicate a bad wine (or a bad bottle). We hope you never meet one.

>> **Vinegar:** In the natural evolution of things, wine is just a passing stage between grape juice and vinegar. Most wines today remain in the wine stage because of technology or careful winemaking. If you find a wine that has crossed the line toward vinegar, it's bad wine.

>> **Chemical or bacterial smells:** The most common are acetone (nail polish thinner) and sulfur flaws (rotten eggs, burnt rubber, bad garlic). Bad wines.

>> **Oxidized wine:** This wine smells flat, inexpressive, or maybe cooked, and it tastes the same. It might have been a good wine once, but air — oxygen — got in somehow and killed the wine. Bad bottle.

>> **Cooked aromas and taste:** When a wine has been stored or shipped in heat, it can actually taste cooked or baked as a result (wine people use the term *maderized* for such wines). Often there's telltale leakage from the cork, or the cork has pushed up a bit inside the bottle. Bad bottle. (Unfortunately, every

other bottle of that wine that experienced the same shipping or storage will also be bad.)

>> **Corky wine:** The most common flaw, *corkiness* comes across as a smell of damp cardboard that gets worse with air, along with diminished flavor intensity. It's caused by a defective cork, and any wine in a bottle that's sealed with a cork is at risk for it. Bad bottle. (Fortunately, only a very small percentage of wines are corky.)

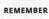

REMEMBER

Let's not dwell too long on what can go wrong with a wine. If you find a bad wine or a bad bottle — or even a wine that's considered a good wine, but you don't like it — just move on to something you like better. Drinking a so-called great wine that you don't enjoy is as time-wasting as watching a television show that bores you. Change the channel. Explore.

Chapter **3**

Pinot Envy and Other Secrets about Grape Varieties

We love to visit wine country. Gazing across manicured rows of grapevines in Napa Valley or pondering craggy terraces of rugged hillside vines in Portugal inspires us — and reinforces for us the fact that wine is an agricultural product, born of the earth, the grapevine, and the hard work of humans. Literally and emotionally, grapes are the link between the land and the wine. As you read in this chapter, grapes also happen to give us one of the easiest ways of classifying wine and making sense of the hundreds of different types of wine that exist.

The Importance of Grape Varieties

Grapes are the starting point of every wine. The grapes that make a particular wine dictate the genetic structure of that wine and how it will respond to everything the winemaker does to it. Think back to the last wine you drank. What color was it? If it was white, the odds are that's because it came from white grapes; if it was pink or red, that's because the wine came from red grapes. Did it smell herbal or earthy or fruity? Whichever, those aromas came mainly from the grapes. Was it firm and tannic or soft and voluptuous? Thank the grapes — with a nod to Mother Nature and the winemaker.

REMEMBER

The specific grape variety (or varieties) that makes any given wine is largely responsible for the sensory characteristics the wine offers — from its appearance to its aromas, flavors, and alcohol-tannin-acid profile. How the grapes grow — the amount of sunshine and moisture they get, for example, and how ripe they are when they're harvested — is also a factor and can emphasize certain grape characteristics rather than others. So can winemaking processes, such as oak aging (see Chapter 5). Each type or *variety* of grape reacts in its own way to the farming and winemaking techniques that it faces.

Of genus and species

By *grape variety*, we mean the fruit of a specific type of grapevine: the fruit of the Cabernet Sauvignon vine, for example, or of the Chardonnay vine.

TECHNICAL STUFF

The term *variety* actually has specific meaning in scientific circles. A variety is a subdivision of a species. Most of the world's wines are made from grape varieties that belong to the species *vinifera* — itself a subdivision of the genus *Vitis*. This species originated in Europe and western Asia; other distinct species of *Vitis* are native to North America.

Grapes of other species can make wine; for example, the Concord grape, which belongs to the native American species *Vitis labrusca*, makes Concord wine and also grape juice and jelly. But the number of non-*vinifera* wines is small because the flavor of those grapes is less popular in wine.

A variety of varieties

Snowflakes and fingerprints aren't the only examples of Nature's infinite variety. Within the genus *Vitis* and the species *vinifera*, as many as 10,000 varieties of wine grapes exist. If wine from every one of these varieties were commercially available and you drank the wine of a different variety every single day, it would take you more than 27 years to experience them all!

Not that you would want to. Within those 10,000 varieties are grapes that have the ability to make extraordinary wine, grapes that tend to make very ordinary wine, and grapes that only a parent could love. Most varieties are obscure grapes whose wines rarely enter into international commerce.

THE PHYLLOXERA THREAT

If endangered-species lists had existed at the end of the 19th century, *Vitis vinifera* certainly would have been on them. The entire species was nearly eradicated by a tiny louse called *phylloxera* that immigrated to Europe from America and proceeded to feast on the roots of vinifera grapevines, wiping out vineyards all across the continent.

To this day, no remedy exists to protect vinifera roots from phylloxera. What saved the species was grafting vinifera vines onto rootstocks of native American species that are resistant to the bug. The practice of grafting the fruit-bearing part of *Vitis vinifera* onto the rooting part of other, phylloxera-resistant species continues today everywhere in the world where phylloxera is present and fine wine is made. Miraculously, each grape variety maintains its own character despite the fact that its roots are alien.

An extremely adventuresome grape nut who has plenty of free time to explore the back roads of Spain, Portugal, Italy, and Greece might be able to encounter only 2,000-plus different grape varieties (over five years' worth of drinking) in his lifetime. The grape varieties you might encounter in the course of your normal wine enjoyment probably number fewer than 50.

How grapes vary

All sorts of attributes distinguish each grape variety from the next. These attributes fall into two categories, which we informally call personality traits and performance factors. *Personality traits* are the characteristics of the fruit itself — its flavors, for example. *Performance factors* refer to how the grapevine grows, how its fruit ripens, and so forth.

Personality traits of grape varieties

REMEMBER

Skin color is the most fundamental distinction among grape varieties. Every grape variety is considered either a white variety or a red (or black) one, according to the skin color of the ripe grapes. (A few red-skinned varieties are further distinguished by having red pulp rather than white pulp, but almost all red varieties have white pulp.) Within the white and black categories, each grape variety has its own hue.

Individual grape varieties also differ from one another in other ways:

>> **Aromatic compounds:** Some grapes (like Muscat) contribute floral aromas and flavors to their wines, for example, while others contribute herbaceous notes (as Sauvignon Blanc can) or fruity character. Some grapes have neutral aromas and flavors and, therefore, make fairly neutral wines.

- » **Acidity levels:** Some grapes are naturally disposed to higher acid levels than others, which makes for crisper, leaner wines.

- » **Thickness of skin and size of the individual grapes (called _berries_):** Black grapes with thick skins naturally have more tannin than those with thin skins; ditto for small-berried varieties compared to large-berried varieties, because their skin-to-juice ratio is higher. More tannin in the grapes translates into a firmer, more tannic red wine.

The composite personality traits of any grape variety are fairly evident in wines made from that grape. A Cabernet Sauvignon wine is usually more tannic and slightly lower in alcohol than a comparable Merlot wine, for example, because that's the nature of those two grapes.

Performance factors of grape varieties

How a particular grape variety performs in the field is vitally important to the grape grower because the vine's growth patterns determine how easy or challenging that variety will be to cultivate in a particular site. The issues include

- » How much time a variety typically needs to ripen its fruit. (In regions with short growing seasons, early-ripening varieties do best.)

- » How dense and compact the grape bunches are. (In warm, humid conditions, dense bunches can have mildew problems.)

- » How much vegetation a particular variety tends to have. (In fertile soils, a vine that's disposed to growing a lot of leaves and shoots can have so much vegetation that the grapes don't get enough sun to ripen.)

THE ROUTE TO RIPENESS

When grapes are not yet ripe, they contain high amounts of acid and very little sugar — which is true for any fruit — and their flavor is tart. As ripening progresses, they become sweeter and less acidic (although they always retain some acid), and their flavors become richer and more complex. Their skins get thinner, and even their seeds and stems "ripen." In red grape varieties, the tannin in the skins, stems, and pips (seeds) becomes richer and less astringent. The stage of ripeness that the grapes attain before being harvested is a big factor in the style of a wine.

THE MARRIAGE OF GRAPEVINE AND SOIL

One key factor in grape variety performance is the soil of the vineyard. Over the centuries, some classic compatibilities between grape varieties and types of soil have become evident: Chardonnay in limestone or chalk, Cabernet Sauvignon in gravelly soil, Pinot Noir in limestone, and Riesling in slatey soil. At any rate, these are the soils of the regions where these grape varieties perform at their legendary best.

Soil affects a grapevine in several ways: It provides nutrition for the grapevine; it can influence the temperature of the vineyard; and it's a water-management system for the plant.

A safe generalization is that the best soils are those that have good drainage and aren't particularly fertile. (An extreme example is the soil — if we can call it that — of the Châteauneuf-du-Pape district in France's Rhône Valley: It's just stones.) The wisdom of the ages dictates that the grapevine must struggle to produce the best grapes, and well-drained, less fertile soils challenge the vine to struggle, regardless of the grape variety.

TECHNICAL STUFF

The reasons some grape varieties perform brilliantly in certain places (and make excellent wine as a result) are extremely complex. The amount of heat and cold, the amount of wind and rain (or lack of it), and the slant of the sun's rays on a hillside of vines are among the factors affecting a vine's performance. In any case, no two vineyards in the world have precisely the same combination of these factors — precisely the same *terroir* (see Chapter 4). The issue simply defies simple generalizations.

Grape royalty

Bees have their queens, gorillas have their silverbacks, and humans have their royal families. The grape kingdom has nobles, too — at least as interpreted by the people who drink the wine made from those grapes. *Noble* grape varieties (as wine people call them) have the potential to make great — not just good — wine. Every noble grape variety can claim at least one wine region where it's the undisputed king. The wines made from noble grapes on their home turf can be so great that they inspire winemakers in far-flung regions to grow the same grape in their own vineyards. The noble grape might prove itself noble there, too, but frequently it doesn't. Adaptability isn't a prerequisite of nobility.

Classic examples of noble grape varieties at their best are

>> The Chardonnay grape and the Pinot Noir grape in Burgundy, France

>> The Cabernet Sauvignon grape in Bordeaux, France

>> The Syrah grape in France's Northern Rhône Valley

>> The Chenin Blanc grape in France's Loire Valley

>> The Nebbiolo grape in Piedmont, Italy

>> The Sangiovese grape in Tuscany, Italy

>> The Riesling grape in the Mosel and Rheingau regions of Germany

A Primer on White Grape Varieties

This section includes descriptions of 14 white *vinifera* varieties whose wines we see a lot today. In describing the grapes, we naturally describe the types of wine that are made from each grape. These wines can be varietal wines or place-name wines that don't mention the grape variety anywhere on the label (a common practice for European wines; see Chapter 4). These grapes can also be blending partners for other grapes, in wines made from multiple grape varieties. We discuss these wines in the rough order of their importance. (Turn to Chapter 2 for a quick review of some of the descriptors we use in this section.)

Chardonnay

Chardonnay is an elite grape variety thanks to its role in producing the greatest dry white wines in the world and the greatest sparkling wines — white Burgundies, in the first case, and Champagnes (where it's usually part of a blend), in the second case. Today, it also ends up in a huge amount of everyday wine. The Chardonnay grape grows in practically every wine-producing country of the world for two reasons: It's adaptable to a wide range of climates, and the name *Chardonnay* on a wine label is a surefire sales tool.

Traditional Chardonnay winemaking involves using oak barrels to ferment the juice or age the wine, and the oak influences the wine's taste. The process can bring smoky, toasty flavors to the wine and diminish the wine's fruitiness. But many Chardonnays these days are either *unoaked* or made in such a way that the oak influence is minor. (See Chapter 5 for more on oak.)

TIP

Chardonnay itself has fruity aromas and flavors that range from apple — in cooler wine regions — to tropical fruits, especially melon or pineapple, in warmer regions. Chardonnay also can display subtle earthy aromas, such as mushroom or minerals (a savory note). Chardonnay wine has medium to high acidity and is generally full-bodied. Classically, Chardonnay wines are dry, but most of the inexpensive Chardonnays these days are actually somewhat sweet.

The top Chardonnay-based wines (except for most Champagnes and similar bubblies) are 100 percent Chardonnay. But less expensive wines that are labeled *Chardonnay* — those selling for less than $12 a bottle in the United States, for example — are likely to have some other, far less distinguished grape blended in, to help reduce the cost of making the wine. (Chapter 4 explains the regulations governing grape variety blending.)

Riesling

The great Riesling wines of Germany and the Alsace region of France have put the Riesling grape on the map as one of the world's greatest varieties. Riesling shows its real class in a few other places, but certainly not everywhere. Austria, Australia's Clare Valley and Eden Valley regions, and New York's Finger Lake region are among the few.

In some ways, Riesling is the antithesis of Chardonnay. While Chardonnay is often oaky, Riesling almost never is; while Chardonnay can be full-bodied and rich, Riesling is more often light-bodied, crisp, and refreshing. Riesling's fresh, vivid personality can make many Chardonnays taste clumsy in comparison.

REMEMBER

Trademarks of Riesling are high acidity, low to medium alcohol levels, and aromas/flavors that range from ebulliently fruity to flowery to minerally.

TIP

The common perception of Riesling wines is that they're sweet, and many of them are — but plenty of them aren't. (Riesling grapes can be *vinified* — made into wine — either way, according to the style of wine a producer wants to make.) And some Riesling wines don't taste as sweet as they might technically be, because their high acidity undercuts the impression of sweetness. Look for the word *trocken* (meaning dry) or *halb-trocken* on German Riesling labels and the word *dry* on U.S. labels if you prefer the dryer style of Riesling. In general, though, we suggest that you not get hung up on the sweetness issue and just focus on how delicious Riesling can be.

TIP

If you consider yourself a trendsetter, check out the Riesling section of your wine shop rather than the Chardonnay aisle. And definitely look for Riesling wines in top restaurants, because they can be delicious with lighter but flavorful foods.

Sauvignon Blanc

Sauvignon Blanc is a white variety with very distinctive character. It's high in acidity and has pronounced aromas and flavors. Besides herbaceous notes (sometimes referred to as *grassy*), Sauvignon Blanc wines display mineral aromas and flavors, vegetal character, or — in certain climates — fruity character, such as ripe melon, figs, or passion fruit. The wines are light- to medium-bodied and dry or dryish. Most of them are unoaked.

France has two classic wine regions for the Sauvignon Blanc grape: the Loire Valley, where the two best-known Sauvignon wines are called Sancerre and Pouilly-Fumé (described in Chapter 10), and Bordeaux. In Bordeaux, Sauvignon Blanc is sometimes blended with Sémillon (described in Table 3-1 in the later section "Other white grapes"); some of the Bordeaux wines that are blends of the two grapes and fermented in oak are among the great white wines of the world.

New Zealand's Sauvignon Blanc wines are particularly renowned for their intensely flavorful style. Sauvignon Blanc is also important in northeastern Italy, South Africa, Chile, and parts of California (sometimes labeled as *Fumé Blanc*).

Pinot Gris/Pinot Grigio

Pinot Gris (pronounced *gree*) is one of several grape varieties called *Pinot:* Others include Pinot Blanc (white Pinot), Pinot Noir (black Pinot), and Pinot Meunier (we don't know how that one translates). Pinot Gris (gray Pinot), called *Pinot Grigio* in Italian, is considered a white grape, although its skin color is coppery pink, and unusually dark for a white variety.

Pinot Gris wines are usually not oaky. Those labeled Pinot Grigio typically are light-bodied and have fairly neutral aromas and flavors, while those called Pinot Gris tend to have more body and more flavor, such as notes of peach, peach-stone, or orange rind.

Pinot Gris is an important grape throughout northeastern Italy, but the only region in France where Pinot Gris figures prominently is Alsace, where it really struts its stuff. Oregon makes a signature style of Pinot Gris that's light, flavorful, and often slightly spritzy. California versions are mainly mass-market wines labeled Pinot Grigio and modeled after the Italian style — but they're less dry, more flavorful, and softer in acidity than the Italian originals.

Other white grapes

Table 3-1 describes some other grapes whose names you see on wine labels or whose wine you could drink in place-name wines without realizing it.

TABLE 3-1   ## Other White Grapes and Their Characteristics

Grape Type	Characteristics
Albariño	An aromatic grape from the northwestern Spanish region of Rías Baixas and Portugal's northerly Vinho Verde region, where it's called Alvarinho. It makes medium-bodied, crisp, stony- peachy- and appley-tasting, usually unoaked white wines whose high glycerin gives them silky texture.
Arneis (ahr-*nase*)	A local variety from the Piedmont region of northwestern Italy, where white varieties are uncommon. It makes soft, flavorful wines with notes of melons, almonds, and flowers.
Chenin Blanc	A noble grape in the Loire Valley of France, for Vouvray and other wines. The best wines have high acidity and a fascinating oily-ish texture (they feel viscous in your mouth). A few good dry Chenin Blanc wines come from California. In South Africa, the wine is historically called Steen.
Gewürztraminer (geh-*vairtz*-trah-mee-ner)	A wonderfully exotic grape that makes fairly deep-colored, full-bodied, soft white wines with aromas and flavors of roses and lychee fruit. France's Alsace region is a classic domain of this variety; the wines have pronounced floral and fruity character but are fairly dry. Italy's Alto Adige region makes dry, minerally Gewürztraminer, as do a few wineries in California and New York.
Grüner Veltliner	A native Austrian variety that boasts complex aromas and flavors (vegetal, spicy, mineral), rich texture, and usually substantial weight.
Muscat/Moscato	An aromatic grape that makes Italy's sparkling Asti (which, incidentally, tastes exactly like ripe Muscat grapes). Extremely pretty floral aromas. Alsace and Austria make a dry Muscat wine, and in lots of places (southern France, southern Italy, Australia) it makes a delicious, sweet dessert wine. Moscato (the Italian name) from California and Australia is a hugely popular mass-market wine in the U.S.
Pinot Blanc	Fairly neutral in aroma and flavors yet can make wines with character. High acidity and low sugar levels translate into dry, crisp, medium-bodied wines. Alsace, Austria, northern Italy, and Germany are the main production zones.
Sémillon (seh-mee-yohn)	Sauvignon Blanc's classic blending partner and a good grape in its own right. Sémillon wine is low in acid relative to Sauvignon Blanc and has attractive but subtle aromas — lanolin sometimes—although it can be slightly herbaceous when young. A major grape in Australia, and southwestern France, including Bordeaux (where it's the key player in the dessert wine, Sauternes).
Verdicchio	A grape from Italy's Adriatic coast that makes varietally-labeled wine with medium body, crisp acidity, and aromas/flavors of lemon and sea air.
Viognier (vee-ohn-yay)	A grape from France's Rhône Valley that's grown in California, the south of France, South America, and elsewhere. Floral aroma, delicately apricot-like flavor, medium- to full-bodied with low acidity.

A Primer on Red Grape Varieties

If you love red wine, lucky you! You have a wide range from which to choose, because so many red grape varieties make good quality, interesting wines. Some of these varieties grow just about everywhere, while others are specialties of certain countries or regions. You'll encounter these grapes in varietal wines, place-name wines, and sometimes in blends. (See Chapter 4 for a chart listing the grape varieties of major place-name wines. Also, check out Chapter 2 for a guide to some of the descriptors we use in this section.)

International superstars

Four red grape varieties are so renowned that winemakers all over the world have tried their hands at growing them and making wine from them. Read on to meet these four superstars.

Cabernet Sauvignon

Cabernet Sauvignon is a noble grape variety that grows well in many climates, except very cool areas. It became famous through the age-worthy red wines of the Médoc district of Bordeaux (which also contain Merlot and Cabernet Franc, in varying proportions; see Chapter 10). But today, California is an equally important region for Cabernet Sauvignon — not to mention Washington, Australia, South Africa, Chile, Argentina, and so on.

The Cabernet Sauvignon grape makes medium- to full-bodied wines that are high in tannin. The textbook descriptor for Cabernet Sauvignon's aroma and flavor is *black currants* or *cassis*. Many of the finest wines have a marked note of savory minerality, and many have toasty or smoky aromas and flavors from oak.

TIP

Cabernet Sauvignon wines come in all price and quality levels. The least-expensive versions are usually fairly soft and very fruity. The best wines are rich and firm with great depth and classic, concentrated Cabernet flavor. Serious Cabernet Sauvignons can age for 15 years or more.

Because Cabernet Sauvignon is fairly tannic (and because of the blending precedent in the home region of Bordeaux), winemakers often blend it with other grapes; usually Merlot — being less tannic — is considered an ideal partner. Australian winemakers have an unusual practice of blending Cabernet Sauvignon with Syrah. (More on that in Chapter 14.)

TIP

Cabernet Sauvignon often goes by just its first name, *Cabernet* (although it isn't the only Cabernet) or even by its nickname, *Cab*.

Merlot

Deep color, full body, relatively high alcohol, and soft tannin are the characteristics of wines made from the Merlot grape. The aromas and flavors can be plummy or sometimes chocolatey, or they can suggest tea leaves.

TIP

Some wine drinkers find Merlot easier to like than Cabernet Sauvignon because it's less tannic. (But some winemakers feel that Merlot isn't satisfactory in its own right, and thus often blend it with Cabernet Sauvignon, Cabernet Franc, or both.) Merlot makes both inexpensive, simple wines and, when grown in the right conditions, very serious wines.

Merlot is actually the most-planted grape variety in France's Bordeaux region. Merlot is also important in Washington, California, New York's Long Island district, northeastern Italy, and Chile, among other regions.

Pinot Noir

Cabernet is the sensible wine to make — a good, steady, reliable wine that doesn't give the winemaker much trouble and can achieve excellent quality — while Pinot Noir is finicky, enigmatic, and challenging. But a great Pinot Noir can be one of the greatest wines ever.

The prototype for Pinot Noir wine is red Burgundy, from France, where tiny vineyard plots yield rare treasures of wine made entirely from Pinot Noir. Oregon, California, New Zealand, and parts of Australia, Chile, and Slovenia also produce good Pinot Noir. But Pinot Noir's production is relatively limited, because this variety is very particular about climate and soil.

Pinot Noir wine is lighter in color than Cabernet or Merlot. It has fairly high alcohol, medium to high acidity, and medium to low tannin (although oak barrels can contribute additional tannin to the wine). Its flavors and aromas can be very fruity — often like a mélange of red berries and black berries — or earthy and woodsy, depending on how it's grown and/or vinified. (You can find Pinot Noir wines in a wide variety of styles.) Pinot Noir is rarely blended with other grapes in making red wine, but most Champagnes combine Pinot Noir with Chardonnay. (Chapter 15 explains how a red grape can make a white sparking wine.)

Syrah/Shiraz

The northern part of France's Rhône Valley is the classic home for great wines from the Syrah grape, but these days, Australia can be considered the grape's second home. Syrah also grows in Washington, California, Italy, Spain, Chile, Argentina, Israel, Greece — you name it.

Syrah produces deeply colored wines with full body, firm tannin, and aromas/flavors that can suggest berries, and sometimes smoked meat, black pepper, tar, or even burnt rubber (believe it or not). In Australia, Syrah (called Shiraz) comes in several styles; some Shirazes are charming, vibrantly fruity wines that are quite the opposite of the northern Rhône's powerful Syrah wines, such as Hermitage and Côte-Rôtie, while others are even more powerful than those classic French wines. Turn to Chapter 14 for more on Shiraz.

Syrah doesn't require any other grape to complement its flavors, although in Australia, it's often blended with Cabernet, and in the southern Rhône Valley, it's often part of a blended wine with Grenache and other varieties (see the later section "Other red grapes" for more about Grenache).

Local heroes

Some red grape varieties don't translate well outside their home regions, usually because growing conditions elsewhere aren't ideal. But they can make exciting wines on their home turf — wines that offer a terrific change of pace from the more standard "international" red varieties. Here are five of these varieties, in random order.

Zinfandel

Zinfandel is one of the oldest grapes in California. Its aura is enhanced by its mysterious history: For decades, authorities were uncertain of its origins and thought that it might exist only in the United States. DNA research finally proved that Zinfandel is an obscure Croatian grape called Crljenak Kastelanski, as is Italy's Prmitivo variety. (In case you're wondering, that's pronounced soorl-*yen*-ak kash-tel-*ahn*-ski.)

BURIED IN THE BLEND

Knowing the grape variety or varieties of a wine — either because it's the name of the wine, or because you remember which grape varieties are approved for use in the wine's specific region — can really boost your understanding of that wine. But a big trend today is blended wines, which contain the juice of several varieties; only the winemaker knows which varieties are in the blend (and he's not telling). The best approach with wines like that is to just taste them and decide whether you like them or not — whatever they might be.

Zin — as lovers of red Zinfandel call it — makes rich, dark wines that are high in alcohol and medium to high in tannin. They can have a blackberry or raspberry aroma and flavor, a spicy or tarry character, or even a jammy flavor. Some Zins are lighter than others and meant to be enjoyed young, and some are serious wines with a tannin structure that's built for aging. (You can tell which is which by the price.) The Zinfandel grape also makes the popular pink wine called White Zinfandel.

Nebbiolo

Outside of scattered sites in northwestern Italy — mainly the Piedmont region — Nebbiolo just doesn't make remarkable wine. But the extraordinary quality of Barolo and Barbaresco, two Piedmont wines, proves what greatness Nebbiolo can achieve under the right conditions.

The Nebbiolo grape is high in both tannin and acid, which can make a wine tough. Fortunately, the grape also gives enough alcohol to soften the wine. Its wines can be deep in color when young but can develop orangey tinges within a few years. Its complex aroma is fruity (strawberry, cherry), earthy and woodsy (tar, truffles), herbal (mint, eucalyptus, anise), and floral (roses).

TIP

Lighter versions of Nebbiolo are meant to be consumed young — wines labeled *Nebbiolo d'Alba* or *Roero,* and some wines labeled *Nebbiolo Langhe,* for example — while Barolo and Barbaresco are wines that really deserve a *minimum* of 8 years' age before drinking.

Sangiovese

Sangiovese is an Italian grape that excels in the Tuscany region of Italy, especially in the Brunello di Montalcino and Chianti Classico districts. Sangiovese makes wines that are medium to high in acidity and firm in tannin; the wines can be light-bodied to full-bodied, depending on exactly where the grapes grow and how the wine is made. The aromas and flavors of the wines are fruity — especially red cherry, often tart cherry — with floral nuances of violets and sometimes a slightly nutty character.

Tempranillo

Tempranillo is Spain's candidate for greatness. It gives wines deep color, fairly low acidity, and only moderate alcohol. Modern renditions of Tempranillo from the Ribera del Duero region and elsewhere in Spain prove what depth of color and fruit intensity this grape has. In the most traditional wines, such as some in the Rioja region, much of the grape's color and flavor is subdued by long wood aging and by blending with varieties that lack color, such as Grenache.

GRAPE VARIETIES THAT SHOULD BE BETTER-KNOWN

Many grape varieties are considered minor in the big picture of the wine world but are worth knowing about. If you encounter wines made from any of the nine whites and four reds we list here, give them a try. We list them alphabetically, with a brief description of the wine made from each one.

White varieties:

- **Aligoté:** Mainly found in Burgundy; makes dry, crisp, inexpensive (for Burgundy) wines.

- **Carricante:** The best Italian white variety you have never heard of. Found in the Mt. Etna region of Sicily, where it's the leading variety in such wines as Etna Bianco.

- **Furmint:** Hungarian variety; the main variety in the dessert wine, Tokaji Aszú; also made as a dry wine.

- **Garganega:** The grape variety of Italy's Soave; occasionally seen as a varietal wine.

- **Godello:** Dry, spicy wine from Spain's Galicia region.

- **Kerner:** Its original home is Germany, but this variety really shines as a viscous varietal wine in Italy's Alto Adige region.

- **Pecorino:** Found in Marche and Abruzzo regions of eastern Italy; often blended, but good enough to stand on its own.

- **Trebbiano:** Common (as in, ordinary) variety used for white wine blends in Tuscany and neighboring regions in Italy, but can really do well as varietal wine in Abruzzo.

- **Vermentino:** Becoming one of Italy's leading white varietal wines, especially in Tuscany, Liguria, and Sardinia. Its wines have good weight and an interesting, oily-like texture.

Red varieties:

- **Dolcetto:** A leading varietal wine in Piedmont, Italy, that makes dry, fairly serious red wines — but less serious than most Nebbiolo-based wines.

- **Montepulcianoo:** The leading red varietal wine in Abruzzo, Italy; also in Marche.

- **Nerello Mascalese:** Main red variety in the Mt. Etna region in Italy. Very underrated. The primary variety in Etna Rosso; also in Faro wine.

- **Petit Verdot:** Excellent Bordeaux variety, being used more and more in blended Bordeaux wines and increasingly as a varietal wine in California, South America, and other places.

Malbec

This grape originated in Bordeaux and is prominent in the southwestern French region of Cahors. But today, we wine drinkers know it far better as Argentina's signature red grape variety. Malbec is a dark variety that makes deeply colored red wines with very firm tannin and spicy, dark-berry aromas and flavors. In the sunny, high elevations of Argentina's Mendoza region, the wines tend to have softer tannin and richer fruit flavors than in France.

Other red grapes

Table 3-2 describes additional red grape varieties and their wines, which you can encounter either as varietal wines or as wines named for their place of production.

TABLE 3-2 **Other Red Grapes and Their Characteristics**

Grape Type	Characteristics
Aglianico	From southern Italy, where it makes Taurasi and other age-worthy, powerful red wines, high in tannin.
Barbera	Italian variety that, oddly for a red grape, has little tannin but very high acidity. When fully ripe, it can give big, fruity wines with refreshing crispness. Many producers age the wine in new oak.
Cabernet Franc	A parent of Cabernet Sauvignon, and often blended with it to make Bordeaux-style wines. Ripens earlier, and has more expressive, fruitier flavor (especially red berries), as well as less tannin. A specialty of the Loire Valley in France, where it makes wines with place-names such as Chinon and Bourgeuil.
Carménère	Originated in Bordeaux, but today is a key player only in Chile. Makes dark, flavorful wines with dark berry and spice notes and fairly soft tannins. Some wines can have herbal flavors if the grapes weren't ripe enough.
Gamay	Excels in the Beaujolais district of France. It makes grapey wines that can be low in tannin — although the grape itself is fairly tannic. Neither the grape called Gamay Beaujolais in California nor the grape called Napa Gamay is true Gamay.
Grenache	A Spanish grape by origin, called Garnacha there. (Most wine drinkers associate Grenache with France's southern Rhône Valley more than with Spain, however.) Sometimes Grenache makes pale, high-alcohol wines that are weak in flavor. In the right circumstances, it can make deeply colored wines with velvety texture and fruity aromas and flavors suggestive of raspberries. Some California wineries make a "White" Grenache that's sweet and pink.

Chapter **4**

Wine Label Lingo

W e browse the shelves of wine stores all the time, not only to shop for dinner but also to keep an eye on what kinds of wines are hitting the shelves. More than ever, we see an amazing proliferation of wine labels. New brands of wine seem to be appearing out of the blue every week. All this choice is terrific — or it's completely paralyzing, depending on how you approach the situation.

One sure way to become more comfortable when confronted by shelf upon shelf of unfamiliar wine labels is to figure out how to decode the information on those labels. Reading wine labels isn't difficult, because regulations specify what items must, can, and cannot appear on a label. Master that with the help of this chapter, and you'll be basking in the richness of choices that today's wine market offers.

The Wine Name Game

All sorts of names appear on wine labels. These names often include the following:

» The name of the *grape* from which the wine was made

» A *brand name,* which is traditionally the name of the company or person that made the wine (called the *producer*); for less expensive wines, it's likely to be an invented name

>> Sometimes a special, fanciful name for that particular wine (called a *proprietary name*)

>> The name of the *place,* or *places,* where the grapes grew (the wine region, and sometimes the name of the specific vineyard property)

Then there's the *vintage* year (the year when the grapes for that wine grew and were harvested), which is part of the wine's identity; and sometimes you see a descriptor like *reserve,* which either has a specific legal definition or means nothing at all, depending on where the wine came from. You discover details about all these items in the following sections.

Grape names and place-names

Most of the wines you find in wine shops or on restaurant wine lists are named in one of two basic ways: either for their *grape variety* or for the *place where the grapes grew.* That information, plus the name of the producer, becomes the shorthand name we use in talking about the wine.

Robert Mondavi Cabernet Sauvignon, for example, is a wine made by the Robert Mondavi Winery and named after the Cabernet Sauvignon grape. Fontodi Chianti Classico is a wine made by the Fontodi winery and named after the place called Chianti Classico.

You may recognize some names as grape names (see Chapter 3) and other names as place-names right off the bat; but if you don't, don't panic. That information is the kind of thing you can look up. (Parts 3, 4, and 5 will help.)

Hello, my name is Chardonnay: Varietal wines

A *varietal* wine is named after either the *principal* or the *sole* grape variety that makes up the wine. Each country (and in the United States, some individual states) has laws that stipulate the minimum percentage of the named grape that a wine must contain if that wine wants to call itself by the grape name. The issue is truth in advertising.

TECHNICAL STUFF

U.S. federal regulations fix the legal minimum percentage of the named grape at 75 percent (which means that your favorite California Chardonnay can have as much as 25 percent of some *other* grape in it). In Australia and in the countries that form the European Union (E.U.), the minimum is 85 percent.

Some varietal wines are made *entirely* from the grape variety for which the wine is named. There's no law against that anywhere.

WARNING

Most of the time, the labels of varietal wines don't tell you whether other grapes are present in the wine — let alone what those grapes are or the percentage of the wine that they account for. All you know is that the wine contains at least the minimum legal percentage of the named variety.

Interestingly, if a wine sold in the United States is named for two or more grape varieties — a wine called Sémillon-Chardonnay, for example — the label must state the percentages of each, and these percentages must total 100 percent. Now that's an honest varietal wine!

Why name a wine after a grape variety? Grapes are the raw material of a wine. Except for whatever a wine absorbs from oak barrels (certain aromas and flavors, as well as tannin) and from certain winemaking processes described in Chapter 5, the juice of the grapes is what any wine *is*. So to name a wine after its grape variety is logical.

Naming a wine for its grape variety is also satisfying to exacting consumers. Knowing what grape a wine is made from is akin to knowing what type of oil is in the salad dressing, whether your cupcake has any high fructose corn syrup, and how much egg is in your egg roll.

Most California (and other U.S.) wines carry varietal names. Likewise, most Australian, South American, and South African wines are named by using the *principal* principle. Even some countries that don't normally name their wines after the grape, such as France, are increasingly jumping on the varietal-name bandwagon for certain, inexpensive wines.

WARNING

A common perception among some wine drinkers is that a varietal wine is somehow *better* than a non-varietal wine. Actually, the fact that a wine is named after its principal grape variety is absolutely *no indication of quality*.

Hello, my name is Bordeaux: Place-name wines

TIP

Unlike American wines, most European wines are named for the *region* where their grapes grow rather than for the grape variety itself. Many of these European wines come from precisely the same grape varieties as American wines (like Chardonnay, Cabernet Sauvignon, Sauvignon Blanc, and so on), but they don't say so on the label. Instead, the labels say Burgundy, Bordeaux, Sancerre, and so on: the *place* where those grapes grow.

Is this some nefarious plot to make wine incomprehensible to English-only wine lovers who have never visited Europe and flunked geography in school? *Au contraire!* The European system of naming wines is actually intended to provide more information about each wine, and more understanding of what's in the bottle, than varietal naming does. The only catch is that to harvest this information, you have to learn something about the different regions from which the wines come. (Turn to Parts 3, 4, and 5 for some of that information.)

In the following sections, we list reasons for naming wines after places, describe the concept of *terroir*, and talk about place-names on labels of American wines (because they do exist).

Why name a wine after a place?

Grapes, the raw material of wine, have to grow somewhere. Depending on the type of soil, the amount of sunshine and rain, and the many other characteristics that each *somewhere* has, the grapes will turn out differently. If the grapes are different, the wine is different. Each wine, therefore, reflects the place where its grapes grow.

In Europe, grape growers/winemakers have had centuries to figure out which grapes grow best where. They've identified most of these grape-location matchups and codified them into regulations. Therefore, the name of a *place* where grapes are grown in Europe automatically connotes the grape (or grapes) used to make the wine of that place. The label on the bottle usually doesn't tell you the grape (or grapes), though.

DECODING COMMON EUROPEAN PLACE-NAMES

The following table lists common place-names on wine labels, the European countries in which the places are located, and the grape varieties used to make the wines.

Wine Name	Country	Grape Varieties
Beaujolais	France	Gamay
Bordeaux (red)	France	Cabernet Sauvignon, Merlot, Cabernet Franc, and others*
Bordeaux (white)	France	Sauvignon Blanc, Sémillon, Muscadelle*
Burgundy (red)	France	Pinot Noir

Wine Name	Country	Grape Varieties
Burgundy (white)	France	Chardonnay
Chablis	France	Chardonnay
Champagne	France	Chardonnay, Pinot Noir, Pinot Meunier*
Châteauneuf-du-Pape	France	Grenache, Mourvèdre, Syrah, and others*
Chianti	Italy	Sangiovese, Canaiolo, and others*
Côtes du Rhône	France	Grenache, Mourvèdre, Carignan, and others*
Port (Porto)	Portugal	Touriga Nacional, Tinta Barroca, Touriga Franca, Tinta Roriz, Tinto Cão, and others*
Pouilly-Fuissé, Mâcon, St.-Véran	France	Chardonnay
Rioja (red)	Spain	Tempranillo, Grenache, and others*
Sancerre/Pouilly-Fumé	France	Sauvignon Blanc
Sauternes	France	Sémillon, Sauvignon Blanc*
Sherry	Spain	Palomino
Soave	Italy	Garganega
Valpolicella	Italy	Corvina, Corvinone, Rondinella*

*Indicates that a blend of grapes is used to make these wines.

The terroir game

Terroir (pronounced ter-wahr) is a French word that has no direct translation in English, so wine people just use the French word, for expediency (not for snobbery). *Terroir* has no fixed definition; it's a concept, and people tend to define it more broadly or more narrowly to suit their own needs. The word itself is based on the French word *terre*, which means soil; so some people define *terroir* as, simply, dirt.

But *terroir* is really much more complex (and complicated) than just dirt. *Terroir* is the combination of immutable natural factors — such as topsoil, subsoil, climate (patterns of sun, rain, wind, and so on), the slope of the hill, and altitude — that a particular vineyard site has. Chances are that no two vineyards in the entire world have precisely the same combination of these factors. So we consider *terroir* to be the *unique* combination of natural factors that a particular vineyard site has.

Terroir is the guiding principle behind the European concept that wines should be named after the place they come from (thought we'd gotten off the track, didn't you?). The thinking goes like this: The name of the place connotes which grapes were used to make the wine of that place (because the grapes are set by regulations), and the place influences the character of those grapes in its own unique way. Therefore, the most accurate name that a wine can have is the name of the place where its grapes grew. It's not some nefarious plot; it's just a whole different way of looking at things.

Place-names on American wine labels

Wine labels from non-European countries also tell you where a wine comes from — usually by featuring the name of a place somewhere on the label. But a few differences exist between the European and non-European systems.

First of all, on an American wine label (or an Australian, Chilean, or South African label, for that matter), you have to go to some effort to find the place-name on the label. The place of origin isn't the fundamental name of the wine, as it is for classic European wines; the grape usually is.

Second, place-names in the United States signify far less than they do in Europe. Some places indicated on a label can be meaningful because they refer to specific, well-defined areas with fairly consistent growing conditions, such as Alexander Valley in California or Red Mountain in Washington. But other places are so large that their name communicates nothing specific — such as California, a territory that's 30 percent larger than the entire country of Italy. Same thing for Australian wines labeled *South Eastern Australia* — an area only slightly smaller than France and Spain *combined*.

PLACES LARGE AND SMALL

When we travel to other countries, we realize that people in different places have different ways of perceiving space and distance. If someone tells us that we'll find a certain restaurant "just up ahead," for example, we figure it's the equivalent of about three blocks away — but they might mean three miles.

Discussing place-names for European wines can be just as problematic. Some of the *places* are as small as several acres, some are 100 square miles big, and others are the size of New Jersey. Certain words used to describe wine zones imply the relative size of the place (in descending order of size and ascending order of specificity): country, region, district, subdistrict, commune, and vineyard.

Wines named in other ways

Even among U.S. wines — where the clear norm is to name wines after their principal grape variety — you will come across wines that go by a non-varietal name. Some of these names reflect tradition and others reflect a very contemporary trend in wine marketing. The first category encompasses *generic wines*, and the second represents *wines with proprietary names*.

» **Generic wines:** A generic name is a wine name that's been used inappropriately for so long that it has lost its original meaning in the eyes of the government. Burgundy, Chianti, Chablis, Champagne, Rhine wine, Sherry, Port, and Sauterne are all wine names that rightfully should apply only to wines made in those specific European places, but they've long ago been adopted by large American wineries. Although the U.S. government has finally agreed that these names can no longer be used for American wines, any wine that bore such a name prior to March 2006 may continue to carry that name for domestic commerce. In time, these generic names will become less common on wine labels.

» **Wines with proprietary names:** Beginning approximately in the 1980s, some American wineries began producing wines with fanciful names such as Tapestry, Conundrum, Insignia, Isosceles, and Trilogy. These are *proprietary names* (often trademarked) created for special wines within that winery's production portfolio. Some European wineries also developed wines with proprietary names. In the case of American wines, the bottles with proprietary names usually contain wines made from a *blend* of grapes, so that no one grape name can be used as the name of the wine. In the case of European wines, the grapes used to make the wine were (originally, at least) probably not the approved grapes for that region; therefore, the regional name couldn't be used on the label.

These wines with proprietary names usually are generally made in small quantities, are quite expensive ($40 to $75 or more a bottle), and are high in quality. Today, however, the proprietary wine trend has taken hold also for moderately priced and inexpensive American wines. One reason is that blended wines, especially blended red wines, are very popular. Made from several different grape varieties, these wines cannot use a single grape name on their labels — nor would they want to, because their proprietary names are more fun and more promotable. An example is Apothic Red, made by E.& J. Gallo.

Decoding the Language of the Label

Once upon a time, wine labels were boring, colorless (literally and in spirit), and the opposite of inviting. Now, many wine labels are fun. They catch your eye, draw you in for a closer look, and maybe make you smile. Although we tend to have classic tastes in wine, we love the variety of wine labels because it makes browsing for wine more enjoyable than ever.

But wine labels have an important purpose besides making their bottles stand out on the shelves. Wine labels contain information about the wine that's inside the bottle — and knowing what the information means can make you a smarter buyer. Sometimes that information is straightforward — like the name of the region where the grapes grew — and sometimes it's tricky, like long phrases in a foreign language that you don't speak.

In the following sections, we discuss the most common wine-label terms, and reveal their meaning (or lack thereof!).

The mandatory sentence

The government authorities in the United States (and other governments) mandate that certain information appear on the main label of all wine bottles — basic stuff, such as the alcohol content, the type of wine (usually *red table wine* or *white table wine*), and the country of origin. Such items are generally referred to as *the mandatory.* These items include the following:

» A brand name

» Indication of class or type (table wine, dessert wine, or sparkling wine)

» The percentage of alcohol by volume (unless it's implicit — for example, the statement *table wine* implies an alcohol content of less than 14 percent; see Chapter 1 for details)

» Name and location of the bottler

» Net contents (expressed in milliliters; the standard wine bottle is 750 milliliters, which is 25.6 ounces)

» The phrase *Contains Sulfites* (with very, very few exceptions)

» The government warning (that we won't dignify by repeating here; just pick up any bottle of wine, and you'll see it on a label)

Figure 4-1 shows you how all the details come together on a label of an American varietal wine.

Wines made outside the United States but sold within it must also carry the phrase *imported by* on their labels, along with the name and business location of the importer.

FIGURE 4-1: The label of an American varietal wine.

Illustration by Lisa S. Reed

WILL THE REAL WINE PRODUCER PLEASE STAND UP?

Although U.S. labeling laws require wine labels to carry the name and address of the bottler, this information doesn't necessarily tell you who made the wine.

Of the various phrases that may be used to identify the bottler on labels of wine sold in the United States, only the words *produced by* or *made by* indicate the name of the company that actually fermented 75 percent or more of the wine (that is, who really *made* the wine); words such as *cellared by* or *vinted by* mean only that the company subjected the wine to cellar treatment (holding it for a while, for example).

The mandatory information required on U.S. and Canadian wine labels is also required by the E.U. authorities for most wines produced in European Union countries (although the wording of the warning label can vary). The labels of those E.U. wines must contain one additional item of information not required on labels of wines from elsewhere. This additional item is a phrase indicating that the wine comes from an officially recognized wine zone (see the next section for the scoop).

Indications of origin

The European Union has set up a system to recognize and protect agricultural products (such as wine, cheese, olives, hams, and so forth) that come from specific places so that companies in other places can't make products with the same name and thus confuse consumers. Wines from all the classic wine regions of E.U. member countries (France, Italy, Spain, Germany, and so forth) are covered under this system. When you see the label of a European wine that's from a recognized, protected place, you'll find a phrase to that effect.

Actually, two different phrases exist because European wines from protected places fall into two categories:

>> Wines named for places where production is highly regulated so that the very place-name of the wine not only defines the territory of production but also connotes the wine's grape varieties, grape-growing methods, and winemaking techniques

>> Wines that carry the protected names of larger places where winemakers have more freedom in terms of the grape varieties and production methods they use

The E.U.'s mandated phrases for these two types of place-name wines are the following:

>> *Protected Designation of Origin (PDO),* for the most regulated wines. The classic wines mentioned in the sidebar "Decoding common European place-names," for example, are all in this category.

>> *Protected Geographic Indication (PGI),* for the less regulated wines from registered regions.

In theory, every bottle of European wine — except for the most broadly sourced, least expensive wines — carries one of these two phrases on its label.

But in practice, the situation is much more complicated, especially at the moment. How so?

>> For one thing, each country can, and does, translate the words *Protected Designation of Origin* and *Protected Geographic Indication* into its own language on its labels.

>> Second, because these E.U. designations went into full effect only in 2012, some wine labels still carry the phrases that were previously used by each country to designate a wine's category of origin.

>> And finally, each country can permit its wineries to continue using the former phrases rather than the new phrases.

TIP

If you're getting into French, Italian, or other European wines and see a long, foreign phrase on the label that's adjacent to the place-name or region of the wine, know that it indicates an officially protected geographic zone. If you really want to know which of the two protected categories the wine falls into, refer to the lists in the next two sections.

TIP

Incidentally, the phrase for a registered place-name in the United States is *American Viticultural Area (AVA)*. But the phrase *doesn't* appear on wine labels (refer to Figure 4-1). Nor does any such phrase appear on labels of Australian or South American wines. Nor do two different degrees of regulations exist, as they do in the European Union. (Refer to the section "Place-names on American wine labels," earlier in this chapter.)

Label terms that mean PDO (Protected Designation of Origin)

TECHNICAL STUFF

Here are the phrases — first in the new terminology and then in the original terminology — that you might find on labels of PDO wines from the major European countries. In all cases, the phrases translate more or less as "Protected Designation of Origin":

>> **France:** Appellation d'Origine Protégée (AOP) or Appellation Contrôlée or Appellation d'Origine Contrôlée (AC or AOC, in short)

>> **Italy:** Denominazione di Origine Protetta (DOP) or Denominazione di Origine Controllata (DOC); and for certain wines of an even higher status, Denominazione di Origine Controllata e Garantita (DOCG)

>> **Spain:** *Denominación de Origen Protegida (DOP)* or *Denominación de Origen (DO)*, as well as *Denominación de Origen Calificada (DOCa)* for regions with the highest status (of which only two exist: Rioja and Priorat; see Chapter 12 for even more words on Spanish labels)

>> **Portugal:** Denominação de Origem Protegida (DOP) or Denominação de Origem Controlada (DOC)

>> **Germany:** *Qualitätswein;* and for wines of higher ripeness, *Prädikatsweine* (see Chapter 12 for more on Germany's complex appellation system)

Figure 4-2 shows a European wine label as it would appear in the United States, using the original place-name terminology.

Label terms that mean PGI (Protected Geographic Indication)

TECHNICAL STUFF

Here are the phrases — first in the new terminology and then in the original terminology — that you might find on labels of PGI wines from the major European countries. In all cases, the phrases translate more or less as "Protected Geographic Indication":

>> **France:** *Indication Géographique Protégée (IGP)* or *Vin de Pays* followed by the name of an approved area

>> **Italy:** Indicazione Geografica Protetta (IGP) or Indicazione Geografica Tipica (IGT) and the name of an approved area

>> **Spain:** *Indicación Geográfica Protegida (IGP)* or *Vino de la Tierra* followed by the name of an approved area

Brand name

Wine name

PDO category

Type

Vintage

Producer information

Net contents

Bottler information
Importer information

Alcohol by volume

Alcohol 15% vol

FIGURE 4-2:
The label of a
European wine to
be sold in the
United States.

Illustration by Lisa S. Reed

>> **Portugal:** *Indicaçõa Geográfica (IG)* to refer to a region, but on a label, the original phrase, *Vinho Regional* (regional wine) and the name of an approved area

>> **Germany:** *Landwein*

Some optional label lingo

Besides the mandatory information required by government authorities, all sorts of other words can appear on wine labels. These words include meaningless phrases intended to make you think that you're getting a special quality wine, and words that provide useful information about what's in the bottle. Sometimes the same word can fall into either category, depending on the label. This ambiguity occurs because some words that are strictly regulated in some producing countries aren't regulated at all in others.

Vintage

The word *vintage* followed by a year, or the year listed alone without the word *vintage*, is the most common optional item on a wine label (refer to Figure 4-2). Sometimes the vintage appears on the label itself, and sometimes it has its own small label closer to the neck of the bottle.

REMEMBER

The *vintage year* is nothing more than the year in which the grapes for a particular wine grew; the wine must have 75 to 100 percent of the grapes of this year, depending on the country of origin. (*Non-vintage* wines contain wines from more than one year.) But an aura surrounds vintage-dated wine causing many people to believe that any wine with a vintage date is by definition better than a wine without a vintage date. *In fact, no correlation exists between the presence of a vintage date and the wine's quality.*

TIP

Generally speaking, *what* vintage a wine is — that is, whether the grapes grew in a year with perfect weather or whether the grapes were meteorologically challenged — is an issue you need to consider (a) only when you buy top-quality wines, and (b) mainly when those wines come from parts of the world that experience significant variations in weather from year to year — such as many European wine regions.

Reserve

Reserve is our favorite meaningless word on U.S. wine labels. The term is used to convince you that the wine inside the bottle is special. This trick usually works because the word *does* have specific meaning and *does* carry a certain amount of prestige on labels of wines from many other countries:

>> In Italy and Spain, the word *reserve* (or its foreign language equivalent, which looks something like *reserve*) indicates a wine that has received extra aging at the winery before release. Implicit in the extra aging is the idea that the wine was better than normal and, therefore, worthy of the extra aging. Spain even has *degrees* of reserve, such as Gran Reserva.

>> In France, the use of *reserve* isn't regulated. However, its use is generally consistent with the notion that the wine is better in quality than a given producer's norm.

REMEMBER

In the United States, the word *reserve* has historically been used in the same sense — as in, Beaulieu Vineyards Georges de Latour Private Reserve, the best Cabernet that Beaulieu Vineyards makes. But these days, the word is bandied about so much that it no longer has meaning. For example, some California wines labeled *Proprietor's Reserve* are the *least* expensive wines in a particular producer's lineup and some of the least expensive wines, period. Other wines are labeled *Special Reserve, Vintage Reserve, Vintner's Reserve,* or *Reserve Selection* — all utterly meaningless phrases.

Estate-bottled

Estate is a genteel word for a wine farm, a combined grape-growing and wine-making operation. The words *estate-bottled* on a wine label indicate that the company that grew the grapes and made the wine also bottled the wine. In other words, *estate-bottled* suggests accountability from the vineyard to the winemaking through to the bottling. In many countries, the winery doesn't necessarily have to own the vineyards, but it has to control the vineyards and perform the vineyard operations.

Estate-bottling is an important concept to those who believe that you can't make good wine unless the grapes are as good as they can possibly be. If *we* made wine, we'd sure want to control our own vineyards.

We wouldn't go so far as to say that great wines *must* be estate-bottled, though. Ravenswood Winery — to name just one example — makes some terrific wines from the grapes of small vineyards owned and operated by private landowners. And some large California landowners are quite serious about their vineyards but don't make wine themselves; they sell their grapes to various wineries. None of those wines would be considered estate-bottled.

TIP

Sometimes French wine labels carry the words *domaine-bottled* or *château-bottled* (or the phrase *mis en bouteille au château/au domaine*). The concept is the same as estate-bottled, with *domaine* and *château* being equivalent to the U.S. term *estate*.

Vineyard name

Some wines in the medium-to-expensive price category — costing about $25 or more — might carry on the label the name of the specific vineyard where the grapes for that wine grew. Sometimes one winery will make two or three different wines that are distinguishable only by the vineyard name on the label. Each wine is unique because the *terroir* of each vineyard is unique (we discuss *terroir* earlier in this chapter). These single vineyards might or might not be identified by the word *vineyard* next to the name of the vineyard.

Italian wines, which are really into the single-vineyard game, will have *vigneto* or *vigna* on their labels next to the name of the single vineyard. Or they won't. It's optional.

Even more optional words on the label

You'll be pleased to know that we have just about exhausted our list of terms that you could find on a wine label.

One additional expression on some French labels is *Vieilles Vignes* (vee-yay veen), which translates as "old vines," and appears as such on some Californian and Australian labels. Because old vines produce a very small quantity of fruit compared to younger vines, the quality of their grapes and of the resulting wine is considered to be very good. The problem is the phrase is unregulated. Anyone can claim that his vines are old.

The word *superior* can appear in French (*Supérieure*) or Italian (*Superiore*) as part of a PDO place-name (refer to the section "Indications of origin," earlier in this chapter, for a refresher on this acronym). It traditionally meant that the wine attained a higher alcohol level than a non-superior version of the same wine would have — a distinction not worth losing sleep over. Now, the term is also used in Italy to designate a specific type of wine. Soave Superiore, for example, is a wine that's distinct from the wine Soave by virtue of its vineyard location, winemaking, and so forth.

The word *Classico* appears on the labels of some Italian PDO wines when the grapes come from the heartland of the named place.

Chapter **5**

Winemaking Matters

The most frustrating thing about wine has got to be the technical lingo. All you want is a crisp, fruity white wine to serve with tonight's mac 'n' cheese. But to find it, you have to fight your way through a jungle of jargon. You encounter it on the back labels of wine bottles, in the words the sales clerk uses to explain his recommendations, and on the signs all around the wine shop. Why on earth is everyone making wine so complicated?

Here's the scoop: Wine is two products. Some wine is just a beverage, and it should taste good — period. Other wine is an art form that fascinates and intrigues people. Many people who make and sell wine want you to think that their wines are in the second category, because those wines are more prestigious. Complicated technical language is supposed to make you think that a wine is special — something more than just a beverage.

How much of this information (if any) is pivotal in helping you get the kind of wine you want, and how much is pretentious technobabble? Read on.

Vineyard Jargon, Winemaking Talk

The taste and the quality of every wine are the result of several factors. The fundamental factors are the grape variety or varieties and the place where the grapes grew (see Chapters 3 and 4 for information on grapes and *terroir*). Two other factors are

>> The manner of cultivating the grapes in the vineyard

>> The techniques used in the winery to process the grapes and handle the wine

Because production techniques *do* affect the quality and taste of a wine, discussion of these techniques is bound to pop up when wine people get going on the subject of wines that they like. You can easily get impressed by the technical words, and conclude that a wine tastes better or is higher in quality because of this or that winemaking detail.

In reality, no winemaking procedure is inherently good or inherently bad. Any technique can be right or wrong depending on the grapes and the type of wine being made — that is, the wine's price level, the taste profile the winemaker is seeking, and the type of wine drinker the winery is targeting (someone who takes wine very seriously or someone more casual about wine drinking).

The technical words that you hear represent isolated winemaking (or grape-growing) steps, which are only *parts* of the total picture of a wine. How the wine tastes is the ultimate validation of any method used to produce a wine: The procedures themselves are meaningless if they don't create a wine that's appealing to the wine drinkers for whom that wine is intended.

REMEMBER

The *taste* of the wine involves not only its flavors but also its aroma, body, texture, length, and so on (see Chapter 2). And the taste of a wine is a subjective experience.

The rest of this chapter explains the meaning behind the isolated elements of winemaking that you're most likely to hear or read about when you're buying wine.

The World of Viti-Vini

Producing wine actually involves two separate steps: the growing of the grapes, called *viticulture,* and the making of the wine, called *vinification.* (In some wine courses, students nickname the dual process *viti-vini.*) Sometimes, one company performs both steps, as is the case with *estate-bottled* wines (see Chapter 4). And sometimes, the two steps are completely separate. For example, some large wineries buy grapes from private grape growers. These growers don't make wine; they just grow grapes and sell them to whatever wine company offers them the highest price per ton.

In the case of the very least expensive wines, the winery named on the label may not have even purchased grapes but rather wine (from bulk wine producers) and then blended the wines and bottled the final product as its own. (As we mention in Chapter 4, only the terms *produced by* or *made by* on the label assure you that the company named on the label actually vinified most of that wine.) In the following sections, we discuss terms that are associated with viticulture and then with vinification.

Vine-growing variations

Growing grapes for wine is a fairly intricate process that viticulturalists are constantly refining to suit their particular soil, climate, and grape varieties. Many of the technical terms spill over into discussions about wine or they crop up on wine labels. Here are expressions you're likely to encounter as you dig further into wine:

>> **Microclimate (known increasingly as *mesoclimate*):** Every wine region has climatic conditions (the amount and timing of sun, rain, wind, humidity, and so on) that are considered the norm for that area. But individual locations within a region — the south-facing side of a particular hill, for example — can have a climatic reality that's different from that of the area as a whole. The unique climatic reality of a specific location is called its *microclimate,* or, in technical circles, its *mesoclimate. Microclimate* is the more common term on back labels and in colloquial usage.

>> **Ripeness:** Harvesting grapes when they're perfectly ripe is one of the crucial points in wine production. (See Chapter 3.) But ripeness is a subjective issue.

In cooler climates, a high degree of ripeness doesn't happen every year; wines from "riper" vintages should, therefore, be richer and fuller-bodied than the norm for that type of wine. In warmer climates, ripeness is almost automatic; the trick becomes not letting the grapes get too ripe too fast, which causes them to be high in sugar but still physiologically immature and undeveloped in their flavors (like a physically precocious but immature teenager). There's no fixed definition of perfect ripeness.

>> **Low yields:** Generally, the more grapes a grapevine produces (the higher its *yield* of grapes), the less concentrated the flavors of those grapes will be, and the lower in quality (and less expensive) their wine will be. Just about any wine producer anywhere can claim that his yields are low, because it's too complicated to prove otherwise. The proof is usually in the wine's concentration of flavor: If the wine tastes thin or watery, we'd be suspicious of the "low yield" claim.

>> **Organic:** Grape growers increasingly farm their vineyards *organically,* that is, without using chemical pesticides, herbicides, and so forth. Their reasons have to do with the health of the land, as well as their belief that organically grown grapes are superior to conventionally farmed grapes and that they

make better wine. For a wine label in the United States to state that the grapes for that wine were grown organically, the vineyard must be certified as organic by a government-approved organization. Many growers who do farm organically see the certification process as an unnecessary hurdle, and wines made from their grapes therefore cannot be labelled as organically grown.

A related term is *biodynamic;* this means that the vineyards are organic and also are farmed in keeping with the principles established in the early 20th century by Austrian philosopher Rudolph Steiner, which involve, among other issues, cosmic aspects such as respecting the movement of the moon and the planets in the timing of the work on the land. Biodynamic wines enjoy almost a cult following. (**Note:** The term biodynamic is actually trademarked and is properly used only by producers who are certified by an organization called Demeter.)

Winemaking wonder words

The vinification end of wine production falls into two parts:

>> **Fermentation:** The period when the grape juice turns into wine

>> **Maturation (or *finishing*):** The period following fermentation when the wine settles down, loses its rough edges, goes to prep school, and gets ready to meet the world

CLONING THE PERFECT GRAPEVINE

Hang around wine people long enough and you're sure to hear talk about *clones* or *clonal selection* of grape varieties. Has the brave new world of grape growing arrived? Not really. In botanical terms, a *clone* is a subdivision of a variety. Within a single variety, such as Chardonnay, differences can exist from one plant to the next. For example, some plants might ripen their fruit slightly more quickly or produce grapes with slightly different aromas and flavors than the next.

When nurseries propagate grapevines by taking cuttings from a *mother plant* and allowing those cuttings to root (until the plant is mature enough to be grafted onto a phylloxera-resistant rootstock, as we discuss in Chapter 3), the new plants are genetically identical to the mother plant. Naturally, grape growers purchase the most ideal plants for their situation, in terms of ripening time, fruit flavor, disease resistance, heartiness — or whatever they're looking for. Voilà! They've made a clonal selection. Increasingly, growers plant several different clones of a grape variety to foster complexity in the wine made from that vineyard's grapes.

Depending on the type of wine being made, the whole process can take three months or five years, or even longer.

Winemakers don't have as many options in making wine as chefs do in preparing food — but almost! Of all the jargon you're likely to hear about fermentation and maturation, information about oak is probably the most common. The following sections give you the details.

When wood becomes magic

Winemakers can use oak barrels, 60 gallons in size, as containers for wine during fermentation and/or maturation. The barrels lend oaky flavor and aroma to the wine, which many people find very appealing; they can also affect the texture of the wine and its color. The barrels are expensive —upwards of $900 per barrel if they're made from French oak. (Most people consider French oak to be the finest.) We suppose the expense is one good reason to boast about using the barrels.

But not all oak is the same. Oak barrels vary in the origin of their oak, the amount of *toast* (a charring of the inside of the barrels) each barrel has, how often the barrels have been used (their oaky character diminishes with use), and even the size of the barrels (larger barrels have a lower oak-to-wine ratio). Even if all oak *were* the same, a wine can turn out differently depending on whether unfermented juice or actual wine went into the barrels, and how long it stayed there.

And sometimes —frequently, in fact, for inexpensive wines—the oak that winemakers use is not a container at all but some other form of oak used to flavor the wine. These *oak alternatives* include planks of oak that are inserted into the wine in stainless steel tanks, large "tea bags" containing oak chips, or even liquid oak flavoring.

WARNING

In fact, the whole issue of oak is so complex that anyone who suggests that a wine is better simply because it's been oaked is guilty of gross oversimplification.

Barrel-fermented versus barrel-aged

You don't have to venture very far into wine before you find someone explaining to you that a particular wine was barrel-fermented or barrel-aged. What in the world does he mean, and should you care?

>> The term *barrel-fermented* means that grape juice went into barrels (almost always oak) and evolved into wine there.

>> The term *barrel-aged* usually means that wine (already fermented) went into barrels and stayed there for a maturation period — from a few months to a couple of years.

Because most wines that ferment in barrels remain there for several months after fermentation ends, *barrel-fermented* and *barrel-aged* are often used together. The term *barrel-aged* alone suggests that the fermentation happened somewhere other than the barrel — usually in stainless steel tanks.

TECHNICAL STUFF

Classic barrel-fermentation — juice into the barrel, wine out — applies mainly to white wines, and the reason is very practical. As we mention in Chapter 2, the juice of red grapes ferments together with the grape skins in order to become red, and those solids are mighty messy to clean out of a small barrel! Red wines usually ferment in larger containers — stainless steel tanks or large wooden vats — and then *age* in small oak barrels after the wine has been drained from the grape skins. (Some light, fruity styles of red wine may not be oaked at all.)

TECHNICAL STUFF

Some winemakers do partially ferment their reds in barrels; they start the fermentation in tanks and then drain the juice from the skins and let that juice finish its fermentation in barrels, without the skins. When a red wine is described as being barrel-fermented, that's usually the process.

REMEMBER

Here's why you might care whether a white wine is barrel-fermented or just barrel-aged. Wines that ferment in barrels actually end up tasting *less* oaky than wines that simply age in barrels, even though they might have spent more time in oak. (A barrel-fermented and barrel-aged Chardonnay might have spent 11 months in oak, for example, and a barrel-aged Chardonnay might have spent only 5 months in oak.) That's because juice interacts with the oak differently than wine does.

WARNING

A lot of people who are supposed to know more about wine than you confuse the effects of the two processes and tell you that the barrel-fermented wine tastes oakier. If you have a strong opinion about the flavor of oak in your wine, be sure you know the real story.

Even More Winemaking Terms

Become a wine expert overnight and dazzle your friends with this amazing array of wine jargon. (Just don't fool yourself into believing that any one of the procedures described here necessarily creates a high-quality wine. The merit of each procedure depends on the complete set of winemaking techniques for that wine and on the particular type of wine being made.)

>> **Temperature control:** The modern age of winemaking began when winemakers were able to control scientifically the temperature of their fermentations by using stainless steel tanks rigged with cooling jackets or by using various computer-operated cooling devices. Because the temperature of the

fermentation affects the final style of the wine, temperature control is critical. (The temperatures are about 54 to 77 degrees Fahrenheit or 12 to 25 degrees Celsius for white wines and 77 to 93 degrees Fahrenheit or 25 to 34 degrees Celsius for reds.) But, hey, this process was revolutionary and exciting half a century ago. Today, it's just par for the course.

>> **Stainless steel:** Large tanks made of shiny, hygienic stainless steel are the vessels of choice for most fermentations, whether for red wine or white. When you hear a winemaker or wine expert say that a particular wine was fermented in stainless steel, understand him to mean that one of two things is true:

- The wine was not oaked at all (which is common for many aromatic-style white wines — such as Rieslings, for example — to preserve the grapes' own flavors).

- The wine was barrel-aged rather than barrel-fermented (see the preceding section).

>> **Lees:** *Lees* is the name for various solids, such as dead yeast cells, that precipitate to the bottom of a white wine after fermentation. These solids can interact with the wine and create more complex flavors in the wine. (Sometimes, the winemaker stirs the lees around in the wine periodically to prevent off flavors.) A white wine with extended lees contact is usually richer in texture and tastes less overtly fruity than it would otherwise.

>> **ML or malolactic:** *Malolactic,* nicknamed *ML* or *malo,* is a secondary fermentation that weakens the acids in a wine, making the wine softer and less acidic. ML usually happens naturally, but a winemaker can also incite it or prevent it.

Most red wines undergo malolactic fermentation, but for white wines, ML is a stylistic judgment call on the winemaker's part. Sometimes, ML can contribute a buttery flavor to a white wine and it can create complex, non-fruity flavors, but it diminishes the wine's fresh, vibrant fruitiness.

>> **pH:** The chemical term *pH* means exactly the same thing for wine as it does in other scientific fields. ("Our facial cream is pH-balanced for sensitive skin.") If you want a technical explanation, look up your former chemistry teacher. If you'll settle for the general concept, *pH* is a measurement of acidity; wines with low pH (approximately 3.4 or less) have stronger acidity, and wines with higher pH have weaker acidity. But all wines have acidity.

>> **Soft tannins:** Tannin in red wines varies not only in its quantity but also in its nature. Some tannins give wines rich texture and an impression of substance without tasting bitter; other tannins are astringent and mouth-drying. *Soft tannins,* or *ripe tannins,* are buzzwords for the good kind. Winemakers achieve soft tannins by harvesting red grapes fully ripe, by controlling fermentation time and temperature, and by using other techniques.

>> **Micro-oxygenation:** You hear this term, sometimes abbreviated as *micro-ox,* thrown around in technical circles. This high-tech winemaking technique involves feeding miniscule, controlled amounts of oxygen into a wine during or after fermentation. It can mimic the gentle, steady exposure to oxygen that barrel-aged red wines receive as they mature in wood and thus can help red wines develop softer tannins and more stable color without any actual use of oak. For some winemakers, it's a useful tool, but some critics consider it manipulative.

>> **Fining and filtering:** Winemakers *fine* and *filter* most wines near the end of their maturation period. The purpose of these procedures is to *clarify* the wine — that is, to remove any cloudiness or solid matter in the wine — and to *stabilize* it — to remove any yeast, bacteria, or other microscopic critters that could change the wine for the worse after it's bottled.

REMEMBER

A popular belief among anti-tech wine lovers is that fining and filtration strip a wine of its character — and that unfined, unfiltered wines are inherently better, even if they're not brilliant in appearance. But it's a complex issue. (For one thing, there are *degrees* of fining and filtration, like *light* fining and *gentle* filtration.) These processes, when carried out carefully, are generally not detrimental to wine.

WARNING

>> **Natural wine:** It's fashionable for winemakers to claim that their wine is *natural* (as if most wines are unnatural?). They mean to suggest that their winemaking techniques — and their grape growing, for that matter — are non-manipulative and low tech. But even the advocates and practitioners of so-called natural wine don't agree about what the term *natural* actually means. For example, some use sulfur to keep their wine sound (read about sulfites in Chapter 1), while others don't, and sometimes to the detriment of the wine. Take the term with a grain of (natural) salt.

>> **Concrete eggs and clay amphorae:** In their quest to leave no stone unturned for a finer wine, some winemakers are now reviving ancient winemaking techniques and using retro fermentation containers. Concrete eggs are egg-shaped vessels used for fermentation or aging; we have seen them in many countries, but generally their use is still experimental. Amphorae are earthen vessels that are narrower at the top and bottom and widest in the middle; some winemakers bury them in the ground for temperature control. Their status is even more experimental.

>> **Blending:** This term usually applies to the process of making a wine from more than one grape variety. Winemakers typically ferment the different grapes separately and then blend their wines together.

One reason for blending wines of different grapes is to improve the wine's quality by using complementary grapes whose characteristics enhance each other. (Many of Europe's traditional wines, such as red Rioja, red Bordeaux, Châteauneuf-du-Pape, and Champagne, are blended wines that owe their personalities to several grapes.) Another reason is to reduce costs by diluting an expensive wine, like Chardonnay or Cabernet, with something else far less expensive.

WINE TERMS THAT MEAN NOTHING

Sometimes winemakers or salespeople use words to describe their wines that, frankly, have no actual meaning. Usually, the use of these words is an attempt to create an aura of quality and rarity around the wines in question, but in fact these terms are free for any producer to use. When you hear these terms, understand them to mean that the person using them really wants you to believe his wine is special. Then decide for yourself, by tasting, whether it is.

- Handcrafted
- Artisanal
- Craft wine
- Limited edition, limited selection, limited release
- Vintner's select, vineyard select, "anything" select

2

Wine and You: Up Close and Personal

Find out what you need to know about buying wine in shops.

Read about issues involved in buying wine in restaurants.

Get the lowdown on how to serve wine correctly.

Maximize enjoyment of your meal by learning which types of foods pair best with various types of wines.

Chapter **6**

Buying Wine to Drink at Home

U nless you're BFFs with a passionate wine expert, most times you have to make your own wine-buying choices. If you're lucky, the shop owner will just happen to be some guy or gal whose life's purpose is to teach people about wine. But the chances are that most of the time you'll feel as if you're lost in a fog, surrounded by strange, mysterious bottles.

In the days when we wrote earlier editions of *Wine For Dummies,* we bought almost all our wine in wine shops that we visited in person. Now the Internet accounts for most of our wine purchases. Convenient as online shopping is, though, there's still much to be said for browsing in person, especially if you're just beginning to learn about wine. And finding a knowledgeable wine merchant can make your wine shopping easier.

In this chapter, we tell you about various types of wine retailers and how to choose those best for you. We also explain how to overcome any fears you might feel about buying wine.

Buying Wine Can Give Anyone the Jitters

Common sense suggests that buying a few bottles of wine should be less stressful than, say, applying for a mortgage or interviewing for a job. What's the big deal? It's only grape juice.

But memories tell us otherwise. One time, we pretended we knew what we were doing and bought a full case — 12 bottles — of a French wine based on the brand's general reputation, not realizing that the particular vintage we purchased was a miserable aberration of the wine's usual quality. (Why didn't we just ask someone in the store, or do a little research in advance?) And we recall the many times we spent staring at shelves lined with bottles whose labels might as well have been written in Chinese, for all that we could understand them. Fortunately, our enthusiasm for wine motivated us to persevere. We eventually discovered that wine shopping can be fun.

TIP

Our experience has taught us that the single, most effective way to ensure that you have more good wine-buying experiences than bad ones is to come to terms with your knowledge — or lack thereof — of the subject.

Too much information about wine — new vintages each year, hundreds of new wineries, new brands, and so on — is changing too quickly for *anyone* to presume that he knows it all, or for anyone to feel insecure about what he or she doesn't know.

Wine Retailers, Large and Small

Buying wine in a store to drink at home is great for a number of reasons, not the least of which is that stores usually have a much bigger selection of wines than restaurants do, and they charge you less for them. You can examine the bottles carefully and compare the labels. And you can drink the wine at home from the glass — and at the temperature — of your choosing. Of course that big selection of wines in the store can be downright daunting.

Depending on where you live, you can buy wine at all sorts of stores: supermarkets, wine superstores, discount warehouses, general wine and liquor stores, or small specialty wine shops. Each type of store has its own advantages and disadvantages in terms of selection, price, or service.

Wine, being an alcohol beverage, is regulated in many countries. Governments dictate where and how wine may be sold. Some states within the United States and some provinces in Canada have raised government control of alcohol beverage sales to a fine art, deciding not only *where* you can buy wine but also *which wines* are available for you to buy. If you love wine and live in one of those areas (you know who you are), take comfort in the fact that (a) you have a vote; (b) freedom of choice lies just across the border; and (c) if cars can drive themselves, there's hope for freedom in wine buying.

We'll assume a healthy, open-minded, free-market economy for wine in our discussion of retail wine sales in the following sections. We hope that scenario applies where you live, because your enjoyment of wine will blossom all the more easily if it does.

Supermarkets, superstores, and so on

In truly *open* wine markets, you can buy wine in supermarkets, like any other food product. Supermarkets and their large-scale brethren, discount warehouses and superstores, make wine accessible to everyone.

In supermarkets, superstores, or discount stores, the mystique surrounding wine evaporates: Who can waste time feeling insecure about a wine purchase when many more critical issues are at hand, such as how much time is left before the kids turn into monsters and which is the shortest line at the checkout? And the prices, especially in large stores, are usually quite reasonable.

WARNING

The downside of buying wine in these stores is that your selection is often limited to wines produced by large wineries that generate enough volume to supply supermarket chains. And you'll seldom get any advice on which wines to buy. Basically, you're on your own.

TIP

Discount stores are good places to find *private label* wines — wines that are created especially for the discount chain and that carry a brand name that's owned by the store. These wines are usually decent, and if you like the wines, they can be excellent values. Some of the "club" chains may also offer — in smaller quantities — higher-end wines that are not the usual supermarket fare.

TIP

The bottom line is that supermarkets and discount warehouses can be great places to buy everyday wine for casual enjoyment. But if what you really want is to become knowledgeable about wine as you buy it, or if you want an unusually interesting variety of wines to satisfy your rapacious curiosity, you'll probably find yourself shopping elsewhere most of the time.

Specialty wine shops

Wine specialty shops are small- to medium-sized stores that sell wine, usually liquor and, sometimes, wine books, corkscrews, wine glasses, and maybe a few specialty foods.

If you decide to pursue wine as a serious hobby, you'll probably end up buying your wine at specialty wine shops because they offer many advantages. For instance, these shops almost always have wine-knowledgeable staffers on the premises. Also, you can usually find an interesting, varied selection of wines at all price levels.

Many times, wine shops organize their wines by country of origin and — in the case of classic wine countries, such as France — by region (Bordeaux, Burgundy, Rhône, and so on). Red wines and white wines are often in separate sections. You can usually find a special section for Champagnes and other sparkling wines and another for dessert wines. Some stores organize their wine sections by style, such as Aromatic Whites, Powerful Reds, and so forth, or by grape variety.

Some wine shops have a special area (or even a super-special, temperature-controlled room) for the finer, more expensive wines. In some stores, this area is a locked, vaultlike room. In others, it's the whole back area of the store.

WARNING

Over in a corner somewhere, often right by the door to accommodate quick purchases, you might see a cold box, a commercial refrigerator where bottles of best-selling white and sparkling wines sit. Unless you really must have an ice-cold bottle of wine immediately, avoid the cold box. The wines are usually too cold and, therefore, might not be in good condition. You never know how long the bottle you select has been sitting there under frigid conditions, numbed lifeless.

TIP

Near the front of the store, you might also see boxes or bins of special sale wines. Sometimes, sale wines are those the merchant is trying to unload because he's had them for too long, or they're wines that he got a special deal on (because the distributor is trying to unload them). When in doubt, try one bottle first before committing to a larger quantity. (We provide more wine shopping strategies later in this chapter.)

Online merchants

The online wine-buying experience today mainly involves purchasing wines from the websites of established brick-and-mortar wine shops or choosing wines from flash sites that offer an ever-changing but limited selection. A few companies do sell wine *only* online — such as Wine.com, ShopWineDirect.com, and Vinfolio.com.

Most websites of established wine shops offer an extensive selection of all types of wines. However, restrictions prevent some retail stores (and their websites) from shipping to consumers who live in other states, which significantly narrows your options in terms of where you shop. At last count, only 14 states and the District of Columbia allow out-of-state retailers to ship wine to their residents. That means that 36 states prohibit alcohol shipments from out-of-state retail stores into their states, including the state we live in, New York! (Wineries have much more latitude regarding shipments to consumers.) Loss of sales taxes and powerful local wine retailer and wholesaler lobbies are the reasons.

Some mega-chains have licensed stores in most states, so that you can receive the wine legally from their local, in-state store. And some stores (and their websites) will agree to ship wine to you even if they shouldn't. (Look for terms and conditions that stipulate that you agree you are buying the wine in their state, and that you are shipping it out of state to yourself; language like this probably lessens the store's risk, but maybe not yours.) The wine you buy from retailers in these 36 states can actually be legally destroyed by shipping companies because the store has no right to ship to out-of-state consumers. Or if the regulatory heat is off, you could receive your order with no problem. The situation is frustrating for both retailers and consumers.

Wine store websites we like include include Flatiron-wines.com; astorwines.com; chambersstwines.com (all in NYC); blmwine.com (Allston, MA); hdhwine.com (Chicago); kermitlynch.com (Berkeley, CA); rarewineco.com (Sonoma, CA); wallywine.com (Los Angeles); and winelibrary.com (Springfield, NJ).

Unlike the websites of established wine stores, flash sites offer a limited selection of wines at any given moment, usually at very affordable prices. Flash sites are the wine equivalent of shopping for sale items at the mall: If you find something you want, buy it before someone else does. Most flash sites enable you to sign up for e-mail alerts so that you can stay abreast of their offerings. You can get real bargains at these flash sites (one is called Wines Til Sold Out [www.wtso.com]), but you have to act quickly because the wines do sell out rapidly.

Criteria for Choosing Wine Merchants

Buying wine on the Internet is terrific *if you know something about wine*. If you're a novice, you're much better off relying on a knowledgeable wine merchant to help you select your wines. But whichever route you prefer, certain guidelines can help you choose a good retailer.

Sizing up a wine merchant is as simple as sizing up any other specialty retailer, whether online or face to face. As you find out in the following sections, the main criteria are fair prices, a wide selection, staff expertise, and service.

In the wine shop

TIP

When you're a novice wine buyer, your best strategy is to shop around with an eye to service and reliable advice more than to price. After you've found a merchant who has suggested several wines you've liked, stick with him, even if he doesn't have the best prices in town. Paying a dollar or so more for wines recommended by a reliable merchant (wines that you'll probably like) makes more sense than buying wines in a cut-rate or discount store and saving a buck, especially if that store has no special wine adviser or if the advice you receive is suspect.

REMEMBER

When you have more knowledge of wine, you'll have enough confidence to shop at stores with the best prices. But even then, price must take a backseat to the storage conditions of the wine (see the section "Judging wine storage conditions," later in this chapter).

TIP

As a starting point, ask a wine-knowledgeable friend what store(s) he or she recommends.

Evaluating selection, expertise, and service

You won't necessarily know on your first visit whether a particular store's selection is adequate for you. If you notice a lot of wines from many different countries at various prices, give the store's selection the benefit of the doubt. If you outgrow the selection as you discover more about wine, you can seek out a new merchant at that point.

WARNING

Don't be too ready to give a merchant the benefit of the doubt when it comes to expertise, however. Although some retailers are extremely knowledgeable about the wines they sell and about wine in general, others know less than their customers. Just as you expect a butcher to know his cuts of meat, you should expect a wine merchant to know wine. Be free with your questions (such as, "Can you give me some specific information about this wine?" or "How are these two wines different?"), and judge how willing and able the merchant is to answer them.

Expect wine merchants to have *personal* knowledge and experience of the wines they sell. Often, retailers use the point-score ratings of a few critics (usually a number like 90 or higher on a scale of 100) as a sales crutch. (See Chapter 19 for details.) Selling by the numbers is a quick way of communicating what one critic thought about the wine — but that doesn't mean *you'll* like the wine! Retailers' knowledge and experience of the wines simply must go beyond the critics' scores, or they're not doing their jobs properly.

Most knowledgeable wine merchants pride themselves in their ability to guide you through the maze of wines and help you find a wine you will like. Trust a merchant's advice at least once or twice and see whether his choices are good ones for you. If he's not flexible enough — or knowledgeable enough — to suggest wine that suits your needs, obviously you need another merchant.

TIP

Any reputable wine merchant will accept a bottle back from you if he's made a poor recommendation or if the wine seems damaged. After all, he wants to keep you as a customer. But with the privilege comes responsibility: Be reasonable. Ask ahead of time about the store's defective and unopened wine policy. You should return an *open* bottle only if you think the wine is defective — in which case the bottle should be mostly full! Hold on to your receipt. In the case of unopened bottles, don't wait several months before returning a wine; by that time, the store may have a hard time reselling the bottle. After a couple of weeks, consider the wine yours.

Judging wine storage conditions

WARNING

Here's a fact about wine that's worth understanding early on: Wine is a perishable product. It doesn't go moldy like cheese, and it can't host E. coli bacteria as meat can. It normally poses no health hazard beyond those associated with alcohol and certain individuals' sensitivities, even when a wine is past its prime. But if wine isn't stored properly, its taste can suffer. (For advice on storing wine in your own home, see Chapter 17.)

Particularly if you plan to buy a lot of wine or expensive wine, check out the store's wine storage conditions. What you don't want to see is wine stored in a warm area, such as near the heaters where it cooks all winter or on the top floor of the building where the sun can smile on it all summer.

The very best shops have climate-controlled storerooms for wine, although, frankly, these shops are in the minority. If a shop does have a good storage facility, the proprietor will be happy to show it off to you because he'll be rightfully proud of all the expense and effort he put into it.

TIP

In better wine shops, you'll see most of the bottles (except the inexpensive, large, juglike bottles) lying in a horizontal position so that their corks remain moist, ensuring a firm closure. A dry cork can crack or shrink and let air into the bottle, which will spoil the wine. A short time upright doesn't affect wine much, so stores with a high turnover can get away with storing their fast-selling wines that way, but slower-selling, expensive bottles, especially those intended for long maturation in your own cellar or storage cabinet, will fare better in the long run when they are lying down from the start.

Of course, many wines these days, even very good wines, have screwcaps on their bottles instead of cork. These bottles can be displayed upright without risk. But normally you will see them lying sideways along with the corked bottles because that's the most practical arrangement for the store.

Unfortunately, the problem of wine spoilage doesn't begin at the retail outlet. Quite frequently, the *wholesaler* or *distributor* — the company from which the retailer purchases wine — doesn't have proper storage conditions. And in some instances, wine has been damaged by extreme weather even before it got to the distributor, while sitting on the docks in the dead of winter (or in the heart of summer). A good retailer will check out the quality of the wine before he buys it, or he'll send it back if he discovers the problem after he's already bought the wine.

On the Internet

When you purchase wine online rather than at a store, the issue of storage is nearly impossible to evaluate. Selection, availability, and price are the criteria that determine which online store deserves your loyalty.

TIP

When we're shopping for a specific wine online, our first stop is Wine Searcher (www.wine-searcher.com). This search engine site enables you to look for specific wines, even specific vintages, and discover which of the site's member retailers (including most major wine shops across the United States and online retailers) are selling that wine, and at what price. You can then contact that retailer online or by phone to purchase the wine. We don't always select the shop with the lowest price, however. Sometimes shipping charges from a distant store negate the lower price.

You won't find offerings from flash sites on Wine Searcher because the wines offered by such sites change too quickly, sometimes several times a day. Some flash sites that you should check out include Wines Til Sold Out(www.wtso.com), Invino.com, GreatWine2U.com, and Last Bottle Wines(lastbottlewines. com). All these sites generally list wines at affordable prices (some highly discounted) and sometimes with conditional free shipping.

Strategies for Wine Shopping

When you begin to get comfortable buying wine, you can really have fun in wine shops, especially when you use the strategies in the following sections.

One key strategy is to be open to new wines. Like most people, when we first started buying wine, we'd buy the same brands again and again. We knew what to expect from them, and we liked them well enough (both good reasons to buy a particular wine). But in retrospect, we let ourselves get stuck in a rut. If wine was really going to be fun, we realized we had to be a little more adventuresome.

TIP

New wines can be interesting and exciting. Now and then you might get a lemon, but at least you'll know not to buy that wine again! Keep in mind that if you're trying a wine for the first time, never buy more than a bottle or two. The wine isn't a great buy unless you like it. Personally, we seldom buy more than two or three bottles of a particular wine, even if we know the wine. We like variety, rather than drinking the same wine over and over.

Explain what you want

Communication is key in the wine–buying experience. The most knowledgeable wine expert in the world can't recommend a wine that you'll like unless you can give him or her some clues about your tastes.

HOW TO AVOID ENCOUNTERS WITH POORLY STORED WINE

If you don't know how a wine has been stored — and let's face it, most of the time you don't — you can do two things to minimize the risk of getting a badly stored bottle:

- First, patronize retailers who seem to care about their wine and who provide their customers with good service.

- Second, be attentive to seasonal weather patterns when buying wine or when having it shipped to you. We think twice about buying wine at the end of, or during, a very hot summer, unless the store has a good temperature-control system. And we never have wine shipped to us (other than quick, local deliveries) at the height of summer or winter.

Another way of knowing that the wine you're buying is sound is just to buy the best-selling, most popular wines (assuming you don't mind being a slave to taste trends). Wines that move through the distribution chain very quickly have less opportunity to be damaged along the way.

The following is a familiar scene in nearly every wine shop:

Customer: I remember that the wine had a yellow label. I had it in this little restaurant last week.

Wine Merchant: Do you know what country it's from?

Customer: I think it's Italian, but I'm not sure.

Wine Merchant: Do you recall the grape variety?

Customer: No, but I think it has a deer or a moose on the label. Maybe if I walk around, I can spot it.

Needless to say, most of the time that customer never finds the wine he or she is looking for.

TIP

When you come across a wine you like in a restaurant or at a friend's house, snap a picture of the label with your cellphone or write down from the label as much information about the wine as you can. Don't trust your memory. If your wine merchant can see the name, he or she can give you that wine or something very similar to it.

Tell your wine retailer anything you can about the types of wines that you've liked previously or that you want to try. Describe what you like in simple terms.

Mention what kind of food you plan to have with the wine. The wine you drink with your halibut isn't the one you want with spicy chili! A good wine merchant is invaluable in helping you match your wine with food. (Chapter 9 tells you more about pairing wine with food.)

Name your price

Because the price of a bottle of wine can range from about $4 to literally hundreds of dollars, it's a good idea to decide approximately how much you want to spend, and say so. Fix two price ranges in your mind: one for everyday purposes and one for special occasions. These prices will probably change over time; the $8 to $12 range you start with for everyday wines often rises to $12 to $20 as you discover finer wines. A good retailer with an adequate selection should be able to make several wine suggestions in your preferred price category.

REMEMBER

A good wine merchant is more interested in the repeat business he'll get by making you happy than he is in trading you up to a bottle of wine that's beyond your limits. If what you want to spend is $15 a bottle, just say so, and stand firm, without embarrassment. Plenty of decent, enjoyable wines can be found at that price.

FIVE QUESTIONS YOU SHOULD ASK IN A WINE SHOP

Here are five questions that can give you vital information about the wine you're planning to buy.

- **If a wine costs more than $20: What kind of storage has this wine experienced?** Hemming and hawing on the part of the wine merchant should be taken to mean *poor*.

- **How long has this wine been in your store?** This question is especially important if the store doesn't have a climate-control system.

- **What are some particularly good buys this month?** (Provided you trust the wine merchant, and you don't think he's dumping some overstocked, closeout wine on you.)

- **If applicable: Why is this wine selling at such a low price?** The merchant may know that the wine is too old or is otherwise defective; unless he comes up with a believable explanation, assume that's the case.

- **Will this wine go well with the food I'm planning to serve?** The more information about the recipe or main flavors you can provide, the better your chance of getting a good match.

Chapter 7

Buying Wine in Restaurants

When you buy a bottle of wine in a restaurant, you get to taste it right then and there — instant gratification. If you've chosen well, you have a delicious wine that pairs beautifully with the food you've selected. You also can delight in the compliments of your family and friends during the entire meal and go home feeling good about yourself. If you haven't chosen well well, we all know *that* feeling! Fortunately, practice *does* make perfect, at least most of the time.

By the Glass or Buy the Bottle

In most restaurants, you have to choose your wine from a menu that tells you nothing but the names of the wines and the price per bottle. Welcome to the *restaurant wine list.*

Restaurant wine lists can be a challenge. Typically, they don't tell you enough about the wines. Sometimes, nothing on the list appeals to you, at least in your price range; other times, you have so many choices that you're immobilized. Some lists simply aren't accurate: You spend ten good minutes of your life deciding which wine to order, only to discover that it's "not available tonight" (and probably hasn't been for months) — or the vintage you want has sold out.

But believe it or not, restaurateurs really do want you to buy their wine. They usually make a sizable profit on every sale; their servers earn bigger tips, and you enjoy your meal more, going home a more satisfied customer. True, sometimes some restaurants have made it difficult for you to choose wine, but fortunately, the old ways are changing.

REMEMBER

Wines available for sale fall into two categories, as you learn in more detail in the following sections:

>> **Wines by the glass:** The glass of wine that you order can be ordinary or finer, inexpensive or higher-priced, depending on the restaurant.

- In some restaurants and in bars, you can buy an anonymous glass of wine called the *house wine.* House wine offerings usually include one white and one red (and sometimes a sparkling wine). These wines can be purchased by the glass or sometimes in a carafe. You get a restaurant's house wine when you simply ask for a glass of white or a glass of red.

- Many restaurants today do not offer a standard house wine, opting instead to give customers a wider choice — premium wines by the glass. These wines by the glass are generally better quality than standard house wines. They're usually also available by the bottle.

>> **Wines by the bottle:** Buying an actual bottle of wine is the historic norm in most restaurants. You usually choose that wine from a wine menu or wine list.

- Standard, or regular, wines are available by the bottle from the restaurant's *standard,* or regular, *wine list.* These wines can range from moderately priced to luxury offerings, depending on the restaurant.

- Reserve wines are those wines featured on a special wine list, sometimes called a *reserve wine list* (not every restaurant has such a list). They include older or rarer wines, usually very expensive.

Just a glass, please

When circumstances are such that a glass of wine makes the most sense (you only want one or possibly two glasses, or you're the only one in your group who's having wine with dinner, for example), chances are you'll need to order a wine by the glass. In our experience, restaurants are now selling more wines by the glass than ever before.

Depending on the restaurant, your options are the house wine or a premium wine by the glass — which, thankfully, is increasingly the norm, and certainly the option we recommend.

A restaurant's premium by-the-glass wines are red, white, sometimes rosé, and sparkling wines that are a lot better in quality than its basic house red or white. As such, a restaurant sells these wines at a higher price, usually in the range of $15 to $25 per glass.

A restaurant might offer only one or two premium whites and reds, or it might offer more choices. These premium wines aren't anonymous beverages, like the house red and white, but are identified for you somehow — on the wine list, on a separate card, verbally, or sometimes even by a display of bottles. Usually you'll find a restaurant's premium glass wines listed on the menu itself, under a heading such as *Wines by the Glass,* or on the wine list, where a by-the-glass price appears in a separate column for a few wines or is listed at the front of the column.

TIP

Ordering premium wines by the glass is a fine idea, especially if you want to limit your consumption or if you and your guests want to experiment by trying several wines. Sometimes, we order a glass of a premium white wine or a glass of Champagne or sparkling wine as a starter and then go on to a bottle of red wine. When we don't agree on which bottle to choose, ordering wines by the glass solves that problem. And sometimes, when we don't want to drink an entire bottle (at lunch, for example), just a glass of wine is perfect.

WARNING

One of the risks in ordering wines by the glass is that they can taste tired (in other words, old or lifeless) if the open bottles have not been stored properly. In those situations, ask the server, "How long has this bottle been open?" Ideally, the wine was opened that day. If not, ask if he or she can open a fresh bottle.

Another downside — one that we encounter increasingly — is that red wines by the glass can be too warm. While the restaurant's full bottles are stored in temperature-controlled conditions, the open bottles of red to be served by the glass often stand on the back bar where they quickly become too warm. Sometimes when we mention that the wine is too warm, the server will offer to pour us a glass from a fresh bottle that's cooler. And sometimes we just ask for a glass of ice cubes and a spoon; swirling a single ice cube in the wine *very* briefly and removing it makes a meaningful difference in the wine's temperature. Of course, we apply the ice-cube remedy only to fairly simple, inexpensive wines.

WINES BY-THE-GLASS: GOING THE EXTRA MILE

It's commendable that so many restaurants offer interesting selections of wine by the glass, particularly in view of the challenges it presents to restaurateurs. Their main problem is preserving the wine in all those open bottles. The more wines a restaurant offers by the glass, the greater the odds that wine will be left over in each bottle at the end of the evening, and those wines won't be fresh enough to serve the next day. Unless a restaurant sets up some sort of wine preservation system, it can waste an enormous amount of wine by selling it by the glass. If their by-the-glass turnover is not very high, smart restaurateurs limit the number of premium wines offered by the glass. Otherwise, its wine profits will go right down the drain (or into the stew)!

WARNING

You will probably end up paying more if you order a bottle's worth of individual glasses than you would if you had ordered a whole bottle to begin with. If two or three of you are ordering the same wine by the glass — and especially if you might want refills — ask how many ounces are poured into each glass (usually 5 to 8 ounces) and compare the price with that of a 25.4-ounce (750-ml) bottle of the same wine. (You usually do have the option of buying an entire bottle.) Sometimes, the cost of only three five-ounce glasses is equivalent to the price of a whole bottle.

TIP

Some restaurants offer an interesting selection of *half-bottles*. We strongly suggest you check out these bottles. Buying half-bottles (which hold two or more large glasses, depending upon the pour) instead of wines-by-the glass will save you money and insure a fresh pour from an unopened bottle. This is especially important for Champagne or sparkling wine.

Choosing from the bottle list

Most of the time, you'll probably end up turning to the restaurant's standard wine list to choose your wine. We use the term *standard wine list* to distinguish a restaurant's basic wine list from the special, or reserve, wine list, which certain restaurants have. Unfortunately, nothing is standard about wine lists at all. They come in all sizes, shapes, and degrees of detail, accuracy, and user friendliness.

Some wine lists offer only wines by the bottle. Others include wines by the glass, either on a separate page or in a separate column that indicates a wine's glass price, where applicable, next to its bottle price. (Later in this chapter, we explain some strategies for dealing with wine lists.)

WHEN THE RESTAURANT DOESN'T HAVE AN ALCOHOL LICENSE, BYOB

In most places, establishments that sell alcoholic beverages — both retail stores and restaurants — must be licensed by the government, to assure that appropriate taxes are paid and to aid in the enforcement of local laws. Some restaurants don't have liquor licenses due to circumstance or choice, and, therefore, can't sell wine. In those restaurants, you can BYOB (bring your own bottle) to enjoy with your meal. (To determine the restaurant's policy on BYOB, call ahead.)

We love BYOB restaurants! Not only do we save money by drinking a wine we purchased less expensively in a shop, but we can also bring any bottle we choose. You might have to pay a small fee when you bring your own wine — after all, the service staff handles your bottle for you — but in most cases, you still get a good deal. (See the later section "Restaurant Wine Tips" for more about *corkage* fees.)

WARNING

These days the wine lists of very fine restaurants, or those that are particularly wine-oriented, might also feature listings of elite wines by the glass with prices you could easily confuse with bottle prices. These selections are likely to be branded as Coravin selections, a reference to a device that enables restaurateurs to pour a glass of wine without removing the cork. Using this device, a restaurant can offer a single glass of very old or rare wine without compromising the remainder of the bottle's contents — but the price for that single glass is commensurate with the wine's reputation, often $50 per glass or more. Sometimes these listings occupy a separate page of the wine list. These elite wines by the glass are a real boon for serious wine lovers; just realize that all you are getting for your money is a glass and not a bottle.

TIP

Some fine restaurants have a *special*, or *reserve*, wine list of rare wines, to supplement their standard wine list. These special lists appeal to two types of customers: very serious wine connoisseurs and "high rollers." If you're not in either category, don't even bother asking whether the restaurant has such a list.

Analyzing the Wine List

Your first step in your encounter with the wine list is to size up the list. You can do so by noting how the wine list is organized.

TIP

As soon as your server comes to the table, ask to see the wine list. Besides communicating to the server that you feel comfortable with wine (whether it's true or not), quickly asking for the list gives you more time to study it. Also, if you wait until the food is served to order a wine, you might get the wine when you're almost finished eating! This has happened to us more than once, and now we always ask for the wine list as soon as we receive our menus. Often, the server brings the wine list with the menus without being asked.

What the wine list should tell you

You can't predict exactly what you'll find on the wine list, other than prices. Generally speaking, though, you might discover the wines arranged in the following categories:

» Champagne and sparkling wines

» (Dry) White wines and Rosé wines

» (Dry) Red wines

» Dessert wines

Some restaurants further subdivide the wines on their list according to country, especially in the white and red wine categories: French red wines, Italian red wines, California reds, and so on. These country sections may then be subdivided by wine region. France, for example, may have listings of Bordeaux, Burgundy, and possibly Rhône all under *French Red Wines. U.S. Reds* may be divided into California wines, Oregon wines, and Washington wines. Some lists organize wines by grape varieties rather than by origin.

The more serious a restaurant is about its wine selection, the more information it gives you about each wine. Here's some information you're likely to find about each wine:

» **Item number:** These numbers are sometimes called *bin numbers,* referring to the specific location of each wine in the restaurant's cellar or wine storage room.

» **The name of each wine:** The names of wines may be grape names or place-names (see Chapter 4 for details on how wines are named), but they had better also include the name of each producer (Château this or that, or such-and-such Winery), or you'll have no way of knowing exactly which wine any listing is meant to represent.

» **A vintage indication — the year the grapes were harvested:** If the wine is a blend of wines from different years, it may say *NV,* for *non-vintage.* (Chapter 4 tells you why non-vintage wines exist.)

WARNING

We're always annoyed when we see lists that don't name the wine's vintage. Or when we order a vintage-specific wine and the server shows up with a different vintage, which suggests that the restaurant didn't update its wine list. This can be a problem if the actual vintage isn't as good as the one we ordered, or if the wine's just too young to drink. We don't hesitate to order a different bottle from the list if this happens.

» **Description of each wine:** Sometimes, you might find a brief description of the wines; however, this is unlikely if dozens of wines are on the list.

» **Food pairings:** Sometimes, a wine list might include suggestions from the restaurateur for certain wines to pair with certain dinner entrées. In our experience, this information can be helpful, but you might not always like — or agree with — the wine suggestion.

» **Prices for each wine:** Wine lists *always* include prices.

WINE LIST POWER STRUGGLES

In many restaurants, the servers don't give you enough time to study the wine list. (Really good restaurants recognize that choosing a bottle of wine can take some time.) If your waiter asks, somewhat impatiently, "Have you selected your wine yet?" simply tell him (firmly) that you need more time. Don't be bullied into making a hasty choice.

Usually, your table will receive only one wine list. An outmoded convention dictates that only the host (the masculine is intentional) needs to see the list. At our table of two, we have *two* thinking, curious, decision-making customers. We usually ask for a second list.

Invariably, the wine list is handed to the oldest or most important-looking male at the table. If you're a female who is entertaining business clients, this situation can be insulting and awkward. Speak up and ask for a copy of the wine list for yourself. If it's important enough to you, slip away from the table and inform the server that you are the host of the table.

Tips for using the wine list

The wine list that you find in your hands might be comprehensive, featuring a large selection of wines and all the information we list in the previous section. Or it might be sparse. Depending on the nature of that list, here are some tips that we hope will be helpful:

TIP

>> **Notice low to high pricing.** Often, you'll find that within each category, the wines appear in ascending order of price with the least expensive wine first. Many a restaurateur is betting that you won't order that first wine out of fear of looking cheap. They figure you'll go for the second, third, or fourth wine down the price column or even deeper if you're feeling insecure and need the reassurance that your choice is a good one. (Meanwhile, that least expensive wine may be perfectly fine. Don't hesitate to order it.)

>> **Check out the regional wines.** If a restaurant features a particular country's cuisine, the wines of that country, say Italian, may be listed first (and given certain prominence), followed by a cursory listing of wines from other areas. You'll usually find the best values among those regional wines.

>> **Notice the appearance.** Once upon a time, the best wine lists consisted of hand-lettered pages inside heavy leather covers embossed with the words *Carte des Vins* in gold. Today, the best wine lists are more likely to be laser-printed pages or cards that more than make up in functionality what they sacrifice in romance.

WARNING

The more permanent and immutable a wine list seems, the less accurate its listings are likely to be — and the less specific.

>> **Don't worry if no separate list exists.** Sometimes, the list of wines is actually part of the restaurant's menu, especially if the menu is a computer-printed page or two that changes from week to week. Restaurants featuring immediate, up-to-date wine listings like this can be a good bet for wine.

>> **Pay attention to the numbers.** Item numbers for each wine make it easier for the server to locate and pull the wine quickly for you. They're also a crutch to help the server bring you the right wine in case he doesn't have a clue about wine — not to mention a crutch for *you* in ordering the wine in case you don't have a clue how to pronounce what you've decided to drink. (You can always pretend that you're using the number for the server's benefit.)

TIP

Many restaurants that are serious about wine publish their wine lists on the Internet. Before a special meal, you can go to the restaurant's website and make a short list of possible wines for your meal — a guaranteed way to boost your comfort level.

THE LOWDOWN ON HIGH WINE PRICES

Most restaurateurs count on wine and liquor sales to provide a sizable percentage of their business profit. The typical restaurant charges two to two-and-a-half (sometimes three!) times the retail store price for a bottle of wine. That means that the restaurant is earning *three to four times* the price it paid for the bottle.

Admittedly, restaurateurs incur costs for wine storage, glasses, breakage, service, and so on. But in the eyes of many wine drinkers, those costs don't justify such extraordinary markups.

Some savvy restaurateurs have discovered that by marking up their wines less, they actually sell *more* wine and make *more money* in the end. We try to patronize *those* restaurants.

The end result: Choosing your wine

If, after sizing up the wine list, you decide that you aren't familiar with most of the wines on it or are confused about which wine to drink, *ask for help with your selection*.

If the restaurant is fairly formal or very wine-focused, ask whether a *sommelier* (pronounced som-mel-yay) is on staff — technically, a specially trained, high-level wine specialist who's responsible for putting the wine list together and for making sure that the wines offered on the list complement the cuisine of the restaurant. (Today, more and more restaurants employ one.) If the restaurant isn't particularly fancy, ask to speak with the wine specialist. Often someone on staff, frequently the proprietor, knows the wine list well.

TIP

If someone on the restaurant staff knows the wine list well, this person is your best bet to help you select a wine. He or she will usually know what wines go best with the food you're ordering. He'll also be extremely appreciative of your interest in the list. For these reasons, even though we're familiar with wine, we often consult the sommelier, proprietor, or wine specialist for suggestions from the wine list. The sommelier (or wine specialist) often can save you money by recommending a good-value wine on the list that you didn't know about.

TIP

Following are a few ways you can request help when choosing a wine:

>> If you aren't sure how to pronounce the wine's name, point to it on the list.

>> Point out two or three wines on the list to the sommelier or server and say, "I'm considering these wines. Which one do you recommend?" Doing so is also a subtle way of communicating your price range.

TWICE THE PRICE

Most servers try to do their job honestly without bilking their customers. But a few profit-minded restaurateurs train their servers to maximize wine sales in every way possible. For example, some servers are trained to refill wine glasses liberally so that the bottle is empty before the main course arrives. (This can happen all the more easily when the glasses are large.) Upon emptying the bottle, the server asks, "Shall I bring another bottle of the same wine?" Depending on how much wine is in everyone's glass and how much wine your guests tend to drink, you may not *need* another bottle, but your tendency will be to say "yes" to avoid looking stingy.

» Ask to *see* one or two bottles; your familiarity with the labels, seeing the name of an importer whose other wines you've enjoyed, or some other aspect of the label might help you make up your mind.

» Mention the food you plan to order and ask for suggestions of wines that would complement the meal.

Managing the Wine Presentation Ritual

The wine presentation used to occur with such ceremony that you'd think you were involved in high church or temple services. The hushed tones of the waiter, the ritualized performance, the seriousness of it all could make you want to laugh (but that seemed wrong — almost like laughing in church). Fortunately, most wine servers aren't taking the ritual so seriously these days. But the process and the logic behind it remain the same. Step by step, the ritual (and the logic) goes like this:

1. The waiter or sommelier presents the bottle to you (assuming that you are the person who ordered the wine) for inspection.

TIP

The point is to make sure that the bottle *is* the bottle you ordered. Check the label carefully. In our experience, 10 to 15 percent of the time, we receive the wrong bottle or vintage — especially when there is no sommelier on staff. Feel the bottle with your hand, if you like, to determine whether its temperature seems to be correct; see Chapter 8 for details on proper serving temperature. If you're satisfied with the bottle, nod your approval to the server.

2. **The server removes the cork and places it in front of you.**

The purpose of this step is for you to determine, by smelling and visually inspecting the cork, whether the cork is in good condition, and whether the cork seems to be the legitimate cork for that bottle of wine.

In rare instances, a wine might be so *corky* (see Chapter 2 for detailed wine taste descriptions) that the cork itself has an unpleasant odor. On even rarer occasions, the cork might be totally wet and shriveled or very dry and crumbly; either situation suggests that air has gotten into the wine and spoiled it.

Once in a while, you might discover an incorrect vintage year or winery name on your cork. But most of the time, the presentation of the cork is inconsequential.

If the cork does raise your suspicions, you should still wait to smell or taste the wine itself before deciding whether to accept the bottle.

Once, when one of our wise-guy friends was presented the cork by the server, he proceeded to put it into his mouth and chew it, and then he pronounced to the waiter that it was just fine!

3. **If your wine needs decanting, the server decants it.**

For more information on decanting, see Chapter 8.

4. **The server pours a small amount of wine into your glass and waits.**

At this point, you're *not* supposed to say, "Is that all I get?!" You're expected to take a sniff of the wine and a little sip, and then either nod your approval to the waiter or murmur, "It's fine." Actually, this step is an important part of the ritual because if something *is* wrong with the wine, *now* is the time to return it — not after you've finished half the bottle! For a review of wine-tasting techniques, turn to Chapter 2 before you head out to the restaurant.

If you're not really sure whether the condition of the wine is acceptable, ask for someone else's opinion at your table and then make a mutual decision. Take as long as you need to on this step.

If you do decide that the bottle is out of condition, describe to the server what you find wrong with the wine, using the best language you can. (*Musty* or *dank* are descriptors that are easily understood.) Be sympathetic to the fact that you're causing more work for him, but don't be overly apologetic. (Why should you be? You didn't make the wine!) Usually, a sommelier will smell or taste the wine himself, as well.

Depending on whether the sommelier or captain agrees that it's a bad bottle or whether he believes that you just don't understand the wine, he might bring you another bottle of the same, or he might bring you the wine list so you can select a different wine. Either way, the ritual begins again from the top.

LADIES FIRST?

Almost all restaurant servers pour, and re-pour, wine for the women at the table first. What's wrong with that? Well, one of us, who otherwise is not a male chauvinist, doesn't like that idea because many times the females at the table aren't drinking as much wine as he is. Quite frequently, the last part of the bottle goes into the glasses of the women, who might already have wine in their glasses, while the males might have empty glasses in front of them, forcing the host to order another bottle or do without. Because we're all for equality between the sexes, how about pouring the wine into the emptiest glasses, regardless of gender?

5. **If you do accept the wine, the waiter pours the wine into your guests' glasses and then finally into yours.**

Now you can relax.

REMEMBER

The sommelier or wine specialist in a restaurant is there to help you make an intelligent choice of wine(s). Don't hesitate to use his (or her) services. We almost always call on the sommelier, when he is available, to ask questions about wines and get advice.

Restaurant Wine Tips

Drinking wine in a restaurant requires so many decisions that you really do need a guidebook. Should you leave the wine in an ice bucket? What should you do if the wine is bad? And can you bring your own wine? Let the following list guide you:

» **Can I kick the ice-bucket habit?** Most servers assume that an ice bucket is necessary to chill white wines and sparkling wines. But sometimes the bottle is already so cold when it comes to you that the wine would be better off warming up a bit on the table. If your white wine goes into an ice bucket and you think it's getting *too* cold, remove it from the bucket, or have the waiter remove it. Just because that ice bucket is sitting there on your table (or next to your table) doesn't mean that your bottle has to be in it!

TIP

Sometimes, a red wine that's a bit too warm can benefit from five or ten minutes in an ice bucket. (But be careful! It can get too cold very quickly.) Just explain to the server that the wine is too warm. The too-warm red-wine problem occurs frequently in over-heated restaurants.

>> **What's with these tiny glasses?** When various glasses are available, you can exercise your right to choose a different glass from the one you were given. If the restaurant's red wine glass is quite small, a stemmed water glass might be more appropriate for the red wine. Ask the server what glassware options you have.

>> **Should the wine "breathe"?** If a red wine you ordered needs aeration to soften its firm tannins (see Chapter 8), merely pulling the cork will be practically useless in accomplishing that (because the air space at the neck of the bottle is too small). Decanting the bottle or pouring the wine into glasses early is the best tactic. Don't hesitate to ask for your wine to be decanted.

>> **Where's my bottle?** We prefer to have our bottle of wine on or near our table, not out of our reach. We can look at the label that way, and we don't have to wait for the server to remember to refill our glasses, either. (Okay, call us controlling.)

>> **What if the bottle is bad?** Refuse any bottle that tastes or smells unpleasant (unless you brought it yourself!). A good restaurateur will always replace the wine, even if he thinks nothing is wrong with it. (See the preceding section for details on returning a bad bottle during the wine presentation ritual.)

>> **May I bring my own wine?** Many restaurants allow you to bring your own wine — especially if you express the desire to bring a special wine or an older wine. Restaurants will usually charge a *corkage* fee (a fee for wine service, use of the glasses, and so on) that can vary from $10 to $35 a bottle, or higher, depending on the policy of the restaurant. You should never bring a wine that's already on the restaurant's wine list; it's cheap and insulting. (Call and ask the restaurant when you're not sure whether the wine is on its list.) Anyway, you certainly should call ahead to determine whether bringing wine is possible — in some places, the restaurant's license prohibits it — and to ask what the corkage fee is.

>> **Can I take the remaining wine home with me?** The answer depends on where the restaurant is located. Some states and municipalities prevent you from leaving a restaurant with an open bottle of wine. Others permit it, often with precautions attached, such as sealing the wine in a bag with a copy of your bill for the meal showing on the outside. Ask your server about the local regulations.

>> **What if I'm traveling abroad?** If you journey to wine-producing countries, such as France, Italy, Germany, Switzerland, Austria, Greece, Spain, or Portugal, by all means try the local wines. They'll be fresher than the imports, in good condition, and the best values on the wine list.

Long Live Wine Bars

Wine bars are everywhere these days. Major cities in the United States have numerous wine bars, and major airports have them, too; New York City alone has more than we can count! Wine bars are establishments that offer an extensive choice of wines by the glass — from 12 to 100 — as well as simple food to accompany the wines. The wine bottles are usually either hooked up to an inert-gas injection system after being opened, which keeps the wine fresh, or are topped up with inert gas from a free-standing dispenser at the end of each evening.

In wine bars, you're sometimes offered a choice of two different *sizes* of wines by the glass. You can have a *taste* of a wine (about 2½ ounces) for one price, or a *glass* of a wine (often 5 ounces) for another price. And you can often order a *flight* of wines — several similar wines served side by side so you can compare them.

Wine bars are the ideal way to try lots of different wines by the glass — an educational as well as delicious experience. We love them! The fact that their numbers are increasing year by year proves that other wine drinkers love them, too. Another plus: Usually the entire wine bar staff will be more knowledgeable about wine than you would find in a restaurant staff.

IN THIS CHAPTER

» **Corkophobia and other barriers to getting the wine out**

» **Breathing lessons for your bottle**

» **Tulips, flutes, trumpets, and other types of wine glasses**

» **Appropriate temperatures and serving suggestions for wine**

» **Survival tactics for leftover wine**

Chapter **8**

Serving Wine

H ave you ever broken a cork while trying to extract it from a bottle? Have you taken an unusually long time to remove a stubborn cork while your guests smiled at you uneasily? These situations have certainly happened to us from time to time — probably to just about everyone else who has ever pulled a cork out of a bottle of wine. It's enough to give anyone a case of corkophobia!

Removing the cork from a wine bottle is the first challenge you face in your quest to enjoy wine, and it's a big one. (Fortunately, when you get the hang of it, it's easy — most of the time.) Then you face other challenges in the niggling details of wine service, such as which type of glass to use and what to do if you don't finish the whole bottle. But help is at hand in this chapter.

Getting the Cork Out

Before you can even think about removing the cork from a wine bottle, you need to deal with whatever covers the cork. Most wine bottles have a colorful covering over the top of the bottle that's called a *capsule.* Wineries place capsules on top of the corks for two reasons: to keep the corks clean and to create a fetching look for their bottles.

Wineries now use colored foil or plastic capsules rather than the traditional lead capsules. Whether the capsule is plastic, foil, or even cellophane, we usually remove the entire capsule so that no wine can possibly come into contact with the covering when we pour. (We use the small knife that's part of most *corkscrews* — the devices that exist solely for opening wine bottles.) Sometimes, we encounter a plastic plug atop the cork rather than a capsule, and we just flick it off with the tip of the knife. Occasionally, the cork is covered with hardened wax; just tap the wax gently until it breaks.

After removing the capsule or plug, we wipe clean the top of the bottle with a damp cloth. Sometimes, in older bottles, the visible end of the cork is dark with mold that developed under the capsule, and in that case, we wipe all the more diligently. (That mold can actually be a good sign: It means that the wine has been stored in humid conditions. See Chapter 17 for info on humidity and other aspects of wine storage.)

Sometimes wine lovers just can't bring themselves to remove the whole capsule out of respect for the bottle's packaging. (In fact, traditional wine etiquette dictates that you do not remove the entire capsule.) In that case, they use a gizmo called a foil cutter that sells for about $6 to $9 in wine shops, kitchen stores, or online. Or they cut off the capsule below the lip of the bottle, about one inch from the top, using the knife on the corkscrew.

Finally, after all the preceding prep, it's time to actually remove the cork. In the following sections, we warn you about the corkscrew you shouldn't use and recommend corkscrews that are worth your time and money.

The corkscrew not to use

The one corkscrew we absolutely avoid happens to be the most common type of corkscrew around. We don't like it for one very simple reason: It mangles the cork, almost guaranteeing that brown flakes of cork will be floating in your glass of wine.

That corkscrew is the infamous Wing Type Corkscrew, a bright silver-colored, metal device that looks like a cross between a pair of pliers and a drill; when you insert this corkscrew into a cork, two "wings" rise up from the side of the corkscrew, which you push down to remove the cork. The major shortcoming of this device is its meager but sharp worm, or *auger* (the curly prong that bores into the cork), which is too short for many corks and overly aggressive on all of them.

TIP

Instead of finding out the hard way that this corkscrew just doesn't cut it (or, literally, cuts it too much!), invest a few dollars in a decent corkscrew right off the bat. The time and hassle you save will be more than worth the investment. There are many good corkscrews available; we recommend the three described in the following sections.

Corkscrews to buy

One very reliable corkscrew, especially good for novices, is the Screwpull. About 6 inches long, it consists of an arched piece of plastic (which looks like a clothespin on steroids) straddling an inordinately long, 5-inch worm that's coated with Teflon (see Figure 8-1). It also comes in chrome or nickel — more expensive but worth it because it will last forever. The plastic one usually breaks after a few years.

Illustration by Lisa S. Reed

To use this corkscrew, you simply place the plastic frame over the bottle top (having removed the capsule), until a lip on the plastic is resting atop the bottle. Screw the worm downward until it touches the cork. Then hold on to the plastic firmly while turning the lever atop the worm clockwise into the cork. Simply keep turning the lever in the same clockwise direction, and the cork magically emerges from the bottle. To remove the cork from the Screwpull, simply turn the lever counterclockwise while holding on to the cork.

The Screwpull comes in many colors and costs about $20 to $25 in wine shops, kitchen stores, and online. The chrome or nickel version costs about $60. It's very simple to use and doesn't require a lot of muscle.

We have two other corkscrews for the corks that the Screwpull can't remove. (Flange-top bottles, for example, really challenge the Screwpull because of their unusual width at the top.) Our two alternative corkscrews (described in the following sections) are smaller devices that — besides often working better — can conveniently fit into a pocket. Their size is one reason that servers in restaurants favor them.

TIP

You can buy some really fancy corkscrews — some which attach to a counter or a bar — that will cost you $100-plus. Yes, most of them work very well after you get the hang of them, but frankly, we don't see the need to spend that much on a corkscrew. We'd rather spend it on the wine!

The two-pronged Ah-So

One corkscrew we recommend is called, unofficially, the Ah-So because — according to legend, anyway — when people finally figure out how it works, they say, "Ah, so that's how it works!" (It's also known as the "Butler's Friend" — but where have all the butlers gone?) The Ah-So sells for around $5 for the simplest version, up to $30 for the fancy ones.

It's a simple device made up of two thin, flat metal prongs, one slightly longer than the other (see Figure 8-2). To use it, you slide the prongs down into the tight space between the cork and the bottle (inserting the longer prong first), using a back-and-forth seesaw motion until the top of the Ah-So is resting atop the cork. Then you twist the cork while gently pulling it up.

FIGURE 8-2:
The Ah-So
corkscrew.

Illustration by Lisa S. Reed

One advantage of the Ah-So is that it delivers an intact cork — without a hole in it — that can be reused to close bottles of homemade vinegar or to make cutesy bulletin boards.

TIP

Although more difficult to operate than the Screwpull, the Ah-So really comes into its own with very tight-fitting corks that no other corkscrews, including the Screwpull, seem to be able to budge. Also, the Ah-So can be effective with old, crumbly corks that don't give other corkscrews much to grip.

WARNING

The Ah-So is useless with loose corks that move inside the bottle's neck when you try to remove them. It just pushes those corks down into the wine. At that point, you'll need another tool called a *cork retriever* (which we describe in the section "Dealing with cork particles in your wine" later in this chapter).

The most professional corkscrew of them all

Our final recommended corkscrew, the most commonly used corkscrew in restaurants all over the world, is simply called the Waiter's Corkscrew. A straight or gently curved base holds three devices that fold into it, like a Swiss Army knife: a lever, a worm, and a small knife (see Figure 8-3). The latter is especially handy for removing the capsule from the bottle.

Illustration by Lisa S. Reed

The Waiter's Corkscrew is definitely the preferred corkscrew of people in the wine business. Using it requires some practice. First, grasp the bottle's neck. The trick then is to guide the worm down through the center of the cork by turning the corkscrew; turn slowly at first, until you're sure that the worm is not off center and is actually descending down the middle of the cork. After the worm is fully descended into the cork, place the lever on the lip of the bottle and push against the lever while pulling the cork up. Give a firm tug at the very end or wiggle the bottom of the cork out with your hand.

TIP

If your cork ever breaks and part of it gets stuck in the neck of the bottle, the Waiter's Corkscrew is indispensable for removing the remaining piece. Use the method we just described, but insert the worm at a 45-degree angle. In most cases, you will successfully remove the broken cork.

The Waiter's Corkscrew sells for a few dollars to about $18 or more for the best versions. We use these corkscrews frequently because they're the fastest to use, after you get the hang of them. And you can carry them in your pocket, if you're going someplace where you might be opening wine bottles. Just remember to remove it from your pocket before you travel by air, as corkscrews with knives are not TSA-approved.

The Durand

A new device is quickly gaining in popularity among serious wine types. It's called the Durand, and it's a hybrid of the Ah-So and the Waiter's Corkscrew. It is especially effective with frail or old corks. You first grip the cork with the Ah-So prongs, and then gently screw down the long worm of the corkscrew. At the moment, however, it is rather expensive ($125).

Dealing with cork particles in your wine

Every now and then, even if you've used the right corkscrew and used it properly, you can still have pieces of cork floating in your wine. They can be tiny dry flakes that crumbled into the bottle, actual chunks of cork, or even the entire cork.

Before you start berating yourself for being a klutz, you should know that "floating cork" has happened to all of us at one time or another, no matter how experienced we are. Cork won't harm the wine. And besides, you can get a wonderful instrument called a *cork retriever* (no, it's not a small dog from the south of Ireland!) that sells for $5 to $10 online.

One type of cork retriever consists of three 10-inch pieces of stiff metal wire with hooks on the ends. This device is remarkably effective for removing floating pieces of cork from the bottle. We have even removed a whole, fallen cork through the neck with a cork retriever.

Alternatively, you can just pick out the offending piece(s) of cork with a spoon after you pour the wine into your glass. (That's one occasion when serving your guest first is rude, because the first glass has more cork pieces in it.) Or you can pour the wine through a paper coffee filter (preferably the natural brown-paper type), into a decanter or pitcher to catch the remaining pieces of cork.

A special case: Opening Champagne and sparkling wine

Opening a bottle of sparkling wine is usually an exciting occasion. Who doesn't enjoy the ceremony of a cold glass of bubbly? But you need to use a completely different technique than you'd use to open a regular wine bottle. The cork even looks different. Sparkling wine corks have a mushroom-shaped head that protrudes from the bottle and a wire cage that holds the cork in place against the pressure that's trapped inside the bottle.

WARNING

Be careful when you remove the wire cage. From the moment you loosen the cage, keep one hand on top of the cork as a precaution. (We had a hole in our kitchen ceiling from one adventure with a flying cork.) Be sure to point the bottle away from people and fragile objects.

If you like to hear the cork pop, just yank it out. When you do that, however, you'll lose some of the precious wine, which will froth out of the bottle. Also, the noise can interfere with your guests' conversation. Besides, it ain't too classy!

Removing the cork from sparkling wine with just a gentle sigh rather than a loud pop is fairly easy. Simply hold the bottle at a 45-degree angle with a kitchen towel wrapped around it if it's wet. (Try resting the base of the bottle on your hipbone.) Twist the bottle while holding on to the cork so that you can control the cork as it emerges. When you feel the cork starting to come out of the bottle, *push down against the cork* with some pressure, as if you don't want to let it out of the bottle. In this way, the cork will emerge slowly with a hiss or sigh sound rather than a pop.

WARNING

Never, ever use a corkscrew on a bottle of sparkling wine. The pressure of the trapped carbonation, when suddenly released, can send the cork *and* corkscrew flying right into your eye, with serious consequences.

Here are some other tips for opening bottles of bubbly:

>> Never shake a bottle of sparkling wine before opening. If your bottle of bubbly has just traveled, let it rest for a day. Controlling the cork is difficult when the carbon dioxide has been stirred up.

If you're in the midst of a sparkling wine emergency and need to open a bottle that has traveled, calm down the carbonation by submerging the bottle in an ice bucket for about 30 minutes. (Fill the bucket with one-half ice cubes and one-half ice-cold water.)

TIP

>> Every once in a while, you'll come across a really tight sparkling wine cork that doesn't want to budge. Try running the bottle neck under warm water for a few moments or wrapping a towel around the cork to create friction. Either action will usually enable you to remove the cork, but keep your thumb on the cork in case it suddenly pops out.

>> Another option for a tight cork is to use a fancy gadget that you place around the part of the cork that's outside the bottle. (Actually, three types of gadgets can do the trick: Champagne Pliers, a Champagne Star, and a Champagne Key.) Or you can probably try using regular pliers, although lugging in the toolbox will surely change the mood of the occasion.

Screw Caps Are "In"

Back in the day, only cheap, lower-quality wines had screw cap closures. But in the past 20 years, more and more wine producers have switched from corks to screw caps for their fine wines. Not only are many wineries now using screw caps for their wines that are meant to be enjoyed young, but also a number of producers, particularly in Australia and New Zealand, are using screw-cap closures even on wines destined for cellaring.

Rather than imitation cork we prefer to see real screw caps on wine bottles. Screw caps are perfectly sound closures, technically speaking, and they're easier to remove than corks. They also prevent *cork taint*, a chemical flaw affecting a small percentage of corks and, consequently, the wine in those bottles. A *corky* wine — that is, one affected with cork taint — is damaged either slightly or flagrantly. In the worst-case scenarios, corky wines give off an offensive odor similar to moldy or damp cardboard.

Don't expect to see bottles of the most elite, age-worthy red wines sporting screw caps anytime soon, because many winemakers are still reluctant to use them for such wines, especially producers in Europe. But don't shy away from screw-capped bottles of other fine wines when you find them.

Does Wine Really Breathe?

Most wine is alive in the sense that it changes chemically as it slowly grows older. When grapes turn into wine, they give off carbon dioxide, just like us. Wine itself absorbs oxygen, and, like our own cells, it oxidizes. So we suppose you could say that wine breathes. But of course that's not what the server means when he asks, "Shall I pull the cork and let the wine breathe?"

WARNING

The term *breathing* refers to the process of aerating the wine, exposing it to air. Generally, the aroma and flavor of a very young wine improves with aeration. But just pulling the cork out of the bottle and letting the bottle sit there is a truly ineffective way to aerate the wine. The little space at the neck of the bottle is way too small to allow your wine to breathe very much.

In the following sections, we explain how to aerate your wine and list the wines that benefit from aerating.

How to aerate your wine

If you really want to aerate your wine, do one or both of the following:

>> Pour the wine into a *decanter* (a fancy word for a glass container that is big enough to hold the contents of an entire bottle of wine). Practically speaking, it doesn't matter what your decanter looks like or how much it costs. In fact, very inexpensive, wide-mouthed carafes are fine.

>> Pour some of the wine into large glasses at least ten minutes before you plan to drink it.

Which wines need aerating?

Many red wines but only a few white wines — and some dessert wines — can benefit from aeration. You can drink most white wines upon pouring, unless they're too cold, but that's a discussion for later (see the section "Not Too Warm, Not Too Cold").

Young, tannic red wines

TIP

Young, tannic red wines (see Chapter 2 for more on tannin) — such as Cabernet Sauvignons, Bordeaux, many wines from the northern Rhône Valley, and many Italian wines — definitely taste better with aeration because their tannins soften and the wine becomes less harsh.

The younger and more tannic the wine is, the longer it needs to breathe. As a general rule, most tannic, young red wines soften up with one hour of aeration. A glaring exception to the one-hour rule would be many young Barolos or Barbarescos (red wines from Piedmont, Italy, which you can read about in Chapter 11). These wines are frequently tannic enough to make your mouth pucker, and can often can benefit from three or four hours of aeration. But some Barolos and Barbarescos with softer tannins are ready to drink sooner. You can taste the wine to find out.

Older red wines with sediment

Many red wines develop *sediment* (tannin and other matter in the wine that solidifies over time) usually after about ten years of age. You want to remove the sediment because it could taste a bit bitter. Also, the dark particles floating in your wine, or the cloudy substance accumulating at the bottom of your glass, don't look very appetizing.

To remove sediment, keep the bottle of wine upright for a day or two before you plan to open it so that the sediment settles at the bottom of the bottle. Then decant the wine carefully: Pour the wine out of the bottle slowly into a decanter while watching the wine inside the bottle as it approaches the neck. You watch the wine so that you can stop pouring when you see cloudy wine from the bottom of the bottle making its way to the neck. If you stop pouring at the right moment, all the cloudy wine remains behind in the bottle.

TIP

To actually see the wine inside the bottle as you pour, you need to have a bright light shining through the bottle's neck. Candles have traditionally been used for this purpose, and they're romantic, but a flashlight standing on end works even better because it's brighter, and it doesn't flicker. (The flashlight app on your cellphone has similar advantages.) Or simply hold the bottle up to a bright light and pour slowly.

If the wine needs aeration after decanting (that is, it still tastes a bit harsh), let it breathe in the open decanter until the wine softens to your taste. Or decant it a second time.

WARNING

The older the wine, the more delicate it can be. Don't give old, fragile-looking wines excessive aeration. (Look at the color of the wine through the bottle before you decant; if it looks pale, the wine could be pretty far along in its life cycle.) The flavors of really old wines will start fading rapidly after 10 or 15 minutes of being exposed to air.

A few white wines

Some very good, dry white wines — such as full-bodied white Burgundies and white Bordeaux wines, as well as the best Alsace and German Rieslings — also get better with aeration. For example, if you open a young Corton-Charlemagne (a great white Burgundy), and it doesn't seem to be showing much aroma or flavor, chances are that it needs aeration. Decant it and taste it again in half an hour. In most cases, the wine dramatically improves. Conversely, most red Burgundies usually don't need aeration or decanting. An exception to not decanting red Burgundy would be a young, dark-colored, tannic Burgundy.

Vintage Ports

One of the most famous fortified wines is Vintage Port (properly called "Porto"). We discuss this wine and others like it in Chapter 16.

For now, we'll just say that, yes, Vintage Port needs breathing lessons, and needs them very much, indeed! Young Vintage Ports are so brutally tannic that they demand many hours of aeration (eight would not be too many). Even older Ports improve with four hours or more of aeration. Older Vintage Ports also require decanting for another reason: They're chock-full of sediment. (Often, large flakes of sediment fill the bottom 10 percent or so of the bottle.) Keep Vintage Ports standing for several days before you open them to allow the sediment to settle.

Does the Glass Really Matter?

If you're just drinking wine as refreshment with your meal, and you aren't thinking about the wine much as it goes down, the glass you use probably doesn't matter much. But if you have a good wine, a special occasion, friends who want to talk about the wine with you, or the boss at your home for dinner, *stemware* (glasses with stems) is called for. Frankly, we use fine glasses just about every night with dinner. And it's not just a question of etiquette and status. Good wine tastes better out of good glasses. Really.

Think of wine glasses as being like stereo speakers. Any old speaker brings the music to your ears, just like any old glass brings the wine to your lips. But can't you appreciate the music so much more, aesthetically and emotionally, from good speakers? The same principle holds true with wine and wine glasses. You can appreciate a wine's aroma and flavor complexities so much more out of a fine wine glass. The medium is the message.

Color, size, and shape

Good wine glasses are always clear. Those pretty pink or green glasses may look nice in your china cabinet, but they interfere with your ability to distinguish the true colors of the wine.

Two other aspects of a glass are important: its size and its shape. The idea that the taste of a wine changes when you drink it from different sizes or shapes of glasses can be difficult to believe. A riot almost broke out at one wine event we organized because the same wine tasted so different in different glasses that the tasters thought we had served them different wines — and that we had just pretended it was all the same wine, to fool them.

For dry red and white wine, small glasses are all wrong — besides that, they're a pain in the neck. You just can't swirl the wine around in little glasses without spilling it, which makes appreciating the aroma of the wine almost impossible. And furthermore, who wants to bother continually refilling them? Small glasses can work adequately only for sherry or dessert wines, which have strong aromas to begin with and are generally consumed in smaller quantities than table wines.

REMEMBER

Matching glass size to wine works like this:

» Glasses for red wines should hold a minimum of 12 ounces; many of the best glasses have capacities ranging from 16 to 24 ounces, or more.

» For white wines, 10 to 12 ounces should be the minimum capacity.

» For sparkling wines, an 8- to 12-ounce capacity is fine.

The shape of the bowl matters because it affects the surface area of the wine that's exposed to air and also the manner in which the wine enters your mouth. Some wine glasses have very round bowls, while others have more elongated, somewhat narrower bowls. We're not physicists, and so we can't explain the phenomenon, but we know from experience that the shape changes our taste perception. When we're having dinner at home, we often try our wine in glasses of different shapes, just to see which glass works best for that wine. The next section discusses the functions of various glass shapes.

Stemware made of very thin, fine crystal costs a lot more than normal glassware. That's one reason many people don't use them, and why some people do. The better reason for using fine crystal is that the wine tastes better out of it. Thick, heavy glass detracts from your tasting experience because it is a rude barrier between your lips and the wine; thin crystal heightens the aesthetic experience of wine drinking.

Tulips, flutes, trumpets, and other picturesque wine-glass names

You thought that a tulip was a flower and a flute and a trumpet were musical instruments? Well, they also happen to be types of glasses designed for use with sparkling wine (see Figure 8-4).

FIGURE 8-4: Glasses for sparkling wine (from left): Tulip, flute, and trumpet.

Illustration by Lisa S. Reed

» The tulip is the ideally shaped glass for Champagne and other sparkling wines. It is tall, elongated, and narrower at the rim than in the middle of the bowl. This shape helps hold the bubbles in the wine longer, not allowing them to escape freely (the way the wide-mouthed, sherbet-cuplike, so-called Champagne glasses do). Riedel's Champagne Veritas glass is a variation of the tulip that is wider yet in the middle of the glass. Actually, it is our favorite Champagne glass right now.

» The flute is another type of sparkling wine glass, but it's less ideal than the tulip because it doesn't narrow at the mouth, and it does little to trap and hold the wine's aromas.

>> The trumpet actually widens at the mouth, making it less suitable for sparkling wine but very elegant looking. Another drawback of some trumpet glasses is that the wine can actually fill the stem itself, which causes the wine to warm up from the heat of your hand as you hold the stem.

We avoid the trumpet glass. We are not fans of flutes, either. When tulip glasses or Riedel's Veritas glasses are not available, we use good white wine glasses for Champagnes and sparkling wines.

An oval-shaped bowl that narrows at its mouth (see Figure 8-5) is ideal for many red wines, such as Bordeaux, Cabernet Sauvignon, Merlot, Chianti, Zinfandel, and most white wines. On the other hand, some red wines, such as Burgundies, Pinot Noirs, and Barolos — and the better Chardonnays and white Burgundies — are best appreciated in wider-bowled, apple-shaped glasses (see Figure 8-5). We urge you to experiment and decide for yourself which shape you prefer for any particular wine.

FIGURE 8-5:
The Bordeaux glass (left) and the Burgundy glass (right).

Illustration by Lisa S. Reed

HALF EMPTY OR HALF FULL?

"Fill 'er up" may be the rule for your gas tank, but not for your wine glass. We are annoyed when servers fill our glasses to the top. We suppose they mean well in giving us our money's worth. But how can we stick our noses into full glasses without looking like idiots?

To leave room for swirling and smelling the wine, fill the glass only partially. One-third capacity is the best fill level for serious red wines. (This goes back to that idea of aerating the wine and trapping the aromas in the glass's airspace.) White wine glasses can be filled halfway, while sparkling wine glasses can be two-thirds full.

Which glasses to buy?

So what's a wine lover to do: Buy a different type of glass for each kind of wine? Fortunately, some all-purpose red and white wine glasses combine the best features of most glasses in terms of size, thickness, and shape. Andrea Robinson, a Master Sommelier, has designed "The One," a glass that comes in two sizes: a larger glass for red wines, and a smaller glass for white wines. The glass shape is trapezoidal, a relatively new shape that some wine people favor for red Burgundy. In fact, we use the larger glass for both red and white wines.

WORTH THE SEARCH

Other glassware options include Riedel or Spiegelau Crystal. Riedel is an Austrian glass manufacturer that specializes in making what it considers the ideal wine glass for each kind of wine. Spiegelau, a German company now owned by Riedel, operates similarly, but its glasses are less expensive than Riedel's.

Another company, Ravenscroft Crystal, based in New York City, offers quality crystal wine glasses at moderate prices. Five other fine crystal wine manufacturers are Schlott Zeisel, Eisch, Gabriel Glas, Stolzle, and Zalto — the latter a fave of many New York sommeliers. You can buy these glasses in many department stores or specialty shops. Eisch promotes its glassware as being particularly good for making young or tannic wines taste readier to drink.

Washing your wine glasses

TIP

Detergents often leave a filmy residue in glasses, which can affect the aroma and flavor of your wine. We strongly advise that you clean your good crystal glasses by hand, using washing soda or baking soda. (Washing soda is the better of the two; it dissolves better than baking soda.) Neither product leaves any soapy, filmy residue in your glass. You can find washing soda in the soap/detergent section of supermarkets.

WHEN PLASTIC IS THE LOGICAL CHOICE

Sometimes, such as at outdoor events, real glassware is just not a good option. The solution is GoVino, a brand of stemless plastic glasses that are really very decent for wine lovers. The glasses have a shape similar to the bowl of all-purpose stemware, and therefore you can swirl and sniff just as you would when you're using stemware. When plastic makes sense, these glasses are the way to go.

Not Too Warm, Not Too Cold

Just as the right glass enhances your wine experience, serving wine at the ideal temperature range is a vital factor in your enjoyment of wine.

Most red wines are best at cool room temperature, 62 to 65 degrees Fahrenheit (16 to 18 degrees Celsius). Once upon a time, in drafty old English and Scottish castles, that was simply room temperature. (Actually, it was probably warm, mid-summer room temperature!) Today when you hear *room temperature,* you think of a room that's about 70 degrees Fahrenheit or higher (21 degrees Celsius), don't you? Red wine served at this temperature can taste flat, flabby, lifeless, and often too *hot* — you get a burning sensation from the alcohol. Many restaurants leave red wines out at their room temperature, which is usually way too warm!

Ten or 15 minutes in the fridge or 5 to 10 minutes in an ice bucket does wonders to revive red wines that have been suffering from heat prostration. But don't let the wine get too cold. Red wines served too cold taste overly tannic and acidic and decidedly unpleasant. Light, fruity red wines, such as the simplest Beaujolais wines and inexpensive Pinot Noirs, are most delightful when served slightly chilled at about 56 to 58 degrees Fahrenheit.

TIP

Are you wondering how to know when your bottle is 56 to 58 degrees Fahrenheit? You can buy a nifty digital thermometer that wraps around the outside of the bottle and gives you a color-coded reading. Or you can buy something that looks like a real thermometer that you place into the opened bottle (in the bottle's mouth, you might say). We have both of those, and we never use them. Just feel the bottle with your hand and take a guess. Practice makes perfect.

While many red wines are served too warm, white wines are often served too cold, judging by our experiences in many restaurants. The higher the quality of a white wine, the less cold it should be so that you can properly appreciate its flavor. Don't use an ice bucket unless your white wine is too warm. Table 8-1 indicates our recommended serving temperatures for various types of wines.

Some people prefer Champagnes colder than other white wines because they warm up quite rapidly.

TIP

To avoid the problem of warm bubbly, keep an ice bucket handy. Or put the bottle back in the refrigerator between pourings.

TABLE 8-1   **Serving Temperatures for Wine**

Type of Wine	Temperature °F	Temperature °C
Most Champagnes and sparkling wines	45°F	7°C
Older or expensive, complex Champagnes	52°F	11°C
Inexpensive sweet wines	50°–55°F	10°–12.8°C
Rosés and blush wines	50°–55°F	10°–12.8°C
Simpler, inexpensive, quaffing-type white wines	50°–55°F	10°–12.8°C
Dry Sherry, such as fino or manzanilla	55°–56°F	12°–13°C
Fine, dry white wines	58°–62°F	14°–16.5°C
Finer dessert wines, such as a good Sauternes	58°–62°F	14°–16.5°C
Light, fruity red wines	58°–60°F	14°–14.5°C
Most red wines	62°–65°F	16°–18°C
Sherry other than dry fino or manzanilla	62°–65°F	16°–18°C
Port and Madeira	62°–65°F	16°–18°C

Entertaining with Wine

When you're hosting a dinner party, you probably serve more wines than you would in the course of a normal dinner. Instead of just one wine all through the meal, you may want to serve a different wine with every course. Many people serve two wines at the table: a white with the first course and a red with the entrée. (And if they love wine, they use a cheese course as an excuse to serve a second, knockout red or a dessert wine.)

REMEMBER

Because you want every wine to taste good — besides blending deliciously with the food you're serving — you should give some thought to the sequence in which the wines will be served. The classic guidelines are the following:

>> Champagne or sparkling wine first

>> White wine before red wine (unless the white wine is clearly superior to the red wine)

>> Light wine before heavy wine

>> Dry wine before sweet wine

>> Simple wine before complex, richly flavored wine

TIP

Each of these principles operates independently. A very light red wine served before a rich, full-bodied white can work just fine. If the food you're serving calls for white wine, there's really no reason that both wines couldn't be white: a simpler, lighter white first and a richer, fuller-bodied white second. Likewise, both wines could be red, or you could serve a dry rosé followed by a red.

We provide more details on how to serve wine when entertaining in the following sections.

First things first

Even if you don't plan to serve hors d'oeuvres, you probably want to offer your guests a drink when they arrive to set a relaxing tone for the evening.

TIP

We like to serve Champagne (notice the capital C) as the apéritif because opening the bottle of Champagne is a ceremony that brings everyone together. Champagne honors your guests. And a glass of Champagne is compelling enough that to spend a thoughtful moment tasting it doesn't seem rude; even people who think it's absurd to talk about wine understand that Champagne is too special to be ignored. Also, Champagne is complex enough that it stands alone just fine, without food. Nonetheless we often accompany the bubbly with nuts or a dip.

How much is enough?

TIP

A simple rule is to figure, in total, a full bottle of wine per guest (total consumption). That quantity may sound high, but if your dinner is spread over several hours and you're serving a lot of food, it isn't necessarily immoderate. If you're concerned that your guests may overindulge, be sure to keep their water glasses full so that they have an alternative to automatically reaching for the wine.

If your dinner party is special enough to have several food courses and several wines, we recommend giving each guest a separate glass for each wine. The glasses can be different for each wine, or they can be alike. All those glasses really look festive on the table. And with a separate glass for each wine, no guest feels compelled to empty each glass before going on to the next wine. (You also can tell at a glance who is drinking the wine and who isn't really interested in it, and you can adjust your pouring accordingly.)

Keeping Leftover Wine

A sparkling-wine stopper, a device that fits over an opened bottle of bubbly wine, is really effective in keeping any remaining Champagne or sparkling wine fresh (often for two or three days) in the refrigerator. But what do you do when you have red or white wine left in a bottle?

You can put the cork back in the bottle if it still fits, and put the bottle into the refrigerator. (Even red wines will stay fresher there; just take the bottle out to warm up about two hours before serving it.) But other methods are also reliable in keeping your remaining wine from oxidizing; these techniques are all the more effective if you put the bottles in the fridge after using them, which slows down the action of oxygen on the wine:

>> If you have about half a bottle of wine left, simply pour the wine into a clean, empty half-sized wine bottle and recork the smaller bottle. We sometimes buy wines in half-bottles, just to make sure that we have the leftover, empty half-bottles around.

>> Buy a can of inert gas, available in some wine stores and online. Just squirt a few shots of the gas into the bottle and put the cork back in the bottle. The gas displaces the oxygen in the bottle, thus protecting the wine from oxidizing. Simple and effective.

AN ASIDE ABOUT ATMOSPHERIC PRESSURE

File this under FYI ("For Your Information") — or maybe under "Believe It or Not."

Several years ago, we were enjoying one of our favorite red wines, an Italian Barbera, in the Alps. It was a perfect summer day in the mountains — crisp, clear, and cool. The wine was also perfect — absolutely delicious with our salami, bread, and cheese. A couple of days later, we had the very same wine at the seashore, on a cloudy, humid, heavy-pressure day. The wine was heavy, flat, and lifeless. What had happened to our wonderful mountain wine? We made inquiries among some of our wine-drinking friends and discovered that they have had similar experiences. For red wines at least, atmospheric pressure apparently influences the taste of the wine: thin, light pressure, for the better; heavy pressure, heavy humidity, for the worse. So the next time one of your favorite red wines doesn't seem quite right, check the barometer!

>> Try using a simple new wine preservation device called Repour. It is a large plastic stopper that you insert into your opened bottle after peeling off a tiny foil cover on the bottom of the stopper. By absorbing oxygen in the airspace of the bottle, the stopper reverses the effects of oxygen interaction that the wine has experienced after being opened. We have tried it on red wines that were open for three days and witnessed the restored freshness of the wine. Repour sells for about $18 for a box of ten stoppers. Each stopper is good for one bottle of wine.

To avoid all this bother, just drink the wine! Or, if you're not too fussy, just place the leftover wine in the refrigerator and drink it in the next day or two — before it goes into a coma.

Chapter **9**

Marrying Wine with Food

Every now and then, we encounter a wine that stops us dead in our tracks. It's so sensational that we lose all interest in anything but that wine. We drink it with intent appreciation, trying to memorize the taste. We wouldn't dream of diluting its perfection with a mouthful of food. But 999 times out of 1,000, we drink our wine with food. Wine is meant to go with food. And good food is meant to go with wine.

Good. We've settled that. Wine goes with food, and food goes with wine. Any questions?

Of course, we're being facetious. The world has thousands of wines, and every one is different. And the world has thousands of basic foods, each one different — not to mention the infinite combinations of foods in prepared dishes (what we really eat). In reality, food-with-wine is about as simple an issue as soul-meets-soulmate. Find out more about pairing wine with food in this chapter.

With Wine and Food, Rules Do Not Apply

Back in the era of the TV show *Mad Men*, a few simple — and simplistic — rules guided people in selecting wines for their meals. Wine was simpler then, and food was simpler too. Today, the enormous range of wines available and the eclectic gamut of food choices render yesterday's easy rules obsolete.

Not only that, but today, science has documented that people have inborn sensitivities or tolerances to some of the fundamental tastes present in foods and wines. The bitterness of strong, black coffee or tannic red wine can be almost painful to people with the most sensitive taste buds, for example, while the most tolerant tasters enjoy that bitterness. The guidelines for pairing food and wine today must be extremely flexible to accommodate individual likes and dislikes.

REMEMBER

We can tell you what we like and what works for us in pairing food and wine. And we can tell you how certain components of food interact with certain styles of wine. But you have to be your own judge of what works for you, through your firsthand experience of eating and drinking.

The Dynamics of Food and Wine

Every dish is dynamic — it's made up of several ingredients and flavors that interact to create a (more or less) delicious whole. Every wine is equally dynamic in its combination of flavors and structural components. When food and wine combine in your mouth, the dynamics of each change; the result is completely individual to each dish-and-wine combination. When wine meets food, several things can happen:

>> The food can exaggerate a characteristic of the wine. For example, if you eat walnuts (which are tannic) with a tannic red wine, such as a Bordeaux, the wine tastes so dry and astringent that most people would consider it undrinkable.

>> The food can diminish a characteristic of the wine. Salt diminishes the impression of tannin, for example, and an overly tannic red wine — unpleasant on its own — could be delightful with a well-salted rare steak or roast beef.

>> The flavor intensity of the food can obliterate the wine's flavor or vice versa. If you've ever drunk a big, rich flavorful white wine with a delicate filet of sole, you've had this experience firsthand.

>> The wine can contribute new flavors to the dish. For example, a red Zinfandel that's gushing with berry fruit can bring its berry flavors to the dish, as if another ingredient had been added.

>> The combination of wine and food can create an unwelcome third-party flavor that wasn't in the wine or the food originally; for example, we get a metallic flavor when we eat plain white-meat turkey with red Bordeaux. (Actually, Burgundy, white or red, works better with turkey.)

THE FIFTH WHEEL: UMAMI

The long-held belief had been that humans can perceive four basic tastes: sweet, sour, salty, and bitter. But people who study food concluded that a fifth taste exists, and maybe many more than that. The fifth taste is called *umami* (pronounced oo-*mah*-me), and it's associated with a savory character in foods. Shellfish, oily fish, meats, mushrooms, and cheeses are some foods high in umami taste.

Umami-rich foods can increase the sensation of bitterness in wines served with them. To counteract this effect, try adding something salty (such as salt itself) or sour (such as vinegar or lemon) to your dish. Although this suggestion defies the adage that vinegar and wine don't get along, the results are the proof of the pudding.

Fortunately, certain elements of food react in predictable ways with certain elements of wine, giving us a fighting chance at making successful pairings. The major components of wine (alcohol, sweetness, acid, and tannin) relate to the basic tastes of food (sweetness, sourness, bitterness, and saltiness) the same way that the principle of balance in wine operates: Some of the elements exaggerate each other, and some of them compensate for each other. (See the discussion of balance in Chapter 2.)

REMEMBER

The following sections note some ways that food and wine interact, based on the components of the wine. Keep in mind that each wine and each dish has more than one component, and the simple relationships we describe can be complicated by other elements in the wine or the food. Whether a wine is considered tannic, sweet, acidic, or high in alcohol depends on its dominant component. (See Chapter 2 for details.)

Tannic wines

Tannic wines include most wines based on the Cabernet Sauvignon grape (including red Bordeaux), northern Rhône reds, Barolo and Barbaresco, and any wine — white or red — that has become tannic from aging in new oak barrels. These wines can

>> Taste astringent, or mouth-drying, when paired with spicy-hot foods

>> Taste bitter with bitter foods

>> Taste less bitter when paired with salty foods

Sweet wines

Many so-called dry wines today actually have some sweetness, particularly inexpensive (about $12 or less) wines from California. Wines with unmistakable sweetness include most Moscato wines, White Zinfandel, many Rieslings (unless they're labeled *dry* or *trocken*), and medium-dry Vouvray. Sweet wines also include dessert wines such as Port, sweetened Sherries, and late-harvest wines. Depending on their level of sweetness, these wines can

>> Taste fruitier when matched with salty foods

>> Make salty foods more appealing

>> Go well with foods as sweet as they are, but not sweeter

Acidic wines

Acidic wines include most Italian white wines; Sancerre, Pouilly-Fumé, and Chablis; traditionally made red wines from Rioja; most dry Rieslings; and fully dry wines based on Sauvignon Blanc. These wines can

>> Counterbalance oily or fatty heaviness in food

>> Taste smoother and less acidic when served with salty foods

>> Stand up to foods that have some acidity

High-alcohol wines

High-alcohol wines include many California wines, both white and red; southern Rhône whites and reds; southern Italian reds; fortified wines such as Port and Sherry; and most wines produced from grapes grown in warm climates. These wines can

>> Overwhelm lightly flavored or delicate dishes

>> Make spicy-hot dishes taste hotter

>> Seem less rich and full with slightly sweet foods

>> Seem less rich and full with umami-rich foods (see the nearby sidebar, "The fifth wheel: Umami")

Other Ways of Pairing Food and Wine

Besides considering the predictable reactions between components of foods and those of wine (see the preceding section), many people choose a wine for a dish (or vice versa) in a more general way, by trying to harmonize particular characteristics of a wine with those in the food.

REMEMBER

The characteristics of a wine that come into play against the characteristics of a dish include the following:

>> **The wine's flavors:** Earthy, herbal, fruity, vegetal, and so on

>> **The weight of the wine:** Light-bodied, medium-bodied, or full-bodied

>> **The wine's intensity of flavor:** Subtle flavor intensity, moderately flavorful, or very flavorful

WARNING

The idea of matching the specific flavors of a wine to those in a food is popular in some circles. In our experience, though, that's just not a reliable way to create a successful pairing because it fails to take into consideration issues such as the flavor intensity of the food and the wine, and the dryness or sweetness of each.

Matching the weight of a wine to the weight of a dish is a more useful practice. You probably use this principle already without realizing it: You choose a light-bodied wine to go with a light dish, a medium-bodied wine to go with a fuller dish, and a full-bodied wine to go with a heavy dish.

The flavor intensity of the food and the wine is another useful consideration. A subtle wine is likely to wimp out on you when you taste it side by side with a very flavorful dish. An Asian stir-fry or Tex-Mex dish bursting with flavor would be at home with a very flavorful (rather than subtle) wine, such as a German Riesling or a rich Zinfandel.

TIP

To harmonize these characteristics of the wine and the food, of course, you have to have a good idea of what the food is going to taste like and what various wines taste like. That second part can be a real stumbling block for people who don't devote every ounce of their free energy to learning about wine. The solution is to ask your wine merchant. He might not have the world's greatest knack in wine and food pairings (then again, he might), but at least he should know what his wines taste like.

"A CHÂQUE SON GOUT" — PERSONAL TASTE RULES

We once happened to discuss food pairings for red Bordeaux wine with the owner of one of the five First Growths of Bordeaux (see Chapter 10 for an explanation of First Growths). "I don't like Bordeaux with lamb," the distinguished gentleman proclaimed. We were confused; "But Bordeaux and lamb is a classic combination!" we said. "No, I don't agree," he answered, holding his ground. After a moment, he added, "Of course, I don't like lamb."

Classic Pairings of Wine and Food

TIP

No matter how much you value imagination and creativity, there's no sense rein-venting the wheel. In wine-and-food terms, it pays to know the time-tested, classic pairings — because they work (assuming that you like the food and you like the wine). Here are some famous and reliable combinations:

>> Oysters and unoaked Chablis

>> Lamb and red Bordeaux (we like Chianti Classico with lamb, too)

>> Port with walnuts and Stilton cheese

>> Salmon with Pinot Noir

>> Amarone with Gorgonzola cheese

>> Foie gras with Sauternes or with late-harvest Gewürztraminer

>> Braised beef with Barolo

>> Dry amontillado Sherry with rich soup

>> Roast chicken with Beaujolais

>> Toasted almonds or green olives with fino or manzanilla Sherry

>> Goat cheese with Sancerre or Pouilly-Fumé

>> Dark chocolate with California Cabernet Sauvignon

Look for various additional suggestions on wine and food pairings scattered throughout Parts 3, 4, and 5.

WINE FROM VENUS, FOOD FROM MARS

TIP

Sooner or later you're bound to experience food-and-wine disaster — when the two taste miserable together. We've had many opportunities to test our solution to food-and-wine disaster, and it works: As long as the wine is good and the food is good, eat one first and drink the other afterward — or vice versa.

3

Wine's Classic Face: The "Old World" of Wine

France is synonymous with wine. Find out about the wines of France's key wine regions, including Bordeaux, Burgundy, Chablis, Champagne, and others — and what makes these wines so special.

Italy is equally wine-famous. Read about the wines from Piedmont, Tuscany, and all the other great Italian regions and let your mouth water.

Spain, Germany, Austria, Portugal, Greece, Croatia, Slovenia, and Hungary all make some impressive wines, too. Explore the wines from these other European hot spots.

Chapter **10**

Knowing the Wines of France

When we think of France, we think of wine. Bordeaux, Burgundy, Beaujolais, Chablis, Champagne, and Sauternes are not only famous wines but also places in France where people live, work, eat, and drink wine. France's wine production is the highest in the world in many years, with Italy running neck and neck. And despite decreasing wine consumption in major European countries, France still has one of the highest per capita wine consumption rates of any major country in the world. The French have set the standard in wine.

The French Model

Why did France become the most famous place in the world for wine?

» For one thing, the French have been doing it for a long time — making wine, that is. Even before the Romans conquered Gaul and planted vineyards, the Greeks arrived in France with their vines.

>> Equally important is French *terroir,* the magical combination of climate and soil that, when it clicks, can yield grapes that make breathtaking wines.

>> And what grapes! France is the birthplace of almost all the renowned varieties in the world — Cabernet Sauvignon, Chardonnay, Merlot, Pinot Noir, Syrah, and Sauvignon Blanc, just to name a few. (See Chapter 3 for more information on these grape varieties.)

France is the model, the standard setter, for the world's wines: Most wine-producing countries now make their own versions of wines from Cabernet Sauvignon, Chardonnay, Merlot, Pinot Noir, and so on, thanks to the success of these grapes in France.

As fine wine production spreads all over the world, France receives less attention in the wine world that it once dominated. But any study of the world's wines must start with France.

The following sections describe the French model for wine in more detail.

Understanding French wine law

Way back in 1935, France developed a system of defining its wine regions, and that system became the legislative model for most other European countries. It's called the *Appellation d'Origine Contrôlée,* or AOC (translated as "regulated place-name" or "regulated origin name") system. The European Union's (E.U.'s) modern framework of wine laws, within which the AOC system now operates, is also modeled on the French system. Knowing about this French system helps you understand a lot about not just French wines but also many other European wines.

TIP

To understand French wine laws, you need to know five things:

>> Most French wines are named after places. (These aren't arbitrary places; they're places registered and defined in French wine regulations.)

>> Most of the time, the wine and the region have the same name (as in Burgundy wine, from Burgundy).

>> The French wine system is hierarchical. Some wines (that is, the wines of some places) officially rank higher than other wines.

>> Generally, the smaller and more specific the place for which a wine is named, the higher its rank.

>> Just because a wine carries a high rank doesn't necessarily mean that it's better than the next wine; it just means that it *should* be better. The laws rate the potential of the place where the wine comes from and are not infallible indications of a wine's actual quality.

TECHNICAL STUFF

Approved and regulated French wine regions fall into two categories. The following French phrases, which appear on the label, indicate the category. (Wines in the first category generally cost more.) From higher to lower, the categories are

» **Appellation Contrôlée,** or AC (or AOC) — known in the new system (described in Chapter 4) as **Appellation d'Origine Protégée,** or AOP. This is the higher grade. On the label, the place-name of the wine usually appears in the middle of the French phrase.

» **Vin de Pays,** meaning "country wine" — known in the new system as **Indication Géographique Protégée,** or IGP. On the label, the phrase is followed by a place-name, such as *Vin de Pays* (or *IGP*) *de l'Hérault,* which indicates the area where the grapes grew; the places or regions are generally much larger than the places or regions referred to in the first category.

TECHNICAL STUFF

One very small category, which fell between these two, was eliminated at the end of 2011. This was *Vin Délimité de Qualité Supérieure,* or VDQS, wine (translated as "demarcated wine of superior quality").

If a French wine does not have one of the preceding official terms on its label — in either the original or new version — then it is simply *Vin de France,* a wine from grapes grown anywhere in France rather than in a specific region. Vin de France is a burgeoning category that enables producers to blend grapes or wines from different regions to create decent, inexpensive wines. These wines are usually labelled with the grape name and carry a vintage.

Fine distinctions in the ranks

France's system of place-naming its wines is actually a bit more complex than the two neat categories described in the preceding section might imply. Although all AOC or AOP wines/places hold exactly the same legal status — say, they're all generals in the French wine army — the market accords some AOCs higher regard (and higher prices) than others, based on the specificity of their *terroirs* and their reputations.

TECHNICAL STUFF

Some large AOC/AOP territories have smaller AOC/AOP zones nestled within them. Wines produced from grapes grown only within the smaller territory can carry the name of that smaller territory, which is a more specific AOC name than that of the larger area. For example, within the large AOC region of Bordeaux, some wines are produced from grapes grown within a smaller district called Haut-Médoc. That district itself encompasses even smaller AOC zones; wines made from grapes grown in these smaller zones may use yet another AOC name, such as Pauillac, a village. (They're all generals, but some of them have more silver stars.)

The more specific the place described in the wine name, the finer the wine is generally considered to be in the eyes of the market, and the higher the price the winemaker can ask. Naturally, a winemaker will generally use the most specific name to which his wine is entitled.

REMEMBER

In increasing order of specificity, an AOC or AOP name can be the name of

>> A region (Bordeaux or Burgundy, for example)

>> A district (Haut-Médoc or Côte de Beaune)

>> A subdistrict (Côte de Beaune-Villages)

>> A village or commune (Pauillac or Meursault)

>> A specific vineyard (Le Montrachet)

Unfortunately, unless you know French geography and place-names, you won't know which type of place an AOC/AOP name refers to just by looking at the label.

France's Wine Regions

France has six wine regions that are extremely important for the quality and renown of their wines. Each region specializes in certain grape varieties for its wines, based on climate, soil, and local tradition.

>> The three major regions for red wine are Bordeaux, Burgundy, and the Rhône Valley.

>> For white wines, Burgundy is again a major region, along with the Loire Valley and Alsace.

>> For sparkling wines, Champagne is the most prestigious wine region —not only in France but also in the world (see Chapter 15 on Champagne).

Apart from these prestigious regions, France has several more regions that make wines worth knowing about. Again, each region cultivates certain grape varieties for its wines according to its climate, soil, and local tradition.

>> Two significant French wine regions are Provence and Languedoc-Roussillon, both in the South of France.

>> Wine districts in southwest France, such as Cahors, produce good-value wines and, in some cases, seriously good wines.

We cover all these regions in this chapter, in more or less detail according to the importance of the region. For more specific information on French wines, see our book *French Wine For Dummies* (Wiley).

Bordeaux: The Legend

To really know wine, you must know French wine — French wines are *that* important in the wine world. Likewise, you must know Bordeaux to know French wine.

Bordeaux is a wine region in southwestern France named after the ninth-largest French city, Bordeaux, a port city on the Garonne River, near the Atlantic Ocean (see Figure 10-1). Bordeaux produces about 900 million bottles a year from about 7,375 producers. (Bordeaux used to boast almost twice as many producers, but larger wineries annexed many of the smaller ones in the past 30 years.) Most Bordeaux wines — about 89 percent of them — are dry reds; the remaining 11 percent of the region's production are dry whites, with some sweet white wines, such as Sauternes, and a tiny amount of rosés and sparkling wines. Red Bordeaux wines are also called *clarets* (mainly a British term).

Because the Bordeaux region is situated on the Atlantic coast, it has a maritime climate, with warm summers and fairly mild winters. The maritime weather brings rain, often during harvest time. As the weather varies from year to year, the character and quality of the vintages also vary; when all goes well, such as in 2005, 2010, 2015, and potentially 2016, the wines can be truly great.

Bordeaux's reputation as one of the greatest wine regions in the world revolves around the legendary elite red wines of Bordeaux — great wines made by historic *châteaux* (wine estates) and capable of improving for many decades (see Chapter 17). Prices for these wines run up to $4,000 a bottle for Château Pétrus — the most expensive red Bordeaux wine. (Great, older vintages of Pétrus can cost even more!)

These legendary wines represent the pinnacle of a red Bordeaux pyramid; quantitatively, they're less than 2 percent of the region's red wine production. Middle-level red Bordeaux wines start at about $45 a bottle retail when they're first available and are ready to drink within 8 to 12 years of the harvest. The least expensive Bordeaux reds can cost as little as $10 to $20 a bottle, and are enjoyable young, within 2 to 5 years of the vintage date. The vast majority of red Bordeaux (about 70 percent) fall into the least expensive category.

FIGURE 10-1:
The wine regions
of France.

Illustration by Lisa S. Reed

THE TASTE OF REALLY GREAT BORDEAUX

When young, the finest red Bordeaux wines have aromas of black currants (cassis), plums, spice, and cedar. For the first 10 years or so, these wines can be dry in texture, sometimes almost austere, with tannin masking their fruity flavors. Eventually, the wines turn from ruby to garnet in color, develop an extraordinarily complex bouquet and flavor, and soften in texture. The very finest red Bordeaux wines will frequently take 20 to 25 years (and longer in great vintages) before reaching their maturity; some have lasted well over 100 years (see Chapter 17 for a discussion of collector-level wines).

The subregions of red Bordeaux

The least expensive Bordeaux reds come from grapes grown anywhere in the Bordeaux region, and thus carry the regionwide AOC designations, Bordeaux and Bordeaux Supérieur. (See "The value end of the Bordeaux spectrum," later in this chapter.) For finer wines, two distinct red wine production zones exist within the Bordeaux region; these two areas have come to be called the Left Bank and the Right Bank — just as in Paris.

Bordeaux's top red wines come from specific AOC *districts* or *communes* (village areas) located in either the Right Bank or the Left Bank.

TECHNICAL STUFF

The Left Bank vineyards lie west of the Garonne River (the more southerly of the two rivers depicted in the Bordeaux inset of Figure 10-1) and the Gironde Estuary, which empties into the Atlantic Ocean. The Right Bank vineyards lie east and north of the Dordogne River (the more northerly of the two rivers depicted in the inset), and east of the Gironde Estuary. (The middle ground in between the two rivers, Entre-Deux-Mers, makes both good value white wine and red wine.)

Of the various wine districts on the Left Bank and the Right Bank, four (two on each bank) are the most important:

>> Left Bank (the western area): Haut-Médoc, Pessac-Léognan

>> Right Bank (the eastern area): St.-Emilion, Pomerol

The Left Bank and the Right Bank differ mainly in soil composition: Gravel predominates on the Left Bank, and clay is dominant on the Right Bank. As a result, Cabernet Sauvignon, which has an affinity for gravel, plays a key role in the Haut-Médoc (oh-may-doc) and Pessac-Léognan (pay-sac-lay-oh-nyahn). Merlot, which does well in clay, dominates the St.-Emilion (sant-ay-meal-yon) and Pomerol (pohm-eh-roll) wines. (Both areas grow Cabernet Sauvignon *and* Merlot, as well as Cabernet Franc and three less significant grapes, Petit Verdot, Malbec, and Carménère, the last two of which are rarely used in Bordeaux today. See Chapter 3 for more information on grape varieties.)

TECHNICAL STUFF

MERLOT TAKES THE LEAD

Merlot is the most widely used variety throughout Bordeaux. Cabernet Sauvignon is second, followed by Cabernet Franc. Even on the Left Bank, a trend exists for a higher amount of Merlot in the blend, thus making the wines more accessible at an earlier age.

Left Bank and Right Bank Bordeaux wines are, therefore, markedly different from one another:

>> The Left Bank generally produces firm, tannic wines with more pronounced black currant and mineral flavor. The top Left Bank wines usually need many years to develop and will age for a long time, often for decades — typical of a Cabernet Sauvignon–based wine.

>> Bordeaux wines from the larger Right Bank are more approachable, because they're mainly Merlot; you can enjoy even the best of them long before their Left Bank cousins, often as soon as five to eight years after the vintage. They're less tannic, richer in texture, and plummier in flavor.

A deep dive into the Haut-Médoc

Historically, the Haut-Médoc district, on the Left Bank, is Bordeaux's most important area, and it deserves special attention. The Haut-Médoc is the southern part of the Médoc peninsula, which is the entire area west of the wide Gironde Estuary (refer to Figure 10-1). The name Médoc also applies to the northern part of that peninsula. In other words (in the same word, actually), Médoc is frequently used as an umbrella term for the combined districts of Médoc and Haut–Médoc.

The Haut–Médoc district is very important because it encompasses four famous wine communes: St.-Estèphe, Pauillac, St.-Julien, and Margaux. Table 10-1 gives a general description of each commune's wines.

TABLE 10-1   The Four Principal Communes in the Haut-Médoc

Commune	Wine Characteristics
St.-Estèphe (sant-eh-steff)	Firm, tannic, earthy, chunky, and slow to mature. Typical wine: Château Montrose
Pauillac (poy-yac)	Rich, powerful, firm, and tannic, with black currant and cedar aromas and flavors; very long-lived. Home of three of Bordeaux's most famous wines: Lafite-Rothschild, Mouton-Rothschild, and Latour
St.-Julien (san-jhoo-lee-ehn)	Rich, flavorful, elegant and finesseful, with cedary bouquet. Typical wine: Château Ducru-Beaucaillou
Margaux (mahr-go)	Fragrant, supple, harmonious, with complex aromas and flavors. Typical wines: Château Palmer and Château Margaux

Two other communes in the Haut-Médoc — Listrac (lee-strahk) and Moulis (moo-lees) — make less-well-known wines. Vineyards that aren't located in the AOC territories of these six communes carry the district-wide appellation, *Haut-Médoc*, rather than that of a specific commune.

REMEMBER

The names of these districts and communes are part of the official name of wines made there and they appear on the label.

Classified information: Left Bank

Some very lucky chateaux on Bordeaux's Left Bank have special bragging rights as *classified growths* because more than 160 years ago, they made the grade.

Back in 1855, the organizers of a Paris exposition (akin to a World's Fair) asked the Bordeaux Chamber of Commerce to develop a classification of Bordeaux wines. The Chamber of Commerce delegated the task to wine brokers, the companies who buy and resell the wines of Bordeaux. These merchants named 61 top red wines — 60 from the Haut-Médoc and one (Château Haut-Brion) from what was then called Graves (and today is known as Pessac-Léognan).

According to the prices and the existing reputations of the wines at that time, the merchants divided these 61 wines into five categories, known as *crus* or *growths*. (In Bordeaux, a *cru* refers to a classified wine estate.) The listing is known as the Classification of 1855; to this day, these classified growths enjoy special prestige among wine lovers. (The Bordeaux wine brokers also classified Sauternes, Bordeaux's great sweet wine; see Chapter 16 for info on Sauternes.) The following list names the five First Growth châteaux:

>> Château Lafite-Rothschild

>> Château Latour

>> Château Margaux

>> Château Haut-Brion

>> Château Mouton-Rothschild (elevated from a Second Growth in 1973)

Additionally, the classification included 14 Second Growths, 14 Third Growths, 10 Fourth Growths, and 18 Fifth Growths.

The 61 ranked wine estates are sometimes referred to as *Great Growths* or *Grands Crus Classés*. To appreciate the honor attached to being one of the 61 Great Growths, bear in mind that more than 7,000 châteaux exist in Bordeaux!

The 1855 Classification has held up remarkably well over time. Sure, a few of the 61 properties are not performing up to their historic level today, while some unclassified châteaux now probably deserve to be included. But because of the politics involved, no changes in classification ranking have been made, with one dramatic exception (see the sidebar "The Mouton exception").

A classification of the wines of Graves/Pessac-Léognan was issued in 1959, following a government-sanctioned process that was similar to that of the 1855 classification. Because this area is famous for its white wines as well as its reds, two lists of classified châteaux emerged, one for white wines and one for reds. The classification recognized Château Haut-Brion as Grand Cru Classé on both lists; 12 other chateaux are Cru Classé for red wine, and 9 are Cru Classé for white wines.

Classified information: Right Bank

TECHNICAL STUFF

Just to confuse things: Although the 1855 Classification completely ignored the wines of the Right Bank, the AOC commission classified the wines of St.-Emilion a century later, in 1955. Unlike the wines covered by the 1855 Classification, St.-Emilion wines are reclassified approximately every ten years. (A reclassification last took place in 2012.) The wines fall into three quality categories, which are indicated on the labels:

» Currently, 18 châteaux in St.-Emilion have the highest ranking, *Premier Grand Cru Classé.* Four of the 18 are on a pedestal as "Category A": Château Ausone, Château Cheval Blanc, Château Angelus, and Château Pavie (Angelus and Pavie were added in 2012). The other 14 are "Category B" *Premier Grand Cru Classé* wines. They include the following, in alphabetical order:

- Château Beausejour Duffau-Lagarrosse
- Château Beau-Sejour Becot
- Château Belair-Monange
- Château Canon
- Château Canon La Gaffeliere
- Château Figeac
- Clos Fourtet

- Château La Gaffeliere
- Château Larcis Ducasse
- La Mondotte
- Château Pavie Macquin
- Château Troplong Mondot
- Château Trotte Vieille
- Château Valandraud

» A middle category, *Grand Cru Classé,* consists of 65 châteaux.

» The third category, simply *Grand Cru,* encompasses some 600 properties.

THE MOUTON EXCEPTION

The one dramatic change to the 1855 Classification occurred in 1973. That year, the late Baron Philippe de Rothschild finally triumphed in his 50-year battle with the French government to have his beloved Château Mouton-Rothschild upgraded from a Second Growth to a First Growth. The Minister of Agriculture decreed that Château Mouton-Rothschild was indeed a First Growth — which many Bordeaux wine lovers considered it to be all along, in quality if not in official status.

The Baron's motto, written in French on his family crest, had to change. Before 1973, it read:

First, I cannot be; second, I do not deign to be; Mouton, I am.

The Baron changed the motto on his 1973 Château Mouton-Rothschild to read:

First, I am; second, I was; Mouton does not change.

A postscript to this heartwarming story: We adopted an adorable little kitten, a Blue Point Siamese, in 1973. Because Mouton-Rothschild is one of our favorite wines, and because our little kitten demonstrated the same firm, tenacious qualities as the wine, we named him Mouton. He was with us for 20 years, proving that he had the same longevity as the wine for which he was named. He is buried in an old wooden case that once held bottles of 1973 Mouton-Rothschild.

WARNING

The second category, Grand Cru Classé, is vastly superior to the rather mundane Grand Cru wines in the third category. If you're thinking that the authorities should rename the St.-Emilion classification categories, you are right: "Grand Cru" is a misnomer for the third category. The wines of Pomerol have never been officially classified.

Bordeaux to try when you're feeling flush

TIP

If you're curious to try a prestigious red Bordeaux, let the following lists guide you. In addition to all five First Growths listed in the previous section, we recommend the following classified growths from the Médoc, as well as some wines from the three other principal districts: Pessac-Léognan, Pomerol, and St.-Emilion. Consult the later section "Practical advice on drinking red Bordeaux" before you drink the wine.

Haut-Médoc wines		
Château Léoville-Las-Cases	Château Clerc-Milon	Château Lynch-Bages
Château Léoville-Barton	Château Pichon-Lalande	Château Ducru-Beaucaillou
Château Palmer	Château Lagrange	Château Grand-Puy-Lacoste
Château Léoville-Poyferré	Château Pichon-Baron	Château Branaire-Ducru
Pessac-Léognan wines		
Château La Mission-Haut-Brion	Château Haut-Bailly	Château de Fieuzal
Château Pape-Clément	Domaine de Chevalier	Château La Louvière
Château La Tour-Haut-Brion	Château Smith-Haut-Lafitte	
Pomerol wines		
Château Pétrus*	Château Trotanoy	Château L'Evangile
Château Lafleur*	Château Clinet	Château La Fleur de Gay
Château Latour à Pomerol	Vieux-Château-Certan	Château La Conseillante
Château Certan de May	Château Lafleur-Pétrus	

Very expensive

St.-Emilion wines		
Château Cheval Blanc	Château La Dominique	Château Canon-La-Gaffelière
Château Ausone	Château Grand Mayne	Château Pavie-Macquin
Château Figeac	Château Troplong Mondot	Château Magdelaine

The value end of the Bordeaux spectrum

As you probably suspected, the best buys in Bordeaux wines are not the illustrious classified growths. As of this writing, the least expensive classified–growth Bordeaux wines retail for about $40 a bottle but can go up to over $1,000 a bottle for First Growths, such as Château Lafite–Rothschild and Château Latour. For really good values (and wines that you can drink within a few years of the vintage), look for Bordeaux wines that were not included in the 1855 Classification.

The middle class of the Médoc

REAL DEAL

Over the years, we have been very impressed with the price-to-quality ratio that *Cru Bourgeois* Bordeaux wines (an unofficial classification) offer. The nine wines that follow are particularly impressive on a consistent basis. They retail for about $30 to $45. We firmly believe that many of these wines would qualify for *Grands Cru* status if the 1855 Classification were revised.

Château Chasse-Spleen	Château Phélan-Ségur	Château Poujeaux
Château Les Ormes-de-Pez	Château Haut-Marbuzet	Château de Pez
Château Labegorce-Zédé	Château Potensac	Château Siran

WORTH THE SEARCH

Another wine often compared to *Grands Crus Classés* wines in quality is Château Gloria, from St.-Julien (now up to $45). Château Sociando-Mallet is an excellent producer from the Haut-Médoc: It's about $39.

Other moderately priced ($30 to $40) Haut-Médoc wines that we recommend include the following:

Château Monbrison	Château Meyney
Château Coufran	Château Lanessan
Château Haut-Beauséjour	Château Fourcas-Hosten
Château d'Angludet	

Fronsac and Canon-Fronsac

When you leave the Médoc peninsula and cross over the Dordogne River into the Right Bank region, the first wine districts you encounter are Fronsac and Canon-Fronsac (refer to Figure 10-1). Of the lesser Bordeaux appellations, Canon-Fronsac and Fronsac have the highest reputations for quality, and they're priced accordingly, in the $30 to $40 range. Like St.-Emilion and Pomerol, Fronsac and Canon-Fronsac produce only red wines, and Merlot is the dominant grape variety.

Petits châteaux

Petits châteaux is the general, catch-all term for the huge category of reasonably priced wines throughout the entire Bordeaux region that have never been classified. The term is somewhat of a misnomer because it suggests that the wines come from a specific château or vineyard estate; in fact, many *petits châteaux* do come from specific estates, but not all do.

Some estates source their grapes from all over the Bordeaux region, and others source only from specific appellations. Many *petits châteaux* red wines hail from noteworthy appellations, all on the Right Bank: Côtes de Bourg, Blaye–Côtes de Bordeaux, Côtes de Bordeaux, and Lalande de Pomerol. Most of the wines from these appellations range from $15 to $30.

TIP

With a couple of exceptions, all these Right Bank wines are primarily Merlot. They are generally fruitier, have softer tannins, and are enjoyable sooner than the Cabernet Sauvignon–dominated wines of the Left Bank. *Petits châteaux* (you'll know them by their price) are the Bordeaux wines of choice when you're looking for a young, inexpensive, approachable Bordeaux with dinner.

Generic Bordeaux

REAL DEAL

Red Bordeaux wines with no more-specific appellation carry the general *Bordeaux* or *Bordeaux Supérieur* appellations. Their grapes are predominantly Merlot and can grow anywhere throughout the Bordeaux region. These are fairly light-bodied wines that sell for $12 to $14. Sometimes, the labels identify the wines as specifically Merlot or Cabernet Sauvignon. Whether leading brands such as Mouton-Cadet and Michel Lynch, or less known brands, generic Bordeaux from good vintages, such as 2015, can be really excellent buys.

Practical advice on drinking red Bordeaux

Because the finest red Bordeaux wines take many years to develop, they're not good choices in restaurants where the vintages available tend to be fairly recent. And when mature Bordeaux wines are available in restaurants, they're usually extremely expensive. Order a lesser Bordeaux when you're dining out, and save the best wines for drinking at home.

REVERSE CHIC: DRINKING INEXPENSIVE BORDEAUX

Some wine snobs wouldn't think of ordering anything but classified-growth Bordeaux in restaurants. But if you're just getting acquainted with these wines, splurging on an expensive, top-rated Bordeaux doesn't make sense. Begin with inexpensive, easier-drinking Bordeaux wines first so you can develop a context for evaluating and appreciating the finer wines. The contrast of simpler Bordeaux really helps you understand the majesty of the great Bordeaux wines. Besides, every dinner doesn't call for great Bordeaux. A modest Bordeaux is perfectly suitable for simpler fare, such as stew or a burger.

Red Bordeaux wines go well with lamb, venison, simple roasts, and hard cheeses, such as Comté, Gruyère, or Cheddar. If you plan to serve a fine red Bordeaux from a good but recent vintage (see Appendix C for information), you should decant it at least an hour before dinner and let it aerate (see Chapter 8). Serve it fairly cool, at about 62 to 64 degrees Fahrenheit (17 to 19 degrees Celsius). Better yet, if you have good storage conditions (see Chapter 17), save your young Bordeaux wine for a few years — it will only get better.

Fine recent Bordeaux vintages are 2016, 2015, 2010, and 2005 — all of which show promise of being great — plus, 1989, 1986, and 1982 for mature vintages.

Bordeaux also comes in white

White Bordeaux wine comes in two styles, dry and sweet. The dry wines themselves fall into two categories: inexpensive wines for enjoying young and wines so distinguished and age-worthy that they rank among the great dry white wines of the world.

Two areas of the Bordeaux region are important for white wine production:

>> The large district south of the city of Bordeaux is known as the Graves (pronounced grahv; see the Bordeaux inset in Figure 10-1). The Graves district and the Pessac-Léognan district (directly north of Graves) are home to the finest white wines of Bordeaux, both dry and sweet. (We cover the great dessert wine from the southern Graves, Sauternes, in Chapter 16.)

>> In the middle ground between the Garonne and Dordogne Rivers, east of Graves and Pessac-Léognan, a district called Entre-Deux-Mers (ahn-truh-duh-mair) is also known for its dry, semi-dry, and sweet white Bordeaux wines as well as for inexpensive red Bordeaux wines.

A few white wines also come from the predominantly red wine Haut-Médoc district, such as the superb Pavillon Blanc du Château Margaux. Although special and expensive, they qualify only for simple Bordeaux Blanc AOC appellation because the more specific, commune-level AOCs of the Haut-Médoc apply only to reds.

Sauvignon Blanc and Sémillon, in various combinations, are the two main grape varieties for elite dry white Bordeaux. It's a fortunate blend: The Sauvignon Blanc component offers immediate charm in the wine, while the slower-developing Sémillon gives the wine richness and depth, enabling it to age well. In general, a high percentage of Sémillon in the wine is a good indicator of the wine's age-worthiness. Many inexpensive white Bordeaux — which are ready to drink young — are entirely Sauvignon Blanc, but so are a few of the best wines.

The top dry white Bordeaux wines are crisp and lively when they're young, but they develop richness, complexity, and a honeyed bouquet with age. In good vintages (see Appendix C for information), the best whites need at least ten years to develop and can live many years more. (See Chapter 17 for more information on older Bordeaux.)

Table 10-2 lists the top 12 white wines of Pessac-Léognan and Graves, in our rough order of preference, and shows their grape blends. We separated the wines into an A and B group because the four wines in the first group literally are in a class by themselves, quality-wise; they possess not only more depth and complexity but also more longevity than other white Bordeaux. Their prices reflect that — the A group wines range from $100 to over $ 800 per bottle, whereas the B group wines cost between $40 and $80 (except Château Smith-Haut-Lafitte, which is around $100). Almost all the producers listed below produce red Bordeaux as well as a white.

TABLE 10-2   **Top 12 Dry White Bordeaux**

Wine	Grape Varieties
Group A	
Château Haut-Brion Blanc *	Sémillon, 50–55%; Sauvignon Blanc, 45–50%
Château La Mission Haut-Brion Blanc *	Sémillon, 80%; Sauvignon Blanc, 20%
Domaine de Chevalier Blanc	Sauvignon Blanc, 70%; Sémillon, 30%
Château Pape-Clément Blanc	Sémillon, 45%; Sauvignon Blanc, 45%; Muscadelle, 10%
Group B	
Château de Fieuzal	Sauvignon Blanc, 50–60%; Sémillon, 40–50%
Château Smith-Haut-Lafitte	Sauvignon Blanc, 100%
Clos Floridene	Sémillon, 70%; Sauvignon Blanc, 30%
Château La Louvière	Sauvignon Blanc, 70%; Sémillon, 30%
Château La Tour-Martillac	Sémillon, 60%; Sauvignon Blanc, 30%; other, 10%
Château Couhins-Lurton	Sauvignon Blanc, 100%
Château Malartic-Lagravière	Sauvignon Blanc, 100%
Château Carbonnieux	Sauvignon Blanc, 65%; Sémillon, 35%

Very expensive

Burgundy: The Incomparable French Wine

Burgundy (or, as the French call it, *Bourgogne*, pronounced boor-guh-nyuh), is a wine region in eastern France, southeast of Paris (refer to Figure 10-1). Burgundy stands shoulder to shoulder with Bordeaux as one of France's two greatest regions for dry, non-sparkling wines.

Unlike Bordeaux, Burgundy's fame is split nearly equally between its white and red wines. Also unlike Bordeaux, good Burgundy is often scarce. The reason is simple: Not counting the Beaujolais area (which is technically Burgundy, but really makes a separate type of wine), Burgundy produces only 25 percent as much wine as Bordeaux, at best. When you consider the fact that less than half of Burgundy's wine production is red, the scarcity of red Burgundy becomes all the more dramatic.

Burgundy's vineyards are smaller and more fragmented than Bordeaux's — because the soils of Burgundy vary from one hillside to the next and even from the middle of each hill to the bottom. You can find two different vineyards growing the same grape but making distinctly different wines only six feet (two meters) apart from each other across a dirt road!

The few large vineyards that do exist have multiple owners, with some families owning only two or three rows of vines in a particular vineyard. (One famous Burgundy vineyard, Clos de Vougeot, has about 82 owners!) The typical Burgundy winemaker's production varies from 50 cases to 1,000 cases of wine a year, per type — far from enough to satisfy wine lovers all over the world. Compare that to Bordeaux, where the average château owner makes 15,000 to 20,000 cases of his principal wine annually.

REMEMBER

In Burgundy, the winemaker calls his property a *domaine*, certainly a more modest name than *château*, and a proper reflection of the size of his winery.

The grapes: Chardonnay, Pinot Noir, and Gamay

Burgundy has a *continental* climate (warm summers and cold winters) and is subject to localized summer hailstorms that can damage the grapes and enable rot. The soil is mainly limestone and clay. Burgundy's *terroir* is particularly suited to the two main grape varieties of the region, Pinot Noir (for red Burgundy) and Chardonnay (for white Burgundy). In fact, nowhere else in the entire world does the very fickle, difficult Pinot Noir grape perform better than in Burgundy.

In Burgundy's southerly Beaujolais district, the soil becomes primarily granitic but also rich in clay and sand, very suitable for the Gamay grape of this area.

Districts, districts everywhere

Burgundy has five districts, all of which make quite distinct wines. The districts, from north to south, are the following (refer to Figure 10-1):

>> Chablis (shah-blee)

>> The Côte d'Or (coat dor)

>> The Côte Chalonnaise (coat shal-oh-naze)

>> The Mâconnais (mack-coh-nay)

>> Beaujolais (boh-jhoe-lay)

The heart of Burgundy, the *Côte d'Or* (which literally means "golden slope"), itself has two parts: Côte de Nuits (coat deh nwee) in the north and the Côte de Beaune (coat deh bone) in the south.

The Chablis district makes only white wines, and the Mâconnais makes mainly white wines. The Côte Chalonnaise and Côte d'Or make both white and red wines. Beaujolais makes almost exclusively red wines from the Gamay grape.

REMEMBER

The term *red Burgundy* refers primarily to the red wines of the Côte d'Or and also to the less-known — and less-expensive — red wines of the Côte Chalonnaise. Likewise, when wine lovers talk about *white Burgundy*, they are usually referring to just the white wines of the Côte d'Or and the Côte Chalonnaise. They'll use the more precise names, Chablis and Mâcon, to refer to the white wines of those other parts of Burgundy. On the other hand, when wine lovers talk about the region, Burgundy, they could very well be referring to the whole shebang, including Beaujolais, or all of Burgundy *except* Beaujolais. When it comes to wine, "Burgundy" is an imprecise word.

WARNING

Don't ever mistake inexpensive red California wines that call themselves *burgundy* — or the inexpensive California wines named *chablis* — for the real McCoys from France. These imposter wines are from various ordinary grapes grown in industrial-scale vineyards 6,000 miles away from the Côte d'Or. We'd be surprised if either one had even a drop of the true grapes of Burgundy — Pinot Noir or Chardonnay — in it.

From the regional to the sublime

Because soils vary so much in Burgundy, a wine's specific vineyard site is extremely relevant to the taste, quality, and price of that wine. A wine from a tiny vineyard with its own particular character is more precious and rare than a wine blended from several vineyards or a wine from a less-favored site.

The AOC/AOP structure for Burgundy wines recognizes the importance of site. While there are regionwide AOCs, districtwide AOCs, and commune AOCs — just as in Bordeaux — there are also AOC names that refer to individual vineyards. In fact, some of these vineyards are recognized as better than others: Some of them are *Premier Cru* (prem-yay crew), meaning "first growth," while the very best are *Grand Cru*, meaning "great growth."

TECHNICAL
STUFF

Bordeaux producers use the terms *premier cru* and *grand cru*, too — but except for St.-Emilion, the terms represent status bestowed by a classification outside the AOC law (see the earlier sections "Classified information" for details). In Burgundy, *Premier Cru* and *Grand Cru* are always official distinctions within the AOC law. Their meaning is extremely precise.

Table 10-3 gives examples of AOC names in Burgundy, listed in order of increasing specificity.

TABLE 10-3   ## The Structure of Burgundy AOC Names

Specificity of Site	Examples
Regionwide	Bourgogne Rouge
Districtwide	Beaujolais; Mâcon; Bourgogne Côte d'Or
Village or commune	Chambolle-Musigny; Gevrey-Chambertin; Puligny-Montrachet
Premier Cru*	Chambolle-Musigny Les Amoureuses; Gevrey-Chambertin Clos St.-Jacques; Puligny-Montrachet Les Pucelles
Grand Cru*	Le Musigny; Le Chambertin; Le Montrachet

Refers to specific vineyard sites.

Bourgogne Côte d'Or is a new, districtwide AOC/AOP introduced in 2017.

The availability and price of a wine varies according to the specificity of its site. Here are some examples, with prices based on Côte d'Or Burgundies:

>> The two broadest categories — regional and district place-names — account for 53 percent of all Burgundy wines. These wines retail for $20 to $45 a bottle. (You can buy affordable Burgundies at this level.)

>> Commune-specific (also referred to as *village*) wines, such as Pommard or Gevrey-Chambertin, make up 30 percent of Burgundy and are in the $50 to $90 per bottle price range. Fifty-three communes in Burgundy have AOC status.

>> Premier Crus, such as Meursault Les Perrières or Nuits-St.-Georges Les Vaucrains, account for 15 percent of Burgundy wines; 561 vineyards have Premier Cru status. Most of these wines retail for $90 to $150 per bottle — but the best can go up to $500 per bottle.

>> The 31 Grand Crus, such as Chambertin, represent only about *2 percent* of Burgundy's wines. Prices for Grand Cru Burgundies — both red and white — start at less than $200 and can go to $10,500, and up to $15,000 a bottle for Romanée-Conti, Burgundy's — and the world's — most expensive wine. But La Tache, almost on the same level as Romanée-Conti, sells for one-fifth of its price — still costly, of course, but a bargain on this level.

TIP

Thankfully, you can usually tell the difference between a Premier Cru and a Grand Cru Burgundy by looking at the label. Grand Cru Burgundies carry only the name of the vineyard on the label, and not its commune. Premier Cru wines generally carry both the name of the commune plus the vineyard name — most often in the same-sized lettering — on the label and, often, the words *Premier Cru* (or *1er Cru*). If a vineyard name is in smaller lettering than the commune name, the wine is generally not a Premier Cru but is a wine from a single-vineyard site in that commune; not all single vineyards have Premier Cru status.

TECHNICAL
STUFF

If a wine contains grapes from two or more Premier Crus in the same commune, it can be called a *Premier Cru*, but it won't carry the name of a specific Premier Cru vineyard. The label will simply carry a commune name and the words *Premier Cru*.

The Côte d'Or: The heart of Burgundy

The Côte d'Or, a narrow 40-mile stretch of land with some of the most expensive real estate in the world, is the region where all the famous red and white Burgundies originate. The northern part of the Côte d'Or is named the Côte de Nuits, after its commercially most important city, Nuits-St.-Georges. This area makes red

Burgundies almost exclusively, although one superb white Burgundy, called Musigny Blanc, and a couple other white Burgundies do exist on the Côte de Nuits. The following wine communes, from north to south, are in the Côte de Nuits; the names of these communes are also the names of their wines:

>> **Marsannay (mahr-sah-nay):** Known for lighter-bodied reds and rosés

>> **Fixin (fee-san):** Sturdy, earthy, firm red wines

>> **Gevrey-Chambertin (jehv-ray-sham-ber-tan):** Full-bodied, rich red wines; nine Grand Crus, such as Chambertin, Chambertin Clos de Bèze

>> **Morey-St.-Denis (maw-ree-san d'nee):** Full, sturdy red wines; Grand Crus are Bonnes Mares (part), Clos de la Roche, Clos St.-Denis, Clos de Tart, Clos des Lambrays

>> **Chambolle-Musigny (shom-bowl-moo-sih-nyee):** Supple, elegant red wines; Grand Crus include Musigny and Bonnes Mares (part)

>> **Vougeot (voo-joe):** Medium-bodied red wines; Grand Cru is Clos de Vougeot

>> **Vosne-Romanée (vone-roh-mah-nay):** Elegant, rich, velvety red wines; the six Grand Crus are Romanée-Conti, La Tâche, Richebourg, Romanée-St.-Vivant, La Romanée, and La Grand Rue

>> **Flagey-Échézeaux (flah-jhay-eh-sheh-zoe):** Hamlet of Vosne-Romanée; Grand Crus are Grands Échézeaux and Échézeaux

>> **Nuits-St.-Georges (nwee-san-johrj):** Sturdy, earthy, red wines; no Grand Crus; fine Premier Crus

The southern part of the Côte d'Or, the Côte de Beaune, is named after its most important city, Beaune (the commercial and tourist center of the Côte d'Or). The Côte de Beaune makes both white and red Burgundies, but the whites are more renowned. The following communes, from north to south, make up the Côte de Beaune:

>> **Ladoix (lah-dwah):** Seldom-seen, inexpensive red and white wines; part of the Grand Cru vineyards, Corton (red) and Corton-Charlemagne (white) are in this commune

>> **Pernand-Vergelesses (per-nahn-ver-jeh-less):** Little-known red and white wines; excellent values

>> **Aloxe-Corton (ah-luss-cor-tohn):** Full, sturdy wines; several red Grand Crus that all include the name Corton and one magnificent white Grand Cru (Corton-Charlemagne) are here

>> **Chorey-lès-Beaune (shor-ay-lay-bone):** Mainly good-value red wine and a little white wine

- » **Savigny-lès-Beaune (sah-vee-nyee-lay-bone):** Mostly red wines; fine values here, too

- » **Beaune (bone):** Supple, medium-bodied reds; some whites; fine Premier Crus here

- » **Pommard (pohm-mahr):** Sturdy, full red wines; some good Premier Crus (Rugiens and Epénots)

- » **Volnay (vohl-nay):** Graceful, elegant red wines; good Premier Crus (Caillerets and Clos des Ducs)

- » **Auxey-Duresses** (awk-see-duh-ress), Monthélie (mohn-teh-lee), St.-Romain (san-roh-man), St.-Aubin (sant-oh-ban): Four little-known villages producing mainly red wines; fine values

- » **Meursault (muhr-so):** The northernmost important white Burgundy commune; full-bodied, nutty wines; some excellent Premier Crus (Les Perrières and Les Genevrières)

- » **Puligny-Montrachet (poo-lee-nyee-mon-rah-shay):** Home of elegant white Burgundies; Grand Crus include Montrachet (part), Chevalier-Montrachet, Bâtard-Montrachet (part), and Bienvenues-Bâtard-Montrachet, plus very fine Premier Crus

- » **Chassagne-Montrachet (shah-sah-nyuh-mon-rah-shay):** A bit sturdier than Puligny; the rest of the Montrachet and Bâtard-Montrachet Grand Crus are situated here, along with Criots-Bâtard Montrachet Grand Cru; also, some earthy, rustic reds

- » **Santenay (sant-nay):** Light-bodied, inexpensive red wines here

- » **Maranges (ma-rahnj):** Little-known, mainly red, inexpensive wines

REMEMBER

All these red wines are entirely Pinot Noir, and the whites are entirely Chardonnay. The different characteristics from one wine to the next are mainly due to the wines' individual *terroirs*.

The red wines of many of the Côte de Beaune villages can carry the specific name of their commune, or they can use the AOC/AOP of Côte de Beaune Villages. Not only does the Villages name provide more recognition than that of a lesser-known village, such as Pernand-Vergelesses or Ladoix, but also use of the Villages name enables blending of wines from multiple villages, which can increase the quantity of wine and make it more marketable.

WORTH THE SEARCH

Tables 10-4 and 10-5 list the best Burgundy producers and their greatest wines, in rough order of quality.

TABLE 10-4 **Best White Burgundy Producers and Their Greatest Wines**

Producer	Recommended Wines
Domaine Ramonet*	Montrachet; Bâtard-Montrachet; Bienvenues-Bâtard-Montrachet; any of its Chassagne-Montrachet Premier Crus
Coche-Dury*	Corton-Charlemagne; Meursault Premier Crus (any)
Domaine des Comtes Lafon	Meursault Premier Crus (any); Le Montrachet
Domaine Leflaive	Chevalier-Montrachet; Bâtard-Montrachet; Puligny-Montrachet Premier Crus (any)
Domaine Étienne Sauzet	Bâtard-Montrachet; Bienvenues-Bâtard-Montrachet; Puligny-Montrachet Les Combettes
Louis Carillon	Bienvenues-Bâtard-Montrachet; Puligny-Montrachet Premier Crus (any)
Michel Niellon	Bâtard-Montrachet; Chevalier-Montrachet; Chassagne-Montrachet Les Vergers
Verget	Bâtard-Montrachet; Chevalier-Montrachet; Meursault Premier Crus (any)
Louis Latour	Corton-Charlemagne; Puligny-Montrachet Premier Crus (any)
Louis Jadot	Corton-Charlemagne; Chassagne-Montrachet Les Caillerets; Beaune Grèves
Joseph Drouhin	All Grand Crus and Premier Crus

These wines are very expensive and rare.

TABLE 10-5 **Best Red Burgundy Producers and Their Greatest Wines**

Producer	Recommended Wines
Domaine Leroy*	Musigny; Richebourg; Chambertin (all of Leroy's Grand Crus and Premier Crus)
Domaine de la Romanée-Conti*	Romanée-Conti; La Tâche; Richebourg; Grands Échézeaux
Domaine Comte de Vogüé	Musigny (Vieilles Vignes); Bonnes Mares
Anne Gros	Richebourg; Clos de Vougeot
Georges et Christophe Roumier	Musigny; Bonnes Mares; Chambolle-Musigny Les Amoureuses
Ponsot	Clos de la Roche (Vieilles Vignes); Chambertin; Clos St.-Denis (Vieilles Vignes); Griotte-Chambertin
Armand Rousseau	Chambertin (all his Grand Crus); Gevrey-Chambertin Clos St.-Jacques
Méo-Camuzet	Vosne-Romanée Premier Crus (any of his three); Clos de Vougeot; Richebourg; Corton
Hubert Lignier	Clos de la Roche; Charmes-Chambertin

(continued)

TABLE 10-5 *(continued)*

Producer	Recommended Wines
Domaine Dujac	Clos de la Roche; Bonnes Mares
Joseph Roty	Any of his Grand Cru Chambertins
Domaine Marquis d'Angerville	Volnay Clos des Ducs
Domaine Hubert & Etienne de Montille	Volnay and Pommard Premier Crus
Michel Lafarge	Volnay Premier Crus; Beaune Les Grèves
Domaine/Maison J. Faiveley	Nuits-St.-Georges and Mercurey Premier Crus
Bouchard Pere & Fils	All Grand Crus and Premier Crus

These wines are very expensive.

THE TASTE OF FINE WHITE BURGUNDY

White Burgundy combines a richness of flavor — peaches, hazelnuts, and honey in Meursault; floweriness and butterscotch in a Puligny- or Chassagne-Montrachet — with lively acidity and a touch of oak. With age, even more flavor complexity develops. The wine leaves a lingering reminder of all its flavors. Chardonnay wines from other regions and countries can be very good, but there's nothing else quite like a great white Burgundy.

TIP

PRACTICAL ADVICE ON BUYING BURGUNDY

It's nice of the Burgundians to make everything so stratified and clear, isn't it? Premier Cru Burgundies are always better than commune wines, and Grand Crus are the best of all, right? Unfortunately, it ain't necessarily so! In order of importance, these are the criteria to follow when you're buying Burgundy:

- **The producer's reputation:** Based on wines he has made in recent years
- **The vintage year:** Quality fluctuates greatly from year to year
- **The appellation:** The name of the commune or vineyard and its specificity

The producer and the vintage are *considerably* more important than the appellation. *Good vintages for red Burgundy are 2015, 2010, 2009, and 2005. For white Burgundy, 2015, 2014, 2010, and 2008 — 2008 especially for Chablis.*

Côte Chalonnaise: Bargain Burgundies

REAL DEAL

The sad fact about Burgundy is that many of its best wines are costly. But one of Burgundy's best-kept secrets is the Côte Chalonnaise, the district that lies directly south of the Côte d'Or. Five villages here are home to some very decent Burgundies. True, Côte Chalonnaise Burgundies are not as fine as Côte d'Or Burgundies (they're a bit earthier and less refined in flavor and texture), but they can still be quality wines — and we're talking $30 to $40 retail per bottle here. Four villages or communes whose names appear on wine labels are the following:

>> **Mercurey (mer-cure-ay):** Mainly red wine, with about 20 percent white; the best wines of the Chalonnaise come from here, and also the most expensive ($35 to $50); three of the best producers of Mercurey are Aubert de Villaine, J.Faiveley, and Antonin Rodet.

>> **Rully (rouh-yee):** Slightly more white wine than red; although a bit earthy, whites are significantly better than the reds; look for the wines of the producer Antonin Rodet.

>> **Givry (gee-vree):** Mostly red wine, with less than 10 percent white; reds are better than the whites (but quite earthy); Domaine Joblot's Givry is especially worth seeking out.

>> **Montagny (mon-tah-nyee):** All white wine; look for Antonin Rodet's and Louis Latour's Montagny.

WORTH THE SEARCH

Another village specializes in the Aligoté grape (a second white grape permitted in Burgundy) that makes a particularly crisp and lively wine called **Bouzeroon** (boo-zer-ohn) from the village of the same name. Aubert de Villaine is the quality producer here; try his Bourgogne Rouge, Bourgogne Blanc (made from Pinot Noir and Chardonnay, respectively), and especially his Aligoté de Bouzeron.

Chablis: Exceptional white wines

The village of Chablis, northwest of the Côte d'Or, is the closest Burgundian commune to Paris (about a two-hour drive). Although Chablis's wines are 100 percent Chardonnay, just like the white Burgundies of the Côte d'Or, they're quite different in style. For one thing, almost all Côte d'Or white Burgundies ferment and age in oak barrels, but many Chablis producers use stainless steel tanks instead, at least for some of their wines. Also, Chablis's climate is cooler, and its soil is different from the rest of Burgundy. These factors result in wines that are intrinsically lighter-bodied, relatively austere in flavor, and crisper.

TIPS ON DRINKING BURGUNDY

Red Burgundy is a particularly good wine to choose in restaurants. Unlike Bordeaux and Cabernet Sauvignon–based wines, red Burgundy is usually approachable young because of its softness and enticing aromas and flavors of red fruits. Moreover, red Burgundy, like all Pinot Noirs, is a versatile companion to food. It's the one red wine that can complement fish or seafood; it's ideal with salmon, for example. Chicken, turkey, and ham are also good matches for Burgundy. With richer red Burgundies, beef and game (such as duck, pheasant, rabbit, or venison) all go well.

Red Burgundy is at its best when served at cool temperatures — about 60 to 62 degrees Fahrenheit (17 degrees Celsius). It should *not* be decanted. Even older Burgundies seldom develop much sediment, and extra aeration would cause you to lose the wonderful Burgundy aroma, which is one of the greatest features of this wine.

On the other hand, white Burgundy often benefits from decanting, especially Grand Cru and Premier Cru white Burgundies from younger vintages (5 years old or younger). Great young white Burgundies, such as Corton-Charlemagne, just don't evolve completely in their first few years; the aeration will help bring out their aromas and flavors. But don't serve them too cold! The ideal temperature range for serving the better white Burgundies is 58 to 62 degrees Fahrenheit (15 to 17 degrees Celsius).

TIP

Chablis wine is classically very dry and sometimes has flinty flavors, without quite the richness and ripeness of Côte d'Or white Burgundies — even if recent vintages such as 2009 and 2007 have been so warm that Chablis wines sport riper fruit flavor than usual. For a classic, cool-climate Chablis, try a bottle from the 2008, 2010, 2012, or 2014 vintage. We are drinking and enjoying 2014 Chablis now. Personally, we buy a lot more Chablis (Premier Cru and Grand Cru) than Côte d'Or white Burgundies. They're much more affordable; standard Chablis, about $25 to $35, are great values.

TIP

Chablis is an ideal companion to seafood, especially oysters. Like all other white Burgundies, Chablis should be served cool (about 56 to 58 degrees Fahrenheit, or 14 to 15 degrees Celsius), not cold.

Beyond standard Chablis

Chablis is at its best at the Premier Cru and Grand Cru level.

The seven Grand Cru Chablis vineyards are Les Clos, Valmur, Les Preuses, Vaudésir, Grenouilles, Bougros, and Blanchot. Another vineyard that's actually — but not technically — Grand Cru is La Moutonne; this vineyard is a part of the Vaudésir and Les Preuses Grand Cru acreage but isn't recognized as a Grand Cru appellation. Grand Cru Chablis wines range in price from $75 to more than $100, depending on the producer. Grand Cru Chablis from good vintages (see Appendix C) can age and improve for 15 years or more.

TIP

The Chablis district has 22 Premier Cru Chablis appellations, but the eight most well known are Fourchaume, Montée de Tonnerre, Vaillons, Mont de Milieu, Montmains, Butteaux, Séchets, and Les Forêts (also known as Forest). Premier Cru Chablis wines range in price from $40 to $70, depending on the producer, and can age up to ten years or more in good vintages.

Nine outstanding producers of Chablis

WORTH THE SEARCH

Nine producers really stand out in Chablis. For a true understanding of this under-rated wine, try to buy their Grand or Premier Cru Chablis. *Try* is the operative word here; these are small producers whose wines are available only in better stores:

>> **François Raveneau** and **René et Vincent Dauvissat:** Both use oak for fermenting and aging; thus the wines are fairly rich and substantial — and also expensive.

>> **Louis Michel:** Uses stainless steel only, making vibrant, crisp wines.

>> **Jean Dauvissat:** Uses mainly stainless steel.

>> **Jean Collet, Jean-Paul Droin, Christian Moreau, William Fèvre, and Verget:** Other consistently fine producers of Chablis.

Mâcon: Affordable whites

REAL DEAL

The best buys in white Burgundies — and many of the best white wine buys in the world — come from the Mâconnais district.

The Mâconnais lies directly south of the Chalonnaise and north of Beaujolais. It has a milder, sunnier climate than the Côte d'Or to the north. Wine production centers around the city of Mâcon, a gateway city to Provence and the Riviera. The hills in the Mâconnais contain the same chalky limestone beloved by Chardonnay that can be found in many Burgundy districts to the north. In Mâcon, you can even find a village called Chardonnay.

Mâcon's white wines, in fact, are 100 percent Chardonnay. Most of them are simply called Mâcon or Mâcon-Villages (a slightly better wine than Mâcon, because it comes from specific villages), and they retail for $15 to $20 a bottle, with a few up to $25. Often better are Mâcons that come from just one village; in those wines, the name of the village is appended to the district name, Mâcon (as in Mâcon-Lugny or Mâcon-Viré).

Mâcon whites are medium-bodied, crisp, fresh, yet substantial wines, often with minerally flavor. They're usually unoaked. You should enjoy them while they're young, generally within three years of the vintage. A few red wines are made in the Mâcon district (mainly from the Gamay grape) and, like the whites, are good values.

TIP

The best Mâcon whites come from the southernmost part of the district and carry AOC names of their communes — **Pouilly-Fuissé** (pwee-fwee-say) and **St.-Véran** (san-veh-rahn).

>> Pouilly-Fuissé is a richer, fuller-bodied wine than a simple Mâcon, is often oaked, and is a bit more expensive (around $28 to $35; up to $45 for the best ones). To try an outstanding example of Pouilly-Fuissé, buy Château Fuissé, which, in good vintages, compares favorably with more expensive Côte d'Or white Burgundies (although different in style).

>> St.-Véran, at $17 to $25, is very possibly the best-value wine in all of Mâcon. Especially fine is the St.-Véran of Verget — one of the best producers of Mâconnais wines.

Beaujolais: As delightful as it is affordable

The Beaujolais district is situated south of the Mâconnais, in the heart of one of the greatest gastronomic centers of the world; good restaurants abound in the area, as well as in the nearby city of Lyon. As a wine, Beaujolais is so famous that it stands apart from the other wines of Burgundy. It even has its own red grape, Gamay. The fact that Beaujolais is part of Burgundy is merely a technicality.

CELEBRATION TIME: BEAUJOLAIS NOUVEAU

Each year on the third Thursday in November, the new vintage of Beaujolais — called Beaujolais Nouveau — is released all over the world with great fanfare. This youngster — only about six weeks old! — is a very grapey, easy-to-drink, delicious wine with practically no tannin but lots of fruitiness. In the United States, Beaujolais Nouveau graces many a Thanksgiving table because of the timing of its annual debut. It sells for $10 to $12 and is at its best during its first year.

The easy-drinking Beaujolais

TIP

If you're a white wine, White Zinfandel, or rosé wine drinker (or even a non-wine drinker!), Beaujolais could be the *ideal* first red wine to drink — a bridge, so to speak, to more serious red wines. Beaujolais wines are the fruitiest red wines in France, although they're dry. Beaujolais is truly a fun wine that's delicious and doesn't require contemplation.

Beaujolais and Beaujolais Supérieur (1 percent higher in alcohol) are the easiest Beaujolais wines. Their AOC zones extend across the whole Beaujolais district, but in practice, these wines come from the southern part of Beaujolais where the soil is mainly clay and sand. They're fresh, fruity, uncomplicated, fairly light-bodied wines that sell for $12 to $16 and are best a year or two after the vintage. They're fine wines for warm weather, when a heavier red wine would be inappropriate.

The serious versions

REAL DEAL

Beaujolais has its serious side, too. The best Beaujolais are made in the northern part of the Beaujolais district where the soil is granite-based, producing fuller, more substantial wine than basic Beaujolais. Beaujolais-Villages is a wine blended from grapes grown in (some of) 39 specific villages. It costs a dollar or two more but can be well worth the difference.

Beaujolais that's even higher quality comes from ten specific areas in the north. The wines of these areas are known as *Cru* Beaujolais, and only the name of the Cru appears in large letters on the label. (The wines aren't actually named Beaujolais.) Cru Beaujolais have more depth and, in fact, need a little time to develop; some of the Crus can age and improve for five or six years or more. They range in price from about $18 to $30. Table 10-6 lists the ten Cru Beaujolais as they are geographically situated, from south to north, along with a brief description of each wine.

TABLE 10-6   ## The Ten Cru Beaujolais

Cru	Description
Brouilly (broo-yee)	The largest Cru in terms of production and the most variable in quality; light and fruity; drink within three years; with a good producer, such as Georges Descombes, can be very fine
Côte de Brouilly	Distinctly better than Brouilly, fuller and more concentrated; vineyards are higher in altitude; drink within three years
Régnié (ray-nyay)	The newest village to be recognized as a Cru; very similar to Brouilly; not quite so good as Côte de Brouilly

(continued)

TABLE 10-6 *(continued)*

Cru	Description
Morgon (mor-gohn)	At its best, full and earthy; can age for five to seven years, or more
Chiroubles (sheh-roob-leh)	One of our favorites; the quintessential, delicate, delicious, perfumed Beaujolais; tastes of young red fruits; very pretty; drink it within two years of the vintage
Fleurie (flehr-ee)	Medium-bodied, rich, with velvety fruitiness; the most popular Cru (and, along with Moulin-à-Vent, the most expensive, at $18 to $27); quite reliable; can age for four years
Moulin-à-Vent (moo-lahn-ah-vahn)	Clearly the most powerful, concentrated Cru, and the one that can age the longest (ten years or more); this is one Beaujolais that really needs three or four years to develop
Chénas (shay-nahs)	Bordering Moulin-à-Vent (in fact, much of it can be legally sold as the more famous Moulin-à-Vent); what is sold as Chénas is usually well priced; drink within four years
Juliénas (jhool-yay-nahs)	The insider's Beaujolais; often the most consistent and the best of the Crus; full-bodied and rich; can last five years or more; seldom disappoints
Saint-Amour (sant-ah-more)	The northernmost Cru; perfectly named for lovers on Valentine's Day (or any other day); supple, light- to medium-bodied, delicious berry fruit; drink within two or three years

Most Beaujolais is sold by large *négociants* — firms that buy grapes and wine from growers and then blend, bottle, and sell the wine under their own labels. Two of the largest Beaujolais *négociants* are Georges Duboeuf and Louis Jadot; Jadot also owns a few very fine domaines, in Moulin–à–Vent and in Morgon. Seek out some of the small Beaujolais producers, such as Jean–Paul Brun and Georges Descombes, to see how good Beaujolais can be.

TIP

BEAUJOLAIS IN ACTION

To really get a feeling for being in France, visit a bistro in Paris or Lyon and order a carafe of young Beaujolais with your charcuterie, pâte, or chicken. No wine slides down the throat as easily! Young, uncomplicated Beaujolais wines should *definitely* be served chilled, at about 55 degrees Fahrenheit (13 degrees Celsius), to capture their fruity exuberance. The fuller Cru Beaujolais, on the other hand, are best at about the same temperature as red Burgundy (58 to 60 degrees Fahrenheit; 14 degrees Celsius).

The Rhône Valley's Hearty Wines

The Rhône (rone) Valley, which takes its name from the Rhône River, lies in southeastern France (refer to Figure 10-1), south of Beaujolais, between the city of Lyon in the north and Avignon directly south (just north of Provence). As the map suggests, the Rhône Valley is actually two distinct areas, a narrow swath of vineyard land in the north and a larger, more open landscape in the south. To varying degrees, the red wines are full, robust, and fairly high in alcohol. Even some of the white wines tend to be full and powerful. But the wines from the southern part of the Rhône are distinctly different from those in the northern Rhône Valley, as you find out in the following sections.

Generous wines of the South

Most (in fact, about 95 percent of) Rhône wines come from the southern Rhône. In a warm, Mediterranean climate, the grapes develop reliable levels of ripeness and make generous, wines that are generally inexpensive and uncomplicated. The wines are mainly red, and they're mainly blends of several grape varieties. The dominant grape variety is Grenache, which makes easygoing wines that are high in alcohol and low in tannin, but some blends contain significant amounts of Syrah or other varieties, which makes for somewhat gutsier wines.

REAL DEAL

The largest AOC/AOP designation is Côtes du Rhone, the Rhône Valley's everyday red wine, which comes mainly from the southern part of the region. For a good, reliable dry red wine that costs about $12 to $18, look for this name. The southern Rhône Valley makes more serious wines — mostly red — but Côtes du Rhône is one of the best inexpensive red wines in the world.

Almost all Côtes du Rhône wines are red: More than 90 percent are red, with the balance being white and rosé.

Besides Côtes du Rhône itself, other southern Rhône wines to look for are

>> **Côtes du Ventoux** (vahn-too), which is similar to but a bit lighter than Côtes du Rhône

>> **Côtes du Rhône-Villages,** from 95 villages, making fuller and a bit more expensive wines than Côtes du Rhône; 19 of these villages are entitled to use their names on the label, such as *Cairanne-Côtes du Rhône-Villages*

>> The single-village wines **Gigondas** (jhee-gohn-dahs) and **Vacqueyras** (vah-keh-rahs)

The last two wines are former Côtes du Rhône-Villages wines that graduated into individual appellations. Additional villages periodically join their rank, but Gigondas and Vacqueyras are those that you see most often.

>> Gigondas ($33 to $43) is quite rich and robust and can live for ten years or more in good vintages.

>> Vacqueyras is less powerful and robust than Gigondas but also less expensive (mainly $23 to $25); Vacqueyras is a particularly good buy.

But **Châteauneuf-du-Pape** (shah-toe-nuf-doo-pahp) is the king in the southern Rhône. Its name recalls the 14th century, when nearby Avignon (not Rome) was the temporary home of the Popes. Almost all Châteauneuf-du-Pape is red wine and a blend of grapes: As many as 13 varieties can be used, but Grenache, Mourvèdre, and Syrah predominate. At its best, Châteauneuf-du-Pape is full-bodied, rich, round, and ripe. In good vintages, it will age well for 15 to 20 years. Most red Châteauneuf-du-Pape wines retail in the $45 to $65 price range, but the best ones can cost up to $90 or more. Two of the finest Châteauneuf-du-Papes are Château Rayas (nearly 100 percent Grenache from very old vines) and Château de Beaucastel (which can age 20 years or more). A small amount of complex, earthy-style white Châteauneuf-du-Pape is also made.

Two interesting dry rosé wines of the southern Rhône are **Tavel** (tah-vel) and **Lirac** (lee-rahk). Lirac is less well known and, therefore, less expensive: Tavel retails mainly from $20 to $30; Lirac, from $15 to $25. Lirac can also be white or red (red Lirac wines can be more than $25), but all Tavel wines are rosés. Both are made from Grenache and Cinsault grapes. They can be delightful on hot, summer days or at picnics. As with most rosé wines, they are best when they're very young.

Noble wines of the north

The vineyards of the northern Rhône cover hillsides and terraces along the Rhône River and have a climate that is cooler than that of the southern Rhône. The two best red wines of the entire Rhône Valley — **Côte-Rôtie** (coat-roe-tee) and **Hermitage** (er-mee-tahj) — hail from the northern Rhône. Like all northern Rhône reds, both are made from the great Syrah grape, the only red grape in the north.

>> Although both are rich, full-bodied wines, Côte-Rôtie is the more finesseful of the two. It has a wonderfully fragrant aroma — which always reminds us of bacon, green olives, and raspberries — and soft, fruity flavors. (A small percentage of white Viognier grapes is permitted and sometimes used in Côte-Rôtie, and this can contribute floral notes.) In good vintages (see Appendix C), Côte-Rôtie can age for 20 years or more. Many Côte-Rôties are in the $49 to $75 price range, but a few of the best ones retail for more than $100.

The most famous producer of Côte-Rôtie is Guigal; his single-vineyard Côte-Rôties — La Mouline, La Landonne, and La Turque — are legendary but rare and expensive (well over $100, and up to $200-plus).

>> Red Hermitage is clearly the most full-bodied, longest-lived Rhône wine. It is a complex, rich, tannic wine that needs several years before it begins to develop, and it ages easily for 30 years or more in good vintages. (**2010, 2009, 2006, 2003, 1999, 1991, 1990, 1989, and 1988** were all *excellent vintages in the northern Rhône*.) The best red Hermitages sell today for $65 to $95, and a few of the top wines are over $100. Hermitages that sell for less than $50 are invariably not as good.

TIP

The three best producers of Hermitage are Jean-Louis Chave; Chapoutier; and Paul Jaboulet Aîné (for its top Hermitage, La Chapelle).

Cornas, made entirely from Syrah, is another fine northern Rhône red wine. Cornas resembles Hermitage in that it is a huge, tannic wine that needs 10 to 20 years of aging. It ranges in price from $50 to $90 for the best examples. Two Cornas producers to look for are Domaine Auguste Clape and Noel Verset; Jean-Luc Colombo is another leading producer.

Two less-expensive red wines from the northern Rhône are **Crozes-Hermitage,** from an area surrounding the Hermitage zone, and **St.-Joseph.** Both sell for $18 to $30 (and higher, for the best examples).

A small amount of **white Hermitage** is produced from the Marsanne and Roussanne grape varieties. White Hermitage is traditionally a full, rich, earthy wine that needs 8 to 10 years to fully develop, and can age for 15 years or more. Chapoutier's fine Hermitage Blanc, Chante Alouette, however, is all Marsanne (about $92 to $99) and made in a more approachable style. The one truly great white Hermitage is Chave's; at about $280 to $300, it's complex, rich, and almost as long-lived as the red Hermitage. Expensive, yes, but truly one of the world's greatest white wines.

WORTH THE
SEARCH

Condrieu (cohn-dree-uh), made entirely from Viognier, is the other white northern Rhône wine to try. It's one of the most fragrant, floral dry wines in existence. Its flavors are delicate but rich, with delicious fresh apricot and peach notes; it makes a wonderful accompaniment to fresh fish. Condrieu (which sells for $60 to $90, with the best over $100) is best young, however. And, because Condrieu is a small wine zone, the best Condrieu wines are hard to find. Look for them in finer wine shops and better French restaurants.

One wine, **Château-Grillet,** made from Viognier, has its own very small appellation. It's difficult to find, and expensive. You might be fortunate to find a few older vintages of Château-Grillet in the $200 to $280 range, depending on the vintage. Like Condrieu, Château-Grillet is a wine to drink young. At its best, Château-Grillet is an exquisite white wine.

The Loire Valley: White Wine Heaven

If you're looking for white wine alternatives to Chardonnay, discover the Loire (l'wahr) Valley wine region. For the record, you can find red wines and some dry rosés, too, but the Loire region is famous for its white wines.

The Loire Valley stretches across northwest France (refer to Figure 10-1), following the path of the Loire River from central France in the east to the Atlantic Ocean in the west. The rather cool climate, especially in the west, produces relatively light-bodied white wines. The Loire Valley has three sections, each of which features different grape varieties.

The Upper Loire

In the eastern end of the Valley (called the Upper Loire), just south of Paris, are the towns of Sancerre and Pouilly-sur-Loire, located on opposite banks of the Loire River. Here, the Sauvignon Blanc grape makes lively, dry wines that have spicy, green-grass and minerally flavors. The two principal wines in this area are **Sancerre** (sahn-sair) and **Pouilly-Fumé** (pwee-foo-may).

>> Sancerre is the lighter and more vibrant of the two. It's perfect for summer drinking, especially with shellfish or light, freshwater fish, such as trout. Look for the Sancerres of Domaines Henri Bourgeois or Lucien Crochet.

>> Pouilly-Fumé is slightly fuller than Sancerre and can have attractive flinty, mineral flavors. Pouilly-Fumé can be quite a fine wine when made by a good producer, such as Didier Dagueneau or Ladoucette. Because of its fuller weight, Pouilly-Fumé goes well with rich fish, such as salmon, or with chicken or veal.

Most Sancerre and Pouilly-Fumé wines sell in the $25 to $40 range, but a few of the better Pouilly-Fumés can cost $50 or more. These wines are at their best when they're young; drink them within four years of the vintage.

The central Loire Valley

The central Loire Valley is known for both its white and red wines. The white Chenin Blanc grape arguably makes better wine here than it does anywhere else in the world. These wines can be dry or sweet, and they carry the names of the areas where their grapes grow.

>> **Savennières,** at its best, is the world's greatest *dry* Chenin Blanc wine, starts at about $23 but can be up to $65 for its best wines.

>> **Coulée de Serrant** is a great dessert white wine made from Chenin Blanc.

» **Bonnezeaux** and **Quarts-de-Chaume** are two other well-known dessert whites.

» **Vouvray** wines come in three styles: dry (*sec*), medium-dry (*demi-sec*), or sweet (called *moelleux,* pronounced m'wah-leuh). Vouvray sec is a less austere and less full-bodied wine than Savennières, however. Vouvray also can be a sparkling wine.

The best wines of Vouvray, the sweet (moelleux), can be made only in warm vintages of unusual ripeness, which occur infrequently. These wines need several years to develop and can last almost forever, thanks to their remarkable acidity; their prices begin in the $50 to $60 range. Three renowned Vouvray producers are Philippe Foreau of Clos Naudain, Gaston Huet-Pinguet, and Didier Champalou.

TIP

Less expensive Vouvrays, priced at about $15 to $18, are pleasant to drink young. Even the drier versions are not truly bone-dry and are a good choice if you don't enjoy very dry wines. They go well with chicken or veal in cream sauce, spicy cuisines, or fruit and soft cheese after dinner.

The central Loire Valley also boasts the region's best red wines. Made mainly from Cabernet Franc, they carry the place-names of the villages where the grapes grow: **Chinon** (she-nohn), **Bourgueil** (boor-guh'y), **St.-Nicolas-de-Bourgueil** (san-nee-co-lah-deh-boor-guh'y), and **Saumur-Champigny** (soh-muhr-shahm-pee-n'yee). They're all spicy, great-value ($18 to $40), medium-bodied reds that are famously food friendly.

Pays Nantais

Close to the Atlantic Ocean is the third wine district of the Loire Valley — Pays Nantais (pay-ee nahn-tay), named after the city of Nantes, right where the Loire River empties into the Atlantic Ocean. This area is the home of the Muscadet grape (also known as Melon de Bourgogne). The wine, which is commonly known as **Muscadet** (moos-cah-day), is light, bracing, and very dry, with apple and mineral flavors — perfect with clams, oysters, mussels, and river fish (and, naturally, ideal for summer drinking).

TECHNICAL
STUFF

Most Muscadet comes from the Sèvre-et-Maine AOC zone, and those words appear on the label. Frequently, you also see the term *sur lie,* which means that the wine aged on its *lees* (dead fermentation yeasts) and was bottled straight from the tank. This procedure gives the wine liveliness, freshness, and sometimes a slight prickle of carbon dioxide on the tongue. In recent years, we have seen the quality of Muscadet improve considerably, and we consider it a wine to keep your eye on.

REAL DEAL

Muscadet is a terrific warm weather white and a great value. You can buy a really good Muscadet for $10 to $12, but the best Mucadets retail for $15 to $20.

Alsace: Unique Region, Unique Wines

Alsace is a picturesque wine region in northeastern France, just across the Rhine River from Germany. Alsace wines are unique among French wines in that almost all of them carry a grape variety name as well as a place-name (that is, Alsace). All Alsace wines come in a long-necked bottle called a *flûte*. The wines of Alsace also happen to represent very good value.

Considering Alsace's northerly latitude, you'd expect the region's climate to be cool. But thanks to the protection of the Vosges Mountains to the west, Alsace's climate is quite sunny and temperate, and one of the driest in France.

Although Alsace makes some red wine and a little rosé (Pinot Noir), 90 percent of Alsace's wines are white. Four are particularly important: Riesling, Pinot Blanc, Pinot Gris, and Gewurztraminer. Each reflects the characteristics of its grape, but they all share a certain aroma and flavor, sometimes called a spiciness, that can only be described as the flavor of Alsace.

REAL DEAL

>> **Riesling** is the king of Alsace wines. Alsace Riesling has a fruity aroma but a firm, dry, almost steely taste. Although it can be consumed young, Riesling from a good vintage can easily age and improve for ten years or more. Rieslings are in the $22 to $50 price range. Grand Cru Rieslings can be more costly.

>> **Alsace Pinot Blanc** is the lightest of the four wines. Some producers make their Pinot Blanc medium-dry to appeal to wine drinkers who are new to the region's wines, while others make classic, bone-dry Pinot Blanc. Either way, it's best young. Pinot Blanc is quite inexpensive, selling for $16 to $24.

>> **Pinot Gris** is made from the same variety that you find in Italy as Pinot Grigio. Here in Alsace, it's a rich, spicy, full-bodied, characterful wine. Alsace's Pinot Gris retails for $20 to $40; it goes well with spicy meat dishes and can work with slightly sweet or sour flavors.

TIP

» The **Gewurztraminer** grape has such intense, exotic, spicy aromas and flavors that it's a love-it-or-leave-it wine. (One of us loves it — the other leaves it!) But it certainly has its followers. If you haven't tried an Alsace Gewurztraminer yet, you haven't tasted one of the most distinctive wines in the world. It's fairly low in acidity and high in alcohol, a combination that gives an impression of fullness and softness. It goes well with *foie gras* and strong cheeses, and some people like it with spicy Asian cuisine. Gewurztraminer sells mainly for $18 to $22, with the best examples over $25. It does not age as well as Riesling; drink it when it's young.

Besides the grape variety name, you'll see many other words on labels of Alsace wines, such as Reserve (an unofficial term) and Grand Cru, as well as single-vineyard names. Most producers make numerous wines from each grape variety because the vineyards can differ markedly, and they use these label designations to distinguish their various wines.

The South and Southwest

The most dynamic wine regions in France are all located in the southern part of the country. Ironically, this is the oldest wine-producing area in France: The Greeks made wine in Provence in the sixth century B.C. The South is also the part of France that makes the most wine. Languedoc-Roussillon, a dual wine region, produces from one-third to 40 percent of France's wine in most years!

Southwest France, the huge area between Bordeaux and the Spanish border, also makes wine (well, it's French, isn't it?), and many wine regions here have also experienced a renaissance. Like the South, it's mainly red wine country, but you can find some interesting whites, rosés, sparkling wines, and dessert wines, as well. You might say that the South and southwestern France are the country's "new" frontiers.

France's bargain wines: Languedoc-Roussillon

The sunny, dry Languedoc-Roussillon (lahn-gweh-doc-roo-see-yohn) region, also known as the Midi (mee-dee), is France's largest wine-producing area. The region (refer to Figure 10-1) makes mainly red wines; in fact, more than half of France's red wines come from here. Traditionally, these robust red wines came from typical grape varieties of the South, such as Carignan, Cinsault, and Grenache. But in the last two decades, more prestigious varieties, such as Syrah, Cabernet Sauvignon, and Merlot, have become quite common. Winemakers use these grapes both for varietal wines and in blends.

From this region, look especially for the red wines from the AOC zones of **Corbières, Minervois, St.-Chinian, Fitou,** and **Costières de Nîmes.** In addition, many varietal wines carrying the designation *Vin de Pays* (or *IGP*) *d'Oc* are often good values. They're made from grapes that come from anywhere in the Languedoc-Roussillon region, rather than from a specific AOC zone. One amazing white varietal wine, **Picpoul de Pinet,** has its own appellation. It is a racy, lively, minerally wine that sells in the $10 to $14 range. Look for it!

Whichever the appellation, most of these wines are in the $10 to $16 price range, although a few of the better ones cost $20 or more.

Timeless Provence

Provence (pro-vahns) — southeast of the Rhône Valley, east of Languedoc-Roussillon, and west of northern Italy — may be France's most beautiful region. Home of the Riviera, Nice, and Cannes, it's certainly the country's most fashionable and touristy region. But it's also an ancient land, with a thriving old capital, Aix-en-Provence. The excellent light and climate have always attracted great artists — such as Vincent van Gogh — who painted many of their best works here.

Wine has always been part of Provence's culture and economy. Provence is best known for its rosés, which so many tourists enjoy on the Riviera. Rosé wines dominate in the region's largest AOC wine zone, Côtes de Provence; but in three other important AOC zones — Coteaux d'Aix-en-Provence, Les Baux-de-Provence, and Bandol — red wines rule. **Bandol,** and its foremost producer, Domaine Tempier, enjoy Provence's greatest reputation for reds. Another amazing producer, Château Simone, from the tiny Palette appellation, is a standout for its white, red, and rosé wines, but especially for its white. **Cassis** (no relation to the black currant liqueur of the same name), a small AOC zone on the Mediterranean coast near Marseilles, makes distinctive, aromatic white wines.

Provence's reds and rosés derive from the same grape varieties used in Languedoc-Roussillon — Grenache, Cinsault, Mourvèdre, Carignan, Syrah, and Cabernet Sauvignon. The main varieties in white Cassis are Clairette and Marsanne.

Southwest France

The large area that borders the Atlantic Ocean south of the Bordeaux region is known as southwest France — but it's actually composed of many individual wine districts. Two of the most significant are situated near Bordeaux.

>> **Bergerac** (ber-jhe-rak) makes Bordeaux-like red and white wines, without the Bordeaux prices. Merlot dominates Bergerac's red wines, while Sémillon and

Sauvignon Blanc are the main varieties for its whites, some of which cost as little as $10 to $12 a bottle.

>> **Cahors** (cah-or) is southwest France's most prestigious red wine district. The main grape variety is Malbec, and that name increasingly appears on labels. Nowhere else in the world, except Argentina, does this variety play such an important role. The everyday red Cahors wines sell or $12 to $14. The best wines of the traditional Cahors producers, such as Château Lagrezette, are dark, tannic reds that need about ten years of aging before they mature. Prices for Château Lagrezette Cahors wines begin at about $ 45. The Malbec variety generally makes a more powerful wine in Cahors than it does in Argentina.

Three other districts in southwest France specialize in white dessert wines: **Gaillac** (gah-yack), **Juraçon** (joo-rahn-sohn), and **Monbazillac** (mon-bah-zee-yak). Gaillac also makes fruity, lightly sparkling wines. Other red wines of note include **Madiran,** a full-bodied, tannic red made from the Tannat variety — along with Cabernet Sauvignon and Cabernet Franc; and **Irouléguy** (ee-roo-leh-gee), a spicy, tannic red wine made from Tannat, Cabernet Franc, and Cabernet Sauvignon, from an area near the Pyrénées Mountains and Spain, where the locals don't speak French, but Basque. Some Irouléguy rosé and white wines are also made.

Other French Wine Regions

Two of France's three most obscure wine regions have something in common: They're located in the foothills and slopes of the Alps in eastern France, next to Switzerland — where skiers are probably the most avid fans. They are the **Jura** (joo-rah) and **Savoie** (sah-v'wah) — sometimes anglicized as *Savoy*. And then there is the island of Corsica, with its own different wines.

Jura makes two interesting wines that are the region's specialties:

>> Yellow Wine (*Vin Jaune*), from the Savagnin grape variety, is comparable to a light Spanish fino Sherry, but it's not fortified (see Chapter 16). **Château Chalon** is the most famous example of Vins Jaunes (van-joh'n).

>> **Vin de Paille** (van deh pah'ee) is known as *Straw Wine* because of the traditional way in which it's made: The grapes (Savagnin, Chardonnay, and others) are harvested late and arranged to dry on straw mats or in baskets in attics — similar to Tuscany's specialty, Vin Santo (see Chapter 16). The resulting wine is rich, concentrated, nutty, and raisiny.

Savoie's wines, mainly white, are typically dry and light-bodied. **Seyssel** (say-sell), Savoie's best-known AOC, is known for its slightly sparkling wines as well as its still whites.

Corsica, renowned historically as the birthplace of Napoleon, is a large, very mountainous island 100 miles southeast of Provence (refer to Figure 10-1). North of the Italian island of Sardinia, Corsica traces its winemaking at least as far back as the 13th century when it was under control of the city-state of Genova. Corsica was ceded to France in 1768.

Corsica came into international prominence for its wines only recently. Its warm, dry climate lends the island to the production of red wines, and it is best known for its medium-bodied, well-priced reds and rosés. The Patrimonio wine region on the northern coast of Corsica became the island's first AOC zone in 1968, and it still produces Corsica's best red wines, called Patrimonio, made from Sangiovese (called Nielluccio, locally). Patrimonio also produces a white wine, Patrimonio Blanc (made from Vermentino), and some rosé wine.

Ajaccio is a second important AOC region on the southwestern coast, mainly known for red wines. Vin de Corse is a broad AOC appellation covering wines on the southern coast. Altogether, Corsica has nine AOC wine zones. Grenache is a major red variety on Corsica, along with many other typical Rhône varieties.

Although much of Patrimonio and its other wines are consumed on the island, Corsica has been developing an export market for its wines in the last decade. They are great-value wines. They start at $14 to $15 and go up to $28 to $40 for the best wines.

Chapter 11

Italy, the Land of Great Vino

More than 2,000 years after Julius Caesar conquered Gaul, the Italians continue to take the world by storm. With passion, artistic flair, impeccable taste, and flawless workmanship as its tools, Italy has infiltrated the arenas of fashion, film, food, and of course wine.

Thanks to the popularity of Italian restaurants, most of us have frequent opportunities to enjoy best-selling Italian wines, such as Pinot Grigio, Prosecco, Barolo, Amarone, and Chianti. But Italy makes other wines, too — many of them among the greatest wines on earth. And just about every one of Italy's thousand-something wines is terrific with food, because Italians make wines specifically to be enjoyed during a meal. That's how they drink them.

In this chapter, we begin with Italy's three most renowned wine regions — Piedmont, Tuscany, and the Veneto. We also discuss other Italian regions, and their wines, that you are likely to encounter in your wine shop or *ristorante*.

The Vineyard of Europe

Tiny Italy — 60 percent the size of France, three-quarters the size of California — is an over-achiever in its wine production. In many years, Italy leads the world in producing wine! (Italy or France always occupy either first or second place.) Wine is the lifeblood of the Italian people. Vines grow all over, in every one of Italy's 20 regions, and no traditional dinner in Italy can possibly occur without a bottle of wine on the table. Italy also has by far more different grape varieties than any other country in the world — over 1,000, with at least 440 presently used for making wines.

The downside of wine's permeation in Italian culture is that Italians often take wine for granted. For example, Italy took 28 years longer than France to develop a wine classification system to codify its wine producing districts.

Another handicap of Italian wines, for wine drinkers in other countries who want to learn about them, is that most Italian wines are made from native grape varieties that don't exist elsewhere (and when transplanted, don't perform nearly as well as in Italy). Grapes such as Nebbiolo, Sangiovese, Aglianico, and Barbera, to name just a few, can make outstanding wine in Italy, but their names are not household words outside of Italy, despite the fact that recognition of Italian wines has grown amazingly over the past four decades.

TIP

Table 11-1 identifies the grape varieties of wines in three of Italy's most important wine regions. Note that many of these wines are blends of two or more grape varieties.

On the upside, Italy is blessed with such a variety of soils and climates — from Alpine foothills in the north to Mediterranean coastlines — that the range of its wines is almost endless. (A curious wine lover could keep busy for many decades, exploring all the wines in Italy!) Italy's hilly landscape provides plenty of high-altitude relief for grapevines, even in the warm south.

In the following sections, we discuss the gamut of Italian wine quality, explain the label terms that appear on labels of Italian wines, and provide an overview of Italy's wine regions.

The ordinary and the elite

REMEMBER

Italy's wines, as we outside of Italy know them, fall into two distinct groups:

>> Inexpensive red and white wines for everyday drinking with meals in the casual Italian fashion

>> The better wines, which range from good to great in quality, for fine dinners and for quality-conscious wine drinkers and collectors

TABLE 11-1   **Grape Varieties of Some Major Italian Wine Regions**

Region /Red Wine	White Wine	Grape Varieties
Piedmont		
Barolo		Nebbiolo
Barbaresco		Nebbiolo
Gattinara		Nebbiolo, Bonarda*
	Gavi	Cortese
Tuscany		
Chianti, Chianti Classico		Sangiovese, Canaiolo, and others*
Brunello di Montalcino		Sangiovese Grosso
Vino Nobile di Montepulciano		Sangiovese, Canaiolo, and others*
Carmignano		Sangiovese, Cabernet Sauvignon*
Super-Tuscans**		Cabernet Sauvignon, Sangiovese, and others*
Veneto		
	Soave	Garganega, Trebbiano di Soave, and others*
Valpolicella		Corvina, Rondinella, Molinara*
Amarone		(Same grapes as Valpolicella; semi-dried)
Bardolino		Corvina, Rondinella, Molinara*
	Bianco di Custoza	Trebbiano, Garganega, Friulano*
	Lugana***	Trebbiano di Lugana

Blended wines, made from two or more grapes.
**Untraditional wines produced mainly in the Chianti district; see the discussion under Tuscany.*
***Much of the Lugana wine zone is actually in Lombardy.*

One of the best-known Italian wines in the first category is Pinot Grigio, the ubiquitous dry white wine that is the largest-selling type of imported wine in the United States. (Another Italian wine, Prosecco, is now this country's largest-selling sparkling wine.)

In the second category is Barolo, one of the world's greatest red wines, along with many other fine Italian wines, such as Brunello di Montalcino.

Categories of Italian wine, legally speaking

TECHNICAL STUFF

Because Italy is a member of the European Union, her official system of categorizing wines (her *appellation* system) must conform to the E.U. system. (See Chapter 4 for more information.) In the upper tier — wines with a Protected Designation of Origin (PDO) — Italy has two categories of wine:

>> DOCG *(Denominazione di Origine Controllata e Garantita)* wines, translated as "regulated and guaranteed place-name," are a group of elite wines. The long Italian phrase corresponding to the initials DOCG appears on the labels of these wines.

>> DOC *(Denominazione di Origine Controllata* or, in the new E.U. lingo, *Denominazione di Origine Protetta, DOP)* wines, translated as "regulated (or protected) place-name," are Italy's basic PDO wines. The phrase *Denominazione di Origine Controllata* (or *Protetta*) appears on the labels of these wines.

REMEMBER

The terms DOC and DOCG refer both to wine zones and to the wines of those zones. The DOC Soave, for example, is both a place (a specific production zone defined and regulated by Italian law, named after a town called Soave) and the wine of that place.

In the lower E.U. tier — wines with a Protected Geographic Indication (PGI) — Italy has another category of wine: IGT *(Indicazione Geografica Tipica* or, in the new E.U. lingo, *Indicazione Geografica Protetta, IGP)* wines. These wines have a geographic name on the label, but that name represents a broader territory than that of DOC/DOCG (DOP) wines. For example, although the DOCG wine Brunello di Montalcino must derive from grapes grown in a very specific section of the region of Tuscany, a wine with the IGT/IGP name of "Tuscany" may come from anywhere in that whole region. Many IGT/IGP wines carry a grape variety name in addition to the name of the protected geographic area.

Italy's wine regions

Italy is said to have 20 wine regions, which correspond exactly to her political regions (see Figure 11-1). In other words, wine is produced everywhere in Italy. What we would call a wine region in France, such as Burgundy or Alsace, we refer to as a wine *zone* in Italy to avoid confusion with the political regions.

FIGURE 11-1:
The wine
zones of Italy.

Illustration by Lisa S. Reed

Many of the finest wines come from the north: the Piedmont region in the northwest, Tuscany in north-central Italy, and the three regions (informally called the
Tre Venezie) of northeastern Italy. But southern Italy also makes some fine wines
that have become better known outside of Italy, as we discuss in the later section
"The Sunny South of Italy."

Reds Reign in Piedmont

Piedmont's claim to wine fame is the Nebbiolo (neb-bee-*oh*-lo) grape, a noble red variety that produces great wine only in northwestern Italy. The proof of Nebbiolo's nobility is its wines: Barolo (bah-*ro*-lo) and Barbaresco (bar-bah-*res*-co) are two of the world's great red wines. But Piedmont's other red grape varieties, such as Barbera (bar-*bear*-ah) and Dolcetto (dohl-*chet*-to), can also make seriously good wines. White wines take a back seat in this region, as you see in the following sections.

Barolo and Barbaresco

Both Barolo and Barbaresco are DOCG wines made entirely from the Nebbiolo grape in the Langhe hills around the town of Alba, and each is named after a village within its production zone. They are robust reds — very dry, full-bodied, and high in tannin, acidity, and alcohol — with an amazing range of flavors. Their aromas and flavors suggest tar, violets, roses, ripe strawberries, and (sometimes) truffles (the kind that grow in the ground, not the chocolate!).

Barolo is more full-bodied than Barbaresco and usually requires a bit more aging; otherwise, the two wines are very similar. Like most Italian wines, they show at their best with food. Good Barolo and Barbaresco wines usually start at $35 to $40 retail and run to well over $100. Most Barbarescos are slightly less expensive than Barolos.

TIP

Barolos and Barbarescos are not meant to drink when they are young. Production rules stipulate that Barolo isn't Barolo until it has aged for at least 3 years at the winery, or for five years if it's called *Riserva.* (Barbaresco's minimum aging is 2 years, or four for Riserva.) Despite this long production regime, both wines benefit from additional aging. When made in a traditional style, Barolo and Barbaresco wines often require 10 to 15 years' total aging, from the year of the vintage — and these wines often benefit from a few hours of aeration before drinking to soften their somewhat tough tannins. (See Chapter 8 for instructions on aerating wine.) But the situation is changing. Both Barolo and Barbaresco are becoming more approachable, with softer tannins than previously. Many Barolos from the 2012 vintage are enjoyable now, for example. Wines from the very good 2010 vintage, however, could use a few more years and will improve with aging.

WORTH THE SEARCH

Both Barbaresco and especially Barolo have something in common with Burgundy in France: *You must find a good producer to experience the wine at its best.* To guide you in that endeavor, we list the producers whom we consider the best of Barolo and Barbaresco, in our rough order of preference.

Barolo

Giacomo Conterno

Giuseppe Rinaldi

Bartolo Mascarello

Giuseppe Mascarello

Bruno Giacosa

Cappellano

Vietti

Elvio Cogno

Gaja

Marcarini

Aldo Conterno

Ceretto (aka Bricco Rocche)

Cavallotto

Roberto Voerzio

Luciano Sandrone

Podere Colla

Renato Ratti

Brovia

E. Pira & Figli

G.B. Burlotto

Oddero

Pio Cesare

Massolino

Prunotto

Elio Altare

Cordero di Montezemolo

Luigi Pira

Manzone

Marchesi di Barolo

Michele Chiarlo

Conterno-Fantino

Giocomo Borgogno

Fontanafredda

Barbaresco

Bruno Giacosa

Gaja

Ceretto (aka Bricco Rocche)

Marchesi di Gresy

Produttori del Barbaresco

DeForville

Roagna

The top seven Barolo producers above are so close in excellence that it is just personal preference that separates them. Some producers — including Giacomo Conterno, both Mascarellos, Giuseppe Rinaldi, Cappellano, and Bruno Giacosa — make traditionally styled wines. Others — such as Gaja and E. Pira — make modern-style wines. See the nearby sidebar "Traditional, new-style, and middle-ground" for more details about these styles.

For years, many of the top Barolo wines have carried the names of specific vineyards, such as Cannubi or Lazzarito, on their labels. Since 2010, the use of site names has been codified into the DOCG regulation for Barolo: 181 site names (11 of them commune names) are now official *Menzioni Geographiche Aggiunti* ("additional geographic mentions," or MGAs). The site name appears on the label but the Italian phrase corresponding to MGA usually does not. Producers can still use a single-vineyard name that is not an MGA, however. In the Barbaresco zone, 66 specific sites are now official MGAs — although it is less common to see a site name on Barbaresco labels than on Barolo labels. The presence or absence of a vineyard or site name does not suggest higher or lower quality. The quality of the producer is your best gauge of the wine's quality.

TIP

In addition to the importance of the producer, the quality of the vintage is also a strong consideration in choosing your Barolo or Barbaresco. The truly great years of the past 25 years for these Nebbiolo-based wines are 2010, 2001, and 1996. Good to very good vintages include 2013, 2006, 2004, and 1999; these vintage Barolos and Barbarescos can be enjoyed now. The lighter 2012 vintage is showing very well now.

REAL DEAL

Two other good Nebbiolo-based wines, the DOCGs **Gattinara** (gah-tee-*nah*-rah) and **Ghemme** (*gae*-mae), come from northern Piedmont, where the Nebbiolo grape is called *Spanna*. Although Gattinara and Ghemme seldom get the praise that the two big Bs (Barolo and Barbaresco) enjoy, they offer the same enticing Nebbiolo aromas and flavors — especially Gattinara — in a less full-bodied style. Priced at $29 to $43 a bottle, Gattinara from a good producer may be one of the world's most underrated wines. Look for the Gattinaras by Antoniolo and Travaglini (Antoniolo is a bit more expensive). Antichi Vigneti di Cantalupo (about $35) is the leading Ghemme producer.

Piedmont offers plenty of wines besides Barolo and Barbaresco; in the following sections, we discuss several red and white wines to try.

TRADITIONAL, NEW-STYLE, AND MIDDLE-GROUND

One Barolo can differ from another (and one Barbaresco from another) not only according to where in each zone the grapes grow but also according to the wineries' production methods. Traditionally made wines are more tannic, need more time to develop, and typically have greater longevity than new-style wines. The new-style wines are fruitier in flavor and tend to have less structural power than the traditional wines, as well as being ready to drink sooner — as soon as three to five years after they're released. We see the new-style wines declining in popularity, and the traditional style more popular than ever. The middle-ground, combining aspects of traditional and new-style winemaking, is becoming an increasingly large category. There are always exceptions; the great producer, Angelo Gaja, although technically making so-called "newer-styled" wines, makes both Barolos and Barbarescos that last as long as the great traditional producers.

Weekday reds

The Piedmontese serve serious wines like Barolo and Barbaresco for Sunday dinner or special occasions. What they drink on an everyday basis are the red wines Dolcetto and Barbera, and also Nebbiolo wines made from grapes grown outside of the prestigious DOCG zones of Barolo and Barbaresco. Of the three, Dolcetto is generally the least complex, and is often the first red wine served in a Piedmontese meal.

Dolcetto

If you know enough Italian to translate the phrase *la dolce vita*, you could think that the name Dolcetto indicates a sweet wine. Actually, the Dolcetto grape tastes sweet, but the *wine* is distinctly dry and has some noticeable tannin, although the tannin isn't strong when you drink the wine with food. The aromas and flavors of Dolcetto include black pepper, spice, and berries.

Most Dolcetto wines sell for $14 to $28. The best Dolcetto wines are from the zones of Dogliani, Diano d'Alba, and Alba; with the exception of Dogliani, a DOCG wine, the labels of these wines carry the grape name, Dolcetto, along with the name of the area. Just about all our recommended Barolo producers make a Dolcetto, usually Dolcetto *d'Alba* (from Alba).

WORTH THE SEARCH

Two favorite Dolcetto producers of ours who both make Dolcetto from the Dogliani area are Quinto Chionetti and Luigi Einaudi.

Barbera

While Dolcetto is unique to Piedmont, the Barbera grape is the one of the most widely planted red grape varieties in all of Italy. (Sangiovese is *the* most planted red variety, followed by Montepulciano and Merlot.) But it's in Piedmont — specifically the Asti, Alba, and Monferrato wine zones — that Barbera excels. It's a red wine with high acidity and generous black-cherry fruit character. The wine's richness and weight vary according to the area where the grapes grow and, of course, the producer's style. Some Barbera wines are impressively rich while others are delightfully easygoing. Barbera happens to be one of our favorite everyday wines, especially with pasta or pizza — or anything tomatoey.

Barbera d'Alba is generally a bit fuller, riper, and richer than the leaner Barbera d'Asti and Barbera di Monferrato. But Barbera d'Asti from certain old vineyards rivals Barbera d'Alba in richness and in power. (Link the *d'* with the word following it when pronouncing these names: *dal*-ba, *dahs*-tee.) What had been a sub-zone of Barbera d'Asti is now a DOCG zone called Nizza. Nizza wine is 100 percent Barbera, but it does not necessarily state the grape name on the label.

Barbera is more popular in the United States than it has ever been, and we couldn't be more delighted, because it's now easier to find. Two general styles of Barbera are available:

>> Wine aged without wood or aged in *casks* (large oak containers that impart little, if any, oak flavor to the wine), which sells for about $14 to $30

>> Oak-influenced Barbera wine aged in *barriques* (small, new barrels of French oak), which sells in the $25 to $66 range

Barbera is an unusual red grape variety in that it has practically no tannin, and so the tannins from the small oak barrels can complement Barbera wines nicely. We do admit that some barrique-aged Barberas are very good but, with a few exceptions, we prefer the simpler, less expensive, traditional style.

WORTH THE SEARCH

Three particularly good producers of Barbera d'Alba are Vietti, Giacomo Conterno, and Cappellano. Vietti makes a terrific single-vineyard Barbera d'Alba called Scarrone and a superb single-vineyard Barbera d'Asti called La Crena. Giacomo Conterno makes two Barbera d'Alba wines from his famed Serralunga vineyards. Cappellano produces a remarkably full-bodied Barbera d'Alba from his estate vineyard, Gabutti. Marchesi di Gresy also makes an excellent Barbera d'Asti in a lighter style.

Nebbiolo

A third weekday red from Piedmont is Nebbiolo (labeled as *Nebbiolo d'Alba* or *Langhe Nebbiolo*). Nebbiolo d'Alba, grown from vineyards outside the Barolo/Barbaresco wine zones, must be 100 percent Nebbiolo. Langhe Nebbiolo, which can come from vineyards in the Barolo/Barbaresco territory and beyond, must have a minimum of 85 percent Nebbiolo.

We find that we are seeing more and more Langhe Nebbiolo wines lately, perhaps because its larger wine zone gives producers more flexibility in choosing their grapes than Nebbiolo d'Alba's does. Both wines are lighter in body and easier to drink than either Barolo or Barbaresco, and they sell for about $20 to $30 a bottle. Drinking varietal Nebbiolo wines is a no-brainer for us, because they have the wonderful aromas and flavors of the Nebbiolo grape and we don't have to wait for several years for the wines to mature. Both 2015 and 2014 have been good vintages for Nebbiolo wines.

Another Nebbiolo-based wine is Roero, made in the Roero DOCG territory north of the town of Alba. Roero Rosso must be made almost entirely from Nebbiolo. The advantages all these Nebbiolo wines have over Barolo or Barbaresco is that you can drink them while they're young, and that they are considerably less expensive.

Piedmont's white wine

Almost all Piedmont's wines are red, but the region does boast a few interesting dry whites:

>> **Arneis** (ahr-*nase*) is a white wine produced in the Roero zone near Alba from a once-forgotten grape also called Arneis, which was rescued from extinction by the late Alfredo Currado of the Vietti winery more than 40 years ago. Arneis is a dry wine with rich texture. It's best when consumed within two years of the vintage. A bottle of Vietti's or Ceretto's Arneis retails for $21 to $22; Bruno Giacosa's Arneis is about $27.

>> **Gavi,** named for a town in southern Piedmont, is a very dry wine with pronounced acidity, made from the Cortese grape. Most Gavis sell for $16 to $20, while a premium Gavi, La Scolca Black Label, costs around $33 to $40.

>> **Timorasso** is another white Piedmontese varietal wine getting attention lately. It's from the Colli Tortonesi region in southwestern Piedmont. Walter Massa, a local prodcer, is championing the cause of Timorasso as a varietal wine. Timorasso is dry with lively acidity and yet rich texture; it sells for about $26.

Tuscany the Beautiful

With the cities of Florence and Siena, Michelangelo's David, and the leaning tower of Pisa, the beautiful region of Tuscany has more than its share of attractions. Only one Italian wine can possibly compare in fame — and that, too, comes from Tuscany: Chianti. In the following sections, we talk about Chianti and other great wines from Tuscany, including the region's super-star, Brunello di Montalcino.

Chianti Classico and Chianti: Italy's iconic red wines

The hills of central Tuscany are some of the most striking vineyard scenery on the face of the earth. And the red wines from this area, based on the Sangiovese grape variety, are among the best known and most loved of all Italian wines. But discussing the wine from this area today is complicated because what was once a single, collective wine zone with several subzones is now officially two distinct wine zones. The name *Chianti* once applied to the entire area, but now it refers specifically to one of two wine zones, and *Chianti Classico* refers to the other.

Chianti Classico

Chianti Classico is a DOCG wine zone where grapes have grown for more than ten centuries. The 100-square-mile zone is hilly and varied: Some parts of the zone, such as the southern part close to the city of Siena, are fairly warm, while other parts are higher in altitude and cooler; the soil varies throughout. Therefore, Chianti Classico wines vary in their degree of richness or delicacy according to where in the zone the grapes grow.

The Sangiovese grape variety must constitute at least 80 percent of any Chianti Classico wine. In practice, some producers use only Sangiovese; of those who use additional grape varieties, many use only native Tuscan varieties, such as Canaiolo or Mammolo, while others use international varieties, such as Cabernet Sauvignon or Merlot.

Besides varying according to their vineyard location and grape blend, Chianti Classico wines also vary in style according to their aging. *Riserva* wines must age for two years or more at the winery; although oak aging is not required for any Chianti Classico wine, some of the aging for Riserva often occurs in French oak barrels. *Gran Selezione* wines, a new, elite category of Chianti Classico that must come only from a winery's own estate-grown grapes, must age at least 30 months. Both Riserva and Gran Selezione bottlings of Chianti Classico have potential for long life.

Chianti Classico wines have aromas and flavors of tart cherries, violets, dry earth, and sometimes a slightly nutty character. They are dry and dry-textured, with firm tannin from the Sangiovese grape. The best Chianti Classico wines have concentrated fruit character, even if the flavor is not pronounced. The wines usually taste best from 5 to 8 years after the vintage — although in good vintages, they have no problem aging for 20 or more years.

Although Chianti Classico is not a powerful wine, today's wines are richer and more concentrated than ever before — in some cases, too rich for us. Recent warm vintages in Europe and new vineyard planting in the region have fed a trend toward ripeness of fruit flavors, fleshiness of texture, and higher alcohol. The addition of international varieties and the use of French oak barriques for aging have amplified this trend. More than ever, you must choose your Chianti Classico producers with care.

TIP

Six exceptional recent vintages to look for in Chianti Classico are 2016, 2013, 2011, 2010, 2007, and 2006. And the best Chianti Classicos of 2008 are very good. Two very good older vintages are the 1999 and 2001.

WORTH THE SEARCH

We've compiled a list of our favorite Chianti Classico producers, Group A (for us, the best) and Group B (our other favorites), in alphabetical order within each group.

Group A	Group B
Badia a Coltibuono	Antinori
Castellare	Castello di Fonterutoli
Castell'in Villa	Castello di Volpaia
Castello dei Rampolla	Cecchi-Villa Cerna
Castello di Brolio	Fattoria La Massa
Felsina	Monsanto-Il Poggio
Fontodi	Nozzole
Il Palazzino	Querciabella
Isole e Olena	Ruffino
Riecine	San Felice
Riseccoli	Villa Cafaggio
San Giusto a Rentennano	

TIP

Another producer we greatly admire is **Montevertine;** this winery chose to drop the Chianti Classico appellation in 1981 in protest against the regulation at that time that white grapes must be part of the blend of the wine, and it uses the IGT Toscana appellation instead. (See the "Super-Tuscans" sidebar later in this chapter for more context.) Montevertine wines are 100 percent Sangiovese.

REAL DEAL

Chianti Classico wines retail generally between $25 and $35 a bottle, while Chianti Classico Riserva and Gran Selezione wines are a bit more costly, ranging from $35 to $60 per bottle. For us, basic Chianti Classico remains the best buy.

Chianti

Chianti is a very large wine zone extending through much of central Tuscany and surrounding the Chianti Classico area. (Think of an irregularly shaped donut formed around the donut hole of Chianti Classico.) The zone — all of it DOCG status, deservedly or not — has seven subzones. Chianti wines may use the name of the subzone where their grapes grow or the simpler appellation, Chianti, if their production does not qualify for a district name (if grapes from two subzones are blended, for example, or if the grapes come from outlying parts of the zone that have no subzone status). The subzone that stands out in quality is the tiny Chianti Rufina (*roo*-fee-nah) area (not to be confused with the famous Chianti Classico producer Ruffino). Of the remaining subzones, the Colli Senesi and Colli Fiorentini areas (Siena hills and Florence hills, respectively) enjoy the best reputation for their wines.

Chianti wine must contain at least 70 percent Sangiovese grapes and can be entirely Sangiovese. Both native and international varieties can be part of the wine, but depending on the subzone, Cabernet Sauvignon or Cabernet Franc is limited to 10 or 15 percent. Riserva wines must age for two years or more at the winery, and for some subzones, six or eight months of wood aging is mandated.

Chianti DOCG wines are a mixed lot, stylistically and qualitatively. Some are easy-drinking, fairly light, and inexpensive reds selling for as little as $14, while others are age-worthy and substantial and can cost up to $35. Like Chianti Classico, Chianti DOCG wines often have aromas of cherries and sometimes violets and have a flavor reminiscent of tart cherries. Like most Italian wines, they're delightful with food.

WORTH THE SEARCH

Two outstanding producers making Chianti DOCG wines are Frescobaldi and Selvapiana, both in the Rufina subzone.

Monumental Brunello di Montalcino

Chianti has been famous for centuries, but another great Tuscan wine, Brunello di Montalcino, exploded on the international scene only some 50 years ago, when the Biondi-Santi family, a leading producer, presented some of its oldest wines to writers. The 1888 and 1891 vintages were still drinking well; in fact, they were in excellent shape! The rest is history, as they say.

Today, Brunello di Montalcino (brew-*nel*-lo dee mon-tahl-*chee*-no), a DOCG wine, is one of the greatest, long-lived red wines in existence. It has a price tag to match: from $65 to $80 for the better examples of Brunello to $150 plus for Biondi-Santi's, and as much as $500 a bottle — for wines by Soldera, arguably Brunello di Montalcino's greatest producer.

Brunello di Montalcino takes its name from the town of Montalcino, a walled fortress town south of the Chianti Classico zone, and from its grape variety, which once was referred to as Brunello. The grape in fact is a particular *clone, or strain,* of Sangiovese, often called Sangiovese Grosso. Brunello di Montalcino is an intensely concentrated, tannic wine that demands aging (up to 20 years) when traditionally made and benefits from several hours of aeration before serving. Lately, some producers in Montalcino have been making a more approachable style of Brunello.

REAL DEAL

Rosso di Montalcino is a less expensive ($18 to $25), readier-to-drink wine made from the same grape, sometimes from younger vines, and grown in the same production area as Brunello di Montalcino. Rosso di Montalcino from a good Brunello producer is a good value, offering you a glimpse of Brunello's majesty without breaking the bank.

WORTH THE SEARCH

To really appreciate Brunello di Montalcino, try a wine from one of the producers recommended in the following list (in our rough order of preference). Traditional winemakers, such as Biondi-Santi, Soldera, Costanti, Canalicchio di Sopra, and Pertimali, make wines that need a minimum of 15 to 20 years of aging in good vintages. (Great vintages include 2012, 2010 2007, 2006, 2004, 2001, 1999, 1997, 1995, 1985, and 1975; the vintages of 1997 and older are ready to drink). Brunellos from avowed modern-style producers, such as Caparzo, Altesino, and Col d'Orcia, can be enjoyed about 10 years from the vintage. Younger than 10 years — drink Rosso di Montalcino instead!

Great Brunello di Montalcino Producers

Soldera, Case Basse (very expensive)	Pertimali di Livio Sassetti
Biondi-Santi (expensive)	Castello Banfi
Cerbaiona	Mazzi
Costanti	Il Greppone
Ciacci Piccolomini	Poggio Antico
Canalicchio di Sopra	Caparzo (La Casa Vineyard)
Il Poggione	La Torre
Altesino (Montesoli Vineyard)	CastelGiocondo
La Fiorita	Col d'Orcia

The noble wine of Montepulciano

Vino Nobile di Montepulciano (*no*-be-lay dee mon-tay-pul-chee-*ah*-no) is a DOCG wine that is often mentioned in the same breath as Chianti Classico and Brunello di Montalcino, because it is a historic wine from a neighboring area.

The Montepulciano wine zone, named after the town of Montepulciano, lies southeast of the Chianti Classico zone and within the confines of the Chianti zone. Vino Nobile's principal grape is the Prugnolo Gentile, a local name for Sangiovese. Of central Tuscany's big three red DOCG wines — Chianti Classico, Brunello di Montalcino, and Vino Nobile di Montepulciano — Vino Nobile is generally the most delicate in style. Like Chianti, it is at least 70 percent Sangiovese, and can be entirely from that grape. Most Vino Nobile producers also make a lighter, readier-to-drink wine, Rosso di Montepulciano.

TIP

Nine Vino Nobile producers we recommend are Boscarelli, Fattoria del Cerro, Avignonesi, Lodola Nuova, La Braccesca, Dei, Tenuta Trerose, Fassati, and Poliziano.

Three more wines of note from Central Tuscany

Three more central Tuscan wine zones whose wines are worth knowing include one red, **Carmignano** DOCG (car-mee-*nyah*-no); one white, **Vernaccia di San Gimignano** DOCG (ver-*nah*-cha dee san gee-mee-*nyah*-noh), Tuscany's most renowned white wine; and a zone that produces both white and red wines, Pomino (po-*mee*-no).

The Carmignano wine region is directly west of Florence. Although Sangiovese is the main grape of Carmignano, Cabernet Sauvignon is also one of this wine zone's traditional grapes. Carmignano's taste is quite elegant and finesseful. Two outstanding producers of Carmignano are Villa di Capezzana and Ambra.

Vernaccia di San Gimignano takes its name from the Vernaccia grape and the medieval walled town of San Gimignano, in the western part of the Chianti territory. Vernaccia is generally a fresh white wine with a slightly oily texture and almondlike flavor; drink it young. Most Vernaccias are in the $13 to $17 range. Producers to seek are Montenidoli, Teruzzi & Puthod, Mormoraia, Cecchi, and Casale-Falchini.

>> Pomino is the name of a red and a white wine from a tiny DOC area of the same name, which lies within the Rufina subzone of Chianti. Pomino has long been a stronghold of French varieties, right in the heart of Sangiovese-land. The Frescobaldi family, the major producer of Chianti Rufina, is also the main landowner in Pomino, and makes both a Pomino Rosso and a Pomino Bianco — the red the more noteworthy of the two. Besides Frescobaldi, another fine producer of Pomino is Selvapiana.

>> Pomino Rosso is a blend of mainly Sangiovese with Pinot Noir and/ or Merlot. The Pinot Nero adds an aromatic, elegant touch to this unique Tuscan wine.

>> Pomino Pinot Nero is mainly Pinot Noir (85-100 percent). Priced at $19 to $25, it's a great value!

>> Pomino Bianco blends Chardonnay, Pinot Blanc, and Pinot Grigio in varying combinations. It's priced in the $15 to $19 range.

The Tuscan coast

Historically, hilly central Tuscany was the region's only important wine producing area. But in recent years, the coast of Tuscany has emerged as a significant wine zone, producing many fine wines too numerous to list here. The wines feature native red and white grape varieties such as Sangiovese and Vermentino as well as international varieties such as Cabernet Sauvignon and Chardonnay.

TIP

SANGIOVESE AT THE TABLE

Lighter Chianti wines go well with pasta, prosciutto, and roast chicken. With Chianti Classicos and riservas, fine accompaniments are lamb, roast turkey, veal, steak, and roast beef, and pasta with rich sauces. For the robust Brunello di Montalcino and super-Tuscan wines, try pheasant, steak, game, or chunks of fresh Parmesan cheese. Serve these wines at cool room temperature, 62 to 66 degrees Fahrenheit (16 to 19 degrees Celsius).

WORTH THE SEARCH

SUPER-TUSCANS

Tuscany has an unofficial category of red wines called "Super-Tuscans" that is important, but also confusing. Super-Tuscan wines came into existence almost five decades ago when some producers in the Chianti Classico zone sought to make a great wine without following the grape-variety constraints that the DOC regulations imposed; as renegade wines, they could not carry the DOC name, and were labeled as merely "Tuscan" wines. Despite having lowly legal status outside the DOC arena, the wines sold for high prices and developed an elite following. Subsequent changes to the regulations (such as the elimination of white grape varieties from the official Chianti Classico blend in 2002) have enabled many of these wines to return to the DOC or DOCG fold, but some still carry the Toscana IGT designation by choice — and you could say that their quality makes them "super" Tuscan wines. (See the section "Categories of Italian wine, legally speaking," earlier in this chapter, for details of the IGT designation.) But many an unremarkable red wine carrying the IGT Toscana designation has jumped on the bandwagon and markets itself as a Super-Tuscan when there is nothing super about it. We foresee that the Super-Tuscan category is becoming meaningless, but many people in the wine business still use the term.

The worthy "Super-Tuscans" come from various grapes. Some wines contain only native Tuscan grapes, mainly Sangiovese, while others contain only international varieties, such as Cabernet Sauvignon, Merlot, or Syrah, and still others are a blend of Italian and international grapes. What these wines have in common is that most are expensive, ranging from $75 to more than $100.

Here are seven significant super-Tuscan wines (listed alphabetically, including their grape blend and the producer's name in parentheses). These wines are some of the best in Tuscany:

- **Cepparello,** IGT Toscana — all Sangiovese (Isole e Elena; owner Paolo DiMarchi insists it isn't a super-Tuscan. Whatever it is, it's a great wine.)

- **Percarlo,** IGT Toscana — 100 percent Sangiovese (San Giusto a Rentennano)

- **Le Pergole Torte,** IGT Toscana — entirely Sangiovese (Montevertine)

- **Sammarco,** IGT Toscana — 80 percent Cabernet Sauvignon, 20 percent Sangiovese (Castello dei Rampolla)

- **I Sodi di San Niccolò,** IGT Toscana — mostly Sangiovese (Castellare di Castellina)

- **Solaia,** IGT Toscana — 80 percent Cabernet Sauvignon, 20 percent Sangiovese (Antinori)

- **Tignanello,** IGT Toscana — 80 percent Sangiovese, 20 percent Cabernet Sauvignon (Antinori)

Of particular note is the Bolgheri DOC zone, where Cabernet Sauvignon, Cabernet Franc, and Merlot are the main red varieties. A separate DOC, Bolgheri–Sassicaia applies to the wines grown on the Sassicaia estate, which are among Italy's most elite wines. Three star–power wines from this area are

>> **Masseto,** IGT Toscana — all Merlot, in fact, one of the world's greatest Merlots. Like Ornellaia, the Masseto estate is owned by the Frescobaldi family.

>> **Ornellaia,** DOC Bolgheri— mainly Cabernet Sauvignon; some Merlot and/or Cabernet Franc (Tenuta dell'Ornellaia).

>> **Sassicaia,** DOC Bolgheri-Sassicaia — 75 percent Cabernet Sauvignon, 25 percent Cabernet Franc (Tenuta San Guido).

These wines are so prized by wine collectors that they can cost more than $200 in good vintages; Masseto, made in small amounts, costs $500 to $600! (See Appendix C.)

The Tuscan coast also is home to affordable wines. Two types of wine that we particularly recommend are the following:

>> **Morellino di Scansano** (moh-rehl-*lee*-no dee scahn-*sah*-no) comes from the hilly area around the town of Scansano in southwest Tuscany. Morellino is the local name for the Sangiovese grape. **Morellino di Scansano** DOCG wines offer an easy-drinking, inexpensive ($14 to $19) alternative to Chianti — although a few high-end wines exist, such as Fattoria Le Pupille and Moris Farms.

>> **Vermentino** is a varietal wine from an aromatic white grape variety also grown in Sardinia and Liguria. Vermentino has become a hot variety in Tuscany, especially along the coast. The wine is a crisp, medium-bodied, flavorful white that's usually unoaked, and sells for $20 to $25. Many leading Tuscan producers, such as Antinori and Cecchi, are making attractive Vermentino wines.

The Tre Venezie

The three regions in the northeastern corner of Italy (refer to Figure 11-1) are often referred to as the *Venezie* — the Venices — because they were once part of the Venetian Empire. Colorful historical associations aside, each of these regions, which we discuss in the following sections, produces white and red wines that are among the most popular Italian wines outside of Italy — as well as at home.

Three gentle wines from Verona, plus two blockbusters

Two generations ago, many wine drinkers were introduced to Italian wines through a trio of popular wines from the region of the Veneto: the white **Soave** (so-*ah*-vay) and the reds, **Valpolicella** (val-po-lee-*chel*-lah) and **Bardolino** (bar-do-*lee*-noh). Soave and Bardolino are each named for towns in the vicinity of the picturesque city of Verona — Romeo and Juliet's hometown — and beautiful Lake Garda; Valpolicella is a wine zone east of Lake Garda. Despite facing ups and down in popularity, these three DOC wines continue to be among the most important wines of northeastern Italy. The *classico* version of all three wines generally represents the best quality, from the best vineyard zones.

TIP

Both Valpolicella and Bardolino are fairly light reds made from three or four native, local grape varieties — but of the two, Valpolicella has more body. Today, in fact, it is difficult to find a Valpolicella wine that is as light as these wines used to be, because producers are focusing on making richer wines. One way that they have made their wines more substantial is by using dried or semi-dried grapes as part of their fermentation. This style now has a separate DOC, **Valpolicella Ripasso.** It's still a medium-bodied red, but richer than a basic Valpolicella. Another, even richer, variant is **Amarone della Valpolicella DOCG** (also simply known as *Amarone*), one of Italy's most popular, full-bodied red wines. It's made from the same grape native Italian varieties as Valpolicella, but the ripe grapes dry indoors for several months before fermentation, thus concentrating their sugar and flavors. The resulting wine is a rich, potent (14 to 16 percent alcohol), long-lasting wine, perfect for a cold winter night and a plate of mature cheeses. Some of the best producers of Amarone are Quintarelli, Bertani, Masi, Tommasi, Le Ragose, and Allegrini.

Bardolino is a lighter wine than basic Valpolicella, named after the charming village of Bardolino, which sits on Lake Garda. It's a delightful warm-weather drink when served slightly cool. Similarly to Valpolicella, some producers are now making Bardolino in a richer style — such as the new DOCG wine, Bardolino Superiore — but that trend diverges from the original, lighthearted style of the wine. One of our favorite types of Bardolino, **Chiaretto** (key-ah-*ret*-toh) — a rosé wine — instead epitomizes the vivacity and charm of the Bardolino area.

TIP

Soave is one of the great success stories of Italian wine: From an inexpensive, standard white wine 40 years ago, it has reemerged as one of Italy's finest whites, in the hands of the best producers. (And it is still a great value.) At its best, Soave is a characterful, medium-bodied, unoaked white with flavors of apricot, citrus, apple, and nuts. Many lackluster Soave wines do still exist, and so your best bet is to look for wines labeled as *Soave Classico*, from the hilly heartland of the Soave area, to experience a Soave wine with the concentration and depth that is bringing new respect to this long-popular area.

WORTH THE SEARCH

Most Valpolicella, Bardolino, and Soave wines are priced from $14 to $20, as are two other white wines of the region, **Bianco di Custoza** and **Lugana**. Some of the better Veronese wines, from the following recommended producers, have slightly higher prices:

>> **Valpolicella:** Quintarelli (expensive), Allegrini, Le Ragose, Bertani, Alighieri, Tommasi, Masi

>> **Bardolino:** Le Fraghe, Guerrieri-Rizzardi, Corte Gardoni, Cavalchina

>> **Soave:** Pieropan, Gini, Inama, Pra, Suavia, Santa Sofia, Coffele

Alpine Italy: Trentino-Alto-Adige

If you have traveled much in Italy, you probably realize that, in spirit, Italy isn't one unified country but 20 or more politically conjoined entities. Consider Trentino-Alto-Adige. Not only is this mountainous region (the northernmost in Italy; refer to Figure 11-1) dramatically different from the rest of Italy, but also the mainly German-speaking Alto-Adige (or South Tyrol) in the north is completely different from the Italian-speaking Trentino in the south. (Before World War I, the South Tyrol was part of the Austro-Hungarian Empire.) The wines of the two areas are different, too.

Alto-Adige produces red wine, but most of it goes to Germany, Austria, and Switzerland. The rest of the world mainly sees Alto-Adige's white wines — Pinot Grigio, Chardonnay, Pinot Bianco, Sauvignon, Kerner, Müller Thurgau, and Gewürztraminer — which are all varietal wines, generally made in an unoaked style, and are priced mainly in the $15 to $25 range.

WORTH THE SEARCH

One local red wine to seek out is Alto-Adige's Lagrein, from a native grape variety of the same name. It's a hearty wine, somewhat spicy and rustic in style, but it offers a completely unique taste experience. Hofstätter and Alois Lageder are two producers who make a particularly good Lagrein.

TIP

Alto-Adige produces some of Italy's best white wines, along with nearby Friuli (see the next section). Four producers to look for are Alois Lageder, Hofstätter, Tiefenbrunner, and Abbazia di Novacella. Here are some highlights of each:

>> Lageder's Pinot Bianco from the Haberle vineyard and his Pinot Grigio from the Porer vineyard are exceptional examples of their grape varieties and are among the best wines from these two varieties that we've tasted.

>> Hofstätter's Gewürztraminer, from the Kolbenhof vineyard, is as fine a wine as you can find from this tricky grape variety. Hofstätter also makes one of Italy's best Pinot Nero (Noir) wines, Villa Barthenau.

>> Tiefenbrunner's Müller Thurgau (*mool*-lair *toor*-gow) from his Feldmarschall Vineyard (the region's highest in altitude) is a surprisingly great wine considering that outside of Alto Adige, Müller Thurgau is a lackluster variety.

>> Abbazia di Novacella, a working Augustinian monastery and Italy's northernmost winery, produces a range of fine white wines, including a world-class Kerner (a viscous, flavorful wine from a Germanic variety), retailing from $19 to $22. Its premium Kerner, Praepositus, is even better ($28 to $33). All of this winery's white wines are excellent.

Trentino, the southern part of the Trentino–Alto-Adige region, is not without its own notable wines. Some excellent Chardonnay wines come from Trentino; Pojer & Sandri and Roberto Zeni make two of the best. Elisabetta Foradori is a Trentino producer who specializes in red wines made from the local variety, Teroldego (teh-*roll*-day-go) Rotaliano. Her best red wines, Granato and Sgarzon, are based on Teroldego and get rave reviews from wine critics. Also, one of Italy's leading sparkling wine producers, Ferrari, is in Trentino. (See Chapter 15 for more information on sparkling wine producers.)

The far side: Friuli-Venezia Giulia

Italy has justifiably been known in the wine world for its red wines, but today, driven by its best-selling Pinot Grigio and Prosecco wines, Italy produces more white wines than reds. In the arena of elite white wines, the region of Friuli-Venezia Giulia (refer to Figure 11-1) was the first to make the world conscious of the indisputable quality of Italy's white wines.

Near the region's eastern border with Slovenia, the districts of Collio Goriziano — usually referred to as simply "Collio" —and Friuli Colli Orientali produce the best white wines of Friuli (as the region is generally called). Red wines do exist in Friuli, but the white wines are renowned. Pinot Grigio, Pinot Bianco, and Sauvignon are among the leading wines, mainly labeled with the grape name. Two local favorite white varietal wines are Friulano (formerly called Tocai Friulano) and Ribolla Gialla (both are rich, full, and viscous).

WORTH THE SEARCH

A truly great white wine made here is Silvio Jermann's Vintage Tunina, a blend of five varieties, including Pinot Bianco, Sauvignon, and Chardonnay. Vintage Tunina is a rich, full-bodied, long-lived white of world-class status. It sells in the $55 to $65 range and, frankly, is worth the money. Give the wine about ten years to age and then try it with rich poultry dishes or creamy pasta.

We list our recommended producers in Friuli alphabetically:

Great Producers in Friuli

Abbazia di Rosazzo/ Filiputti	Ronco del Gelso
Borgo Conventi	Ronco del Gnemiz
Girolamo Dorigo	Ronco dei Rosetti, of Zamò
Livio Felluga	Ronco dei Tassi
Gravner	Russiz Superiore, of Marco Felluga
Jermann	Mario Schiopetto
Miani	Venica & Venica
Lis Neris-Pecorari	Vie di Romans
Plozner	Villa Russiz
Doro Princic	Volpe Pasini
Radikon	

PINOT GRIGIO, THE PEOPLE'S CHOICE

Pinot Grigio — the biggest-selling imported still wine in the United States (with Prosecco now the biggest-selling sparkling wine) — is produced in all three of the Venezie regions. Santa Margherita was the first brand to establish itself solidly on the American market, and that brand still sells extremely well in restaurants. Cavit, Folonari, and MezzaCorona are other leading producers, among dozens of brands.

Obviously, wine drinkers like the taste of Pinot Grigio. It's fairly light-bodied, with crisp acidity and fresh, fairly neutral aromas and flavors — an easy-drinking wine that goes well with most foods. Pinot Grigio is so successful, in fact, that many California wineries now grow the Pinot Gris grape and use the Italian name, Pinot Grigio, on their wine labels. The Californian versions tend to be fruitier, fuller-bodied, and sometimes slightly sweet compared to the Italian wines.

The Sunny South of Italy

Rome is generally regarded as the dividing line between northern and southern Italy. Northern Italy is more industrial and affluent, with several major cities, such as Milan and Turin, and it is the home of Italy's most renowned wines — Barolo, Chianti Classico, Brunello di Montalcino, Soave, Amarone, and so forth (as we discuss earlier in this chapter). Southern Italy is mainly agricultural, and besides Rome has only one important city, Naples, but it also boasts the beautiful, heart-stopping Amalfi Coast. Until recently, few "important" wines came from southern Italy.

Italy's South used to produce more wine than the North. Two southern regions, Puglia and Sicily, for decades were the most productive in all of Italy — until they were eclipsed in recent years by Veneto, thanks to Pinot Grigio and Prosecco production. (See Chapter 15 for information on Prosecco.)

Historically, many southern Italian wines were pedestrian in quality, and much of the huge production was sold in bulk to northern Italy and nearby countries. But a wine renaissance has clearly taken place in Southern Italy in the past 20 to 25 years. Sicily and Campania in particular are now making some of Italy's best wines. The richness of the South today encompasses both white wines and red wines.

Here we give you a portrait of southern Italy's four most important wine regions:

>> **Sicily:** One of Sicily's most exciting wine zones is Etna, on the slopes of the active volcano, Mount Etna, in the northeastern part of the island. This zone produces superb cool-climate red and white wines. The reds, called **Etna Rosso,** are based on Nerello Mascalese, a grape variety indigenous to the area. The same grape is the mainstay of other red wines in eastern Sicily, including the great **Faro** wine produced by Palari near the city of Messina. Nerello Mascalese wines resemble Pinot Noirs in their weight and aromas but have greater acidity. Many of Sicily's other top reds come from the island's superb variety, Nero d'Avola, and some excellent wine comes from the native Frappato grape; the DOC **Vittoria** wines blend both grapes. Back in the Etna zone, the indigenous white variety called Carricante makes some of Italy's finest white wines, including **Etna Bianco** — of which Pietra Marina has been a stellar example.

Sicily's established wineries, such as Duca di Salaparuta (also known as Corvo), Regaleali, and Planeta, now have the company of exciting, new wineries, such as COS, Morgante, Palari, Salvo Foti, and Benanti.

>> **Campania:** The Avellino province, near Naples, produces some of the finest wines in southern Italy. A full-bodied, tannic red, **Taurasi** — a DOCG wine

from the great Aglianico variety — is one of the legendary, long-lived red wines in Italy. Premium producers are Mastroberardino (look for his single-vineyard Taurasi, called Radici), Feudi di San Gregorio, and Terredora. The same producers also make two unique whites, **Greco di Tufo** and **Fiano di Avellino.** They're flavorful, viscous wines with great aging capacity that sell in the $18 to $25 range. Falanghina ($14 to $20) is another noteworthy white Campania grape variety and wine, less noble than Fiano or Greco.

>> **Basilicata:** Mountainous, cool Basilicata is the home of southern Italy's greatest red variety, Aglianico, which produces **Aglianico del Vulture.** The wine is similar to Taurasi but not quite so intense and full-bodied. D'Angelo and Paternoster are leading producers.

>> **Apulia:** Better known by its Italian name, Puglia, this generally hot region is one of the leading producers of red wine in Italy — mainly inexpensive, full-bodied red wines, such as **Salice Salentino** (from the native variety, Negroamaro) and **Primitivo,** which is actually the same grape as Zinfandel. Leading producers include Cosimo Taurino, Leone de Castris, Agricole Vallone, and Antinori (whose Puglia estate and wines are named Tormaresca).

Snapshots from the Rest of Italy

Italy's wines are by no means confined to the regions we discuss individually in the earlier sections of this chapter. A quick tour of some of Italy's other regions proves the point. (For more complete info on the wines of these other regions, see *Italian Wine For Dummies* [Wiley].) Refer to Figure 11-1 for the location of each of the following regions:

>> **Lombardy:** Italy's most populated region, with its chic fashion capital, Milan, Lombardy (known as *Lombardia* in Italian) is the source of a vast array of wines. In the northern part of this northerly region, near the Swiss border, the Valtellina wine district produces a relatively light-bodied red wine from the Nebbiolo grape, **Valtellina Superiore DOCG;** you can find the sub-zone names Sassella, Inferno, Grumello, Valgella, or Maroggia on some labels. Most of these wines are moderately priced ($20 to $32) and, unlike Barolo, can be enjoyed fairly young. Lombardy is also the home of Italy's best sparkling wine district, **Franciacorta** (see Chapter 15).

>> **Emilia-Romagna:** This region in central-western Italy is the home of **Lambrusco,** a sweetish red that has been one of Italy's most successful wine exports. Lambrusco also comes in a delicious, dry style, which complements

the rich Bolognese cuisine. Bologna and Parma, two gastronomic meccas, are in this region.

» **Liguria:** This narrow region south of Piedmont, along the Italian Riviera, is the home of Cinque Terre, one of Italy's most picturesque areas. The region's two fine white wines, Vermentino and Pigato, are ideal with Liguria's pasta with pesto, its signature dish.

» **Marches (or Marche):** Verdicchio is a dry, inexpensive white wine that's widely available and seems to improve in quality with every vintage. Try the Verdicchio from Villa Bucci, Fazi-Battaglia, Colonnara, Garofoli, Sartorelli, Tavignano, Bonci, or Umani Ronchi, great values at $12 to $20. Marche's best red wine, Cònero DOCG, made mainly from Montepulciano, is one of Italy's fine red wine buys at $16 to $33.

» **Umbria:** Home to the towns of Perugia and Assisi, Umbria makes several good reds and whites. Orvieto, a white, is widely available for $11 to $12 from Tuscan producers, such as Antinori and Ruffino. Two interesting red wines are Torgiano, a Chianti-like blend (try Lungarotti's Rubesco Riserva DOCG), and Montefalco Sagrantino DOCG, an intense, characterful wine made from the local Sagrantino grape.

» **Lazio:** This region around Rome makes the ubiquitous, inexpensive **Frascati,** a light-bodied white from the Trebbiano grape, which has improved in quality; Fontana Candida is a popular brand.

» **Abruzzo: Montepulciano d'Abruzzo,** an inexpensive, easy-drinking, flavorful low tannin red wine, comes from here; it's a terrific everyday red, especially from a quality producer such as Masciarelli. Abruzzo is also home to two other fine producers, Cataldi Madonna and the late, great Edoardo Valentini, whose sought-after Trebbiano d'Abruzzo is arguably the world's greatest white wine from the otherwise ordinary Trebbiano grape; the Valentini family also makes a fantastic rosé, Cerasuolo, from the Montepulciano grape variety.

» **Sardinia:** This large Mediterranean island off the eastern coast of Italy makes delicate white wines and characterful reds from native grape varieties and from international varieties, such as Cabernet Sauvignon. Sella & Mosca, Argiolas, and Santadi are three leading producers. Two of the more popular Sardinian wines are the white Vermentino and the red Cannonau (a local version of Grenache), both of which sell in the $12 to $18 range.

Chapter **12**

Spain, Portugal, Germany, Austria, Greece, and Other European Hot Spots

Europe is a treasure land of wines, from one end to the next. France and Italy, which we cover in Chapters 10 and 11, are the most famous wine countries of Europe, and Spain is a close #3, especially for its red wines, but more recently for its white wines from Galicia. Portugal is finally being discovered for its great value red wines. Germany's renaissance is in dry wines, now far more numerous than its amazing sweet wines. Austria has emerged as a great source of fine dry white wines and unique reds. Greece, one of the oldest winemaking countries, ironically is now being regarded as a new source of wines — white, red, rosé, and sparkling.

We also take a look at three emerging winemaking countries, Hungary, Croatia, and Slovenia. All three have long winemaking traditions, but have only recently caught attention on the world's wine stage.

These countries share a common legislative umbrella which is the European Union, and each country therefore boasts numerous protected place names for its wines (see Chapter 4). But separately, they have produced wine for centuries, and even today each country clings to its own traditions and grape varieties. That's what makes exploring the wines of Spain, Germany, Austria, Portugal, Greece, Hungary, Croatia, and Slovenia exciting: The wines of each country are unique from those of the next. Not only that — the wines also vary quite a lot within each country, from one wine region to another.

In this chapter, we discuss the main wine regions and wines of Spain, Portugal, Germany, Austria, and Greece and also reveal a few additional European countries — Hungary, Croatia, and Slovenia — whose wines are beginning to turn heads.

Intriguing Wines from Spain

Spain is a hot, dry, mountainous country with more vineyard land than any other nation on earth. It ranks third in the world in wine production, after France and Italy (or Italy and France, depending on the year; each takes turns being first).

After a long period of dormancy and underachievement, Spain is now one of the wine world's most vibrant arenas. For decades, only Spain's most famous red wine region, Rioja (ree-*oh*-ha), and the classic fortified wine region, Sherry, had any international presence for fine wines. (For more on Sherry, see Chapter 16.) Now, many other wine regions in Spain are making seriously good wines. Besides Rioja, which we explore in the next section, the following regions are an important part of the wine quality picture in Spain today, and their wines are generally available (see Figure 12-1):

>> **Ribera del Duero** (ree-*bear*-ah dell *dwair*-oh), famous for its high quality red wines, has helped to ignite world interest in Spanish wines.

>> **Priorato** (pree-oh-*rah*-to), mountainous and inaccessible, and one of the world's "hot" regions for red wine, is southwest of the city of Barcelona, in northeast Spain.

>> **Penedés** (pen-eh-*dais*) produces both red and white wines and is famous for its sparkling wines (known as *Cava;* see Chapter 15).

FIGURE 12-1:
The wine regions of Spain.

Illustration by Lisa S. Reed

>> The **Rías Baixas** (*ree*-ahse *byche*-ahse) region of Galicia (gah-*leeth*-ee-ah) has gained acclaim for its exciting white varietal wine, Albariño. Galicia is also the home of another exciting white variety, Godello.

>> **Navarra** (nah-*var*-rah), an area long known for its dry rosé wines, is an increasingly strong red wine region.

>> **Bierzo** (bee-*ur*-zoh), in northwestern Spain, boasts an exciting native grape called Mencia that makes vibrant dry red wines.

>> **Toro** is quickly emerging as one of Spain's important red wine regions.

>> **Rueda** (roo-*ae*-dah) is known for well-made, inexpensive white wines.

TECHNICAL STUFF

Spain's wine laws provide for a multilevel Protected Designation of Origin (PDO) category — or, as they call it in Spanish, the *Denominación de Origen Protegida (DOP)* category:

>> The fundamental level is *Denominación de Origen (DO);* 69 wine zones hold this status.

>> A higher classification, *Denominación de Origen Calificada (DOC;* formerly *DOCa)*, "Qualified Designation of Origin," has existed since 1991; so far, Rioja and Priorato are the only two regions that have been awarded the DOC.

>> *Vino de Calidad con Indicación Geográfica,* or "Quality Wine with a Geographic Indication," applies to a handful of wine areas, and ranks lower than DO in status.

>> The *Vino de Pago* designation refers to individual wine estates *(pago)* that have earned special status apart from whichever DO zone the estate is located within. Fourteen wine estates are in this category, including the very fine Dominio de Valdepusa estate.

Other Spanish wines with geographic indications fall into the Protected Geographic Indication (PGI) category, or *Indicación Geográfica Protegida (IGP)* in Spain — or, in the traditional parlance, *Vino de la Tierra.* See Chapter 4 for more about appellation systems.

Spain's classic wines start with Rioja

Rioja, in north-central Spain (see Figure 12-1), has historically been the country's preeminent red wine region. Red wines dominate: About 85 percent of the region's wines are red, while 15 percent are *rosado* (rosé) and white. About 600 wineries now exist in Rioja.

The principal grape in Rioja is Tempranillo (tem-prah-*nee*-yoh), Spain's greatest red variety. Regulations permit another three varieties for reds — Garnacha (known elsewhere as Grenache), Graciano (known elsewhere as Carignan), and Mazuelo. Red Rioja wine is typically a blend of varieties. Marqués de Riscal is one of a few wineries legally allowed to use Cabernet Sauvignon in its Rioja blend, because this variety was growing on its property before regulations for Rioja existed.

The Rioja region has three districts: the cooler, Atlantic-influenced Rioja Alavesa and Rioja Alta areas and the warmer Rioja Baja zone. Most of the best Riojas are made from grapes in the two cooler districts, but some Riojas are blended from grapes of all three districts.

Traditional production for red Rioja wine involved many years of aging in small barrels of American oak before release, which created pale, gentle wines that lacked vibrant fruitiness. The more current trend has been to replace some of the oak aging with bottle aging, resulting in wines that taste much fresher. Another trend, among more progressive winemakers, is to use barrels made of French oak along with barrels of American oak — the American oak has traditionally given Rioja its characteristic vanilla aroma. (See Chapter 5 for a discussion of oak barrels.)

Red Rioja wines come in several versions, according to how long they age before being released from the winery.

>> Some wines receive no oak aging at all and are released young; the name for these fresh, youthful wines is *joven,* which means "young." (Often, producers use the term *sin crianza,* "without aging." And sometimes only the absence of one of the three terms below tells you that the wine is not aged.) Most *rosado* and white wines are *joven.*

>> Some wines age in oak and in bottle for two years at the winery and are labeled *crianza;* these wines are still fresh and fruity in style.

>> Other wines age for three years and carry the designation *reserva.*

>> The finest wines age for five years or longer, earning the status of *gran reserva.*

The aging terms appear on the labels — if not on the front label, then on a rear label, which carries the seal of authenticity for Rioja wines.

TIP

Prices start at $12 to $14 for the youngest Riojas, including *rosados* and whites, $14 to $17 for *crianza* reds, and $20 to $25 for Rioja Reservas, and they go from $25 to $55 for some *gran reservas.* The best recent vintages for Rioja are 2010, 2009, 2005, 2004, and 2001. Both 2004 and 2001 are exceptional Rioja vintages that are ready to drink.

TIP

The following Rioja producers are particularly consistent in quality for their red wines (listed in our rough order of preference):

>> R. Lopez de Heredia, particularly for its older vintage wines, Viña Tondonia and Viña Bosconia

>> Bodegas Muga

>> La Rioja Alta

>> CVNE (Compañía Vinícola del Norte de España), commonly referred to as CUNE (*coo*-nay)

>> Marqués de Murrieta Ygay

>> Marqués de Riscal

>> Roda

WORTH THE SEARCH

White Rioja also exists. Most of them are fresh, clean, fairly neutral wines, but Marqués de Murrieta and R. Lopez de Heredia still make *traditional* white Rioja, golden-colored and oak-aged, from a blend of local white grape varieties, predominantly Viura. Perhaps an acquired taste, but we love them. They are great with *paella* or seafood. Older vintages of R. Lopez de Heredia whites are wines to seek out.

Ribera del Duero's serious red wines

Ribera del Duero, two hours north of Madrid by auto, is one of Spain's most dynamic wine regions. Perhaps nowhere else in the world does the Tempranillo grape variety (called Tinto Fino here) reach such heights, making wines with body, deep color, and finesse. For many years, one producer, the legendary *Vega Sicilia*, dominated the Ribera del Duero area. In fact, Spain's single most famous great wine is **Vega Sicilia's Unico** (mainly Tempranillo, with 20 percent Cabernet Sauvignon) — an intense, concentrated, tannic red wine with enormous longevity; it ages for ten years in casks and then sometimes ages further in the bottle before it's released. Unico is available mainly in top Spanish restaurants; its latest vintage in the U.S., 2008, sells for nearly $400 in retail stores. Even Unico's younger, less intensely concentrated, more available sibling, Vega Sicilia Tinto Valbueno 2013, retails for about $160.

REAL DEAL

But the days are long gone since Vega Sicilia was the only renowned red wine in Ribera del Duero. Alejandro Fernández's **Pesquera,** entirely Tempranillo, has earned high praise over the past few decades. Pesquera is a big, rich, oaky wine that has intense fruit character and ages amazingly well. The reserva sells for about $45 while the younger Pesquera Crianza is $32. The reserva of Fernández's other winery in the area, Condado de Haza, sells in the $20 to $22 range. Three other fine producers of Ribera del Duero are Bodegas Mauro, Viña Pedrosa, and Bodegas Téofilo Reyes, who all make red wines that rival Pesquera.

Priorato: Emerging from the past

Back in the 12th century, monks founded a monastery (or *priory*) in the harsh, inaccessible Sierra de Montsant Mountains in the Catalonia region, about 100 miles southwest of Barcelona, and planted vines on the steep hillsides. When the monastery eventually closed, the vineyards became abandoned because life was simply too difficult in this area. In time, the area became known as Priorat, or Priorato.

Cut to the 20th century — in fact about 60 years ago, when winemaking finally began again in a small way, and then about 30 years ago, when enterprising winemakers, among them Alvaro Palacios, rediscovered the area. They decided that conditions were ideal for making powerful red wines, especially from old vines planted by locals early in the 20th century.

All of a sudden, previously unheard of Priorato became the Spanish wine region in the spotlight. The region's volcanic soil, composed mainly of slate and schist, is so infertile that not much other than grapes can grow there. The climate is harshly continental: very hot, dry summers and very cold winters. The steep slopes are terraced, and many vineyards, therefore, can be worked only by hand. And grape yields are very low, giving the wines intensity.

Amazingly rich, powerful red wines — made primarily from Garnacha and Carignan, two of Spain's native varieties — have emerged from this harsh landscape. Many are as rugged as the land, with high tannin and alcohol; some wines are so high in alcohol that they have an almost Port-like sweetness. Because winemaking in Priorato isn't cost-effective, to say the least, and the quantities of each wine are so small, the wines are necessarily quite expensive (prices begin at about $40). Clos Erasmus, arguably the finest Priorato, retails in the $190 to $200 range.

Priorato reds to look for include Clos Mogador, Clos Erasmus, Alvaro Palacios, Clos Martinet, Morlanda, Mas d'En Gil, Marco Abella, and Pasanau. For us, Pasanau Priorato is a particularly good value.

Other Spanish regions to know

The action in Spanish wines definitely doesn't end with Rioja, Ribera del Duero, and Priorato — especially when value is your concern. Here, we discuss a few more noteworthy Spanish wine regions.

Penedés

The Penedés wine region is in Catalonia, southwest of Barcelona (refer to Figure 12-1). It is the home of most Spanish sparkling wines, known as *Cava*, which we discuss in Chapter 15.

Any discussion of Penedés's non-sparkling wines must begin with **Torres,** one of the world's great family-owned wineries. Around 1970, Miguel Torres pioneered the making of wines in Spain from French varieties, such as Cabernet Sauvignon and Chardonnay, along with local grapes, such as Tempranillo and Garnacha.

All the Torres wines are clean, well made, reasonably priced, and widely available. Prices start around $10 for the red called Sangre de Toro (Garnacha-Carignan), $11 to $12 for Coronas (Tempranillo–Cabernet Sauvignon), and $14 for the white Viña Sol. The top-of-the-line Mas La Plana Black Label, a powerful yet elegant Cabernet Sauvignon, costs about $65 to $70.

Freixenet, the leading Cava producer, is now also in the still wine business. Its wines include the inexpensive René Barbier brand of varietal wines.

Rías Baixas: Galicia's white wine region

Galicia — a province in northwest Spain, next to the Atlantic Ocean and Portugal — historically was not known for its wine, probably because of its cool, damp climate. But a small area in southern Galicia (refer to Figure 12-1), called Rías Baixas (*ree-ahse byche*-ahse), has achieved international fame for an exciting white wine called Albariño, made from the Albariño grape.

This region now boasts about 200 wineries, compared to only 60 wineries in 1990. Modern winemaking, the cool local climate, and low-yielding vines have combined to make Albariño wines a huge success, especially in the United States, its leading market. We love this lively, (mainly) unoaked white, with its vivid, floral aromas and flavors reminiscent of apricots, white peaches, pears, and green apples. It's a perfect match with seafood and fish. The Albariño grape — known as Alvarinho in northern Portugal (south of Rías Baixas) — produces wines that are fairly high in acidity, which makes them fine apéritif wines.

TIP

Albariños to look for include Bodega Morgadío, Pazos de Lusco, Fillaboa, Pazo de Señorans, Pazo San Mauro, Pazo de Barrantes, Condes de Albarei, Terras Gauda, Valminor, and Vionta; all are in the $15 to $28 range.

WORTH THE
SEARCH

Another white varietal wine, Godello, grows mainly in Galicia (outside of Rías Baixas) and nearby locations in northwest Spain. The Cinderella story is that Godello was practically extinct in 1970, but then rediscovered and replanted. Now it is one of the hottest wines in Spain; it is spicy, fruity, and it ages well. It has drawn raves from no less a wine authority than wine expert, Jancis Robinson, on her website Jancis Robinson.com.

Navarra

Once upon a time, the word *Navarra* conjured up images of inexpensive, easy-drinking dry rosé wines (or, to the more adventurous, memories of running the bulls in Pamplona, Navarra's capital city). Today, the Navarra region, just northeast of Rioja, is known for its red wines, which are similar to but somewhat less expensive than the more famous wines of Rioja.

TIP

Many Navarra reds rely on Tempranillo, along with Garnacha, but you can also find Cabernet Sauvignon, Merlot, and various blends of all four varieties in the innovative Navarra region. Look for the wines of the following three Navarra producers: Bodegas Julian Chivite (*hoo*-lee-ahn cha-*vee*-tay), Bodegas Guelbenzu (gwel-ben-*zoo*), and Bodegas Magana. Prices run in the $12 to $25 range for all three wines.

Bierzo

This small region is in northwest Spain, east of Rías Baixas. Bierzo is a mountainous area with steep vineyard slopes, growing the red Mencia grape. Wine production is fairly small, but Bierzo's wines are gaining renown and developing something of a cult following among those who love Spanish wines. The wines are what we would call "spicy reds," with lively acidity and aromas and flavors of red fruits. Most Bierzo wines retail in the $14 to $20 range, although a few are quite expensive.

El Toro

The Toro region in northwest Spain, northwest of Ribera del Duero, made wines in the Middle Ages that were quite famous in Spain. But it's a hot, arid area with poor soil, and so winemaking was practically abandoned there for centuries. In Spain's current wine boom, Toro has been rediscovered. Winemakers have determined that the climate and soil are actually ideal for making powerful, tannic red wines — mainly from the Tempranillo variety (called Tinto del Toro here) — which rival the wines of Toro's neighbors in Ribera del Duero. Toro wines to buy include those of Bodegas Fariña, Vega Sauco, Estancia Piedra, Bodegas y Viñas Dos Victorias, Gil Luna, and Dehesa La Granja (owned by Pesquera's Alejandro Fernandez). Retail prices start at about $15, but the best examples can be $50 and higher.

The Verdejo from Rueda

REAL DEAL

The Rueda region, west of Ribera del Duero, produces one of Spain's best white wines from the Verdejo grape. The wine is clean and fresh, has delicious fruiti-ness, and sells for an affordable $12 to $15. The Rioja producer Marqués de Riscal makes one of the leading and most available examples.

DECODING SPANISH WINE LABELS

You may see some of the following terms on a Spanish wine label; here's what they mean:

- **Blanco:** White.
- **Tinto** (*teen*-toe): Red.
- **Bodega**: Winery.
- **Cosecha** (coh-*say*-cha) or **Vendimia** (ven-*dee*-me-yah): The vintage year.
- **Crianza** (cree-*ahn*-zah): For red wines, this means that the wine has aged for two years with at least six months in oak; for white and rosé wines, *crianza* means that the wines aged for a year with at least six months in oak. (Some regions have stricter standards.)
- **Reserva:** Wines produced in the better vintages; red *reservas* must age a minimum of three years, including one year in oak; white *reservas* must age for two years, including six months in oak.
- **Gran reserva:** Wines produced only in exceptional vintages; red wines must age at least five years, including a minimum of two years in oak; white *gran reservas* must age at least four years before release, including six months in oak.

Other noteworthy Spanish regions

Spanish wines are in demand more than ever in international markets because they're such great values — often selling for $10 to $15. Look for wines from the regions of Jumilla (hoo *me* yah), Valdepeñas, Alicante, Valencia, and La Mancha — all offering excellent, good-value wines. Although Jumilla does make many low-priced wines, a few of its finest wines sell for up to $50.

Portugal: More than Just Port

Portugal is justifiably famous for its great dessert wine, Port (which we discuss in Chapter 16). But Portuguese wine boasts so many other dimensions — particularly dry reds. Most Portuguese wines come from native Portuguese grape varieties, of which the country has hundreds, and thus the wines taste unique. *If ever a wine producing country deserved more attention from red and white wine lovers, it is Portugal.* Find out more about Portuguese wines in the following sections.

TECHNICAL
STUFF

The E.U.'s highest, Protected Designation of Origin (PDO) level of wines is called *Denominação de Origem Protegida* in Portuguese, or *Denominação de Origen* (DOC), the traditional term. At the E.U.'s Protected Geographic Indication (PGI) level, where wine producers have more flexibility in their grape varieties and winemaking techniques, Portugal has the category of *Indicação Geográfica (IG)*, also called *Vinho Regional (VR)*.

Portugal's "green" white

TIP

On hot summer evenings, the most appropriate wine can be a bottle of bracing, slightly effervescent, white *Vinho Verde* (*veen*-yo vaird). The high acidity of Vinho Verde refreshes your mouth and particularly complements grilled fish or seafood.

The Minho region, Vinho Verde's home, is in the northwest corner of Portugal, directly south of the Rías Baixas wine region of Spain that we talk about earlier in this chapter. (The region is particularly verdant because of the rain from the Atlantic Ocean — one theory behind the wine's name.)

Two styles of white Vinho Verde exist on the market:

>> One style is that of the most commonly found brands (Quinta da Aveleda and Casal Garcia); these sell for $7 to $10 and are medium-dry wines of average quality that are best served cold. The Quinta da Aveleda is the slightly more expensive of the two brands.

WORTH THE SEARCH

>> The more expensive Vinho Verdes ($11 to $20) are varietal wines made from either the Alvarinho grape (the same as Albariño in Rías Baixas), or the Loureiro or Trajadura grapes. They're more complex, dryer, and more concentrated than basic Vinho Verde, and are Portugal's best whites. Unfortunately, these finer wines are more difficult to find than the inexpensive ones; look for them in better wine shops or in Portuguese neighborhoods.

WARNING

At one time, the majority of wines from Vinho Verde were red. Now, red Vinho Verde is in the minority, less than one-third of production, and mainly consumed locally. These red Vinho Verde wines are *highly* acidic; you definitely need to acquire a taste for them. (We haven't acquired it yet!)

Noteworthy Portuguese red wines

REAL DEAL

The Douro in northern Portugal is the region for sweet Port wine, but it also makes very good dry reds. These wines are fairly new to Portugal's wine scene because of the traditional dominance of sweet, fortified Port wine. But the category of dry Douro reds is exploding, because the average quality of the wines is so high, and the retail price for most red Douro wines is under $15.

The Port house of Ramos Pinto, now owned by Roederer Champagne, pioneered one of the earliest Douro reds, called Duas Quintas; it's an inexpensive ($14), top-quality, dry red that is fairly easy to find. The Douro region boasts other terrific dry red wines, most of them based on grapes traditionally used for Port. Brands to look for include Quinta do Vallado, Quinta do Vale D. Maria, Quinta do Crasto, Quinta de la Rosa, the great Quinta do Vale Meão ($80 to $90), Quinta de Roriz, and Chryseia.

TIP

Here are some other good red Portuguese wines to try:

>> **Quinta do Carmo:** This huge, beautiful wine estate, which dates back to the 17th century, is in the dynamic Alentejo region in southern Portugal. Its red *reserva,* a rich, full-bodied wine, sells for about $18 to $22. Quinta do Carmo also produces a white wine and a less expensive red named Don Martinho.

>> **Quinta de Pancas:** One of the few Cabernet Sauvignons in Portugal, Quinta de Pancas comes from the Alenquer region, north of Lisbon; it sells for $8 to $12.

>> **Quinta da Bacalhôa:** An estate-bottled Cabernet Sauvignon–Merlot from the esteemed Portuguese winemaker Joào Pires in Azeitao (south of Lisbon), Bacalhôa has the elegance of Bordeaux; it sells for about $12.

RECOGNIZING PORTUGUESE WINE TERMS

The following terms may appear on Portuguese wine labels:

- **Colheita** (col-*yay*-tah): Vintage year

- **Garrafeira** (gar-ah-*fay*-rah): A *reserva* that has aged at least two years in a cask and one in a bottle if it's red; six months in a cask, six months in a bottle if it's white

- **Quinta** (*keen*-ta): Estate or vineyard

- **Reserva:** A wine of superior quality from one vintage

- **Tinto** (*teen*-toe): Red

>> **Luis Pato:** This winemaker produces stunning, medium-bodied red wines in the Barraida region, in western Portugal, from the local Baga grape. His finest wine is Vinha Pan (about $35).

>> **Joao Portugal Ramos:** A tireless winemaker who consults for various wineries and also owns three properties, Ramos has a golden touch and yet maintains typicity in his wines. Some wines sell under his own name; others include Marquês de Borba and Vila Santa, both in Alentejo.

Arguably the best dry red wine in Portugal, *Barca Velha*, comes from the Douro region. Made by the Ferreira Port house, Barca Velha is a full-bodied, intense, concentrated wine that needs years to age — Portugal's version of Vega Sicilia's Unico (from Spain). Like Unico, not much is made, and it's produced only in the best vintages. Barca Velha retails at about the same price as Unico or even slightly more — in the $400 to $500 range.

Germany: Europe's Individualist

German wines march to the beat of a different drummer. They traditionally have come in mainly one color: white. They're fruity in style, low in alcohol, rarely oaked, and many of them are off-dry or sweet — although today dry wines have become the most popular style produced in Germany. Also, German labels carry grape names, which is an anomaly in most of Europe.

Germany is the northernmost major wine-producing country in Europe — which means that its climate is cool. The climate is also erratic from year to year, meaning that vintages do matter for fine German wines. Many of Germany's finest vineyards are situated along rivers such as the Rhine and the Mosel, and on steep, sunny slopes, to temper the extremes of the weather and help the grapes ripen.

Except in warmer pockets of Germany, red grapes traditionally did not ripen adequately. Beginning around 1997, red grapes have experienced more ripeness, thanks to climate change. Now we are seeing more and more German red wines, particularly Pinot Noir.

Riesling and company

In Germany's cool climate, the noble Riesling (*reese*-ling) grape finds true happiness. Riesling represents almost 25 percent of Germany's vineyard plantings, the largest of any variety. In fact, 50 percent of the world's Riesling wines are produced in Germany.

A less distinguished German variety is Müller-Thurgau (pronounced *mool*-lair-*toor*-gow), a man-made crossing between the Riesling and Madeleine Royale grapes. It used to be the country's largest-growing variety (and is still second in plantings at 13 percent) but is losing ground because Müller-Thurgau wine has become less popular, and, being prone to vineyard diseases, the grape is challenging to grow. Its wines are softer than Riesling's, less flavorful, and less interesting.

After Riesling and Müller-Thurgau, the most-planted grape in Germany now, believe it or not, is Pinot Noir (locally called Spätburgunder). When we first wrote *Wine For Dummies* back in 1995, Pinot Noir was an afterthought in Germany — accounting for 2 to 3 percent of the country's plantings. Now Pinot Noir accounts for 11.5 percent of Germany's vineyard acreage, and it is gaining ground rapidly. German Pinot Noirs (Spätburgunders) are real values, with retail prices beginning at $16. After Pinot Noir, another red variety, Dornfelder, is fourth in plantings with 8 percent; like Muller-Thurgau, it is a crossing engineered from two other varieties.

Two white varieties that are making inroads are Weissburgunder (Pinot Blanc) and Ruländer (Pinot Gris). Weissburgunder acreage has doubled in recent years, and Ruländer wine production is also on the rise. Another white variety, Silvaner, is still popular enough that it ranks third among white grapes in Germany.

The modern trends in Germany, wine-wise, are clear:

>> Rieslings still rule, but the majority are dry; increasingly, the off-dry style of Riesling, which the Germans call the "fruity" style, is made for export markets such as the U.S.

- » Pinot Blanc and Pinot Gris are becoming popular alternatives to Riesling but not yet major competition.

- » Red wine, especially Pinot Noir, has become much more popular since the turn of the century.

The wine regions of Baden and the Pfalz, Germany's two warmest, are leading the way in red wine production. (We talk about Germany's wine regions in more detail later in this chapter.)

Germany's wine law

Like most European wines, German wines carry place-names. The place named can be an entire wine region, such as Mosel, or it can be a smaller area. For the best wines, the place-name is usually a combination of a village name and a vineyard name, such as Piesporter (town) Goldtröpfchen (vineyard).

Unlike most European wines, however, the grape name is also usually part of the wine name (as in Piesporter Goldtröpfchen *Riesling*). And the finest German wines have yet another element in their name — a *Prädikat* (*pray*-di-cat), which is an indication of the ripeness of the grapes at harvest (as in Piesporter Goldtröpfchen Riesling *Spätlese*). Wines with a Prädikat hold the highest rank in the German wine system.

Germany's system of assigning the highest rank to the ripest grapes is completely different from the concept behind most other European systems, which is to bestow the highest status on the best vineyards or districts. Germany's system underscores the country's traditional grape-growing priority: Ripeness — never guaranteed in a cool and variable climate — is the highest goal.

TECHNICAL STUFF

German wine law divides wines with a Prädikat into six levels, from the least ripe to the ripest (that is, from the lowest to the highest):

- » Kabinett (*kab*-ee-net)

- » Spätlese (*shpate*-lay-seh)

- » Auslese (*ouse*-lay-seh)

- » Beerenauslese (*beer*-en-*ouse*-lay-seh), abbreviated as *BA*

- » Eiswein (*ice*-vine)

- » Trockenbeerenauslese (*troh*-ken-*beer*-en-*ouse*-lay-seh), abbreviated as *TBA*

REMEMBER

At the three highest Prädikat levels, the amount of sugar in the grapes is so high that the wines are inevitably sweet. Many people, therefore, mistakenly believe that the Prädikat level of a German wine is an indication of the wine's sweetness. In reality, the Prädikat is an indication of the amount of sugar in the *grapes at harvest*, not the amount of sugar in the wine. At lower Prädikat levels, the sugar in the grapes can ferment fully, to dryness, and for those wines, there's no direct correlation between Prädikat level and sweetness of the wine.

TECHNICAL STUFF

Wines whose (grape) ripeness earns them a Prädikat are categorized as *Prädikatswein*, translated as "wines with special attributes" (their ripeness). They are Protected Designation of Origin (PDO) wines in the eyes of the European Union (see Chapter 4 for more about this and other designations, including the full phrases in German). When the ripeness of the grapes in a particular vineyard isn't sufficient to earn the wine Prädikat status, the wine can still qualify as a PDO (protected place-name) wine in Germany's second tier, called *Qualitätswein*, translated as "quality wine"; each label carries the name of one of Germany's 13 wine regions in addition to the word *Qualitätswein* and usually the name of a grape variety. (See the later section "Germany's wine regions" for the names of the main regions.)

A very small amount of Germany's wine production falls into the looser Protected Geographic Indication (PGI) category. These are called *Landwein* in Germany, and they carry a geographic indication that's broader than a region name.

German wine styles

Although the common perception of German wines has been that they're sweet, and although a movement toward dry wines has swept over Germany, the truth is that many German wines have always tasted dry, or fairly dry. In fact, you can find German wines at just about any sweetness or dryness level you like. The following sections cover German wine styles in more detail.

Gentle, half-dry, and dry wines

Most inexpensive German wines, such as the once hugely popular Liebfraumilch, are light-bodied, fruity wines with pleasant sweetness. The traditional German term for this style of wine is *lieblich*, which translates as "gentle" — a poetic but apt descriptor — but these days, many Germans use the term *fruity style*. The very driest German wines are called *trocken* (dry). Wines that are sweeter than trocken but dryer than lieblich are called *halbtrocken* (half-dry). The words *trocken* and *halbtrocken* sometimes appear on the label, but not always. *Halbtrocken* wines have not sold well, and seem to be disappearing.

TIP

You can take a good stab at determining how sweet a German wine is by reading the alcohol level on the label. If the alcohol is low — about 9 percent or less — the wine probably contains grape sugar that didn't ferment into alcohol and is, therefore, somewhat sweet. Higher alcohol levels suggest that the grapes fermented completely, to dryness.

Although we generally prefer dry white wines, we find that a bit of sweetness in German wines can be appealing — and, in fact, can improve the quality of the wine. Sweetness undercuts the wines' natural high acidity and can give the wines better balance. In practice, most off-dry German wines don't really taste as sweet as they are, thanks to their acidity.

TECHNICAL
STUFF

One way that German winemakers keep some sweetness in their wines is called the *süssreserve* (sweet reserve) method. In this method, a winemaker holds back as much as 25 percent of his grape juice and doesn't allow it to ferment. He then ferments the rest of his juice fully, until it's dry wine. Later, he blends the unfermented grape juice into his dry wine. The grape juice (the süssreserve) contributes a natural, juicy sweetness to the wine. Alternatively, some winemakers ferment all their Riesling juice but block the fermentation process before all the grape sugar has converted to alcohol.

What's noble about rot?

Wine connoisseurs all over the world recognize Germany's sweet, dessert-style wines as among the greatest wines on the face of the earth. Most of these legendary wines owe their sweetness to an ugly but magical fungus known as *botrytis cinerea* (pronounced bo-*try*-tis sin-eh-*ray*-ah), commonly called *noble rot.*

Noble rot infects ripe grapes in late autumn if a certain combination of humidity and sun is present. This fungus dehydrates the berries and concentrates their sugar and their flavors. The wine from these infected berries is sweet, amazingly rich, and complex beyond description. It can also be expensive: $100 or more per bottle.

TECHNICAL
STUFF

Wines at the BA and TBA Prädikat levels are usually made entirely from grapes infected with noble rot (called *botrytised* grapes) and are generally richly textured and sweet. *Auslese*-level wines often come from some partially botrytised grapes, and when they do, they are likely to be sweet, although never to the extent of a BA or TBA.

Another way that nature can contribute exotic sweetness to German wines is by freezing the grapes on the vine in early winter. When the frozen grapes are harvested and pressed, most of the water in the berries separates out as ice. The sweet, concentrated juice that's left to ferment makes a luscious sweet Prädikat-level wine called *Eiswein* (literally, ice wine). Eisweins differ from BAs and TBAs because they lack a certain flavor that derives from botrytis, sometimes described as a honeyed character.

TIP

Both botrytised wines and Eisweins are referred to as *late-harvest wines*, not only in Germany but all over the world, because the special character of these wines comes from conditions that normally occur only when the grapes are left on the vine beyond the usual point of harvest.

Germany's wine regions

Germany has 13 wine regions — 11 in the west and 2 in the eastern part of the country (see Figure 12-2).

FIGURE 12-2: The wine regions of Germany.

Illustration by Lisa S. Reed

The most famous of these 13 are the Mosel region, named for the Mosel River, along which the region's vineyards lie, and the Rheingau region, along the Rhine River. The Rhine River lends its name to three other German wine regions, Rheinhessen, the Pfalz (formerly called the Rheinpfalz), and the tiny Mittelrhein region. The Nahe and Baden are two other renowned regions.

Mosel

The Mosel, formerly known as Mosel-Saar-Ruwer (*moh*-zel-*zar*-*roo*-ver) to include the names of the river's two tributaries, is a dramatically beautiful region, its vineyards rising steeply on the slopes of the twisting and turning Mosel River. The wines of the region are among the lightest in Germany (often containing less than 10 percent alcohol); they're generally delicate, fresh, and charming. Riesling dominates the Mosel with over 60 percent of the plantings. Wines from this region are instantly recognizable because they come in green bottles rather than the brown bottles that other German regions use. The Mosel is Germany's fifth-largest wine-producing region.

TIP

The Mosel boasts dozens of excellent winemakers who produce really exciting Riesling wines. Some of our favorites include, in alphabetical order:

Egon Müller	J.J. Prüm
Dr. Fischer	Reichsgraf Von Kesselstatt
Friedrich Wilhelm Gymnasium	Willi Schaefer
Karlsmühle	Schloss Leiser
Dr. Loosen	Schloss Saarstein
Maximin Grünhauser	Selbach-Oster
Merkelbach	Zilliken
Meulenhof	

Rheingau

The Rheingau (*ryne*-gow) is among Germany's smaller wine regions. It, too, has some dramatically steep vineyards bordering a river, but here the river is Germany's greatest wine river, the Rhine. The Riesling grape occupies about 80 percent of the Rheingau's vineyards, many of which are south-facing slopes that give the Riesling grapes an extra edge of ripeness. Rheingau wine styles tend toward two extremes: trocken wines on the one hand and sweet late-harvest wines on the other. Recommended Rheingau producers include Georg Breuer, Knyphausen, Franz Küntsler, Schloss Schönborn, Leitz, and Robert Weil.

A SECRET CODE OF GERMAN PLACE-NAMES

If you're like most of us who don't speak German or know German geography intimately, deciphering German wine names can be tricky, to say the least. But here's a bit of information that can help. In the German language, the possessive is formed by adding the suffix *-er* to a noun. When you see names like Zeller or Hochheimer — names that end in *-er* — on a wine label, the next word is usually a vineyard area that "belongs" to the commune or district with the *-er* on its name (Zell's Swartze Katz, Hochheim's Kirchenstück). The name of the region itself always appears on labels of Qualitätswein and Prädikatswein wines.

Rheinhessen

Rheinhessen (*ryne-hess-ehn*) is Germany's largest wine region, producing huge quantities of simple wines for everyday enjoyment. Liebfraumilch originated here, and it's still one of the most important wines of the region, commercially speaking. The Rheinhessen's highest-quality wines come from the Rheinterrasse, a vineyard area along the river. The Rheinhessen's image today has greatly improved, because it now produces many exciting, dry Rieslings. Producers from that area who are particularly good include Gunderloch, Heyl Zu Herrnsheim, and Strub.

Pfalz

Almost as big as the Rheinhessen, the Pfalz (*fallz*), Germany's second-largest wine producer, is making both fine Rieslings and red wines. Some of Germany's best dry Rieslings come from the cooler, northern part. (The Pfalz has more Riesling planted than any other German region.) Other major white varieties of the Pfalz include Müller-Thurgau and Grauburgunder (another name for Pinot Gris), but a local speciality is Scheurebe (*schoy* reh beh).

Today, almost 40 percent of the Pfalz's wines are red, and they come from the warmer southern part. Dornfelder, a dark-colored, fruity, tannic, quite full-bodied wine, is the largest-planted red variety, followed by Pinot Noir and Blauer Portugieser.

To experience the best of the Pfalz, look for wines from Dr. Bürklin-Wolf, Rainer Lingenfelder, Müller-Catoir, and Basserman-Jordan.

Nahe

Another German region of importance for the quality of its wines, especially Riesling, is Nahe (*nah-heh*), named for the Nahe River and situated west of Rheinhessen. The Riesling wines here are relatively full and intense. Favorite producers include Diel, Kruger-Rumpf, Prinz zu Salm-Dahlberg, and Dönnhoff.

Baden

Now Germany's most important region for Pinot Noir, Baden (*bah*-den) is capitalizing on the recent warm climate that undoubtedly has played a large role in its greatly improved red wines. Today, 44 percent of Baden's wines are red — primarily Pinot Noir. While tasting in Germany, we were astounded by the quality of Baden's Pinot Noirs, certainly a far cry from the very light, thin German Pinot Noir wines of the past.

The somewhat cooler, northern part of Baden produces some fine Weissburgunder (Pinot Blanc) and Grauburgunder as well as dry Rieslings. Although co-ops make 80 percent of Baden's wines, independent producers to look for in Baden include Weingut Heitlinger (for Riesling), and Weingut Dr. Heger (for Weissburgunder and Riesling).

REAL DEAL

One Baden producer, Weingut Bernhard Huber, is making Pinot Noirs that compare favorably to France's Côte de Beaune Burgundies, and at a lower price. Huber's Pinot Noirs start at $30.

Austria's Exciting Whites (and Reds)

Austria is one of the wine countries that most excites us. Apart from the gorgeous vineyard regions, the warmth of the people, and the classic beauty of Vienna, we love so many of the wines. What makes Austrian wines all the more interesting is how they are evolving, as winemakers gradually discover how to best express their land and their grapes through wine.

Austria makes less than 1 percent of all the wine in the world — about 27 million cases a year. Most of this small quantity, more than 75 percent of it, is consumed within Austria, leaving a really small amount for the rest of the world. That fact, and the fact that the Austrians have embraced a high-quality image, explains why many Austrian wines command premium prices.

All of Austria's wine comes from the eastern part of the country, where the Alps recede into hills, and most of it comes from small wineries. Austria's sweet whites have long had a reputation for excellence, but her dry whites and reds have gained recognition only in the past three decades.

>> Reds are still in the minority but growing, now claiming 34 percent of the country's production. Because many of Austria's wine regions are too cool for growing red grapes, red wines hail mainly from the area of Burgenland (bordering Hungary), one of the warmest parts of the country. They're

medium- to full-bodied, often engagingly spicy, with vivid fruity flavor and often the international touch of oaky character. Many of them are based on unusual, native grape varieties such as the spicy Blaufänkisch (also known as *Lemberger*), the gentler St. Laurent, or Blauer Zweigelt, (a crossing of the other two, commonly known as Zweigelt), which is the most-planted red grape in Austria.

» Austria's white wines — apart from the luscious, late-harvest dessert wines made from either botrytised, extremely ripe, or dried grapes — are dry wines ranging from light to full-bodied, and are generally unoaked.

Find out more about the world of Austrian wine in the following sections.

Grüner Veltliner and company

The country's single most important grape variety is the native white Grüner Veltliner. Its wines are full-bodied yet crisp with rich texture and flavors that are herbal or sometimes spicy-vegetal (especially green pepper). They're extremely food-friendly and usually high quality. Some people in the wine trade have nick-named Grüner Veltliner "GruVe"; we agree with that characterization!

Another key grape for quality whites is Riesling, grown mainly in the region of Lower Austria, in the northeast. In fact, some experts believe that Austria's finest wines are its Rieslings (while others prefer Grüner Veltliner).

Other grape names that you may see on bottles of white Austrian wine include Müller-Thurgau, which makes characterful dry whites; Welschriesling, a grape popular in Eastern Europe for inexpensive wines that achieves high quality only in Austria; and Pinot Blanc (also known as Weissburgunder), which can excel here. Sauvignon Blanc is a specialty of the region of Styria, in the south, bordering Slovenia; of all the Sauvignon Blanc wines in the world, these rank among the finest.

Austrian wine names and label terms

The naming protocols for Austrian wines vary because Austria's place-name system is in flux. In some parts of Austria, for example in the Wachau district, along the Danube River, some wines are still named in the German system — a town name ending in -*er* followed by a vineyard name and a grape variety, along with the name of the region. In other parts of Austria, wine names are generally a grape name (or a proprietary name) followed by the name of the region. Increasingly, the naming of wines for specific, controlled regions or districts — similar to France's "Burgundy" or Italy's "Chianti Classico," for example — is emerging.

Austria's wine classification laws fall under the E.U. umbrella explained in Chapter 4, whereby the top wines fall into a category of Protected Designation of Origin (PDO in English), and second-tier wines fall into the looser category of Protected Geographic Indication (PGI in English). The higher tier is *Qualitätswein*; these must come from any of Austria's 9 federal states, or from 16 specific wine regions. The second-tier category is *Landwein*; these wines carry the origin of one of three collective wine-growing areas.

Within the *Qualitätswein* PDO category are the *Prädikatswein* group — a throwback to the Germanic system of recognizing wines whose grapes have attained various levels of ripeness — and the *DAC* group, which applies to wines that show the regional character of specific DAC (*Districtus Austria Controllatus*) areas.

The DAC category classifies Austria's wines based on *terroir*. Authorities introduced the *Districtus Austria Controllatus (DAC)* system in early 2003, and wine regions have gradually applied for recognition of their wines under this system. Ten DAC zones now exist (their permitted grape varieties are noted in parentheses):

>> Weinvertel (Grüner Veltliner)

>> Traisental (Grüner Veltliner or Riesling)

>> Kremstal (Grüner Veltliner or Riesling)

>> Kamptal (Grüner Veltliner or Riesling)

>> Mittelburgenland (Blaufränkisch)

>> Eisenberg (Blaufränkisch)

>> Leithaberg (for white wines: Pinot Blanc, Chardonnay, Neuburger, Grüner Veltliner, or a blend of these varieties; and for reds, Blaufränkisch)

>> Neusiedlersee (Zwiegelt)

>> Wiener Gemischter Satz (various grapes, planted in one vineyard)

>> Schilcherland (for Schilcher, pronounced *shil* ker, an iconic rosé from Blauer Wildbacher)

The Glory That Is Greece

We find it ironic that a country that practically invented wine, way back in the 7th century B.C., could be an emerging wine region today. But that's the way it is. Greece never stopped making wine for all those centuries, but her wine industry took the slow track, inhibited by Turkish rule, political turmoil, and other real-life issues. The modern era of Greek winemaking began only in the 1960s, and it has made particularly strong strides in the past two decades. Today, Greek wines are worth knowing; we introduce you to them and all their glory in the following sections.

Greek grapes

Although Greece is a southern country and famous for its sunshine, its grape-growing climate is actually quite varied, because many vineyards are situated at high altitudes where the weather is cooler. (Most of Greece is mountainous, in fact.) Its wines are mainly (60 percent) white; some of those whites are sweet dessert wines, but most are dry.

One of Greece's greatest wine assets — and handicaps, at the same time — is its abundance of native grape varieties, more than 300 of them. Only Italy has more indigenous grape varieties. These native grapes make Greek wines particularly exciting for curious wine lovers to explore, but their unfamiliar names make the wines challenging to sell. Greece also produces wines from internationally famous grape varieties, such as Chardonnay, Merlot, Syrah, and Cabernet Sauvignon, but these days producers seem more committed than ever to their native varieties rather than to international grapes.

Of Greece's many indigenous grape varieties, four in particular stand out as the most important — two white and two red varieties:

>> **Assyrtiko (ah-*seer*-tee-koe):** A white variety that makes delicate, bone-dry, crisp, very long-lived wines with citrusy and minerally aromas and flavors. Although Assyrtiko grows in various parts of Greece, the best Assyrtiko wines come from the volcanic island of Santorini. Any wine named Santorini is made from at least 90 percent Assyrtiko. Two outstanding Santorini producers are Domaine Sigalas and Gaia (*yea*-ah).

>> **Moschofilero (mos-cho-*feel*-eh-roe):** A very aromatic, pink-skinned variety that makes both dry white and pale-colored dry rosé wines grows mainly around Mantinia (man teh *nee* ah), in the central, mountainous Peloponnese region. If a wine is named Mantinia, it must be at least 85 percent Moschofilero. Wines made from Moschofilero have high acidity and are fairly low in alcohol, with aromas and flavors of apricots and/or peaches. Because they're so easy to drink, Moschofilero wines are a great introduction to Greek wines.

>> **Agiorghitiko (eye-your-*yee*-tee-koe):** The name of this grape translates in English to "St. George," and a few winemakers call it that on the labels of wines destined for English-speaking countries. Greece's most planted and probably most important native red variety, it grows throughout the mainland. Its home

turf, where it really excels, is in the Nemea district of the Peloponnese region; any wine with the place-name Nemea is entirely Agiorghitiko. Wines from this variety are medium to deep in color, have complex aromas and flavors of plums and/or black currants, and often have a resemblance to Cabernet Franc or spicy Merlot wines. Agiorghitiko also blends well with other indigenous or international varieties.

>> **Xinomavro (ksee-*no*-mav-roe):** This is the most important red variety in the Macedonia region of northern Greece. Xinomavro produces highly tannic wines with considerable acidity that have been compared to Nebbiolo wines of Piedmont, Italy. Wines made from Xinomavro have complex, spicy aromas, often suggesting dried tomatoes, olives, and/or berries. Xinomavro wines are dark in color but they lighten with age and have great longevity. Their home base is the Naoussa district of Macedonia; any wine named Naoussa is entirely Xinomavro.

Other important white indigenous varieties in Greece include Roditis (actually a pink–skinned grape), which makes Patras white; and Savatiano, the most widely planted white grape. Retsina, a traditional Greek wine made by adding pine resin to fermenting grape juice (resulting in a flavor not unlike some oaky Chardonnays), is made mainly from Savatiano. Mavrodaphne is an indigenous Greek red variety that's becoming increasingly important, both for dry and sweet red wines.

Wine regions, producers, and label lingo in Greece

Some of the wine regions of Greece whose names you're likely to see on wine labels include

>> **Macedonia:** The northernmost part of Greece, with mountainous terrain and cool climates. Naoussa wine (from the Xinomavro grape) comes from here.

>> **The Peloponnese:** A large, mainly mountainous, peninsula in southwestern Greece with varied climate and soil. Noteworthy wines include the soft, red Nemea; the dry whites Patras and Mantinia; and the sweet wines Mavrodaphne de Patras (red) and Muscat de Patras (white).

>> **Crete:** The largest Greek island, which makes both white and red wines, many of which are varietally named along with the place-name of Crete.

>> **Other Greek islands:** Besides Crete, the four most important islands that make wine are Santorini, Rhodes, Samos, and Cephalonia.

Many Greek wines today are top quality, especially the wines of small, independent wineries. The following are some of our favorite Greek wine producers (listed alphabetically within regions):

>> **From Macedonia:** Alpha Estate, Domaine Gerovassilou, Kir Yianni Estate, and Tsantali-Mount Athos Vineyards

>> **From the Peloponnese:** Antonopoulos Vineyards, Gaia Estate (pronounced *yea*-ah, it has wineries also on Santorini), Katogi & Strofilia (with operations also in Macedonia), Mercouri Estate, Papantonis Winery, Domaine Skouras, Domaine Spiropoulos, and Domaine Tselepos

>> **From the islands:** Boutari Estates (six estates throughout Greece, including Crete and Santorini), Gentilini (on Cephalonia), and Domaine Sigalas (Santorini)

Greece's appellation system for wine, which had involved separate tiers for dry wines and sweet wines, has been simplified by the country's complete adaptation of the new E.U. system. Twenty-nine wine zones fall into the PDO category, and most will carry the phrase *Protected Designation of Origin* in English. PGI wines mainly carry the phrase *Protected Geographic Indication* in English.

Other terms that have formal definitions under Greek wine regulations include *reserve* (PDO wines with a minimum one or two years aging, for whites and reds respectively), *grande reserve* (two years of aging for whites and four years for reds), and *cava* (non-PDO wines with one year of aging for whites and three years for reds). All these terms require that a specified portion of the wines' aging takes place in barrel.

Three Other European Wine Hot Spots

Just about every European country makes wine, with the exception of the cool Scandanavian countries. Three countries, in particular, have caught our attention: Hungary, Croatia, and Slovenia. Of the three, Hungary is the most established. Croatia and Slovenia, on the other hand, have recently emerged as serious wine-producing countries, even though both also have a long history of winemaking.

Hungary: Unique Old World wines

Hungary's central European location makes it the entryway into Eastern Europe. Romans first planted vines here about 2,000 years ago. Hungary has developed its own traditional grape varieties over the centuries, some of which originated from nearby Germany and Austria. Hungary turned to the popular French varieties in the 20th century, after the phylloxera epidemic hit its vineyards very hard in 1882, Hungary began growing Chardonnay, Cabernet Sauvignon, Merlot, Cabernet Franc, and Pinot Noir. Wines are still being made from these varieties in Hungary, but the traditional grape varieties of Central and Eastern Europe make the most interesting wines today.

Hungary's wine production is about 60 percent white wines and 40 percent red. Its most renowned wine, by far, is its dessert wine, Tokaji Aszú, based on its native white Furmint grape variety; we discuss this wine in Chapter 16. Hungary's dry white wines are quite full-bodied and unique. Furmint, the main variety in Tokaji Aszú, is also Hungary's most prominent white varietal wine; it is dry, distinctive, and reasonably priced. The dry version of Furmint retails mainly for $10 to $15, and up to $18 for the best examples. Furmint also makes a late-harvest wine, retailing for $20 or more. Hungary produces other white wines from native varieties, but Furmint is the one you are most likely to see.

Two of Hungary's leading red varieties are Kékfrankos (Austria's Blaufränkisch) and Blauer Portugieser. Both are made as varietal wines and also used in blends; the wines are medium-bodied, spicy, and food-friendly. Another red wine, Egri Bikavér, produced around the town of Eger, and often labeled by its nickname, "Bull's Blood," is an inexpensive ($10), field-blended wine; it is Hungary's best-known red wine.

Croatia: A wine renaissance in Eastern Europe

Croatia, the country situated opposite Italy across the Adriatic Sea, has been producing wines since at least 2500 B.C., when Greeks settled in the region. Like all European wine countries, Croatia grows many traditional grape varieties. Croatia today has one of the fastest growing wine industries in Europe, and boasts one of the world's highest per capita consumption levels, higher even than that of France.

Croatia's modern wine renaissance began in the early 1990s, when the country separated from Communist Yugoslavia. Croatia quickly transitioned from large wine cooperatives producing ordinary wines to private ownership of vineyards and more distinctive wines. Croatian wines are 67 percent white, 32 percent red, and 1 percent rosé. Despite its rather small size, Croatia has over 300 separate wine zones.

Croatia has two distinctive wine areas:

>> **Continental Croatia:** Hilly areas in the interior part produce rich, fruity white wines, while areas farther south near the Mediterranean Sea produce medium-bodied red wines. The best-known wine region in continental Croatia is Slavonia — also the source of a famous oak forest where many wine-producing countries source oak for wine barrels.

>> **Coastal Croatia:** The coastline and the many Dalmatian islands grow grapes in a sunny, warm ideal climate with mild winters.

Coastal Croatia and its islands make the country's most renowned wines. The area ranges from Istria in the north — known for its distinctive white wines made from Malvasia, perhaps better here than anywhere else in the world — to the area known as Dalmatia and its islands in the south, including the picturesque city of Dubrovnik. Croatia's most renowned red varietal wine, Plavac Mali, a close relative of Zinfandel and Primitivo, grows along the coast. Excellent, unique white wines, however, predominate along the Coast and on the islands. A standout white wine, Grk, from the indigenous variety of the same name, made a real impact on us when we first discovered it on the Dalmatian island of Korčula.

Slovenia: A surprisingly large wine country

Slovenia is north of Croatia and east of northern Italy. As in Croatia, evidence of Slovenia's winemaking goes back to the fifth century B.C. The only reason that you might have heard little about Slovenian wine is that this fairly small European country drinks most of its own wine. The U.S. and Slovenia's neighbors receive almost all of what little wine Slovenia exports.

Winemaking is very diverse because of a wide variety of microclimates. Surprisingly (at least to us), Slovenia has more than 28,000 operating wineries today.

About 75 percent of Slovenia's wine is white. Two of Slovenia's main red wine varieties, Blaufränkisch and Blauer Portugieser, are thought to have originated here, but many neighboring countries, including Germany, Austria, and Hungary, now also use these varieties. Slovenia also grows three white varieties and one red variety, all popular with its neighbor, Northeast Italy: Malvasia, Rebula (called Ribolla Gialia in Italy), Friulano, Sivi Pinot (Pinot Grigio), and Refosco (a deeply colored red variety) — all made as varietal wines. Slovenia grows all of the renowned international varieties as well, and also produces sparkling wines, using the *méthode champenoise*.

We highlight here some of Slovenia's noteworthy producers and wines to look for. From the Slovenian part of the Istria peninsula, adjoining Friuli-Venezia Giulia in Italy, look for the red and white wines of Santomas, one of Slovenia's pricier producers, but greatly admired locally. For Pinot Noir, which is quite successful in Slovenia, look for Movia's Modri Pinot from the Brda region, well-priced for a Pinot of this quality (about $35), and Tilia's Modri Pinot (about $30). Both producers are among the best in Slovenia and their wines are available in the U.S.

In general, Slovenia's white wines are its stars, among the best values in the wine world. They are often aged for a long time (up to six years). Those who favor "natural wines" (see Chapter 5) will want to know that many of these wines are made with little or no added sulfur.

We predict that Slovenian wines will definitely become better known internationally in the near future.

4
Wine's Modern Face: The "New World" of Wine

Get the lowdown on the top wine regions and producers in the United States. California is, of course, at the top of the list, but other areas might surprise you.

Discover some wines you simply must try from other New World wine countries, such as Australia, New Zealand, Chile, Argentina, and South Africa.

Chapter 13

America, America

When the *conquistadors* came to the New World of America in search of gold, Spanish missionaries accompanied them and planted the first wine grapevines in what is now Southern California. These "Mission" grapes, as they were called, still exist, but the noble grape varieties — Cabernet Sauvignon, Chardonnay, and the rest of the gang — have supplanted them to produce today's fine wines. One thing that hasn't changed is that California is still the focus of the American wine scene, although most of the wine business has moved to the northern part of the state.

In this chapter, we cover American wines, paying particular attention to California's most famous wine regions, Napa Valley and Sonoma, but also discussing California's other wine regions, along with other notable regions outside California: Oregon, Washington, and New York.

The New World of American Wine

Even though the United States produced wine commercially in the 19th century, the modern beginnings of the U.S. wine industry date only to the late 1960s and 1970s. Prohibition from 1919 to 1933, the Great Depression, and World War II were serious blows to the wine business, and recovery was slow.

In 1960, only 256 operating wineries existed in all of California, less than 25 percent of the pre-Prohibition number. By 2016, the state had 4,653 bonded wineries (about a dozen or so "giants," but mainly small, family-owned operations) — more than five times as many wineries as existed just 20 years before, in 1996!

The growth of California's wine business has stimulated interest in wine all across the country. Today, wineries exist in all 50 United States. But wine production is an important industry in only four states: California (the largest wine-producing state, by far), Washington, Oregon, and New York. For information on wines in other states, check out Paul Lukacs' two books on U.S. wines, *The Great Wines of America* and *American Vintage*, W.W. Norton & Company.

The United States currently ranks fourth in world wine production — although well behind all three leaders, Italy, France, and Spain. The following sections cover two interesting aspects of the world of American wine: the emphasis on a wine's grape variety and an appellation system that's different from the European model.

The grape variety as star

The wines of the United States — especially California — embody New World wine-think. Wine producers may plant whatever grape variety they wish, wherever they wish, without restrictions imposed by tradition or regulations. Which is not to say that the choice of grape variety is haphazard: With increased awareness of the importance of *terroir* (the grape-growing environment), U.S. producers today are mindful about where to plant vineyards, and which variety to grow there.

U.S. wines have elevated grape varieties to celebrity status. Until California began naming wines after grapes, Chardonnay, Merlot, Pinot Noir, and Cabernet Sauvignon were just behind-the-scenes ingredients of wine — but now wine drinkers all over the world recognize these grape names as actual wine names.

American Viticultural Areas

An appellation system for wines does exist in the United States, and like the classic French model (see Chapter 10), it identifies numerous vineyard regions. But the U.S. system of *American Viticultural Areas* (AVAs) establishes only the geographical boundaries of wine zones; it doesn't stipulate which grape varieties can be planted, the maximum yield of grapes per acre (see Chapter 5), or anything else that would link the geography to a particular style of wine. Thus, AVA names — the names of the regions of production — have secondary importance on wine labels after the grape name.

BROADER OR MORE SPECIFIC AVAs?

In naming their wines, winemakers often choose to use a broader AVA designation rather than a smaller, more specific one, in order to widen their options in buying grapes and wine. For example, a winery in Alexander Valley, within Sonoma County, could use the broader *Sonoma County* AVA rather than *Alexander Valley* if it sources grapes from other areas of the county. It could use the larger *North Coast* AVA if it blends in grapes or wine from neighboring counties, like Napa. And if low price is a goal, the winery could even use the broadest AVA, *California,* in order to buy less expensive grapes from the industrially farmed vineyards of the Central Valley (the San Joaquin Valley) or other parts of the state where grapes and wine are less expensive than in Sonoma County.

Sometimes, wineries use the *California* appellation even for their better wines, for name recognition and to give themselves complete freedom in sourcing their grapes. While specificity of place is admired, on the one hand, making a good wine at a good price through geographical blending is also admired. The relative merits depend on who's doing the admiring.

Traditional or not, America's way of making and naming wine sits just right with its local wine drinkers: American wines now account for 69 percent of all wine sales in the U.S., with imported wines at about 31 percent of sales.

REMEMBER

Wines labeled with the name of a grape variety in the United States must contain at least 75 percent of that grape variety, according to federal law. Wines with an AVA indication must be made at least 85 percent from grapes of that viticultural area. Wines with vintage years must derive at least 85 percent from the named vintage.

California, U.S.A.

When most wine drinkers think about American wine, they think of California. That's not surprising — since the wines of California make up about 90 percent of U.S. wine production.

In sunny California, there's no lack of warm climate for growing grapes. For fine wine production, the challenge is to find areas cool enough, with poor enough soil, so that grapes don't ripen too quickly, without full flavor development (see Chapter 5). Nearness to the Pacific Coast and relatively high altitudes are more important determinants of cooler climates than latitude is. Fine wines, therefore, come from vineyards up and down almost the whole length of the state.

California's Gallo Winery is the largest winery in the state. In fact, until recently, it was the largest wine company in the world, producing one out of every four bottles of wine sold in the United States. (Within the last decade, a large New York–based corporation, Constellation Brands, became the world's largest wine company through a series of acquisitions.)

It was another California company, the Robert Mondavi Winery, however, that stimulated fine wine production in the United States. In 1966, Robert Mondavi left his family's winery (Charles Krug) to start his own operation, a winery dedicated to making premium wines. These finer wines — his own and those of the many producers who would follow in his steps — would be varietally named Cabernet Sauvignon, Chardonnay, and so on. Identifying the wines by their grape varieties was a reaction against the low-priced jug wines that were then popular, wines labeled with names borrowed from Europe's wine regions, such as Burgundy and Chablis. Today, even Gallo is very much in the varietal wine business. And Robert Mondavi Winery is now part of the huge Constellation Brands corporation.

The most important fine wine areas and districts include the following (see Figure 13-1):

>> **North Coast:** Napa Valley, Sonoma County, Mendocino County, and Lake County

>> **North-Central Coast:** Livermore and Santa Clara Valleys (San Francisco Bay area), Santa Cruz Mountains, Monterey County

>> **Sierra Foothills**

>> **South-Central Coast:** San Luis Obispo County, Santa Barbara County

We discuss all these regions in this chapter, but we cover them in even more detail in our book *California Wine For Dummies* (Wiley).

Weather variations from year to year do exist in California but they tend to be far less dramatic than they are in most European wine regions. One major reason is that rain doesn't fall during the growing season in much of California. (Rain at the wrong time is the usual cause of Europe's poorer vintages.) Using irrigation, winemakers in effect control the water to their vines. Ironically, one example of weather variation in California is drought, which can limit the amount of water for irrigation.

SIGNIFYING NOTHING

The words *reserve, special selection, private reserve, barrel select, vintners reserve, classic,* and so on have no legal definition in the United States. Although many premium wineries use these terms to indicate their special or better wines, most of the larger wineries use the same terms on their inexpensive bottlings as marketing tools (see Chapter 4).

FIGURE 13-1:
The wine regions
of California.

PACIFIC OCEAN

Illustration by Lisa S. Reed

That said, the effects of global climate change have certainly impacted California in recent years, and the future could see more vintage variation than the past has.

RED WINES FINALLY CATCHING UP WITH CHARDONNAY

Chardonnay has been the perennial sales leader among domestic varietal wines in the United States. But Americans are drinking more red wine these days, and red wine sales have finally caught up (47 percent red wine sales, 40 percent white, 13 percent blush/pink). In addition to Cabernet Sauvignon — still the leading red domestic varietal wine in sales — and Merlot, other red wines are gaining in popularity, including Pinot Noir, red Zinfandel, and Syrah/Shiraz. The growth of domestic rosé wines is a related trend. This category has been growing so fast that statistics now track these wines separately, rather than as part of the red wine category.

Napa Valley: As Tiny as It Is Famous

Napa Valley is about a 90-minute drive northeast of the beautiful bay city of San Francisco. Many of California's most prestigious wineries — and certainly its most expensive vineyard land — are in the small Napa Valley, where about 475 wineries have managed to find space. (In 1960, Napa Valley had only 25 wineries.) Hundreds more brands of Napa Valley wine exist, including producers who make wine in shared winemaking facilities. Despite these numbers, the region's wine production is actually much tinier than its reputation: Napa Valley produces 4 percent of California's wine — and much of that is fine wine.

The Napa Valley floor is only 30 miles long and 5 miles wide at its widest point. The southern part of the valley, especially the Carneros district, is the coolest area, thanks to ocean breezes and mists from the San Pablo Bay. Carneros — which extends westward into Sonoma County — is the vineyard area of choice for grape varieties that enjoy a cooler climate: Chardonnay, Pinot Noir, Merlot, and grapes for sparkling wines. North toward Calistoga — away from the bay influence — the climate can get quite hot (but always with cool nights). Cabernet Sauvignon is the most planted variety in Napa Valley.

Wineries and vineyards occupy almost every agricultural part of Napa Valley. Many vineyards are on the valley floor, some are in the hills and mountains to the west (the Mayacamas Mountains), and some are in the Vaca Mountains to the east (especially Howell Mountain). Napa winemakers and grape growers have 16 sub-AVAs besides the broad Napa Valley AVA itself (which always appears on the label alongside a sub-AVA, if any):

>> Spring Mountain, Diamond Mountain, and Mt. Veeder (all in the Mayacamas Mountains)

>> Howell Mountain, Stags Leap District, and Atlas Peak (all hilly or mountainous areas in eastern Napa Valley)

>> Chiles Valley (in the easternmost part of Napa County)

>> Oak Knoll District, Yountville, Oakville, Rutherford, St. Helena, and Calistoga (from south to north along the valley floor)

>> Wild Horse Valley (in southeastern Napa Valley)

>> Coombsville (east of the city of Napa)

>> Los Carneros (part in Napa Valley, part in Sonoma)

The following sections discuss the wines, grapes, and important producers of Napa Valley.

TIP

FROM LESS THAN $10 TO MORE THAN $200

You can find Chardonnays, Cabernet Sauvignons, Pinot Noirs, and Merlots from California at prices less than $10 a bottle. Better wines can be quite expensive, however. Most mid-range varietal wines are in the $25 to $60 range. Special bottlings and limited-production wines such as reserve bottlings, and single-vineyard wines generally can cost $60 to $200 and up.

Sauvignon Blanc wines — somewhat less in demand than Chardonnay, Pinot Noir, and Merlot — are the best values among California's premium wines. You can find some Sauvignon Blancs for less than $16, with many good ones from $18 to $20, although a few are priced as high as $30. Red Zinfandels are also still a bargain, but their prices are climbing as they become more popular. You can still buy many red Zins from $15 to $20, although a few premium Zinfandels are well over $20. If you like White Zinfandels, which are distinctly sweeter than the reds, you can save yourself a bundle; they're in the $7 to $10 range.

The grapes of Napa

Almost everyone in Napa who makes red or white wine makes a Cabernet Sauvignon and a Chardonnay, and many others also make a Merlot.

Cabernet Sauvignon is Napa Valley's most important wine in terms of production, followed by Chardonnay, Merlot, Sauvignon Blanc (sometimes labeled Fumé Blanc), Pinot Noir (mainly from cool Carneros), and Zinfandel. Most critics regard Cabernet Sauvignon as Napa Valley's finest varietal wine.

Blended wines, which do not carry the name of a single grape variety, are also important. If red, these blends are usually made from red Bordeaux varieties (Cabernet Sauvignon, Cabernet Franc, Merlot, and sometimes even Malbec, and Petit Verdot). If white, they're usually made from the white Bordeaux grapes (Sauvignon Blanc and Sémillon). Some of these blends are referred to as Meritage wines — not just in Napa but across the United States — although few carry the word *Meritage* on their labels. (The term *Meritage*, promoted by the Meritage Alliance, can be used only for red or white wines that utilize grape varieties traditional for making red or white Bordeaux wine; see Chapter 10 for info on Bordeaux.)

Who's who in Napa (and for what)

If just about every winery in Napa makes a Chardonnay and a Cabernet Sauvignon, how can you distinguish the wineries from one another? Good question — with no easy answer. The following alphabetical list indicates some of the better wine producers in Napa Valley, as well as their best wines, and can help steer you in the right direction.

>> **Anderson's Conn Valley:** Cabernet Sauvignon, Chardonnay

>> **Araujo Estate:** Cabernet Sauvignon (Eisele Vineyard), Syrah

>> **Beaulieu Vineyard:** Cabernet Sauvignon Private Reserve (G. de Latour)

>> **Beringer Vineyards:** Cabernet Sauvignon, Chardonnay

>> **Bryant Family Vineyards:** Cabernet Sauvignon (small winery; very scarce)

>> **Cain Cellars:** Cain Five (five Bordeaux varieties), Cain Cuvée

>> **Cakebread Cellars:** Cabernet Sauvignon, Sauvignon Blanc, Chardonnay

>> **Chappellet:** Chenin Blanc, Cabernet Sauvignon

>> **Charles Krug:** Cabernet Sauvignon, Chardonnay (Limited Releases)

>> **Chateau Montelena:** Cabernet Sauvignon, Chardonnay

>> **Clos du Val:** Cabernet Sauvignon, Sémillon, Chardonnay

>> **Corison:** Cabernet Sauvignon

>> **Dalla Valle:** Cabernet Sauvignon, Maya (Cabernet Sauvignon, Cabernet Franc)

>> **Dominus Estate:** Dominus (mainly Cabernet Sauvignon), Napanook

>> **Duckhorn:** Merlot, Cabernet Sauvignon, Sauvignon Blanc

>> **Dunn Vineyards:** Cabernet Sauvignon (especially Howell Mountain)

>> **Far Niente:** Cabernet Sauvignon, Chardonnay

>> **Forman Vineyard:** Chardonnay, Cabernet Sauvignon

>> **Freemark Abbey:** Cabernet Sauvignon (Bosché and Sycamore)

>> **Frog's Leap Winery:** Cabernet Sauvignon, Zinfandel, Sauvignon Blanc

>> **Grgich Hills Cellar:** Chardonnay, Cabernet Sauvignon, Fumé Blanc

>> **Harlan Estate:** Cabernet Sauvignon (small winery; very scarce)

>> **Heitz Wine Cellars:** Cabernet Sauvignon (Martha's Vineyard)

>> **Hess Collection Winery:** Cabernet Sauvignon, Chardonnay

>> **Inglenook** (formerly Niebaum-Coppola): Rubicon

>> **Joseph Phelps Vineyards:** Insignia (Cabernet blend)

>> **Mayacamas Vineyards:** Cabernet Sauvignon

>> **Mount Veeder Winery:** Cabernet Sauvignon, Reserve Red

>> **Newton Vineyard:** Chardonnay, Merlot, Cabernet Sauvignon

>> **Nickel & Nickel:** Cabernet Sauvignon (all single-vineyard wines)

>> **Opus One:** Opus One (mainly Cabernet Sauvignon)

>> **Pahlmeyer Winery:** Red (Cabernet blend), Merlot, Chardonnay

>> **Quintessa Estate:** Quintessa (Bordeaux blend)

>> **Robert Mondavi Winery:** Cabernet Sauvignon, Pinot Noir (Reserves)

>> **Saintsbury:** Pinot Noir (all), Chardonnay

>> **Shafer Vineyards:** Cabernet Sauvignon, Merlot

>> **Smith-Madrone:** Riesling, Chardonnay, Cabernet Sauvignon

>> **Spottswoode Winery:** Cabernet Sauvignon, Sauvignon Blanc

>> **Stag's Leap Wine Cellars:** Cask 23 (Cabernet blend)

>> **Stony Hill Vineyard:** Chardonnay, Riesling

>> **Trefethen Vineyards:** Cabernet Sauvignon, Chardonnay, Riesling (dry)

>> **Turley Wine Cellars:** Zinfandel, Cabernet Sauvignon (new)

Down-to-Earth in Sonoma

If you leave San Francisco over the beautiful Golden Gate Bridge, you'll be in Sonoma in an hour. The differences between Napa and Sonoma are remarkable. Many of Napa's wineries are showy (even downright luxurious), but most of Sonoma's are rustic, countrylike, and laid back (with some exceptions, of course).

As examples of the exceptions, the famously successful Gallo company, based in the Central Valley, also owns vineyards and wineries in Sonoma; also here are Sebastiani, Glen Ellen, Korbel, Kendall-Jackson, Simi, Ravenswood, Francis Ford Coppola, and Jordan wineries — not exactly small-time operations! We have the sneaking suspicion that at some point in the future, Sonoma will bear a striking resemblance to Napa. We hope not; we like it just the way it is.

Find out more about Sonoma's viticultural areas, grapes, and important producers in the following sections.

Sonoma's AVAs

Sonoma is more than twice as large as Napa, it's more spread out, and it has almost as many wineries — more than 425. Its climate is similar to Napa's, except that some areas near the coast are definitely cooler. Although there's plenty of Chardonnay, Cabernet Sauvignon, and Merlot in Sonoma, the region's varied microclimates and terrain have allowed three other varieties — Pinot Noir, Zinfandel, and Sauvignon Blanc — to excel. In fact, Sonoma produces more Pinot Noir than does any other county in the U.S.

The following are the viticultural areas (AVAs) of Sonoma County listed roughly from south to north with their principal grape varieties and wines:

>> **Los Carneros** (partly in Napa Valley): Pinot Noir, Chardonnay, sparkling wine, and Merlot

>> **Sonoma Valley:** Chardonnay, Pinot Noir, Cabernet Sauvignon

>> **Moon Mountain** (in Sonoma Valley): Cabernet Sauvignon, Zinfandel

>> **Sonoma Mountain** (in Sonoma Valley): Cabernet Sauvignon

>> **Bennett Valley:** Chardonnay, Sauvignon Blanc, Merlot

>> **Fort Ross-Seaview** (on the extreme Sonoma Coast): Pinot Noir, Chardonnay

>> **Russian River Valley:** Pinot Noir, Chardonnay, Zinfandel

>> **Green Valley** (within Russian River Valley): Sparkling wine, Chardonnay, Pinot Noir

>> **Chalk Hill** (within Russian River Valley): Chardonnay, Sauvignon Blanc

>> **Dry Creek Valley:** Zinfandel, Cabernet Sauvignon, Sauvignon Blanc

>> **Alexander Valley:** Cabernet Sauvignon, Chardonnay, Sauvignon Blanc

>> **Pine Mountain-Cloverdale Peak:** Cabernet Sauvignon, Merlot, Cabernet Franc

>> **Knight's Valley:** Cabernet Sauvignon, Sauvignon Blanc

>> **Rockpile** (northwestern part of Sonoma County): Zinfandel, Cabernet Sauvignon, Syrah, Petite Sirah

Sonoma County has two more AVAs: **Northern Sonoma**, a patchwork area encompassing Russian River Valley, Alexander Valley, Dry Creek Valley, and Knight's Valley; and **Sonoma Coast,** a hodgepodge of land in western Sonoma, along the coast. Also, the large North Coast AVA includes Sonoma County. The largest three specific Sonoma AVAs, in terms of vineyard acreage and number of wineries, are Russian River Valley, Sonoma Valley, and Alexander Valley.

Pinot Noir lovers should look for wines from Russian River Valley producers, such as Williams Selyem, Rochioli, and Dehlinger. Another new, "hot" area for Pinot Noir — an area referred to informally as the Extreme Sonoma Coast or the True Coast — is ideal for growing Pinot Noir. See the nearby sidebar "The True Coast" for details.

THE TRUE COAST

Called by its fans simply, "The True," the *True Sonoma Coast,* also known as the *Extreme Sonoma Coast,* refers to a section of the huge Sonoma Coast AVA along the Pacific Ocean, from the town of Fort Ross north to Annapolis. It includes the towns of Occidental and Freestone, and the Sebastopol hills. The name evolved because wine producers and growers in that area felt the need to distinguish their area from the rest of the Sonoma Coast AVA: Their coastal *terroir* is unique, and so are its wines. The first step toward formally redefining the overly broad Sonoma Coast AVA took place in January 2012, when the Fort Ross-Seaview AVA was created, covering an important vineyard area on the Extreme Sonoma Coast, close to the Pacific Ocean.

One of the main climatic influences in the True Coast area is the Petaluma Gap, a 15-mile virtual wind tunnel of ocean breezes that sweep through an opening in the mountain ranges at Bodega Bay (a village hugging the Pacific Ocean). This cool, windy effect, along with plenty of sun, makes an ideal growing climate for Pinot Noir and Chardonnay. Pinot Noir grapes ripen later on the True Coast, and the wines are typically lower in alcohol than Pinot Noirs from other, warmer parts of Sonoma. True Coast Pinot Noirs tend to be somewhat lighter in color and weight than most other California Pinot Noirs. They possess elegance and balance, plus a delicacy and finesse not usually found in U.S. Pinots.

Quite a few top wineries specializing in Pinot Noir — such as Williams Selyem, Littorai, Hartford Court, Failla, DuNah Vineyard, and Willowbrook Cellars — purchase grapes from True Coast growers and make their own single-vineyard Sonoma Coast Pinot Noirs. The wineries actually situated in the True Coast area are so miniscule, producing only a few thousand cases of wine annually (mainly Pinot Noir), that we don't list their names in the section "Sonoma producers and wines." Flowers Vineyard & Winery is the largest producer on the Extreme Sonoma Coast, and its wines are rather easier to find than those of the smaller wineries. Other wineries whose wines we urge Pinot Noir lovers to seek out include Hirsch Vineyards, Cobb Winery (including Coastland Vineyard), Peay Vineyards, Wild Hog Vineyard, Freestone, Fort Ross Vineyard, Lioco, Drew Family Estate, B. Kosuge, and Red Car. Wines from this special area are difficult to find in retail shops; your best bet is to look for them online or to contact the wineries directly.

Sonoma producers and wines

The following list of recommended producers includes some of Sonoma's better wineries, listed alphabetically, along with their best wines.

>> **Arrowood Vineyards:** Chardonnay, Cabernet Sauvignon, Syrah

>> **Benziger Family Winery:** Cabernet Sauvignon, Sauvignon Blanc

>> **Chalk Hill Estate:** Sauvignon Blanc, Chardonnay, Cabernet Sauvignon

>> **Château St. Jean:** Chardonnay (Robert Young, Belle Terre Vineyards)

>> **Cline Cellars:** Mourvèdre, Zinfandel

>> **Clos du Bois:** Marlstone (Cabernet blend), Chardonnay

>> **Dehlinger Winery:** Pinot Noir, Chardonnay, Syrah

>> **Dry Creek Vineyard:** Fumé Blanc, Chenin Blanc, Zinfandel

>> **Fisher Vineyards:** Chardonnay, Cabernet Sauvignon

>> **Flowers Vineyard & Winery:** Pinot Noir, Chardonnay

>> **Foppiano Vineyards:** Petite Sirah, Cabernet Sauvignon, Merlot

>> **Gallo Family Vineyards:** Chardonnay (Laguna Ranch), Zinfandel

>> **Hanzell Vineyards:** Chardonnay

>> **Hartford Court:** Pinot Noir (all), Zinfandel

>> **Jordan Vineyard:** Cabernet Sauvignon, Chardonnay

>> **Joseph Swan Vineyards:** Pinot Noir, Zinfandel

>> **Kendall-Jackson:** Cabernet Sauvignon, Chardonnay, Zinfandel

>> **Kistler Vineyards:** Chardonnay, Pinot Noir

>> **La Crema Winery:** Chardonnay, Pinot Noir

>> **La Follette Wines:** Pinot Noir, Chardonnay

>> **Laurel Glen Vineyard:** Cabernet Sauvignon

>> **Littorai Wines:** Pinot Noir, Chardonnay

>> **Marcassin:** Chardonnay (all vineyards; very scarce, by mailing list)

>> **Marimar Torres Estate:** Chardonnay, Pinot Noir

>> **Martinelli Vineyard:** Zinfandel, Chardonnay (Russian River Valley)

>> **Merry Edwards Winery:** Pinot Noir, Sauvignon Blanc

>> **Peter Michael Winery:** Chardonnay, Les Pavots (Cabernet blend)

>> **A. Rafanelli Winery:** Zinfandel, Cabernet Sauvignon (mailing list)

>> **Ramey Wine Cellars:** Cabernet Sauvignon, Chardonnay, Syrah

>> **Ravenswood:** Zinfandel, Merlot (Sangiacomo Vineyard), Pickberry

>> **J. Rochioli Vineyard:** Pinot Noir (all), Sauvignon Blanc, Zinfandel

>> **Sebastiani Vineyards:** Cabernet Sauvignon, Merlot, Chardonnay

>> **Seghesio Family Estates:** Zinfandel (all), Sangiovese, Barbera

>> **Sonoma-Cutrer Vineyards:** Chardonnay (all selections)

>> **Williams Selyem Winery:** Pinot Noir (all), Zinfandel, Chardonnay

Mendocino and Lake Counties

Mendocino County is directly north of Sonoma County. Lake County (dominated by Clear Lake), a region with few wineries, is Napa's neighbor to the north. If you have the chance, it's worth your while to drive up the beautiful California coast-line from San Francisco on Route 1 to the quaint, old town of Mendocino — perhaps with a side trip to view the magnificent, giant redwoods of the Pacific Coast. Tourists are scarcer up here than in Napa or Sonoma, and that makes it all the nicer: You'll be genuinely welcomed at the wineries.

The cool Anderson Valley in Mendocino County is ideal for growing Chardonnay, Pinot Noir, Gewürztraminer, and Riesling, and for the production of sparkling wine. The wily Louis Roederer Champagne house bypassed Napa and Sonoma to start its sparkling wine operation, Roederer Estate, here, and has done extremely well — as have Scharffenberger Cellars (now owned by Louis Roederer) and Handley Cellars, two other successful producers of sparkling wine in Anderson Valley (see Chapter 15 for more sparkling wine producers).

The following list includes recommended producers and their best wines. We list the producers alphabetically in each county.

>> **Mendocino County:**

- **Brutocao Cellars:** Zinfandel, Barbera, Dolcetto

- **Edmeades:** Zinfandel (especially single vineyards)

- **Elke Vineyards:** Pinot Noir

- **Fetzer Vineyards:** Pinot Noir, Cabernet Sauvignon Reserves

- **Frey Vineyards:** Petite Sirah, Zinfandel
- **Goldeneye Winery (Duckhorn):** Pinot Noir
- **Greenwood Ridge Vineyards:** Riesling, Pinot Noir, Zinfandel
- **Handley Cellars:** Pinot Noir, Chardonnay, Gewürztraminer
- **Husch:** Pinot Noir, Sauvignon Blanc, Gewürztraminer
- **Lazy Creek Vineyards:** Gewürztraminer, Riesling
- **Lolonis Winery:** Cabernet Sauvignon (all), Zinfandel
- **McDowell Valley Vineyards:** Syrah, Viognier
- **Navarro Vineyards:** Gewürztraminer, Chardonnay (Reserve)

» **Lake County:**

- **Guenoc Winery:** Cabernet Sauvignon, Chardonnay, Langtry Meritage Red (Cabernet blend), Petite Sirah Reserve
- **Langtry Estate & Vineyards:** Petite Sirah, Sauvignon Blanc
- **Steele Wines:** Chardonnay, Zinfandel, Pinot Noir, Pinot Blanc

The San Francisco Bay Area

The San Francisco Bay area includes wine regions north, east, and south of the city: Marin County to the north; Alameda County and Livermore Valley to the east; and San Mateo County to the south.

The urban spread east and south of San Francisco, from the cities of Palo Alto to San Jose (Silicon Valley) and eastward, has taken its toll on vineyards in the Livermore and Santa Clara Valleys (all just about gone from Santa Clara Valley). Livermore Valley, cooled by breezes from the San Francisco Bay, is now relatively small. In Livermore, directly east of San Francisco, Sauvignon Blanc and Sémillon have always done well.

We list our recommended wineries alphabetically, by locality.

» **Marin County:**

- **Kalin Cellars:** Sauvignon Blanc, Sémillon, Chardonnay, Pinot Noir; grapes from diverse areas, including Livermore Valley
- **Sean H. Thackrey:** Orion Old Vines Red (Syrah blend), Sirius (Petite Sirah); grapes come from several different areas

» **Alameda County/Livermore Valley:**

- **A Donkey and Goat Winery:** Chardonnay, Mourvèdre
- **Concannon Vineyard:** Chardonnay, Petite Sirah
- **Dashe Cellars:** Zinfandel, Grenache, dry Riesling
- **Edmunds St. John:** Syrah, Rocks and Gravel (Rhône blend)
- **Murrieta's Well:** Zinfandel, Red Meritage (Cabernet blend)
- **Wente Family Estates:** Chardonnay, Sauvignon Blanc

» **San Mateo County:**

- **Cronin Vineyards:** Chardonnay, Cabernet Sauvignon
- **Thomas Fogarty Winery:** Gewürztraminer, Chardonnay, Pinot Noir

The Santa Cruz Mountains

Standing atop one of the isolated Santa Cruz Mountains, you can quickly forget that you're only an hour's drive south of San Francisco. The rugged, wild beauty of this area has attracted quite a few winemakers, including some of the best in the state. (Paul Draper of Ridge Vineyards and Randall Grahm of Bonny Doon are but two.) The climate is cool on the ocean side, where Pinot Noir thrives. On the San Francisco Bay side, Cabernet Sauvignon is the important red variety. Chardonnay is a leading variety on both sides.

We list our recommended Santa Cruz Mountains wine producers alphabetically, along with their best wines:

» **Bargetto:** Chardonnay, Pinot Noir, Cabernet Sauvignon, Merlot

» **Bonny Doon Vineyard:** Le Cigare Volant Red (Rhône blend)

» **David Bruce Winery:** Pinot Noir

» **Cinnabar Vineyards:** Chardonnay, Cabernet Sauvignon

» **Kathryn Kennedy Winery:** Cabernet Sauvignon, Syrah

» **Mount Eden Vineyards:** Chardonnay Estate, Pinot Noir Estate

» **Ridge Vineyards:** Cabernet Sauvignon Monte Bello, Geyserville (Zin blend), Zinfandel

» **Santa Cruz Mountain Vineyard:** Pinot Noir, Cabernet Sauvignon

What's New in Old Monterey

Monterey County has a little bit of everything — a beautiful coastline; the chic town of Carmel; some very cool (as in temperature) vineyard districts, and some very warm areas; mountain wineries and Salinas Valley wineries; a few gigantic wine firms and lots of small ones. Like most California wine regions, Monterey has been changing rapidly during the past three decades, and now nine official sub–viticultural areas (AVAs) exist here — with the larger Monterey AVA, covering close to 100 wineries at present (but that number is changing rapidly). The smaller AVAs are the following

>> Arroyo Seco

>> Carmel Valley

>> Chalone

>> Hames Valley

>> Monterey

>> San Antonio Valley

>> San Bernabe

>> San Lucas

>> Santa Lucia Highlands

Santa Lucia Highlands, in particular, is now one of the prime Pinot Noir regions in California.

Chardonnay is the leading varietal wine in Monterey County — as it is in most of the state. But the cooler parts of Monterey are also principal sources of Riesling and Gewürztraminer. Cabernet Sauvignon and Pinot Noir are the leading red varieties in the mountain areas.

The following are our recommended producers in Monterey County, listed alphabetically, along with one producer from neighboring San Benito County:

>> **Albatross Ridge**

>> **Bernardus Winery:** Chardonnay, Sauvignon Blanc, Marinus (mainly Cabernet Sauvignon), Pinot Noir

>> **Calera (San Benito County):** Pinot Noir (especially single-vineyard selections), Viognier, Chardonnay, Aligoté

>> **Chalone Vineyard:** Chardonnay, Pinot Blanc, Pinot Noir

>> **Château Julien:** Chardonnay, Merlot, Cabernet Sauvignon

- **Estancia Estates:** Chardonnay, Cabernet Sauvignon, Merlot, Pinot Noir
- **Hahn Estates/Smith & Hook Winery:** Chardonnay, Pinot Noir, Smith & Hook Cabernet Sauvignon
- **Jekel Vineyards:** Riesling, Chardonnay, Pinot Noir
- **Morgan Winery:** Chardonnay, Pinot Noir, Syrah
- **Paraiso Vineyards:** Pinot Noir, Chardonnay, Riesling, Syrah
- **Robert Talbott Vineyards:** Chardonnay

Gold Country: The Sierra Foothills

No wine region in America has a more romantic past than the Sierra Foothills. The Gold Rush of 1849 carved a place in history for the foothills of the Sierra Nevada Mountains. It also brought vineyards to the area to provide wine for the thirsty miners. One of the vines planted at that time was certainly Zinfandel — still the region's most famous wine. Many of the oldest grapevines in the United States, some more than 100 years old and mainly Zinfandel, are here in the Sierra Foothills.

In fact, very little has changed in the Sierra Foothills over the years. This is clearly the most rustic wine region on the West Coast. Therein lies its charm. A visit to the Sierra Foothills is like a trip into the past, when life was simple.

The Sierra Foothills is a sprawling wine region east of Sacramento, centered in Amador and El Dorado Counties, but spreading north and south of both. Two of its best-known viticultural areas are Shenandoah Valley and Fiddletown. Summers can be hot, but many vineyards are situated as high as 1,500 feet — such as around Placerville in El Dorado — and evenings are very cool. Soil throughout the region is mainly volcanic in origin.

The following are our recommended producers in the Sierra Foothills (listed alphabetically), along with their best wines:

- **Amador Foothill Winery:** Zinfandel
- **Boeger Winery:** Zinfandel, Barbera, Sauvignon Blanc
- **Karly Winery:** Zinfandel, Sauvignon Blanc
- **Lava Cap Winery:** Barbera, Cabernet Sauvignon, Petite Sirah
- **Montevina Winery:** Zinfandel, Barbera, Syrah
- **Renaissance Vineyard:** Cabernet Sauvignon, Riesling (Late Harvest)

>> **Shenandoah Vineyards:** Zinfandel, Sauvignon Blanc

>> **Sierra Vista Winery:** Zinfandel, Syrah

>> **Sobon Estate:** Zinfandel, Viognier

San Luis Obispo: Paso Robles to Edna Valley

San Luis Obispo County — in the heart of California's Central Coast, about equidistant from San Francisco and Los Angeles — encompasses vastly diverse viticultural areas. These include, for example, the warm, hilly Paso Robles region (north of the town of San Luis Obispo) where Zinfandel, Cabernet Sauvignon, and Syrah reign, and the cool, coastal Edna Valley and Arroyo Grande (south of the town), home of some very good Pinot Noirs and Chardonnays.

Paso Robles is one of California's fastest-growing wine regions, with 200-plus wineries — more than twice as many as it had just eight years ago. Its wines are very different from those of the two coastal areas.

We recommend the following producers in San Luis Obispo (listed alphabetically, along with their best wines):

>> **Paso Robles:**

- **Adelaida Cellars:** Pinot Noir, Zinfandel, Cabernet Sauvignon
- **Caparone Winery:** Sangiovese, Aglianico, Nebbiolo
- **Clayhouse Wines:** Petite Sirah, Syrah, Malbec
- **Daou Vineyards:** Cabernet Sauvignon Reserve, Pinot Noir
- **Eberle Winery:** Zinfandel, Cabernet Sauvignon, Syrah, Viognier
- **Justin Vineyards:** Isosceles (Cabernet blend)
- **J. Lohr Winery:** Chardonnay, Cabernet Sauvignon, Syrah
- **Meridian Vineyards:** Chardonnay (especially Reserve), Syrah
- **Peachy Canyon Winery:** Zinfandel
- **Robert Hall Winery:** Rhône blends, Viognier, Sauvignon Blanc
- **Tablas Creek Vineyard:** Mourvèdre, Grenache, Syrah, Roussanne
- **Hope Family Wines/Treana:** Treana Red, Treana White

>> **Edna Valley and Arroyo Grande:**

- **Alban Vineyards:** Viognier (Estate), Roussanne, Syrah, Grenache

- **Claiborne & Churchill:** Riesling, Pinot Gris, Pinot Noir

- **Edna Valley Vineyard:** Chardonnay, Pinot Noir

- **Laetitia Vineyard:** Chardonnay, Pinot Noir

- **Saucelito Canyon Vineyard:** Zinfandel

- **Talley Vineyards:** Chardonnay, Pinot Noir

WORTH THE SEARCH

Special Paso Robles finds: **Adelaida Cellars** and **Daou Vineyards** are making some of the finest wines in California from their hillside vineyards. Look especially for their Cabernet Sauvignons and Pinot Noirs.

And do you like Italian red wines but haven't had much luck finding good "Cal-Ital" wines in California? In their small **Caparone Winery** outside of Paso Robles, Dave Caparone and his son Marc are making authentic California wines from Italian varieties. Caparone's Sangiovese and Aglianico are possibly the best examples of these challenging Italian varietal wines in the United States, in our opinion. Caparone's Nebbiolo is also very good but needs some aging in some vintages to be at its best.

Santa Barbara, Californian Paradise

The most exciting viticultural areas in California — if not in the entire country — are in Santa Barbara County. Even though Spanish missionaries planted vineyards there 200 years ago, it wasn't until 1975 that the first major winery (Firestone Vineyards) opened. In light of what we now know — that is, how well suited Santa Barbara County is to grape growing — 1975 was a late start.

The main growing areas of the county are the Santa Maria, Santa Ynez, and Los Alamos Valleys, which lie north of the city of Santa Barbara. Unusually in California, these cool valleys run east to west, opening toward the Pacific Ocean and channeling in the ocean air. The cool climate is ideal for Pinot Noir and Chardonnay. In the Santa Maria Valley, for example, the average temperature during the growing season is a mere 74 degrees Fahrenheit.

The southernmost of the three valleys is the Santa Ynez Valley. It boasts a cool climate on its western end, while the eastern end of the valley is warm enough to grow red grapes, such as Grenache and Syrah. The Sta. Rita Hills AVA in the cool, western end is particularly known for Pinot Noir and Chardonnay, and is one of the three important Santa Barbara AVAs. (The other two are the Santa Maria Valley AVA and the Santa Ynez Valley AVA.)

Pinot Noir has earned Santa Barbara County much of its acclaim as a wine region. Santa Barbara is generally recognized as one of the six great American wine regions for Pinot Noir — the other five being Carneros, the Russian River Valley, the Sonoma Coast, Mendocino County's Anderson Valley, and Oregon's Willamette Valley (which we discuss later in this chapter). In Santa Barbara, Pinot Noir wines seem to burst with luscious strawberry fruit, laced with herbal tones. These wines tend to be precocious; they're delicious in their first four or five years and are not the "keepers" that the sturdier, wilder-tasting Russian River Pinot Noirs or the True Sonoma Coast seem to be. But why keep them when they taste so good?

The following are some recommended producers in Santa Barbara (listed alphabetically), and their best wines:

>> **Alma Rosa:** Chardonnay, Pinot Gris, Pinot Noir

>> **Au Bon Climat:** Pinot Noir, Chardonnay

>> **Babcock Vineyards:** Sauvignon Blanc, Chardonnay, Pinot Noir

>> **The Brander Vineyard:** Sauvignon Blanc

>> **Byron Vineyard:** Chardonnay (especially Nielson Vineyard), Pinot Noir

>> **Cambria Winery:** Chardonnay, Pinot Noir (Julia's Vineyard), Syrah

>> **Cottonwood Canyon:** Pinot Noir, Chardonnay

>> **Daniel Gehrs:** Chenin Blanc, Dry Riesling, Gewürztraminer, Syrah

>> **Fiddlehead Cellars:** Pinot Noir, Sauvignon Blanc

>> **Foxen Vineyard:** Pinot Noir, Syrah, Chardonnay, Chenin Blanc

>> **Gainey Vineyard:** Chardonnay, Pinot Noir, Sauvignon Blanc

>> **Lane Tanner Winery:** Pinot Noir

>> **Longoria Wines:** Pinot Noir, Syrah

>> **The Ojai Vineyard:** Pinot Noir, Syrah, Chardonnay

>> **Presqu'ile Winery:** Pinot Noir, Chardonnay

>> **Qupé Cellars:** Syrah, Chardonnay, Roussanne, Marsanne, Viognier

>> **Sanford Winery:** Pinot Noir (especially Sanford & Benedict Vineyard)

>> **Santa Barbara Winery:** Pinot Noir, Chardonnay, Syrah

>> **Sea Smoke Cellars:** Pinot Noir, Sparkling Sea Smoke, Chardonnay

>> **Zaca Mesa Winery:** Syrah, Roussanne, Chardonnay, Viognier

Oregon: A Tale of Two Pinots

Because Oregon is north of California, most people assume that Oregon's wine regions are cool. And they are. But the main reason for Oregon's relatively cool climate is that no high mountains separate its vineyards from the Pacific Ocean. The ocean influence brings low temperatures and rain. Grape growing and winemaking are really completely different in Oregon and California.

Winemaking has grown rapidly in Oregon. From five wineries in 1970, the state now has about 750, with about 500 in its main wine region, the Willamette (*wil LAM ette Valley*). Most of Oregon's wineries are small, family-owned operations. The exception in terms of size is King Estate, Oregon's largest winery, but even King Estate is relatively small compared to some of the wine behemoths of California.

Oregon first gained respect in wine circles for its Pinot Noir, a grape that needs cool climates to perform at its best (see Chapter 3). The Eyrie Vineyards released Oregon's first Pinot Noir in 1970, but national recognition for the state's Pinots came only after the excellent 1983 and 1985 vintages. Pinot Noir is still Oregon's flagship wine, and a vast majority of the state's wineries produce it. Oregon's Pinot Noirs, with their characteristic black-fruit aromas and flavors as well as depth and complexity, have won accolades as some of the very best Pinots in the United States.

Red wine encompasses 60 percent of Oregon's wine production today; the 40 percent of production that is white wine features mainly Pinot Gris, Chardonnay, and Riesling. In recent years, Oregon's Chardonnays have surged in quality, thanks to the replanting of many vineyards with French clones of the Chardonnay grape, as opposed to the original plantings that were more suited to California's warmer climate.

In the following sections, we discuss Oregon's Pinot Gris, and we talk about the state's main wine regions: the Willamette Valley, the Umpqua Valley, and the Rogue River Valley.

Oregon's other Pinot

Because Chardonnay is the companion grape to Pinot Noir in France's Burgundy region (see Chapter 10), and because Chardonnay wine is hugely popular in America, it's an important variety in Oregon. However, Pinot Gris actually outproduces Chardonnay in Oregon — although Chardonnay is catching up. (Read about Pinot Gris in Chapter 3.)

The late David Lett, founder and winemaker of The Eyrie Vineyards and Oregon's Pinot Noir pioneer, is also the man who made Oregon's first Pinot Gris, around 1970, followed by Ponzi Vineyards and Adelsheim Vineyard. Today, most wineries in the Willamette Valley make Pinot Gris, along with Pinot Noir.

Two styles of Oregon Pinot Gris exist:

>> A lighter, fruity style, from early-harvested grapes, always made without oak; these wines can be consumed as soon as they are released.

>> A medium-bodied, golden-hued wine from grapes left longer on the vine, which sometimes has a little oak aging; these wines can age for five or six years or longer.

In general, Oregon Pinot Gris has aromas reminiscent of pears, apples, and sometimes of melon, and surprising depth for an inexpensive wine. It's an excellent food wine, even when it's slightly sweet; it works especially well with seafood and salmon — just the kind of food that it's paired with in Oregon. Pinot Gris is also great with many Asian cuisines. Most of Oregon's Pinot Gris wines are in the $14 to $22 range in retail stores.

Now, more and more California wineries are also making Pinot Gris. But in California, most wineries are producing a light wine in the style of Italian Pinot Grigio, and they usually call the wine by that Italian name — hoping, no doubt, to capitalize on the popularity of the Italian wine. Oregon's richest Pinot Gris wines resemble Alsace's flavorful Pinot Gris style.

But the U.S.'s most popular white variety, Chardonnay, is now making better Chardonnay wines than ever in Oregon. It seems inevitable that Oregon, too, will eventually make Chardonnay its most popular white variety, despite the state's excellent Pinot Gris wines.

Who's who in Willamette Valley

The main home of Pinot Noir and Pinot Gris in Oregon is the Willamette Valley, directly south of the city of Portland in northwestern Oregon. The Willamette Valley has established itself in the last 45-plus years as one of the most important wine regions in the U.S; in fact, two-thirds of Oregon's wineries are situated there.

TIP

Willamette Valley is a convenient wine destination to visit because the vibrant city of Portland, with all its fine restaurants, hotels, and shops, is just 30-plus minutes north.

Willamette Valley is huge and encompasses several counties. Yamhill County, directly southwest of Portland, has the greatest concentration of wineries, all of which produce Pinot Noir; its county seat, McMinnville, is a destination point for wine tourists. But quite a few wineries are located in Washington County, west of Portland, and in Polk County, south of Yamhill. In addition to the general Willamette Valley AVA, six specific AVAs now exist in the Willamette Valley:

Chehalem Mountains, Dundee Hills, Yamhill–Carlton District, Ribbon Ridge, McMinnville Foothills, and Eola–Amity Hills. The diverse soils of the Willamette Valley have inspired winemakers to differentiate the area and formalize these AVAs. Another five AVAs are under proposal.

TIP

Here are some of the best producers in the Willamette Valley, primarily for Pinot Noir and Pinot Gris (but sometimes also Chardonnay or Riesling):

Adelsheim Vineyard	Brick House Vineyards
Archery Summit	Broadley Vineyards
Argyle Winery	Cameron Winery
Beaux Frères	Chehalem Winery
Benton Lane Winery	Cooper Mountain Vineyards
Bethel Heights Vineyard	Cristom Vineyards
Domaine Drouhin Oregon	Patricia Green Cellars
Domaine Serene	Penner-Ash Wine Cellar
Duck Pond Cellars	Ponzi Vineyards
Edgefield Winery	Redhawk Vineyard
Elk Cove Vineyards	Ken Wright Cellars
Eola Hills Wine Cellars	Rex Hill Vineyards
Erath Winery	St. Innocent Winery
The Eyrie Vineyards	Shafer Vineyard Cellars
Firesteed Winery	Sokol Blosser Winery
Hamacher Wines	
Hinman Vineyards/Silvan Ridge	Stangeland Vineyards
King Estate Winery	Torii Mor Winery
Kramer Vineyards	Tualatin Vineyards
Lange Estate Winery	Van Duzer Wines
Montinore Estate Vineyards	WillaKenzie Estate
Oak Knoll Winery	Willamette Valley Vineyards
Panther Creek Cellars	Yamhill Valley Winery

Two other Oregon wine regions

Two other wine regions of note in Oregon are both in the southwest part of the state: the Umpqua Valley (around the town of Roseburg) and the Rogue River Valley farther south, next to California's northern border.

Considerably warmer than Willamette, the Umpqua Valley is the site of Oregon's first winery, Hillcrest Vineyard, founded in 1962. The main grape varieties in Umpqua are Pinot Noir, Chardonnay, Riesling, and Cabernet Sauvignon. Major wineries are Henry Estate and Girardet Wine Cellars, known for their Pinot Noir and Chardonnay.

The Rogue River Valley is warmer still; Cabernet Sauvignon and Merlot often perform better here than Pinot Noir. Chardonnay is the leading white wine, but Pinot Gris is becoming popular. Bridgeview Vineyards, the region's largest winery, is doing an admirable job with Pinot Gris as well as Pinot Noir. Four other vineyards to watch are Ashland Vineyards, Valley View Winery, Sarah Powell Wines, and Foris Vineyards — the latter a specialist in Merlot and Cabernet Sauvignon.

Washington State Reaches New Heights

Like Oregon, Washington got off to a late start in the wine business. With the exception of Château Ste. Michelle and Columbia Winery, both founded in the 1960s, very few (only 19) of the current over-850 wineries existed before 1980. Washington is now second in the country in wine production.

Although Washington and Oregon are neighboring states, their wine regions have vastly different climates due to the location of the vineyards relative to the Cascade Mountains, which cut through both states from north to south.

On Washington's western, coastal side, the climate is maritime — cool, plenty of rain, and a lot of vegetation. (In Oregon, almost all the vineyards are located on the coastal side.) East of the mountains, Washington's climate is continental, with hot, very dry summers and cold winters. Most of Washington's vineyards are situated in this area, in the vast, sprawling Columbia Valley, which encompasses the important Yakima Valley. Because it's so far north, Washington also has the advantage of long hours of sunlight, averaging an unusually high 17.4 hours of sunshine during the growing season.

More than 80 grape varieties grow in Washington, with the big five being Cabernet Sauvignon, Riesling, Chardonnay, Merlot, and Syrah. Washington first became well known for the quality of its Merlots. Two wineries, Château Ste. Michelle and

Columbia Crest, dominate U.S. sales of Merlot in the over $8 price category. But Washington's Riesling and Syrah are among the country's sales leaders for these varietal wines — and quality leaders as well. One winery, Château Ste. Michelle, makes the largest-selling Riesling wine in the United States.

Woodinville, an eastern suburb of Seattle and a part of Seattle's metropolitan area, has become an exciting center of winery tasting rooms, particularly for small wineries. Woodinville is also the home of the beautiful Château Ste. Michelle winery, as well as Columbia Winery.

The types of wine produced in Washington have dramatically changed during the past two decades. In 1993, about two-thirds of Washington's wines were white, one-third red. Reflecting Americans' changing tastes, Washington's wines are now about 60 percent red, 40 percent white.

Château Ste. Michelle, along with the even larger Columbia Crest (both under the same corporate ownership), are the giants in the state; they account for more than 50 percent of all Washington's wines at present. Two other large Washington wineries are The Hogue Cellars and Washington Hills Cellars.

Check out the following sections for more about Washington's wine regions, important producers, and wines.

Washington's wine regions

Washington has 14 AVAs. One of them is the gigantic **Columbia Valley** AVA which encompasses ten other AVAs within its macro-appellation. These ten (listed in order of their general importance) are:

>> **Yakima Valley:** This region is the second largest in acreage, behind the huge Columbia Valley itself; more wineries are located here than in all the rest of Columbia Valley.

>> **Walla Walla Valley:** Although only 5 percent of the state's *vinifera* grapes grow here, this fast-growing region in the southeast corner of Washington, extending into northeast Oregon, is home to some of the state's top wineries, such as Leonetti Cellar, Woodward Canyon, Waterbrook Winery, Canoe Ridge Vineyard, and L'Ecole No 41 — as well as some of the state's best red wines.

>> **Red Mountain:** The tiny Red Mountain area is actually within the Yakima Valley AVA, but its red clay soil and high altitude earned it a separate appellation in 2001. About nine wineries, including Hedges and Kiona Vineyards, concentrate on red varieties: Cabernet Sauvignon, Merlot, Cabernet Franc, and Syrah.

>> **Horse Heaven Hills:** Recognized as a separate AVA in 2005, this area in the southernmost part of the Columbia Valley, just north of the Columbia River, has long been known as an ideal location for Cabernet Sauvignon. Many of Washington's leading wineries, including Château Ste. Michelle, use grapes from vineyards here.

>> **Wahluke Slope:** A fairly new AVA (2006), the Wahluke Slope is one of the state's warmer appellations, known for its Merlot and Cabernet Sauvignon, and home to Snoqualmie Vineyards.

>> **Rattlesnake Hills:** A tiny appellation established in 2006, Rattlesnake Hills is actually a sub-appellation of Yakima Valley that boasts Yakima's highest elevation (more than 3,000 feet). The wineries number 17, all small. Temperatures are moderate in this beautiful region, thanks to the altitude.

>> **Snipes Mountain:** This AVA (2009) is another sub-appellation of Yakima Valley. Snipes Mountain is the first region in the state of Washington to have grown wine grapes.

>> **Lake Chelan:** Located in northern Columbia Valley, with 15 wineries, Lake Chelan became the state's tenth AVA in 2009. It boasts high elevation and temperate climate.

>> **Naches Heights:** The smallest appellation (with 37 acres and seven vineyards), Naches Heights is a high plateau, ranging up to 2,100 feet, with volcanic soil. It is within the Columbia Valley, west of the city of Yakima. It's been an AVA since 2012.

>> **Ancient Lakes of Columbia Valley:** An AVA (approved in November 2012), Ancient Lakes is also known as Quincy Basin. It's in the northwest part of Columbia Valley. Chardonnay and Riesling grow especially well here.

Columbia Gorge, a beautiful area in southwest Washington crossing into Oregon, is another Washington AVA; it actually has an equal number of Oregon and Washington wineries. The **Greater Puget Sound/Seattle Area AVA** encompasses the Puget Sound Islands and has more than 50 wineries; in this cool, moist climate, Pinot Gris and Pinot Noir are leading varieties, as well as Riesling and Gewürztraminer.

Finally, 11 wineries, including Arbor Crest, are located in **Lewis Clark Valley** (shared with Idaho): This newest Washington AVA is in the Spokane area in eastern Washington.

A WASHINGTON ODDITY

When was the last time you had a Lemberger? No, we don't mean the cheese! Lemberger is a little-known grape variety from Germany that's also grown in Austria, where it's called Blaufränkisch. Don't feel bad if you haven't heard of it, because few people in the United States — outside of Washington — have tasted it. Lemberger is a hardy red variety that does well in the Yakima Valley; it makes a fruity but dry, medium-bodied inexpensive wine in the Beaujolais style. Hoodsport, Covey Run, Kiona Vineyards, and The Hogue Cellars are four good producers of Lemberger — the wine! The Hogue Cellars calls its version "Blue Franc."

Who's who in Washington

No, we're not talking about cabinet members and senators here! The following are our recommended wine producers in Washington, grouped alphabetically, along with some of their best wines:

>> **Andrew Will Cellars:** Cabernet Sauvignon, Merlot

>> **Arbor Crest Wine Cellars:** Sauvignon Blanc, Chardonnay, Riesling

>> **Badger Mountain Winery:** Chardonnay, Cabernet Franc

>> **Barnard Griffin Winery:** Sémillon, Chardonnay, Fumé Blanc, Merlot

>> **Betz Family Winery:** Cabernet Sauvignon, Merlot blend, Syrah

>> **Bookwalter Winery:** Cabernet Sauvignon, Merlot

>> **Canoe Ridge Vineyard:** Merlot, Cabernet Sauvignon

>> **Château Ste. Michelle:** Merlot, Cabernet Sauvignon, Chardonnay (especially Cold Creek Vineyard), "Eroica" Riesling (with Dr. Loosen)

>> **Chinook Winery:** Sauvignon Blanc, Sémillon, Chardonnay

>> **Col Solare Winery:** Meritage (mainly Cabernet Sauvignon; a Château Ste. Michelle/Piero Antinori collaboration)

>> **Columbia Crest Winery:** Reserve Red (Cabernet-Merlot blend), Sémillon, Syrah, Merlot, Cabernet Sauvignon, Sémillon-Chardonnay

>> **Columbia Winery:** Cabernet Sauvignon, Cabernet Franc, Syrah, Merlot (especially Red Willow Vineyard of all four)

>> **Covey Run Winery:** Chardonnay, Lemberger

>> **DeLille Cellars:** Chaleur Estate (Bordeaux-style blend), Chaleur Estate Blanc (Sauvignon Blanc–Sémillon blend), D2 (second label of Chaleur Estate), Harrison Hill (Cabernet Sauvignon), Syrah

>> **Gordon Brothers Cellars:** Chardonnay, Merlot, Cabernet Sauvignon

>> **Gramercy Cellars:** Syrah, Cabernet Sauvignon

>> **Hedges Cellars:** Red Mountain Reserve (Bordeaux-style blend), Cabernet/Merlot, Fumé/Chardonnay, Three Vineyard Red

>> **The Hogue Cellars:** Merlot, Cabernet Sauvignon (Reserve), Blue Franc (Lemberger), Chenin Blanc, Sémillon-Chardonnay, Sémillon

>> **Hoodsport Winery:** Lemberger, Sémillon

>> **Hyatt Vineyards:** Merlot, Cabernet Sauvignon

>> **Januik/Novelty Hill Winery:** Merlot, Cabernet Sauvignon

>> **Kiona Vineyards:** Lemberger, Cabernet Sauvignon, Merlot

>> **L'Ecole No 41:** Merlot (Seven Hills), Cabernet Sauvignon, Sémillon

>> **Leonetti Cellar:** Cabernet Sauvignon (especially Seven Hills Vineyard), Merlot, Sangiovese

>> **Long Shadows Winery:** Merlot, Syrah, Riesling

>> **Matthews Cellars:** Merlot, Yakima Valley Red (Bordeaux-style blend)

>> **McCrea Cellars:** Chardonnay, Syrah

>> **Northstar Winery:** Merlot

>> **O-S Winery (also known as Owen-Sullivan):** Syrah, Cabernet Franc, Merlot

>> **Pacific Rim:** Riesling

>> **Pepper Bridge Winery:** Cabernet Sauvignon, Merlot

>> **Preston Wine Cellars:** Cabernet Sauvignon, Merlot (Reserves)

>> **Quilceda Creek Vintners:** Cabernet Sauvignon, Merlot

>> **Sagelands Vineyard:** Cabernet Sauvignon, Merlot

>> **Savage Grace:** Cabernet Franc

>> **Seven Hills Winery:** Merlot, Cabernet Sauvignon

>> **Snoqualmie Vineyards:** Cabernet Sauvignon, Merlot, Syrah

>> **Tamarack Cellars:** Merlot, Cabernet Sauvignon, Firehouse Red

>> **Tefft Cellars:** Sangiovese, Cabernet Sauvignon

>> **Thurston Wolfe Winery:** Syrah

>> **Washington Hills Cellars:** Cabernet Sauvignon, Merlot, Chardonnay, Sémillon, Cabernet Franc ("Apex" is this winery's premium label; it also uses the "W. B. Bridgman" label)

>> **Waterbrook Winery:** Cabernet Sauvignon, Merlot, Chardonnay, Cabernet Franc, Sauvignon Blanc

>> **Woodward Canyon Winery:** Chardonnay, Cabernet Sauvignon, Merlot

The Empire State

New York City may be the capital of the world in many ways, but its state's wines haven't always received the recognition they deserve, perhaps because of California's overwhelming presence in the U.S. market. New York ranks as the fourth-largest wine producing state in the United States, after California, Washington, and Oregon. Wineries have burgeoned in recent decades and now number more than 400.

Brotherhood, America's Oldest Winery, the oldest continuously operating winery in the United States, opened its doors in New York's Hudson Valley in 1839. More recent milestones have included the development of vineyards planted with vinifera-species grapes in the Finger Lakes region and the emergence of Long Island as a key wine region.

The Finger Lakes region

Common wisdom held that the relatively cold New York winters could not support *Vitis vinifera* (the species of the world's main grape varieties). But a Russian immigrant, the great Dr. Konstantin Frank, proved all the naysayers wrong when he succeeded in growing Riesling (followed by many other vinifera varieties) in 1953 in Hammondsport, in the Finger Lakes region. The first wines from vinifera grapes were made in 1961 at his winery, Dr. Frank's Vinifera Wine Cellars. His son, Willy Frank, ran one of the most successful wineries in the state, with an entire line of fine vinifera wines and excellent sparkling wines; the winery carries on today under the leadership of Dr. Frank's grandson, Fred.

The Finger Lakes region, where four large lakes temper the otherwise cool climate, is still New York's most important wine region. This AVA produces the largest number of New York's wines and has more than 120 wineries. Riesling, the Finger Lakes region's most renowned (and best) wine, is available from most Finger Lakes' wineries, which are almost exclusively small operations.

Long Island and the Hudson Valley

The second important region is Long Island, which has three AVAs: North Fork of Long Island (the most important); the Hamptons, on the island's South Fork; and Long Island itself, applicable to wines made with grapes from all over Long Island. There are about 60 wineries on Long Island, mainly in the North Fork AVA.

Long Island's wine roots date back to 1973, when Alec and Louisa Hargrave got the idea that Long Island's North Fork —about a two-hour drive east of New York City — had the ideal climate and soil for vinifera grapes. They founded Long Island's first winery, Hargrave Vineyards. Some believe that Long Island is particularly suited to Merlot, but Chardonnay, Riesling, Cabernet Sauvignon, Cabernet Franc, and Sauvignon Blanc are also grown, plus some Gewürztraminer, Pinot Noir, and numerous other varieties.

Another AVA is Hudson Valley, situated along the Hudson River north of New York City. In the early days (prior to 1960), most wines in the Hudson Valley and in the Finger Lakes were made from indigenous American varieties, such as Concord, as well as French-American hybrid grapes, such as Seyval Blanc. Wines from native American species and from hybrid varieties are still produced in the Hudson Valley, but their popularity is waning. Now most Hudson Valley producers make wines from the classic European grapes, such as Chardonnay.

Who's who in New York

TIP

Most wineries in New York State are small, family-run operations. The following are lists of recommended producers in New York's three major wine regions, mentioned alphabetically.

The Finger Lakes Region	
Anthony Road Wine Company	Knapp Winery
Atwater Estate Vineyards	Lakewood Vineyards
Casa Larga Vineyards	Lamoreaux Landing Wine Cellars
Dr. Frank's Vinifera Wine Cellars (and its affiliate, Chateau Frank, for sparkling wines)	Lucas Vineyards
Fox Run Vineyards	McGregor Vineyard
Glenora Wine Cellars	Prejean Winery
Hazlitt 1852 Vineyards	Ravines Wine Cellars
Hermann J. Wiemer Vineyard	Sheldrake Point Winery

Heron Hill Vineyards	Standing Stone Vineyards
Hosmer Winery	Swedish Hill Vineyard
Hunt Country Vineyards	Wagner Vineyards
Hudson River Valley Region	
Adair Vineyards	Clinton Vineyards
Baldwin Vineyards	Magnanini Winery
Benmarl Vineyards	Millbrook Vineyards
Brotherhood Winery	Rivendell Winery
Cascade Mountain Vineyards	
Long Island Region *(North Fork, Unless Otherwise Noted)*	
Bedell Cellars	Osprey's Dominion
Channing Daughters (Hamptons)	Palmer Vineyards
Corey Creek Vineyards	Paumanok Vineyards
Duck Walk Vineyards (Hamptons)	Peconic Bay Vineyards
Jamesport Vineyards	Pelligrini Vineyards
Laurel Lake Vineyards	Pindar Vineyards
Lenz Winery	Pugliese Vineyards
Lieb Family Cellars	Raphael
Lieb Cellars	Shinn Estate Vineyards
Macari Vineyards	Sparkling Pointe
Martha Clara Vineyards	Wolffer Estate (Hamptons)

Chapter **14**

The Southern Hemisphere Explodes with Wine

Two generations ago, the Northern Hemisphere owned the action in wine: The classic wines of the world came from Europe, and most of the other important wines came from North America. Wines from Southern Hemisphere countries — Chile, Argentina, South Africa, Australia, and New Zealand — enjoyed popularity in their home markets, but the world stage belonged to European wines.

Time has certainly changed that scenario! The rise of the Southern Hemisphere has altered the world of wine profoundly, and the drinking habits of wine lovers will never again be the same. In the future, Malbec from Argentina, Shiraz from Australia, or Sauvignon Blanc from New Zealand might rise further in international popularity or they might fall off a bit, but their place as classic wines is certain.

In this chapter, we explore the wines of Australia, New Zealand, Chile, Argentina, and South Africa.

Australian Wine Power

Australia is one of the world powers of wine. The wine industry of Australia is one of the most technologically advanced, forward-thinking on earth, and some of the most popular wine brands over recent years have been Australian.

Vitis vinifera grapevines first came to Australia in 1788, from South Africa. Historically, most Australian wines were rich and sweet, many of them fortified with alcohol. But today, Australia is famous for its fresh, fruity, flavorful red and white table wines. Australia now ranks fifth in the world in wine production, having slipped past Argentina in 2016 and 2017, and also ranks fifth in exports. Although Australia makes slightly more than half as much wine as the United States, it exports almost twice as much as the U.S. does.

Approximately the same size as the continental United States but with less than 10 percent the population, Australia has almost 2,500 wineries. Many of these wineries are small, family-owned companies, but a handful of mega-companies are responsible for about two-thirds of Australia's wine production. The dramatic sales growth of inexpensive wine brands from these large Australian producers drove the worldwide popularity of Aussie wine for close to two decades. But that success backfired, resulting in overproduction and low profitability. Australia's wine industry has now refocused and is shifting attention to the country's smaller-production wines as well as to its many unique wine regions. This is an exciting time for wine drinkers to explore the depth of what Australia has to offer. You can start investigating Australian wines with the help of the following sections.

Winemaking, grapes, and terroir

Australia's wine regions are mainly in the southern, cooler (but still warm) part of the country, with many of them clustered in the state of Victoria, the southern part of South Australia, the southern part of Western Australia, the cooler parts of New South Wales, and the island of Tasmania. (See Figure 14-1.)

The success of Australia's wines stems from a generally warm, dry climate, which provides winemakers with excellent raw material for their work — although drought can seriously challenge their work. The country's renowned research programs in grape growing and winemaking also contribute greatly by enabling winemakers to stay on the cutting edge of their craft.

Australia's number-one grape for fine wine is Syrah, locally called *Shiraz,* followed by Cabernet Sauvignon and Chardonnay and, at some distance, Merlot, Sauvignon Blanc, Semillon (pronounced *sem*-eh-lon in Australia, as opposed to the French seh-mee-yohn elsewhere in the world), Pinot Noir, and Riesling. The wines are generally labeled with the name of their grape variety, which must constitute at least 85 percent of the wine.

TIP

Shiraz wines are particularly interesting because they come in different styles, from inexpensive, juicy wines brimming with ripe plum and blackberry fruit to serious wines that express specific regional characteristics, such as spice and pepper from cool-climate areas (such as Yarra Valley and the Adelaide Hills) or sweet-fruit ripeness from warmer areas (such as McLaren Vale, Barossa Valley, and Clare Valley).

FIGURE 14-1:
The wine regions of Australia.

Illustration by Lisa S. Reed

The wines of Australia have two distinct faces:

>> Inexpensive varietal wines that sell for under $10 a bottle fed the boom of Australian wines on international markets, but also suffered from the subsequent fall-off in sales. These most inexpensive of Australian wines generally are labeled as coming from *South Eastern Australia,* meaning that the grapes can come from any of three states, a huge territory. Often sporting whimsical labels, they are user-friendly wines that preserve the intense flavors of their grapes and are soft and pleasant to drink young.

>> Higher-priced wines carry more focused regional designations, such as single states (South Australia or Victoria, for example) or even tighter region-specific designations (such as Barossa Valley, Coonawarra, or Yarra Valley). Although these wines are also enjoyable when released, many of them are more serious wines that can age, and that offer a more complex, nuanced style.

TIP

Australia now has more than 100 Geographic Indications (GIs) whose names are becoming more visible on labels of exported wine. Some of the official geographic areas are large zones, but most are specific regions or sub-regions. We mention some of the more famous regions of Australia, state by state, in the following section. If you're interested in finding out about these areas — and the many others that we don't mention — in more detail, consult the Halliday Wine Companion, 2018 by James Halliday, and his *Wine Atlas of Australia* (Hardie Grant Books, 2006).

Australia's wine regions

Australia has five states that are major wine producing territories. In order of importance, they are South Australia, Victoria, New South Wales, Western Australia, and Tasmania. We explore these regions in the following sections.

South Australia

Australia's most important state for wine production is South Australia, whose capital is Adelaide (see Figure 14-1). South Australia makes about half of Australia's wine. While many vineyards in South Australia produce inexpensive wines for the thirsty home market, vineyards closer to Adelaide make wines that are considered among Australia's finest. Its main fine wine regions include the following:

>> **Barossa Valley:** North of Adelaide, this is one of Australia's oldest areas for fine wine; it's a relatively warm area famous especially for its robust Shiraz, Cabernet Sauvignon, and Grenache, as well as rich Semillon and Riesling (grown in the cooler hills). Most of Australia's largest wineries, including Penfolds, are based here.

>> **Clare Valley:** North of the Barossa Valley, this climatically and soil-diverse area makes the country's signature Rieslings in a dry, weighty yet crisp style, as well as fine Shiraz and Cabernet Sauvignon.

>> **Adelaide Hills:** This fairly cool, high-altitude region east of Adelaide is the home to some very good Sauvignon Blanc, Chardonnay, Pinot Noir, and Shiraz.

>> **McLaren Vale:** South of Adelaide and situated on the coast, with a relatively mild climate influenced by the ocean, this region is particularly admired for its red wines such as Shiraz, Cabernet Sauvignon, and, increasingly, Grenache.

>> **Limestone Coast:** This large zone along the southern coast of South Australia is an important area for fine wine, both red and white, thanks to the prevalence of limestone in the soil and the cool maritime climate. Two of the six regions within the Limestone Coast zone are famous in their own right — the warm **Coonawarra** area for some of Australia's best Cabernet Sauvignon wines, and **Padthaway** for its popular Chardonnay, as well as Merlot and Cabernet Sauvignon.

Victoria

Bordering South Australia to the east is Victoria, a smaller state that makes about 25 percent of Australia's wines. Although South Australia is home to most of Australia's largest wineries, Victoria has more wineries than any other Aussie region, most of them small. Victoria's fine wine production ranges from rich, fortified dessert wines to delicate Pinot Noirs. Principal wine regions include the following, from north to south (refer to Figure 14-1):

>> **Murray Darling:** Formerly known as Murray River, this area stretches into New South Wales. This region is particularly important for growing grapes for Australia's good-value wines, but drought has affected its viability.

- **>> Rutherglen:** In the northeast, this long-established, warm climate zone is an outpost of traditional winemaking and home of an exotic Australian specialty, fortified dessert Muscats and Tokays (the latter now renamed in Australia as Topaque) that are world renowned.

- **>> Goulburn Valley:** In the center of the state, Goulburn Valley makes a specialty of white varieties that are best known in France's Rhône Valley, specifically Marsanne, Roussanne, and Viognier.

- **>> Heathcote:** East of Goulburn and due north of Melbourne (the capital of Victoria), this area boasts high altitudes and unusual soils that make distinctive, rich yet elegant Shirazes and also Cabernet.

- **>> Yarra Valley:** In southern Victoria, and close to Melbourne, Yarra Valley boasts a wide diversity of climates due to altitude differences of its vineyards. The Yarra is noted for its Cabernet, Pinot Noir, Shiraz, Chardonnay, and Sauvignon Blanc, as well as its sparkling wines. It is one of Australia's most dynamic winemaking scenes.

- **>> Mornington Peninsula and Geelong:** South of Melbourne and separated from each other by Port Phillip Bay, these two cool, maritime regions specialize in fine Pinot Noir and Chardonnay.

New South Wales

New South Wales, with its capital, Sydney, is Australia's most populous state, and the first to grow vines. High-volume production of everyday wines comes from an interior area called the Riverina. (We get a kick trying to pronounce its alternate name, Murrumbidgee.) Fine wine, for now, comes from three other areas (refer to Figure 14-1):

- **>> Hunter Valley:** A historic grape-growing area that begins 80 miles north of Sydney. The Lower Hunter, with a warm, damp climate and heavy soils, produces long-lived Semillon as its best wine. The Upper Hunter is a drier area farther from the coast. Shiraz, Cabernet Sauvignon, and Merlot thrive here.

- **>> Mudgee:** An interior area near the mountains. Mudgee specializes in reds such as Merlot and Cabernet Sauvignon but also makes Chardonnay.

- **>> Orange:** A cool, high-altitude area making distinctive white wines and also very good reds.

Western Australia

Western Australia, the largest state in area, has the country's most isolated wine zones, in its southwest corner. It grows only two percent of the country's wine grapes, but wine quality is very high. The warm, dry Swan Valley is the state's historic center of wine production, but two cool to moderate climate regions have become more important (refer to Figure 14-1):

>> **Margaret River:** This is a fairly temperate region near the Indian Ocean. Among the wines that various wineries here excel in are Sauvignon Blanc–Semillon blends (especially Cape Mentelle), Chardonnay (especially Leeuwin Estate), and Cabernet Sauvignon (from Mosswood, Voyager, Cape Mentelle, and Howard Park).

>> **Great Southern:** Cooler than Margaret River, Great Southern's specialty is crisp, age-worthy Riesling — a favorite of ours. This huge, diverse region also produces intense, aromatic Cabernet Sauvignon as well as fine cool-climate Shiraz and Chardonnay; on the southern coast, Pinot Noir is successful. Definitely worth a visit.

Tasmania

Tasmania, an island south of Victoria (refer to Figure 14-1), has cool microclimates in both its northern and southern sections. Producers are increasingly proving what potential exists for delicate Pinot Noirs, Chardonnays, and sparkling wines. Two of the better-known producers are Pipers Brook and Pirie.

The Rise of New Zealand

The history of fine winemaking in New Zealand is relatively short, having been hampered by conservative attitudes toward alcohol. In the 1980s, New Zealand finally began capitalizing on its maritime climate, ideal for producing high-quality wines, and started planting grapes in earnest. Today, it makes about one-quarter of the wine of its nearest neighbor, Australia. Unlike Australia, New Zealand has managed to maintain an elite image for its wines from the start, as opposed to a good-value-for-everyday image, which enables New Zealand wine producers to obtain sustainable prices for their wines. Up to 86 percent of New Zealand's wines are exported.

Four large producers dominate New Zealand's wine production: Montana (sold in the United States under the Brancott label, to avoid confusion with the state of Montana), Corbans, Villa Maria, and Nobilo. But in the past 25 years, numerous small, boutique wineries have sprung up, especially on the South Island. At last count, New Zealand's wineries numbered more than 840.

In the following sections, find out more about the world of wine in New Zealand.

Kiwi geography

New Zealanders are nicknamed "Kiwis," because for a long time their country led the world in kiwi production. (Italy is now the largest producer, followed by New Zealand.) Situated farther south than Australia, New Zealand is, in general, cooler. Of New Zealand's two large islands, the North Island is the warmer. Red grapes grow around the capital city, Auckland, in the north and around Hawke's Bay farther south on the North Island (especially known for its Cabernet Sauvignon, grown on gravelly soil). Chardonnay and Sauvignon Blanc are the North Island's main white varieties. Martinborough, a cooler district at the southern end of North Island, makes excellent Pinot Noir.

On the South Island, Marlborough — the country's largest and commercially most important wine region — is New Zealand's largest production zone especially for Sauvignon Blanc, and also for Chardonnay. The interior, hilly Central Otago zone is famous for its Chardonnay and Pinot Noir.

Sauvignon Blanc, Pinot Noir lead the way

The Sauvignon Blanc grape as of 2016 comprises 72 percent of all wine production in New Zealand. The first New Zealand Sauvignon Blancs to be exported were generally unoaked wines with pronounced flavor, rich texture, and high acidity. They were so distinctive — pungent, herbaceous, with intense flavors suggestive of asparagus, lime, or cut grass — that New Zealand became recognized almost overnight in the late 1980s for a new prototype of Sauvignon Blanc. This style of New Zealand Sauvignon Blanc is still very popular worldwide, although they are a bit less intense in aroma lately. These are the least expensive Kiwi Sauvignon Blancs, retailing for $9 to $19, with many priced around $15 to $16.

Another style of New Zealand Sauvignon Blanc involves the use of oak barrels and/or blending with Semillon. Riper, less assertive, and softer in texture, these wines have fruitier flavors, usually passion fruit or ripe grapefruit. New Zealand wine producers correctly foresaw that wine drinkers could want an alternative to the herbaceous style. The riper, fruitier, less herbaceous New Zealand Sauvignon Blancs are frequently labeled as *Reserve* wines or as single-vineyard wines. They generally retail for $20 to $30.

Pinot Noir is increasingly significant in New Zealand — and New Zealand is increasingly significant in the world of Pinot Noir. In fact, this grape now ranks second only to Sauvignon Blanc in volume of wine produced. In addition to its stronghold in Martinborough, on the North Island, Pinot Noir now grows throughout the South Island. Many wine producers in Marlborough make Pinot Noir in addition to Sauvignon Blanc. And the small, inland Central Otago wine zone, farther south on the South Island, has emerged as one of the world's key Pinot Noir regions.

WORTH THE SEARCH

Central Otago is the world's most southerly major wine region. Vines are planted on hillsides for more sunshine and less frost risk. The low-yielding vines here produce highly concentrated Pinot Noir wines. Mt. Difficulty and Felton Road, both from Central Otago, are currently two of New Zealand's best Pinot Noir producers.

New Zealand Pinot Noirs vary in taste from region to region; the wines of Martinborough, for example, are a bit more savory and minerally than those of Marlborough, which tend to be soft and fruity, while the wines of Central Otago tend to have more weight and concentrated fruit character.

Chile's Rapid Rise to Wine Fame

The Spanish first established vineyards in Chile in the mid-16th century, and the country has maintained a thriving wine industry for its home market for several centuries. But the modern story of Chilean wine is barely 40 years old. Starting in the mid-1980s, Chile's wine industry has developed rapidly through focusing on export markets and through embracing classic French grape varieties such as Cabernet Sauvignon, Merlot, and Chardonnay — with an almost-forgotten red Bordeaux variety called Carménère definitely in the running, on the outside post position. Not a very large country, Chile is now the ninth-largest wine-producing country in the world.

With the Pacific Ocean to its west and the Andes Mountains to the east — not to mention the Atacama Desert to the north and the ice glaciers of Patagonia to the south — Chile is an isolated country. This isolation has its advantages in terms of grape growing: The phylloxera louse hasn't yet taken a strong hold in Chile — as it's done in just about every other winemaking country — and *vinifera* vines can, therefore, grow on their own roots, although some producers plant vines grafted onto American rootstocks, as a precaution. (For an explanation of phylloxera, see Chapter 3.) Chile's other viticultural blessings include the ocean's general tempering influence on a relatively hot climate; a range of low mountains along the coast, which blocks the ocean dampness from most vineyards; cool night air from the Andes to moderate temperatures in the interior hills; and many mineral-rich soils.

TECHNICAL
STUFF

Red grape varieties represent the lion's share of Chile's production, with Cabernet Sauvignon accounting for more than 30 percent of all grapes. Merlot and Carménère, Chile's signature red, together account for another 16 percent. Syrah also now figures prominently in Chile's red grape picture, moving close to Carménère in production, and Pinot Noir is also on the rise. Among white varieties, Sauvignon Blanc is the most significant, followed by Chardonnay, and together these two varieties dominate the white wine scene.

The following sections describe Chile's wine regions and specific wines in more detail.

Chile's wine regions

As in every other country, wine producers in Chile originally planted vineyards in the most obvious locations, places where vines would grow prolifically and were close to commercial centers. With experience, they have discovered the less obvious locations that enable the production of truly distinctive wines. Grape growing has expanded beyond the heart of the country's Central Valley into outlying areas closer to the Pacific coast, farther north toward the desert, and up slopes in the foothills of the Andes. As a result, a wider range of wine styles has emerged, including fresher, crisper whites and more powerful reds.

Maipo Valley was initially considered the ideal place to plant grapes, and it's still the source of excellent wines. It surrounds Santiago, which is Chile's capital and its largest and only important city. Maipo Valley marks the northern part of Chile's vast Central Valley, which lies between the coastal range and the Andes. Despite expansion into outlying areas, most of Chile's vineyards are still in the Central Valley.

TECHNICAL
STUFF

In 2012, Chile adopted a new *Denominación de Origen* (DO) system for identifying vineyard areas. This new system divides the vineyards into six broad regions, three of which are relevant today. Each region contains several sub-regions whose names appear on wine labels, and some sub-regions have specific zones within them. The new classification further distinguishes the location relative to the coast, with three zones: *Costa* areas (coastal), *Entre Cordilleras* areas (between the coastal mountains and the Andes), and *Andes* areas (interior, in the hills of the Andes). Costa and Andes areas are those that benefit the most from cooling climate influences.

From north to south, here's a summary of Chile's wine regions and sub-regions today:

>> **Coquimbo Region:**

- **Elqui Valley:** Close to the Atacama Desert, which covers much of northern Chile, this coastal valley runs east to west. The climate of this tiny, fairly undeveloped sub-region is cool and damp near the ocean and much warmer inland, where skies are so clear that major astronomical research facilities are situated here. For the past decade, the pioneering Falernia winery has been making impressive Syrah wines from this area.

- **Limarí Valley:** A small, semi-arid territory about 250 miles northwest of Santiago. Proximity to the Pacific brings cool morning fog and ocean breezes that blow through the Valley during the day. Parts of this sub-region are classified as *Entre Cordilleras* but mainly it is coastal. Chile's three largest wineries, Concha y Toro, San Pedro, and Santa Rita, all own land in Limarí. Promising wines so far are Sauvignon Blanc, Chardonnay, and Syrah. This is one of the country's "hot" emerging regions.

>> **Aconcagua Region:**

- **Aconcagua Valley:** North of Santiago, the dramatic Aconcagua Valley is named for the continent's highest mountain, Mount Aconcagua, and is one of the warmest areas for fine grapes. But Aconcagua also includes many cooler high-altitude sections, and in fact has vineyards in all three east-west zones. Cabernet Sauvignon grows especially well here, and more recently, Syrah. A new development is fine white wine from vineyards planted in Aconcagua Costa. Viña Errázuriz is Aconcagua Valley's most important winery.

- **Casablanca Valley:** This sub-region was the first of Chile's newer coastal wine regions. Some of Chile's finest Chardonnays and Sauvignon Blancs grow in one part of Casablanca, while good Merlots and Pinot Noirs come from a higher-altitude part. Veramonte is Casablanca's best-known winery; Casas del Bosque and Loma Larga are two other noteworthy wineries. Many wineries elsewhere in Chile own vineyards in this region or buy grapes from here, and they turn to this area particularly for Chardonnay.

- **San Antonio Valley and Leyda Valley:** These two coastal areas (technically Leyda is part of San Antonio, but you can find it mentioned in its own right on wine labels) are south of Casablanca Valley and are exciting new wine zones. The maritime influence produces impressive Sauvignon Blancs and Chardonnays in Leyda, while Pinot Noir and Syrah are growing especially well on the cool, steep slopes. Now making one of the world's better Pinot Noirs outside of Burgundy and perhaps even a better Syrah, Viña Matetic is a winery to watch in San Antonio Valley. Viña Leyda and Garces Silva are standouts in Leyda.

» **Central Valley Region:**

- **Maipo Valley:** Chile's most established wine zone, almost surrounding Santiago, Maipo Valley is home to most of the country's famous wineries. Concha y Toro, Santa Rita, Carmen, Almaviva, and Viñedos Chadwick are a few of Maipo's premium producers. Cabernet Sauvignon is king in this region, and Merlot also does very well. Some vineyards in Maipo Valley are classified as Andes area, but mainly they are *Entre Cordilleras* areas.

- **Rapel Valley:** The large Rapel Valley, south of Maipo Valley, has two wine *zones*, Cachapoal Valley and Colchagua Valley.

  Cachapoal Valley, nearer the Andes, is a red wine area whose soil and climate vary according to proximity to the mountains. Cabernet Sauvignon is particularly significant here, followed by Merlot and Carménère. Morandé and Altair are two rising star wineries here.

  Colchagua Valley is very diverse because it features vineyards on the slopes of the Andes and all the way westward toward the sea. Cabernet Sauvignon, Merlot, Carménère, and Syrah grow especially well here, and the region abounds with well-known wineries. Colchagua's leading wineries include Casa Lapostolle, Montes, Mont Gras, Casa Silva, and Emiliana.

- **Curicó Valley:** One of Chile's oldest and largest wine areas, the Curicó Valley is directly south of Rapel Valley. Because of its diverse microclimates, both red and white varieties grow well here. The huge San Pedro Winery and Viña Miguel Torres are located in Curicó.

» **Maule Valley:** Maule Valley is Chile's largest wine sub-region in area, and also the southernmost of the major zones. Because it's so huge, it has many diverse microclimates, and both red and white varieties grow well, especially Sauvignon Blanc, Cabernet Sauvignon, and Merlot. Two wineries making very good wine here are O. Fournier and J. Bouchon.

The face and taste of Chilean wines

Before Chilean wineries began making wines from grapes grown in the country's cooler regions, the style of Chilean wines was a bit easier to generalize: The wines could be described as generally lacking the exuberant fruitiness of Californian and Australian wines, yet not quite so subtle and understated as European wines. That generalization is still applicable to many of Chile's red wines, especially from the Central Valley sub-regions, but you can now find many an exuberantly fruity Sauvignon Blanc or Pinot Noir from cooler coastal regions and fruity, vibrant Syrah from cooler, Andes-influenced zones.

Chile's Sauvignon Blanc wines are generally unoaked, while most of the Chardonnays are oaked. Red wines vary from simple everyday styles to elite, age-worthy wines.

Chile's wines are usually named for their grape varieties. The reasonable prices of the basic wines — mainly from $10 to $15 in the United States — make these wines excellent values. The wineries whose wines are easiest to find in export markets include, in alphabetical order, Calina, Caliterra, Carmen, Casa Lapostolle, Concha y Toro, Cousiño Macul, Errázuriz, Los Vascos, Mont Gras, Montes, Santa Carolina, Santa Rita, and Undurraga.

Many wineries produce multiple tiers of wine that rise in price (and ideally, in quality) from a basic line to a higher-level line and ultimately what the wineries call their *icon wine,* a super-premium wine, usually a red. Ironically, many of the basic-level reds are labeled as *Reserve* wines (a regulated term but with a rather broad application).

The super-premium reds tend to be in the $60 to $100 price range. These elite Chilean wines are often blends rather than varietal wines, and many are styled along international lines — made from very ripe grapes that give rich, fruity flavors and high (14 percent or higher) alcohol levels and aged in small French oak barrels. What some elite Chilean wines have lacked is a sense of place: They don't taste particularly Chilean. But as the wineries push the envelope of growing regions into the hilly foothills of the mountains and increasingly focus on soil types, Chile increasingly produces fine wines that signal their origins and merit their high prices.

Keep an eye out for some of Chile's top super-premium red wines:

>> Concha y Toro's Don Melchor Cabernet Sauvignon ($85 to $110)

>> Errázuriz's Don Maximiano Founder's Reserve (mainly Cabernet Sauvignon, about $85)

>> Montes Alpha M (a "Bordeaux blend," about $75)

>> Viña Almaviva (a sleek and subtle red, mainly Cabernet Sauvignon with Carménère and Cabernet Franc, $115 to $135)

>> Santa Rita's Casa Real Cabernet Sauvignon, one of Chile's pioneering elite wines (about $75)

>> Casa Lapostolle's Clos Apalta (a blend of Carménère, Merlot, and Cabernet Sauvignon, $85 to $110)

>> Seña, from an estate in Aconcagua that was originally a partnership between the Robert Mondavi and Eduardo Chadwick (of Viña Errázuriz) families and is now owned by the Chadwicks (Cabernet Sauvignon, Merlot, and Carménère, $135)

For us, a particularly good value among Chile's super-premium wines is Casa Lapostolle's Clos Apalta.

Argentina, a Major League Player

Argentina boasts the largest wine production in South America and ranks sixth in the world among wine-producing countries, having been surpassed recently by Australia. Argentina is also a major wine consuming country; only in the last 30 years have producers looked beyond their own borders to develop a strong export trade. Now, Argentine wines have become so popular in North America and Europe that we would have to describe Argentina's ascendancy as meteoric. Not only is Argentina now a major player in the world wine market, but it's also one of the world's most exciting countries for wine production.

Wine grapes have grown in Argentina since the mid-16th century, as they have in Chile (we talk about Chile earlier in this chapter). Argentina's source of vines was more diverse, however; for example, many vines came to Argentina with the vast numbers of Italian and Basque immigrants. As a result, Argentina boasts grape varieties, such as Bonarda and Malbec, which are not important in Chile.

The following sections describe Argentina's wine regions, grapes, and wines in more detail.

Regions and grapes

Argentina's traditional wine regions are situated in the western part of the country, where the Andes Mountains divide Argentina from Chile, but eastern regions are emerging, including some coastal zones. In the west, high altitude tempers the climate. Nevertheless, most of the vineyards are still very warm by day, quite cool by night, and dessert dry. Rivers flowing down from the Andes are the source of water for irrigation.

The vast majority of Argentina's vineyards are in the western province of Mendoza, which lies at roughly the same latitude as Santiago, Chile. Within the Mendoza region are various wine districts (the names of which sometimes appear on wine labels) such as Luján de Cuyo, Maipú, Tupungato, Uco Valley, and San

Raphael. Most of Argentina's oldest wineries and their vineyards are clustered close to Mendoza city, but Uco Valley, in the southern part of the province and close to the Andes, has attracted many newcomers as well as several established wineries that have relocated there.

The province of San Juan, just north of Mendoza and considerably hotter, is Argentina's second-largest wine province. La Rioja province, Argentina's oldest wine-producing region, is east of San Juan, while the mountainous Salta province sits at the extreme northwest of the country.

Salta is particularly famous for Torrontés, a variety that's Argentina's signature white grape. Actually, as many as three different types of Torrontes grow in Argentina, in various regions; the best grape is Torrontes Riojano, and some wine labels might specify this name.

REAL DEAL

Torrontes is generally an inexpensive ($10 to $15), light-bodied, high-acid, aromatic white wine that's especially fine with appetizers, seafood, and fish. But some distinguished Torrontes wines also exist. Salta's sub-region, Cafayate, which has many vineyards growing at altitudes over 5,000 feet, has emerged as a prime area for this grape. The Torrontés wines from these vineyards have bracing acidity and are gaining a reputation as Argentina's best Torrontés. It's not a stretch to say that Torrontés could be the new "hot" white wine coming from South America.

One of Argentina's newest wine areas is in the southerly Patagonia region, including the provinces of Rio Negro and, farther west, Neuquén. This remote part of the country is slowly emerging as a favorable area for Pinot Noir, Chardonnay, and sparkling wines. So far, Patagonia's sparkling wines are doing particularly well and are arguably among the best bubblies in all of South America.

Argentina's red wines are generally more interesting than its whites and far more numerous. For red wines, the once little-known Malbec grape variety — now seldom used in Bordeaux, where it originated — has emerged as Argentina's flagship variety. Malbec has adapted extremely well to the Mendoza region, and winemakers are discovering the nuances its wines develop when the grape grows in the region's various subzones. Argentine Cabernet Sauvignon has its fans, but the fact remains that Malbec is Argentina's signature wine.

Apart from Torrontés, most of the white wines are Chardonnay and Sauvignon Blanc. Red wines include Malbec, Cabernet Sauvignon, Bonarda (which actually exceeds Cabernet in plantings but is less evident among exports), and several Italian varieties, such as Barbera, Dolcetto, and Sangiovese, which also are uncommon in exported wines.

MALBEC'S BIG MOVE

At one point in the 19th century, the Malbec grape variety was a major player in France's Bordeaux region. Then natural disasters all but wiped out Malbec there. The first of these was the phylloxera affliction in the late 19th century. (See Chapter 3 for an explanation of phylloxera.) When replanting the vineyards, many producers planted less Malbec because Bordeaux's cool, maritime climate doesn't always provide the amount of sun and warmth that Malbec needs to ripen fully. Malbec is also prone to vine diseases and is vulnerable to frost. The second natural disaster, the catastropic 1956 frost in Bordeaux, wiped out 75 percent of the Malbec crop. Very few Bordeaux producers bothered to replant Malbec after that. (Ironically, a similar fate happened to Bordeaux's Carménère variety, which ripens too late for Bordeaux's climate; Carménère found a new home in Argentina's next-door neighbor, Chile.) In France, Malbec is still the important grape variety in the Cahors region in southwestern France, where it makes dark-colored, tannic wines.

Meanwhile, Malbec has been flourishing in Argentina's Mendoza region, where a French agronomist introduced it in the mid-19th century. Today, more Malbec grows in Mendoza than any other wine region in the worldy. Mendoza's warm, dry climate is perfect for Malbec, and the grape does particularly well in districts such as Luján de Cuyo and the Uco Valley, in the foothills of the Andes, where vineyards are situated as high as 5,000 feet in altitude. Malbec makes dark, fruity wines in Argentina that are less tannic than the Malbec wines in Cahors, France, and more immediately drinkable.

Names to know

Thanks in part to its high altitudes and sunny days, Argentina's natural resources for grape growing are among the strongest in the world. Foreign investment continues to bring the capital and the winemaking know–how to make the most of these natural resources.

>> Bodega Norton, a winery that was purchased by Austrian crystal producer Swarovski in 1989, makes distinctive wines in Mendoza.

>> Moët & Chandon, a French immigrant since 1999, is Argentina's largest sparkling wine producer and makes varietal wines from its Terrazas de los Andes winery.

>> Bordeaux's elite Cheval Blanc winery partnered with Terrazas de Los Andes in 1999 to create Argentina's iconic Cheval des Andes, a blend of Malbec, Cabernet Sauvignon, and Petit Verdot.

>> A Dutchman owns the state-of-the-art Bodegas Salentein winery and its sister winery, Finca El Portillo.

» Bordeaux's Lurton family owns Bodega J. & F. Lurton.

» In 2002, Bordeaux enologist Michel Rolland created Clos de los Siete, an enclave of wineries in the Uco Valley, most of which are owned by Bordeaux families, including Rolland himself. (He also makes a collective red wine from the group of wineries called Clos de Los Siete, a very refined wine, for about $19.)

TIP

On the homegrown front, Catena Zapata is a true leader among Argentina's top wine producers. Besides creating the Catena Institute of Wine, a research center, Catena has developed the exceptional Adrianna vineyard at extreme altitude to grow Malbec and Chardonnay at an unprecedented quality level. Catena's Cabernet Sauvignon, Malbec, and Chardonnay ($18 to $20) are the winery's basic labels, while the super-premium Catena Alta line, priced about $44, covers higher-end wines, among the finest being made in South America today. The Adrianna Vineyard wines sell for $125. Catena's affiliated winery, Alamos, makes a Malbec that, at $9 a bottle, is one of the greatest wine values around.

REAL DEAL

Trapiche is Argentina's leading export brand, and its wines offer very good quality with amazing value at the lower price points. Trapiche's Oak Cask Cabernet Sauvignon and Oak Cask Malbec, for example, are each $9 to $10.

TIP

Argentine producers we recommend include, in alphabetical order, Achaval Ferrer, Alamos, Bodega J. & F. Lurton, Bodega Norton, Bodega Weinert, Bodegas Salentein, Catena Zapata, Cheval des Andes, Clos de Los Siete, DiamAndes, Doña Paula, El Portillo, Etchart, Finca Sophenia, Las Terrazas, Mendel, Navarro Correas, Riccitelli, Rutini, Santa Julia, Susanna Balbo, Trapiche, Valentín Bianchi, and Zuccardi. Some of Argentina's basic wines are priced in the $8 to $12 range, but you can expect to pay closer to $20 for the better wines. Elite wines such as Cheval des Andes sell for $80 and up.

The South African Wine Safari

Vines came to South Africa in the 1650s with the Dutch, the first European settlers; in the same period, French Huguenots (Protestants) escaping religious persecution brought winemaking expertise. At the end of the 18th century, South Africa was producing a luscious fortified wine called Constantia, which became sought after in European royal courts. The country began focusing seriously on table wine production only in the 1980s, however. Today, South Africa ranks eighth in the world in wine production.

Most of South Africa's wines come from the Western Cape, in the southwestern part of the country. The Western Cape encompasses several wine regions, the most important of which is the Coastal Region, around the Cape of Good Hope. Traditionally, large firms dominated South Africa's wine industry, and they con-tinue to do so. KWV, formerly a wine growers' cooperative, is one of the country's largest wineries. South Africa's largest wine company, the gigantic Distell firm, produces and markets wines from numerous wineries that it owns. Increasingly, however, small producers are emerging, many of whom make exciting wines.

You can find out more about South Africa's regions and wines in the following sections.

South Africa's principal wine regions

South Africa has some vineyard areas with cool microclimates, especially around the southern coast, near the Cape of Good Hope (most of its vineyards are within 32 miles of the ocean) and in higher altitudes, but the climate in its wine regions is otherwise warm and dry. Almost all the country's vineyards are within 90 miles of Cape Town, the country's most fascinating and picturesque city.

TECHNICAL STUFF

South Africa's Wine of Origin legislation in 1973 created wine zones of various sizes. The largest is a Geographical Unit, such as Western Cape; when such a name appears on a label, it can indicate that grapes from various regions were blended together. *Regions* are the next category, followed by Districts, and then the most specific area, a Ward.

Following are four major Districts in the Coastal Region area:

>> **Stellenbosch:** East of Cape Town; the most important wine district in quantity and quality, especially for fine red wines.

>> **Paarl:** North of Stellenbosch, with warmer days and cool nights; home of the famous, beautiful Nederburg Estate; the second-most important wine district.

>> **Franschhoek Valley:** Southeast of Paarl, this district is surrounded on three sides by mountains; many innovative winemakers and culinary attractions are here.

>> **Swartland:** This large district north of Cape Town has evolved in recent years from an area known for inexpensive wines to an exciting center of innovative, high-quality winemaking by small producers; Syrah and old-vine Chenin Blanc are particularly important.

Not a District but a free-standing Ward, Constantia is the oldest wine-producing area in the country, located south of Cape Town and cooled by ocean breezes.

The small, cool Walker Bay district is part of the Cape South Coast region. Bordering the Indian Ocean, it is a key area for production of Pinot Noir and Chardonnay, led by the innovative Hamilton Russell Winery. Another district, Elgin, is on the coast between Stellenbosch and Walker Bay; a cool plateau area, Elgin is known for its intensely flavored Sauvignon Blancs and for Pinot Noirs.

Three other districts of note are Darling, north of Cape Town, in the Coastal Region; Robertson, in the more interior Breede Valley Region; and Worcester, in that same region.

TECHNICAL STUFF

Varietal wines in South Africa must contain at least 75 percent of the named grape variety; exported wines (complying with the stricter European Union regulations) must contain 85 percent of the named variety. About 35 percent of South Africa's wines qualify as Wine of Origin (WO). WO wines must be made 100 percent from grapes of the designated area on the label. Wine of Origin regulations are based on the French *Appellation Contrôlée* laws (see Chapter 10), and they strictly designate vineyards, allowable grape varieties, vintage-dating, and so on.

Steen, Pinotage, and company

The most-planted grape variety in South Africa is Chenin Blanc, sometimes locally called *Steen.* This versatile grape primarily makes medium-dry to medium-sweet wines but also dry wines, sparkling wines, and late-harvest botrytis wines. It is South Africa's signature white variety and is gaining in renown for wines made from old vines.

Cabernet Sauvignon, Merlot, Shiraz, and Pinot Noir have become increasingly important red varieties, while Sauvignon Blanc and Chardonnay are popular white varieties. Cabernet Sauvignon and Sauvignon Blanc do particularly well in South Africa's climate. (Producers here make a very assertive version of Sauvignon Blanc.)

And then you have Pinotage. Uniquely South African, Pinotage is a grape born as a crossing between Pinot Noir and Cinsaut (the same grape as Cinsault, the Rhône

CHAPTER 14 **The Southern Hemisphere Explodes with Wine** 279 variety) back in 1925. However, Pinotage didn't appear as a wine until 1959. Pinotage wine combines the cherry fruit of Pinot Noir with the earthiness of a Rhône wine. It can be a truly delicious, light- to medium-bodied red wine that makes for easy drinking, or it can be a more powerful red. Although many good Pinotage wines sell for $9 to $20, the best Pinotages cost more. Kanonkop Estate, a specialist in this variety, makes classic Pinotages in the $35 to $40 range. Simonsig Estate makes a fine Pinotage for $16 to $18.

While Pinotage is a pleasant wine, certainly worth trying, we believe South Africa's future is with Cabernet Sauvignon, Merlot, and Shiraz (and blends of these grapes) for its red wines and Sauvignon Blanc and Chardonnay for its whites, along with high-end Chenin Blanc.

SOUTH AFRICA: THE FUTURE

Chenin Blanc and Pinotage represent South Africa's recent past. Cabernet Sauvignon, Merlot, and Chardonnay are its present and are definitely making fine wines now. But Sauvignon Blanc and Shiraz seem to hold the most promise for the future.

- Sauvignon Blanc is a no-brainer; some of the world's best Sauvignon Blanc varietal wines are already being made here. The flavorful character of Sauvignon Blanc asserts itself in South Africa, especially in Constantia and in a new cool-climate ward, Elim, in the Cape Agulhas district. Although South African Sauvignon Blancs resemble those from New Zealand to some extent, they are easier to drink and not quite as assertive as some from New Zealand.

- Shiraz has become the hot, new variety of the Southern Hemisphere and indeed throughout the world. What South African winemakers love about Shiraz is its versatility: It can grow well in cool and in warm climates. Right now, Shiraz is the fastest-growing variety being planted in South Africa. In ten years or less, it may be the country's biggest-selling varietal wine.

5

Wine's Exotic Face

Discover the joy that is real Champagne, but also learn the charms of other sparkling wines from all over the world.

Go far beyond Pinot Grigio and Cabernet Sauvignon and discover the exciting world of fortified and dessert wines.

IN THIS CHAPTER

» **All "champagne" is not Champagne**

» **When *extra dry* means "not all that dry"**

» **The lowdown on how Champagne is made**

» **Sparkling wines from $8 to $300-plus**

» **Marrying bubblies with food**

Chapter **15**

Champagne and Other Sparklers

I n the universe of wine, sparkling wines are a solar system unto themselves. They're produced in just about every country that makes wine, and they come in a wide range of tastes, quality levels, and prices. Champagne, the sparkling wine from the Champagne region of France, is the brightest star in the sky, but by no means the only one.

Sparkling wines are distinguished (and distinguishable) from other wines by the presence of bubbles — *carbon dioxide* — in the wine. In the eyes of most governments, these bubbles must be a natural byproduct of fermentation in order for a wine to be officially considered a sparkling wine.

In many wine regions, sparkling wines are just a sideline to complement the region's table wine production, but in some places, sparkling wines are the main business. At the top of that list is France's Champagne region (where sparkling wine was — if not invented — made famous). Italy's Prosecco and Asti wine zones are other important regions as are France's Loire Valley, northeastern Spain, and parts of California.

All That Sparkles Is Not Champagne

Champagne, the sparkling wine of Champagne, France, is the gold standard of sparkling wines for a number of reasons:

>> Champagne is the most famous sparkling wine in the world; the name has immediate recognition with everyone, not just wine drinkers.

>> A particular technique for making sparkling wine was perfected in the Champagne region.

>> Champagne is not only the finest sparkling wine in the world but also among the finest wines of any type in the world.

WARNING

Within the European Union, only the wines of the Champagne region in France can use the name *Champagne.* In some other places, the name *champagne* can appear on labels of all sorts of sparkling wines that don't come from the Champagne region and that don't taste like Champagne. Wineries call their bubbly wines *champagne* to make the wines more marketable. Despite tighter regulations regarding the use of the term, some wineries in the United States may still use *champagne* on their labels. Many wine drinkers also use the word *champagne* indiscriminately to refer to all wines that have bubbles.

(Interestingly, the recent success of the Italian sparkling wine, Prosecco, has caused the same generic usage to occur with that wine name. Bartenders and servers, especially in northern Italy, are starting to call all sparkling wines *prosecco*, regardless of their origin.)

Ironically, much of the sparkling wine sold in the United States that's called champagne is not even made with the same techniques as true Champagne. Most imitation champagnes are made by a process that takes only a few months from beginning to end (compared to a few years to make Champagne), is less costly, and works more effectively on an industrial scale.

THE COOL RULE

Many sparkling wine regions are very cool areas, where grapes generally don't ripen sufficiently for *still* (non-sparkling) wine production. Vinified normally, the wines of these regions would be extremely high in acid, disagreeably tart, and very thin; the reds would lack color. But the elaborate process of sparkling wine production (the *traditional method* of production as practiced in the Champagne region, described later in this chapter) turns the climate's deficits into virtues and transforms the ugly-duckling grapes into graceful swans.

REMEMBER

Whenever we use the word *Champagne* (with a capital *C*), we are referring to true Champagne, from the region of the same name; we use the generic term *sparkling wine* to refer to bubbly wines collectively, and sparkling wines other than Champagne.

Sparkling Wine Styles

All sparkling wines have bubbles, and nearly all of them are either white or pink (less common than white). That's about as far as broad generalizations take us in describing sparkling wines.

Some sparkling wines are downright sweet, some are bone-dry, and many fall somewhere in the middle, from medium-dry to medium-sweet. Some have toasty, nutty flavors, and some are fruity; among those that are fruity, some are just non-descriptly grapey, while others have delicate nuances of lemons, apples, cherries, berries, peaches, or other fruits.

TIP

The sparkling wines of the world fall into two broad styles, according to how they're made, and how they taste as a result:

>> Wines that express the character of their grapes; these wines tend to be fruity and straightforward, without significant layers of complexity.

>> Wines that express complexity and flavors (yeasty, biscuity, caramel-like, honeyed) that derive from winemaking and aging, instead of expressing overt fruitiness.

The sweetness factor

Nearly all sparkling wines are (technically) not completely dry, because they contain small amounts of sugar, usually as the result of sweetening added at the last stage of production. But all sparkling wines don't necessarily taste sweet. The perception of sweetness depends on two factors: the actual amount of sweetness in the wine (this varies according to the wine's style) and the wine's balance between acidity and sweetness.

TECHNICAL STUFF

Here's how the balance factor operates. Sparkling wines are usually very high in acidity, because the grapes grew in a cool climate and therefore are not very ripe at harvest. The wine's carbon dioxide accentuates the acidic impression in the mouth. But the wine's sweetness counterbalances its acidity and vice versa. Depending on the actual amount of sugar and the particular acid/sugar balance a sparkling wine strikes, the wine may taste dry, very slightly sweet, medium sweet, or quite sweet.

Champagne itself is made in a range of sweetness levels, the most common of which is a dry style called *brut* (see the section "Sweetness categories," later in this chapter). Other sparkling wines made by the *traditional method* used in Champagne (see "How Sparkling Wine Happens," later in this chapter) are made in similar sweetness ranges.

TIP

Inexpensive sparkling wines tend to be medium-sweet in order to appeal to the many wine drinkers who enjoy some sweetness in their wines. Sweetness can often mask imperfections that would be more noticeable otherwise.

The quality factor

REMEMBER

When you taste a sparkling wine, the most important consideration is whether you like it — just as for a still wine. If you want to evaluate a sparkling wine the way professionals do, however, you have to apply a few criteria, such as the following, that don't apply to still wines (or are less critical in still wines than in sparkling wines):

>> **The appearance of the bubbles:** In the best sparkling wines, the bubbles are tiny and float upward in a continuous stream from the bottom of your glass. If the bubbles are large and random, you have a clue that the wine is a lesser-quality sparkler. If you don't see many bubbles at all, you could have a bad bottle, a poor or smudged glass, or a wine that may be too old. Tiny variations in glassware can drastically affect the flow of bubbles. If the wine in your glass looks almost flat, but another glass of wine from the same bottle is lively with bubbles, blame the glass and not the wine. (In this case, you should be able to *taste* the bubbles, that is, to feel them on your tongue, even if you can't *see* many of them.) See Chapter 8 for our recommendations about glasses for Champagne and other sparkling wines.

>> **The feel of the bubbles in your mouth:** The finer the wine, the less aggressive the bubbles feel in your mouth. (If the bubbles remind you of a soft drink, we hope you didn't pay more than $8 for the bottle.)

>> **The balance between sweetness and acidity:** Even if a bubbly wine is too sweet or too dry for your taste, to evaluate its quality you should consider its sweetness/acid ratio and decide whether these two elements seem reasonably balanced.

>> **The texture:** Traditional-method sparkling wines should be somewhat creamy in texture as a result of their extended lees aging. (See the next section for an explanation of *traditional method* and *lees.*)

>> **The finish:** Any impression of bitterness on the finish of a sparkling wine is a sign of low quality.

How Sparkling Wine Happens

**TECHNICAL
STUFF**

For all wines, when yeasts convert sugar into alcohol, carbon dioxide (CO_2) is a natural byproduct. If fermentation takes place in a closed container, the carbon dioxide cannot escape into the air. With nowhere else to go, the carbon dioxide becomes trapped in the wine in the form of bubbles.

Most sparkling wines actually go through *two* fermentations: one to turn the grape juice into still wine without bubbles (called a *base wine*) and a subsequent one (conveniently called the *second fermentation*) to turn the base wine into bubbly wine. The winemaker has to instigate the second fermentation by adding yeasts and sugar to the base wine. The added yeasts convert the added sugar into alcohol and CO_2 bubbles.

TIP

Beginning with the second fermentation, the longer and slower the winemaking process, the more complex and expensive the sparkling wine will be. Some sparkling wines are years in the making; others are produced in only a few months. The slow-route wines can often cost well over $100 a bottle, while bubblies at the opposite end of the spectrum can sell for as little as $4.

Although many variations exist, most sparkling wines are produced in one of two ways: through *second fermentation in a tank* or through *second fermentation in a bottle*.

Tank fermentation: Economy of scale

The quickest, most efficient way of making a sparkling wine involves conducting the second fermentation in large, closed, pressurized tanks. This method is called the *bulk method, tank method, cuve close* (meaning "closed tank" in French), or the *charmat method* (after a Frenchman named Eugene Charmat, who championed this process).

Sparkling wines produced in the charmat (pronounced *shar-mah*) method are usually the least expensive to make, and to buy. That's because they're usually made in large quantities and they're ready for sale soon after harvest. Also, the grapes used in making sparkling wine by the charmat method (Chenin Blanc, for example) are usually *far* less expensive than the Pinot Noir and Chardonnay typically used in the *traditional* or *Champagne method* described in the next section.

**TECHNICAL
STUFF**

The following occurs in the charmat method:

1. A base wine (already fermented) is seeded with sugar and yeast, and it ferments a second time. The carbon dioxide created by the fermentation becomes trapped in the wine, thanks to the closed tank as well as pressure within the tank and cold temperature.

2. The wine — now a sparkling wine with higher alcohol than the base wine had — is filtered (under pressure) to remove the solid deposits (the *lees*) from the second fermentation.

3. Before bottling, some sweetness is often added to adjust the wine's flavor, according to the style desired.

The whole process can take just a few weeks. In some exceptional cases, it can be extended to a few months, allowing the wine to rest between the second fermentation and the filtration.

Bottle fermentation: Small is beautiful

The charmat method that we describe in the preceding section is a fairly new way of producing sparkling wines, dating back about 100 years. The more traditional method is to conduct the second fermentation in the individual bottles in which the wine is later sold.

Champagne has been made this way for more than 300 years and, according to French regulations, can be made in no other way. Many other French sparkling wines produced outside of the Champagne region use the same process, but are not allowed to call themselves Champagne because they do not come from that region; they use the term *Crémant* to indicate their production method. The best sparkling wines from Spain, California, and elsewhere also use Champagne's traditional method.

The technique of conducting the second fermentation in the bottle is called the *classic* or *traditional method* in Europe; in the United States, it's called the *Champagne method* or *méthode champenoise*.

Bottle fermentation (or, more accurately, second fermentation in the bottle) is an elaborate process in which every single bottle is an individual fermentation vessel, so to speak. Including the aging time at the winery before the wine is sold, this process requires a minimum of 15 months (in the case of Champagne) and usually takes 3 years or more. Bottle-fermented sparkling wines are always more expensive than tank-fermented bubblies.

TECHNICAL
STUFF

The elements of bottle fermentation are as follows:

1. Each bottle is filled with a mixture of base wine and a sugar-and-yeast solution, closed securely, and laid to rest in a cool, dark cellar.

2. The second fermentation slowly occurs inside each bottle, producing carbon dioxide and fermentation lees.

3. As the bottles lie in the cellar, the interaction of the lees and the wine gradually changes the wine's texture and flavor.

4. Eventually — 12 months to several years after the second fermentation — the bottles undergo a process of a quick, slight shaking and turning so that the lees fall to the neck of each upside-down bottle.

5. The lees are flash-frozen in the neck of each bottle and expelled from the bottle as a frozen plug, leaving clear sparkling wine behind.

6. A sweetening solution (called a *dosage,* pronounced *doh-sahj*) is added to each bottle to adjust the flavor of the wine, and the bottles are corked and eventually labeled for sale.

Actually, the classic method as practiced in Champagne involves several processes that occur way before the second fermentation. For example, the pressing to extract the juice from the grapes must be gentle and meticulous to prevent the grape skins' bitter flavors — and their color, in the case of black grapes — from passing into the juice. Another step crucially important to the quality of the sparkling wine is blending various wines after the first fermentation to create the best composite base wine for the second fermentation.

TECHNICAL STUFF

After the first fermentation, each Champagne *house* (as the producers are called) has hundreds of different still wines, because the winemaker keeps the wines of different grape varieties and different vineyards separate. To create his base wine, or *cuvée,* he blends these wines in varying proportions, often adding some *reserve wine* (older wine purposely held back from previous vintages). More than 100 different wines can go into a single base wine, each bringing its own special character to the blend.

What's particularly tricky about blending the base wine — besides the sheer number of components in the blend — is that the winemaker has to see into the future and create a blend *not* for its flavor today but for how it will taste in several years, after it has been transformed into a sparkling wine. The men and women who blend sparkling wines are true artists of the wine world.

Tasting the difference

Tank-fermented sparklers tend to be fruitier than traditional-method sparkling wines. This difference occurs because the route from grape to wine is shorter and more direct in tank fermentation than in bottle fermentation. Some winemakers use the *charmat,* or tank, method precisely because their goal is a fresh and fruity sparkling wine. *Prosecco* and *Asti,* two of Italy's most famous sparkling wines, are perfect examples. You should drink charmat-method sparklers young, when their fruitiness is at its max.

Second fermentation in the bottle makes wines that tend to be less overtly fruity than charmat-method wines. Chemical changes that take place as the wine develops on its fermentation lees diminish the fruitiness of the wine and contribute aromas and flavors such as toastiness, nuttiness, caramel, and yeastiness. The texture of the wine can also change, becoming smooth and creamy. The bubbles themselves tend to be tinier, and they feel less aggressive in your mouth than the bubbles of tank-fermented wines.

Champagne and Its Magic Wines

Champagne. Does any other word convey such a sense of celebration? Think of it: Whenever people want to celebrate, you can hear them say, "This calls for Champagne!" ("This calls for iced tea!" just isn't quite the same.)

Champagne, the real thing, comes only from the region of Champagne (*sham-pahn-yah*) in northeast France. Champagne is the most northerly vineyard area in France. Many of the important Champagne houses are located in the city of Rheims (French spelling, *Reims*) — where 17-year-old Joan of Arc had Prince Charles crowned King of France in 1429 — and in the town of Epernay, south of Rheims. Around Rheims and Epernay are the main vineyard areas, where three permitted grape varieties for Champagne flourish. (The names of these areas do not appear on the wine labels.) These areas, and the grapes they specialize in, are

>> The Montagne de Reims (south of Rheims), where the best Pinot Noir grows

>> The Côte des Blancs (south of Epernay), home of the best Chardonnay

>> The Valleé de la Marne (west of Epernay), most favorable to Pinot Meunier (a black grape), although all three grape varieties grow there

Most Champagne is made from all three grape varietiese. Pinot Noir contributes body, structure, and longevity to the blend; Pinot Meunier provides precociousness, floral aromas, and fruitiness; and Chardonnay offers delicacy, freshness, elegance, and aging potential.

In the following sections, we delve into the details of Champagne: what makes it special, different types and sweetness levels, and recommended producers.

What makes Champagne special

The cool climate in Champagne is marginal for grape growing, and the grapes struggle to ripen sufficiently in some years. The cool climate and the region's chalky, limestone soil are the leading factors contributing to Champagne's excellence.

THE FATHER OF INVENTION

Dom Pérignon, the famous monk who was cellar master at the Abbey of Hautvillers, didn't invent Champagne, but he did achieve several breakthroughs that are key to the production of Champagne as we now know it. He perfected the method of making white wine from black grapes, for example, and, most important, he mastered the art of blending wines from different grapes and different villages to achieve a complex base wine. (See the earlier section, "How Sparkling Wine Happens," to find out what base wine is.)

Three other elements help distinguish Champagne from all other sparkling wines:

>> The number and diversity of vineyards (more than 300, *crus,* or individual sites, each consisting of multiple vineyards), which provide a huge range of unique wines for blending

>> The cold, deep, chalky cellars — many built during Roman times — in which Champagnes age for many years

>> The 300 years of experience the *Champenois* (as the good citizens of Champagne are called) have in making sparkling wine

The result is an elegant sparkling wine with myriad tiny, gentle bubbles, complexity of flavors, and a lengthy finish. Voilà — Champagne!

Non-vintage Champagne

Non-vintage (NV) Champagne — any Champagne without a vintage year on the label — is the basic style of Champagne. This category accounts for about 85 percent of all Champagne. The wine has no specific vintage year because wine from three or more harvests typically goes into the "non-vintage" blend; some producers argue that "multi-vintage" would be a more accurate descriptor than non-vintage.

A typical grape blend for these basic Champagnes is two-thirds black grapes (Pinot Noir and Pinot Meunier) and one-third white (Chardonnay), but it can vary from year to year. Besides containing multiple grape varieties and wines from multiple vintages, these wines can also contain base wines from 30 or 40 different villages (or more). The Champagne winemaker is by necessity a master blender.

Each Champagne house blends its non-vintage Champagne to suit its own house style. (For example, one house may seek elegance and finesse in its wine, another may opt for fruitiness, and a third may value body, power, and longevity.)

Most major Champagne houses age their non-vintage Champagne for 2 and 1/2 to 3 years before selling it, even though the legal minimum for non-vintage is just 15 months. The extra aging prolongs the marrying time for the blend and enhances the wine's flavor and complexity. If you have good storage conditions (see Chapter 17), aging your non-vintage Champagne for one to three years after you purchase it usually improves the flavor, in our opinion.

TIP

Most non-vintage Champagnes retail for $35 to $65 a bottle. Often, large retailers buy large quantities of a few major brands, obtaining a good discount that they pass on to customers. Seeking out stores that do a large-volume business in Champagne is worth your while.

Vintage Champagne

Vintage Champagne is made entirely from the grapes of a single year, and is not blended with reserve wines from previous years. Historically, only about four or five years of every decade had weather good enough to make a Vintage Champagne — that is, the grapes were ripe enough that some wine could be made without the help of reserve wines. The early '90s were typical: One vintage was good enough, while four years — 1991, 1992, 1993, and 1994 — were unremarkable and not particularly suitable for vintage Champagne. But since 1995, the climate in Champagne has changed, and producers have been able to make Vintage Champagne almost every year. In the 18 years from 1995 to 2012, only five vintages would be considered generally unsuitable for producing a Vintage Champagne.

Here are some specifics of great vintages and their readiness to drink:

>> Since 1995, the Champagne region has had a string of five really fine vintages, especially 1996. The three years that followed 1996 were all good and are now ready to drink (although 1997 was a bit too warm, and its Champagne might be past its peak).

>> 2002 is a very good vintage, suitable for aging. The 2006 vintage is perfect for drinking now.

>> The best recent vintages are 2008 and 2012, with the potential to rank with 1996 and 2002 (as of this writing, very few 2012s have been released in the U.S. yet).

>> Buying older Champagne vintages can be a problem. Not many are available, they tend to be expensive, and you must know how they have been stored. It makes more sense to buy the 2008 and 2012 (when the latter becomes available) and to store them yourself in a cool, dark place.

Although the warming climate has enabled more frequent production of Vintage Champagne, additional warming might not necessarily be a positive factor for regions such as Champagne whose wines epitomize cool climate characteristics. In fact, we usually prefer Vintage Champagnes made in cooler vintages.

Champagne houses decide for themselves whether to make a Vintage Champagne in any given year. Factors other than the quality of the vintage might come into consideration; these include the need to designate some wine as reserve wines for their future non-vintage Champagnes (85 percent of their business, after all), and/or whether a particular vintage's style suits the "house style." For example, although 1989 was a rather good vintage, a few houses decided that Champagnes made from this vintage would be too soft (low in acidity) for them and did not choose to make a Vintage Champagne in 1989. In the end, 1989 produced some very nice Vintage Champagnes, but not as good as the magnificent 1988s.

The minimum aging requirement for vintage Champagne is three years, but many houses age their vintage Champagnes for four to six years in order to enhance the wines' flavor and complexity. Vintage Champagnes fall into two categories:

>> Regular vintage, with a price range of $65 to $90 a bottle; these wines simply carry a vintage date in addition to the name of the producer.

>> Premium vintage (also known as *prestige cuvée* or *tête de cuvée*), such as Moët & Chandon's Dom Pérignon, Roederer's Cristal, or Veuve Clicquot's La Grande Dame; the typical price for prestige cuvées ranges from $125 to $200, with a few even more expensive.

Vintage Champagne is almost always superior to non-vintage for the following reasons:

>> The best grapes from the choicest vineyards are put into Vintage Champagne (this is *especially* true for prestige cuvées).

>> Usually, only the two finest varieties (Pinot Noir and Chardonnay) are used in Vintage Champagne. Pinot Meunier, a less noble variety, is present mainly in non-vintage Champagne.

>> Most Champagne houses age Vintage Champagnes at least two years more than their non-vintage wines. The extra aging assures more complexity.

>> The grapes all come from a year that's above average, at least — or superb, at best.

Vintage Champagne is more intense in flavor than non-vintage Champagne. It is typically fuller-bodied and more complex, and its flavors last longer in your mouth. Being fuller and richer, these Champagnes are best with food. Non-vintage Champagnes — usually lighter, fresher, and less complicated — are suitable as apéritifs, and they can be good values.

Blanc de blancs and blanc de noirs

A small number of Champagnes derive only from Chardonnay; that type of Champagne is called *blanc de blancs* — literally, "white (wine) from white (grapes)." A blanc de blancs can be a vintage Champagne or a non-vintage. It usually costs more than other Champagnes because the Chardonnay variety is costly and prized in the region. Since they are often lighter and more delicate than other Champagnes, most blanc de blanc Champagnes make ideal apéritifs.

Not every Champagne house makes a blanc de blancs. Five of the best blanc de blancs — all Vintage Champagnes — are Taittinger Comte de Champagne, a prestige cuvée; Billecart-Salmon Blanc de Blancs (also made as an NV), Deutz Blanc de Blancs, Pol Roger Blanc de Blancs, and Louis Roederer Blanc de Blancs. Two *exceptional* Blanc de Blancs, both prestige cuvées and quite expensive, are Krug Clos du Mesnil and Salon.

WORTH THE SEARCH

Blanc de noirs Champagne (made entirely from black grapes, usually just Pinot Noir) is fairly rare but does exist, especially among smaller producers (see "Grower Champagnes" section later in this chapter). Bollinger's Blanc de Noirs *Vieilles Vignes Francaises* ("old vines") is clearly one of the best, but it is very expensive ($850 to $925) and difficult to find. The 1985 Bollinger Blanc de Noirs is one of the two best Champagnes we've ever had; the other is the 1928 Krug. The first modern-era Blanc de Noirs from the prestigious house of Krug is the 1995 Prestige Cuvée Krug Clos d'Ambonnay, a single-vineyard Champagne — also made in 1996 and 1998. These three Krug Blanc de Noirs gems range in price from $1,900 to $2,400 a bottle at retail, making it, as far as we know, *the* most expensive of any recently released Champagnes.

Rosé Champagne

Rosé Champagnes — pink Champagnes — can also be vintage or non-vintage. Usually, Pinot Noir and Chardonnay are the only grapes used, in proportions that vary from house to house.

Winemakers create a rosé Champagne usually by including some red Pinot Noir wine in the blend for the base wine. A few actually vinify some of their red grapes into pink wines, the way that you would make a rosé still wine, and use that as the base wine. Colors vary quite a lot, from pale onion skin to salmon to rosy pink. (The lighter-colored ones are usually dryer.)

Rosés are fuller and rounder than other Champagnes and are best enjoyed with dinner. Because they have become associated with romance, they're popular choices for wedding anniversaries and Valentine's Day, but many Champagne lovers, like us, drink them at any time of the year.

WORTH THE SEARCH

Like blanc de blancs Champagnes (see the previous section), rosés usually cost a few dollars more than regular Champagnes, and not every Champagne house makes one. Some of the best rosés are those of Louis Roederer (including its *Cristal* Rosé), Billecart-Salmon, Delamotte, Gosset, Moët & Chandon (especially its Dom Pérignon Rosé), and Paul Bara (its Special Club Rosé).

Sweetness categories

WARNING

Champagnes always carry an indication of their sweetness on the label, but the words used to indicate sweetness are cryptic: Extra dry is not really dry, for example. In ascending order of sweetness, Champagnes are labeled

>> Extra brut, or brut nature: Totally dry

>> Brut: Dry

>> Extra dry: Medium dry

>> Sec: Slightly sweet

>> Demi-sec: Fairly sweet

>> Doux: Sweet

The most popular style for Champagne and other serious bubblies is brut. Brut and, trailing well behind, extra dry, are the two types of Champagne you find most. But recently, very dry Champagnes (extra brut, or brut nature) have become quite popular among connoisseurs.

Recommended Champagne producers

The Champagne business — especially the export end of it — is dominated by 25 or 30 large houses, most of whom purchase (from private growers) the majority of grapes they need to make their Champagne. Of the major houses, only Roederer and Bollinger own a substantial portion of the vineyards from which they get their grapes — a definite economic and quality-control advantage for them.

TIP

Moët & Chandon is by far the largest Champagne house in terms of worldwide sales. Other large brands are Veuve Clicquot, Nicolas Feuillatte, Mumm, Laurent-Perrier, Piper-Heidsieck, Taittinger, Pommery, Lanson, and Perrier-Jouët. The following lists name some of our favorite producers, grouped according to the style of their Champagne: light-bodied, medium-bodied, or full-bodied. (For an understanding of the term *body* as it applies to wine, see Chapter 2.)

Light, elegant styles	
Laurent-Perrier	G.H. Mumm
Ruinart	Perrier-Jouët
Jacquesson	J. Lassalle*
Ayala	Henriot
Piper-Heidsieck	Bruno Paillard
Medium-bodied styles	
Charles Heidsieck	Deutz
Pol Roger	Taittinger
Moët & Chandon	Philipponnat
Alfred Gratien	Lanson
Full-bodied styles	
Krug	Veuve Clicquot
Louis Roederer	Delamotte
Bollinger	Salon*
Gosset	Paul Bara*

Small producer; may be difficult to find.

WORTH THE SEARCH

The following list names Champagne producers whose Vintage Champagnes and Prestige Cuvées have been in top form. For more info on Champagne, see Ed McCarthy's book, *Champagne For Dummies* (Wiley):

>> **Louis Roederer:** Cristal, Cristal Rosé

>> **Krug:** Clos du Mesnil, Vintage, NV Rosé, Grande Cuvée

>> **Bollinger:** Grande Année, Blanc de Noirs Vieilles Vignes

>> **Philipponnat:** Clos des Goisses

>> **Moët & Chandon:** Dom Pérignon

>> **Salon:** Blanc de Blancs

>> **Charles Heidsieck:** Blanc des Millenaires, Vintage, NV Brut

>> **Henriot:** Cuveé des Enchanteleurs, Blanc de Blancs

>> **Gosset:** Celebris, Celebris Rosé, Celebris Blanc de Blancs

>> **Georges Laval:** Brut Nature, Brut Nature Rosé

>> **Ayala:** La Perle d'Ayala Nature, Cuvée Rosé Nature

>> **Bruno Paillard:** Blanc de Blancs Réserve Privée

>> **Veuve Clicquot:** Vintage, La Grande Dame

>> **Pol Roger:** Cuvée Sir Winston Churchill, Blanc de Blancs

>> **Paul Bara:** Special Club Rosé, Special Club Blanc de Noirs

>> **Taittinger:** Comtes de Champagne, Comtes de Champagne Rosé

>> **Billecart-Salmon:** Vintage Blanc de Blancs, Cuvée Elisabeth Salmon Rosé

>> **Deutz:** Cuvée William Deutz, Cuvée William Deutz Rosé, Deutz Blanc de Blancs

>> **Pommery:** Cuvée Louise, Cuvée Louise Rosé

>> **Jacquesson:** Avize Grand Cru, all of its other Champagnes

>> **Laurent-Perrier:** Grand Siècle

>> **Ruinart:** Dom Ruinart Blanc de Blancs, Dom Ruinart Rosé

>> **Perrier-Jouët:** Belle Epoque Blanc de Blancs, Belle Epoque Rosé

>> **Lanson:** Noble Cuvée, Noble Cuvée Blanc de Blancs

>> **Piper-Heidsieck:** Champagne Rare

>> **Alfred Gratien:** Cuvée Paradis (NV)

>> **Delamotte:** Vintage Blanc de Blancs, NV Rosé

>> **Cattier:** Clos du Moulin (NV)

MADAME LILY BOLLINGER'S ADVICE ON DRINKING CHAMPAGNE

When Jacques Bollinger died in 1941, his widow, Lily Bollinger, carried their famous Champagne house through the difficult years of the German occupation of France. She ran the company until her death in 1977. Bollinger prospered under her leadership, doubling in size. She was a beloved figure in Champagne, where she could be seen bicycling through the vineyards every day. In 1961, when a London reporter asked her when she drank Champagne, Madame Bollinger replied:

"I only drink Champagne when I'm happy, and when I'm sad. Sometimes I drink it when I'm alone. When I have company I consider it obligatory. I trifle with it if I am not hungry and drink it when I am. Otherwise I never touch it — unless I'm thirsty."

The redoubtable Madame Lily Bollinger died at the age of 78, apparently none the worse for all that Champagne.

Grower Champagnes

A phenomenon has occurred in the world of Champagne during the last three decades: the availabilty of so-called *grower Champagnes* in export markets. A *grower-producer* is someone who makes Champagne only from the grapes that he has grown in his own vineyards — as opposed to a Champagne house, which typically purchases most of the grapes for its wines. (You can recognize a grower Champagne by the initials *RM* or *RC* in small print on the bottom of the label.)

While a few growers, such as Paul Bara, have been making and selling Champagne for many decades, two-thirds of the region's 15,000 growers are content to sell their grapes rather than make wine. Around 5,000 growers who now sell the Champagnes that they themselves have made account for about 22 percent of all Champagne sales. Most of these sales take place in France; only a very small percentage of growers are large enough to export their Champagnes around the world. But the number is growing.

When co-author Ed wrote *Champagne For Dummies* in 1999, about 50 grower Champagnes were available in the United States. Today that number is well over 200. But this category accounts for only 5 percent of U.S. Champagne sales (up from 2 percent 20 years ago), for two reasons: Grower Champagne production is very small compared to that of the Champagne houses; and the growers' brands are not widely available in the U.S. Another reason could be that only the more knowledgeable Champagne drinkers even know about these wines: Growers don't have the budget to advertise.

Some of the better-known grower Champagnes in the United States include the following: Agrapart, Paul Bara, Bereche et Fils, Henri Billiot, Guy Charlemagne, Chartogne-Taillet, Gaston Chiquet, Diebolt-Vallois, Pascal Doquet, Egly-Ouriet, René Geoffroy, Pierre Gimonnet, Guy Larmandier, Larmandier-Bernier, J. Lasalle, Georges Laval, A. Margaine, Serge Mathieu, Pierre Moncuit, Pierre Peters, Alain Robert, Jacques Selosse, and Vilmart.

Most of these producers make 7,000 or fewer cases per year, a pittance compared to the production of the Champagne houses. Pierre Gimonnet and Gaston Chiquet are the two largest in this group and are probably the most available.

Some people think that because grower Champagnes are made by small producers, the wines are inherently of better quality than other Champagnes. Not true, although many of them are consistently of high quality and have the distinctive taste of their own *terroir.*

On the non-vintage level (by far the largest type of grower Champagne), prices are about the same as other Champagnes. But grower Champagnes generally are lower priced at the premium Champagne level compared to wines of the Champagne houses.

TIP

One word of warning about grower Champagnes: They are generally not aged as long at the winery as major brands, because growers don't have the storage facilities. When you buy these wines, they might taste a bit "green"; they are simply too young, and ideally you should hold on to them a while (we suggest about a year) before you open them.

Other Sparkling Wines

Wineries all over the world have emulated Champagne by adopting the techniques used in the Champagne region. Their wines differ from Champagne, however, because their grapes grow in *terroirs* different from that of the Champagne region and because, in some cases, their grapes are different varieties.

Other wineries in many parts of the world make their bubblies by using the tank fermentation rather than the bottle fermentation method specifically to attain a certain style or to reduce production costs. (We discuss these methods in the earlier section "How Sparkling Wine Happens.")

Italian spumante: Dry and Sweet

Spumante is simply the Italian word for "sparkling." It often appears on bottles of American wines that are sweet, fruity spinoffs of Italy's classic Asti, once called Asti Spumante. But actually, Italy makes many fine, dry spumante wines, including a very popular sparkling wine called *Prosecco*. For more info on Italian sparkling wines, check out our book *Italian Wine For Dummies* (Wiley).

Prosecco

This quintessential Italian sparkling wine has become all the rage in the U.S., which is now its leading export market. In fact, in 2014 Prosecco even surpassed Champagne in U.S. sales! Perhaps even more surprising, Prosecco is selling extremely well in the U.K., long a bastion of Champagne sales. And all this success has occurred in the last 20 years.

Prosecco comes from grapes grown in the central Veneto and the Friuli regions. The dominant grape variety was formerly called Prosecco but is now known as Glera. To clarify, Glera is the grape variety; Prosecco is the name of the DOC zone and the wine.

Prosecco is a straightforward, delicious bubbly wine, moderate in alcohol (about 11 to 12 percent) and boasting aromas and flavors of apple, pear, and other fruits. It is produced mainly by the tank method, and comes in dry, off-dry, and sweet styles. Besides the fully-sparkling *spumante* version, Prosecco also comes as a *frizzante* (lightly sparkling) style, which is less common. Prosecco is the perfect wine to enjoy with Italian antipasto, such as pickled vegetables, calamari, anchovies, or spicy salami. Its fresh, fruity flavors cleanse your mouth and get your appetite going for dinner.

The finest Prosecco comes not from the large DOC zone but from a much smaller DOCG territory called Conegliano Valdobbiadene Prosecco *(coh-nel-L'YAH-no val-doh-be-AH-deh-nay)*; this name refers to two villages in the northern Veneto and applies to the hillside vineyards surrounding them. Another Prosecco DOCG appellation is Asolo Prosecco, just south of Conegliano-Valdobbiadene, around the picturesque town of Asolo *(AH-so-lo)*.

Prosecco wines labeled simply as DOC, from the largest of the three territories, cost about $12 a bottle. Prosecco DOCG wines are a few dollars more — up to $18, with a few of the better Proseccos over $20 — but well-worth it, because the DOCG Proseccos come from vineyards in the best areas, and the higher quality of the wines is evident.

TIP

Recommended producers (alphabetically) include Adami, Bisol, Bisson, Carpenè Malvolti, Mionetto, Nino Franco, and Zardetto. Large producers, such as Mionetto, make both DOC and DOCG Proseccos. Producers stressing high quality, such as Nino Franco and Bisol, concentrate on DOCG Proseccos. For example, although Nino Franco's best-selling Prosecco, Rustico, is $18, he also produces a high-end Prosecco, Vintage Grave di Stecca, with Glera grapes grown in an ancient vineyard on a pre-Alp slope; it is on another, high-quality level, well-worth its $45 to $46 price.

Asti and Moscato d'Asti

Asti is a delicious, fairly sweet, exuberantly fruity DOCG sparkling wine made in the Piedmont region from Moscato grapes. It is normally made via the tank method, but a *Methodo Classico* version (classic method of second fermentation in the bottle) has recently come to be. It's one bubbly that you can drink with dessert (fantastic with wedding cake!).

TIP

Because freshness is essential in Asti, buy a good brand that sells well. (Asti is not vintage-dated, so there's no other way to determine how old the wine is.) We recommend Martini & Rossi and Cinzano (about $11 to $12).

WORTH THE SEARCH

For Asti flavor with fewer bubbles, try the *Moscato d'Asti variation of Asti*. It's a delicate and delicious medium-dry vintage-dated *frizzante* (slightly sparkling) wine that makes a refreshing apéritif. It's also good with dessert and is a great brunch wine. And it has just 5 to 7 percent alcohol!

Moscato d'Asti is popular in the U.S., and we are thrilled, because we love it! Vietti makes a good one, called Cascinetta. Other good producers of Moscato d'Asti are Dante Rivetti and Paolo Sarocco: All these sell for $15 to $19. Again, freshness is essential. With Moscato d'Asti, let the vintage date guide you; buy the youngest one you can find.

Dry spumante: Francicorta and others

Using the traditional method, Italy produces a good deal of dry sparkling wine in the Oltrepò-Pavese zone, in the Franciacorta DOCG zone of Lombardy, and in the Trentino region. Italy's dry sparkling wines tend to be very dry with little or no sweetening dosage. They come in all price ranges:

>> A good mid-priced bubbly from Trento is Ferrari Brut (at $25). Ferrari's Premium Brut, Giulio Ferrari, arguably Italy's best sparkling wine, is in the $125 to $135 price range.

>> Franciacorta's two upscale (and very good) bruts, $35 to $36 and up, are Bellavista NV Franciacorta Brut and Cà del Bosco NV Franciacorta Brut. The premium sparklers of these two houses, single-vineyard bruts, are over $100.

>> Bruno Giacosa Winery, known for its outstanding Barbarescos and Barolos, makes a 100 percent Pinot Noir Extra Brut (about $45) in its spare time, for kicks. Like everything else Giacosa produces, it's superb.

Spanish sparkling wines (Cava)

What if you want to spend about $10 or less for a decent sparkling wine? The answer is Spain's sparkling wine, Cava, which sells mainly for $9 to $12 a bottle. Almost all of it comes from the Penedès region in Catalonia, near Barcelona.

Cava is a traditional method sparkling wine, fermented in the bottle. Most Cavas use Spanish grape varieties— specifically Macabeo, Parellada, and Xarello (pronounced *cha-REL-yo*) along with Chardonnay and two red grapes— and as a result, they taste distinctly different (a nicely earthy, mushroomy flavor) from California bubblies and from Champagne. Cava wines come in all sweetness levels, from Brut Nature to Dulce, and in various aging categories, including Reserva and Gran Reserva.

TIP

Two gigantic wineries dominate Cava production — Freixenet (pronounced *fresh-net*) and Codorníu. Freixenet's frosted black Cordon Negro bottle has to be one of the most recognizable wine bottles in the world. Other Cava brands to look for are Mont Marçal, Paul Cheneau, Jaume Serra Cristalino, Marqués de Monistrol, and Segura Viudas. Juve y Camps, a vintage-dated, upscale Cava, is a worthwhile buy ($16 to $23).

French sparkling wine

France makes many other sparkling wines besides Champagne, especially in the Loire Valley, around Saumur, and in the regions of Alsace and Burgundy. Sparkling wine made by the traditional method (second fermentation in the bottle) often carries the name *Crémant*, as in Crémant d'Alsace, Crémant de Loire, Crémant de Bourgogne, and so on. Grape varieties are those typical of each region (see Chapter 10).

REAL DEAL

Some of the leading brands of French sparkling wines are Langlois-Château, Gratien & Meyer (both from the Loire Valley)t, Kriter, and Saint Hilaire. These wines sell for $10 to $20 and are decent. They're perfect for parties and other large gatherings when you may want to serve a French bubbly without paying a Champagne price. For more info on French sparkling wines, take a look at our book *French Wine For Dummies* (Wiley).

American sparkling wine

Almost as many states make sparkling wine as make still wine, but California and New York are the most famous for it. Dr. Konstantin Frank's Château Frank is a fine producer of New York State sparkling wines, white and rosé, made in the traditional method. It's a value at $18.

One sparkling wine, Gruet, deserves special mention because it hails, improbably, from New Mexico. Owned by France's little-known Champagne Gruet, the New Mexican winery makes three fine bubblies: a NV Brut and NV Blanc de Noirs, both $11 to $14, and a top Vintage Blanc de Blancs, $23 to $24. Another fine sparkling producer is Oregon's Argyle Winery. Its vintage bubblies start at $19 and can go up to over $30 for its finer vintage bruts. Other wineries in Oregon are beginning to make some good sparkling wines.

California bubbly is definitely a different wine from Champagne. It tastes fruitier even when made by a Champagne-trained winemaker, using the same methods and the same grape varieties as in Champagne. Good California sparkling wines, the ones made in the traditional Champagne method, cost as little as $15, but can go up to $40 and more.

Most of California's finest sparkling wines do not call themselves Champagne, but the less-expensive, best-selling ones still do. In that second category, Korbel California Champagne, about $12, is the only brand that is actually fermented in the bottle. Korbel also makes a dryer version, "Natural," for a few dollars more.

We recommend the following California sparkling wine producers, listed in our rough order of preference within each category.

WORTH THE SEARCH

» U.S.-owned producers:

- **Schramsberg Vineyards:** Now sourcing its grapes from the coolest areas in Napa and Sonoma, Schramsberg, has emerged as one of the premium sparkling wine houses in the United States. From its NV Blanc de Blancs and Blanc de Noirs ($36), its NV Rosé ($39), to its premium J. Schram Teté de Cuvée Vintage Brut ($100) and its J.Schram Vintage Rosé ($134 to $140), its sparklers are superb indeed.

- **Iron Horse:** In Green Valley, the coolest part of Sonoma (temperature wise, that is), Iron Horse is clearly making some of California's finest sparkling wine. Look for its better cuvées, such as the Wedding Cuvée or Russian Cuvée, for about $35.

» French- or Spanish-owned producers:

WORTH THE SEARCH

- **Roederer Estate:** Louis Roederer is such a fine Champagne house that we're not surprised at the smashing success of its Anderson Valley winery, near the town of Mendocino. Some critics think it's California's best. Wines include a good-value brut ($23), a delicate rosé ($28) that's worth seeking out, and outstanding premium cuvées, Vintage L'Ermitage ($47) and dVintage L'Ermitage Rosé ($70).

- **Mumm Napa:** Mumm has established itself as one of California's best sparkling wine houses. Much of its production comes from the cool Carneros District; look for the Brut Prestige ($19) and especially for the cherrylike Blanc de Noirs (about $26).

- **Domaine Carneros:** Champagne Taittinger's California winery makes an elegant, high-quality Vintage Brut and Rosé ($30) in cool Carneros. Its premium cuvée, Le Rêve ($105), a Vintage 5 blanc de blancs, is stunning but expensive.

- **Domaine Chandon:** This Napa Valley winery, one of the earliest to specialize in sparkling wine, is part of the Moët & Chandon empire. Chandon continues to make solid, consistent sparkling wines at reasonable prices ($19). Look especially for its premium Etoile (about $31), one of the most elegant sparkling wines in the United States, and the delicious Etoile Rosé ($38). Domaine Chandon also produces a limited bottling of its Vintage Carneros Brut ($45).

- **Gloria Ferrer:** Spain's Freixenet built a beautiful winery in windswept Carneros, named Gloria Ferrer. Most of its sparkling wines are priced right, such as its Sonoma Brut ($19), and its Vintage Royal Cuvée ($30). Gloria Ferrer's premium sparkler, its vintage-dated Carneros Cuvée ($74), is expensive, but worth the price. The winery itself is definitely worth a visit.

- **Scharffenberger:** In the cool Anderson Valley, Scharffenberger, now owned by Champagne Louis Roederer, makes a Chardonnay-based Excellence brut ($19) and a rosé brut ($24).

English sparkling wines

The biggest news in the sparkling wine world is the rather dramatic rise of English sparkling wines. The Brits have always had a love affair with French Champagne and have long been France's largest export market for Champagne. And so it should not be a complete surprise that sparkling wine is now being made in England and in Wales. But its success was once thought improbable. The general thinking had been that the UK was too cool and rainy for wine production. Thanks to climate warming, however, several regions in England have been making seriously good sparkling wines — perhaps not yet up to the best of Champagne, but the sparkling wine industry in the UK is still in its early stages.

Sparkling wine production in England started in the 1960s, but accellerated in the mid-1980s, after Pinot Noir, Chardonnay, and Pinot Noir grapes were planted. Already the production of English sparkling wine is one-third that of the Champagne region. Right now, only 5 percent of its wine is being exported, but that figure should rise in the near future.

Actually, the *terroir* (particularly soil and climate) is very similar to the Champagne region. And the Champenois are very much aware of English sparklers; already Champagne Taittinger and Pommery have invested in English vineyards.

Prices of the best English sparklers are comparable to those of Champagne, perhaps slightly lower. One English sparkling wine that we do hear about and see in the U.S. is Nyetimber. Its NV Classic Brut is about $60, and its Vintage Blanc de Blancs is priced at $75. Others include Ridgeview, Chapel Down and Gusbourne.

Buying and Serving Bubbly

Sparkling wine is best served cold, about 45 degrees Fahrenheit (7 to 8 degrees Celsius), although some people prefer it less cold. We like it colder because the cold helps the wine hold its effervescence — and the wine warms up so quickly in the glass, anyway. Because older Champagnes and Vintage Champagnes are more complex, you should chill them less than young, non-vintage Champagne or sparkling wine.

TIP

Never leave an open bottle of sparkling wine on the table unless it's in an ice bucket (filled with half cold water, half ice) because it will warm up quickly. An exception to this rule is the time when you have a large group of drinkers (six or more), because they will finish the bottle in ten minutes or less. Use a sparkling wine stopper to keep leftover bubbly fresh for a couple of days — in the fridge, of course.

If you're entertaining, you should know that the ideal bottle size for Champagne is the *magnum,* which is equivalent to two bottles. The larger bottle enables the wine to age more gently in the winery's cellar. Magnums (or sometimes double magnums) are usually the largest bottles in which Champagne is fermented; all really large bottles have had finished Champagne poured into them, and the wine is, therefore, not as fresh as it is in a magnum or a regular bottle.

WARNING

Be wary of half-bottles (375 ml) and — chancier yet — *splits* of 187 ml! Champagne in these small bottles is often not fresh. (Exception: fine restaurants that store their wines properly.) If you're given a small bottle of Champagne or any bubbly as a wedding favor, for example, open it at the first excuse; do not keep it around for a year waiting for the right occasion!

Champagne and other good, dry sparkling wines are extremely versatile with food — and they are the essential wine for certain kinds of foods. For example, no wine goes better with egg dishes than Champagne. Indulge yourself next time you have brunch. And when you're having spicy Asian cuisine, try sparkling wine, particularly a fruity style. For us, no wine matches up better with spicy Chinese or Indian food!

Fish, seafood, pasta with cream or oil-based sauces, risotto, and poultry are excellent with Champagne and sparkling wine. If you're having lamb (pink, not well done) or ham, pair rosé Champagne with it. With aged Champagne, chunks of aged Asiago, aged Gouda, or Parmesan cheese go extremely well. Champagne is also great with fried foods and popcorn!

TIP

Don't serve a brut (or extra dry) sparkling wine with dessert. These styles are just too dry. With fresh fruit and desserts that aren't very sweet, try a Prosecco or a demi-sec Champagne. With sweeter desserts (or wedding cake), we recommend Asti. (For more info on Champagne with food, see co-author Ed's *Champagne For Dummies*, published by Wiley.)

IN THIS CHAPTER

» **Sherry: The world's most versatile wine**

» **Port: 80 grapes for one wine**

» **Madeira: A wine that lasts 200 years or more**

» **Sauternes: Liquid gold from rotted grapes**

» **Tokaji Aszú and Essencia: Hungary's great after-dinner wines**

Chapter **16**

Wine Roads Less Traveled: Fortified and Dessert Wines

The wines we lump together as *fortified wines* and *dessert wines* aren't mainstream beverages that you want to drink every day. Some of them are much higher in alcohol than regular wines, and some of them are extremely sweet (and rare and expensive!). They're the wine equivalent of really good candy — delicious enough that you can get carried away if you let yourself indulge daily. So you treat them as treats: a glass before or after dinner, a bottle when company comes, a splurge to celebrate the start of your diet — tomorrow.

Pleasure aside, from a purely academic point of view, you owe it to yourself to try these wines. Seriously! Learning about wine is hard work, but it's also a lot of fun.

Timing Is Everything

Many wines enjoyed before dinner, as apéritif wines, or after dinner, as dessert wines, fall into the category of *fortified wines* (called *liqueur wines* by the European Union, or E.U.; see Chapter 1 for an explanation of E.U. terms). Fortified wines all have alcohol added to them at some point in their production, giving them an alcohol content that ranges from 16 to 24 percent.

TECHNICAL STUFF

The point at which alcohol is added determines whether the wines are naturally sweet or dry.

>> When fortified with alcohol *during* fermentation, the wines end up being sweet, because the added alcohol stops fermentation, leaving natural, unfermented sugar in the wine. (See Chapter 1 for an explanation of fermentation.) Port is the classic example of this process.

>> When fortified *after* fermentation (after all the grape sugar has been converted to alcohol), the wines are dry (unless they're subsequently sweetened). Sherry is the classic example of this process.

Some of the wines we call dessert wines don't have added alcohol. Their sweetness occurs because the grapes are at the right place at the right time — when noble rot strikes. (See the discussion of German wines in Chapter 12 for more about noble rot.) Other dessert wines are sweet because winemakers pick very ripe (but not rotten) grapes and dry them before fermentation to concentrate their juice, or they let the grapes freeze — just other ways of turning grape juice into the nectar of the gods.

The Growing Popularity of Sherry

The late comedian Rodney Dangerfield built a career around the line, "I get no respect!" His wine of choice should have been Sherry, because it has shared the same plight. Sherry is a wine of true quality and diversity, but it remains undiscovered by most of the world, including much of Spain itself, its home country. (Try getting a glass of Sherry in a bar in Madrid or Barcelona!). But even as wine drinkers find pleasure elsewhere, some wine connoisseurs are becoming ever more passionate about Sherry, and gradually raising awareness for this wine.

The Jerez triangle

Sherry comes from the Andalucía region of sun-baked, southwestern Spain. The wine is named after Jerez (her-*eth*) de la Frontera, an old town of Moorish and

Arab origin where many of the Sherry *bodegas* are located. (*Bodega* can refer to the actual building in which Sherry is matured or to the Sherry firm itself.)

Actually, the town of Jerez is just one corner of a triangle that makes up the Sherry region. Another corner is Puerto de Santa María, a beautiful, old coast town southwest of Jerez and home to a number of large bodegas. The third point of the triangle, Sanlúcar de Barrameda (also on the coast but northwest of Jerez), is so blessed with sea breezes that the lightest and driest of Sherries, *manzanilla* (mahn-zah-nee-yah), can legally be made only there. Aficionados of Sherry swear that they can detect the salty tang of the ocean in manzanilla.

Traveling from Sanlúcar to Jerez, you pass vineyards with dazzling white soil. This soil is *albariza,* the region's famous chalky earth, rich in limestone from fossilized shells. Summers are hot and dry, but balmy sea breezes temper the heat.

The Palomino grape — the main variety used in Sherry — thrives only here in the hot Sherry region on albariza soil. Palomino is a complete failure for table wines because it is so neutral in flavor and low in acid, but it's perfect for Sherry production. Two other grape varieties, Pedro Ximénez (*pay*-dro he-*main*-ehz) and Moscatel (Muscat), are used for dessert types of Sherry.

The phenomenon of flor

Sherry consists of two basic types: *fino* (light, very dry) and *oloroso* (rich and full, but also dry). Sweet Sherries are made by sweetening either type.

After fermentation, the winemaker decides which Sherries will become finos (*fee*-nos) or olorosos (oh-loh-*roh*-sohs) by judging the appearance, aroma, and flavor of the young, unfortified wines. If a wine is to be a fino, the winemaker fortifies it lightly (until its alcohol level reaches about 15.5 percent). He strengthens future olorosos to 18 percent alcohol.

At this point, when the wines are in casks, the special Sherry magic begins: A yeast called *flor* grows spontaneously on the surface of the wines destined to be finos. The flor eventually covers the whole surface, protecting the wine from oxidation. The flor feeds on oxygen in the air and on alcohol and glycerin in the wine. It changes the wine's character, contributing a distinct aroma and flavor and rendering the wine thinner and more delicate in texture.

Flor doesn't grow on olorosos-to-be, because their higher alcohol content prevents it. Without the protection of the flor (and because the casks are never filled to the brim), these wines are exposed to oxygen as they age. This deliberate oxidation protects olorosos against further oxidation — for example, after you open a bottle.

Communal aging

Both fino and oloroso Sherries age in a special way that's unique to Sherry making.

TECHNICAL STUFF

The young wine isn't left to age on its own (as most other wines would) but is added to casks of older wine that are already aging. To make room for the young wine, some of the older wine is emptied out of the casks and is added to casks of even older wine. To make room in those casks, some of that wine is transferred to casks of even older wine, and so on. At the end of this chain, four to nine generations away from the young wine, some of the finished Sherry is taken from the oldest casks and is bottled for sale.

This system of blending wines is called the *solera* system. It takes its name from the word *solera* (floor), the term also used to identify the casks of oldest wine.

As wines are blended — younger into older, into yet older, and eventually into oldest — no more than a third of the wine is emptied from any cask. In theory, then, each solera contains small (and ever-decreasing) amounts of very old wine. As each younger wine mingles with older wine, it takes on characteristics of the older wine; within a few months, the wine of each generation is indistinguishable from what it was before being refreshed with younger wine. Thus, the solera system maintains infinite consistency of quality and style in Sherry.

Because the casks of Sherry age in dry, airy bodegas above ground (rather than humid, underground cellars like most other wines), some of the wine's water evaporates, and the wine's alcoholic strength increases. Some olorosos aged for more than ten years can be as much as 24 percent alcohol, compared to their starting point of 18 percent.

Two makes 12+

So far, so good: two types of Sherry — delicate fino aged under its protective flor and fuller oloroso aged oxidatively — and no vintages, because the young wines are blended with older wines. But now Sherry begins to get a bit confusing. Those two types are about to branch into at least 12. New styles occur when the natural course of aging changes the character of a Sherry so that its taste no longer conforms to one of the two categories. Deliberate sweetening of the wine also creates different styles.

Among dry Sherries, these are the main styles:

>> **Fino:** Pale, straw-colored Sherry, light in body, dry, and delicate. Fino Sherries are always matured under flor, either in Jerez or Puerto de Santa María. They have 15 to 17 percent alcohol. After they lose their protective flor (by bottling),

finos become very vulnerable to oxidation spoilage, and you must, therefore, store them in a cool place, drink them young, and refrigerate them after opening. They're best when chilled.

» **Manzanilla:** Pale, straw-colored, delicate, light, tangy, and very dry fino-style Sherry made only in Sanlúcar de Barrameda. (Although various styles of manzanilla are produced, *manzanilla fina,* the fino style, is by far the most common.) The temperate sea climate causes the flor to grow thicker in this town, and manzanilla is thus the driest and most pungent of all the Sherries. Handle it similarly to a fino Sherry.

» **Manzanilla pasada:** A manzanilla that has been aged in cask about seven years and has lost its flor. It's more amber in color than a manzanilla fina and fuller-bodied. It's close to a dry amontillado (see the next item) in style, but still crisp and pungent. Serve cool.

» **Amontillado:** An aged fino that has lost its flor in the process of cask aging. It's deeper amber in color and richer and nuttier than the previous styles. Amontillado (ah-moan-tee-*yah*-doh) is dry and retains some of the pungent tang from its lost flor. True amontillado is fairly rare. Most of the best examples are in the $30 to $90 price range; if you encounter cheaper Sherries labeled *amontillado* that costs less than $15 a bottle, be suspicious of its stylistic authenticity. Serve amontillado slightly cool and, for best flavor, finish the bottle within a week.

» **Oloroso:** Dark gold to deep brown in color (depending on its age), full-bodied with rich, raisiny aroma and flavor, but dry. Olorosos lack the delicacy and pungency of fino (flor) Sherries. They're usually between 18 and 20 percent alcohol and can keep for a few weeks after you open the bottle because they have already been oxidized in their aging. Serve them at room temperature.

» **Palo cortado:** The rarest of all Sherries. In general, it starts out as a fino, with a flor, and develops as an amontillado, losing its flor. But then, for some unknown reason, it begins to resemble the richer, more fragrant oloroso style, all the while retaining the elegance of an amontillado. In color and alcohol content, palo cortado (*pah*-loe-cor-*tah*-doh) is similar to an oloroso, but its aroma is quite like an amontillado. Like amontillado Sherry, beware of cheap imitations. Serve at room temperature. It keeps as well as olorosos.

Sweet Sherry is dry Sherry that has been sweetened. The sweetening can come in many forms, such as the juice of Pedro Ximénez grapes that have been dried like raisins. All the following sweet styles of Sherry are best served at room temperature:

» **Medium Sherry:** Amontillados and light olorosos that have been slightly sweetened can no longer be labeled with those names. They are light brown in color.

» **Pale Cream:** Made by blending fino and light amontillado Sherries and lightly sweetening the blend. They have a very pale gold color. Pale Cream is a fairly new style.

» **Cream Sherry:** Cream and the lighter "milk" Sherries are rich *amorosos* (the term for sweetened olorosos). They vary in quality, depending on the oloroso used, and can improve in the bottle with age. These Sherries are a popular style.

» **Brown Sherry:** Very dark, rich, sweet, dessert Sherry, usually containing a coarser style of oloroso.

» **East India Sherry:** A type of Brown Sherry that has been deeply sweetened and colored.

» **Pedro Ximénez and Moscatel:** Extremely sweet, dark brown, syrupy dessert Sherries. Often lower in alcohol, these Sherries are made from raisined grapes of these two varieties. As varietally labeled Sherries, they are quite rare, but Pedro Ximémez (its nickname is PX) is starting to appear more lately. Delicious over vanilla ice cream (really!).

WARNING

Some wines from elsewhere in the world, especially the United States, also call themselves *Sherry.* Many of these are inexpensive wines in large bottles. Occasionally, you can find a decent one, but usually, they're sweet and not very good. Authentic Sherry is made only in the Jerez region of Spain and carries the official name, *Jerez-Xérès-Sherry* (the Spanish, French, and English names for the town), on the front or back label.

Serving and storing Sherry

The light, dry Sherries — fino and manzanilla — must be fresh. Buy them from stores with rapid turnover; a fino or manzanilla that has been languishing on the shelf for several months will not give you the authentic experience of these wines.

WARNING

Although fino or manzanilla can be an excellent apéritif, be careful when ordering a glass in a restaurant or bar. Never accept a glass from an already-open bottle unless the bottle has been refrigerated. Even then, ask how long it has been open — more than two days is too much. After you open a bottle at home, refrigerate it and finish it within a couple of days.

TIP

Manzanilla and fino Sherry are ideal with almonds, olives, shrimp or prawns, all kinds of seafood, and those wonderful tapas in Spanish bars and restaurants. Amontillado Sherries can accompany tapas before dinner but are also fine at the table with light soups, cheese, ham, or salami (especially the Spanish type, *chorizo*). Dry olorosos and palo cortados are best with nuts, olives, and hard cheeses (such as the excellent Spanish sheep-milk cheese, Manchego). All the sweet Sherries can be served with desserts after dinner or enjoyed on their own.

NUT'N SHERRY

TIP

The aroma of fino Sherry is often compared with almonds. Amontillados are said to smell like hazelnuts, and olorosos, like walnuts. And, by the way, the named nuts make ideal accompaniments to each particular Sherry.

TIP

We like to buy half–bottles of fino and manzanilla so that we don't have leftover wine that oxidizes. These, and all Sherries, can be stored upright. Try not to hold bottles of fino or manzanilla more than three months, however. The higher alcohol and the oxidative aging of other types of Sherry (amontillado, oloroso, palo cortado, all the sweet Sherries) permit you to hold them for several years.

Recommended Sherries

REAL DEAL

Sherries are among the great values in the wine world: You can buy decent, genuine Sherries for $9 to $10. But if you want to try the best wines, you may have to spend $15 or more. The following are some of our favorite Sherries, according to type.

» **Fino:**

- González Byass's Tío Pepe (*tee*-oh *pay*-pay), $19
- Pedro Domecq's La Ina (*een*-ah), $15
- Emilio Lustau's Jarana (har-*ahn*-ah), $16
- Valdespino's Inocente ($12, half-bottle; $24, bottle)

» **Manzanilla:**

- Hidalgo's La Gitana (a great buy at $17 for 500-ml bottle); also, Hidalgo's La Gitana Manzanilla Pasada, $25

» **Amontillado:** You find a great number of cheap imitations in this category. For a true amontillado, stick to one of the following brands:

- González Byass's Del Duque, 30 years old (the real thing; half-bottle, $45; $90, 750 ml bottle)
- Emilio Lustau (any of its amontillados labeled *Almacenista,* $30, 500 ml bottle; $43, 30 years old, 750 ml bottle)
- Hidalgo's Napoleon, 30 years old, $80 to $95

- **» Oloroso:**
  - González Byass's Matusalem, 30 years old (half-bottle, $48; full bottle, $98)
  - Emilio Lustau (any of its olorosos labeled *Almacenista,* $35 to $40)
- **» Palo cortado:** You find many imitations in this category, too. True palo cortados are quite rare.
  - González Byass's Apostoles 30 years old (half-bottle, $48; .750 bottle, $98)
  - Emilio Lustau (any of its palo cortados labeled *Almacenista,* $58)
  - Hidalgo's La Gitana Cortado, 30 years old ($98 to $100)
- **» Cream:**
  - Sandeman's Armada Cream (about $15)
  - Emilio Lustau's Rare Cream Solera Reserva ($25)
- **» East India, Pedro Ximénez, Moscatel:**
  - Emilio Lustau (quality brand for all three Sherries; all $29)
  - González Byass's Pedro Ximénez "Noe" (half-bottle, $49; .750 bottle, $98)

Montilla: A Sherry look-alike

Northeast of the Sherry region is the Montilla-Moriles region (commonly referred to as Montilla, pronounced mon-*tee*-yah), where wines very similar to Sherry are made in fino, amontillado, and oloroso styles. The two big differences between Montilla and Sherry are

» Pedro Ximénez is the predominant grape variety in Montilla.

» Montillas usually reach their high alcohol levels naturally (without fortification).

REAL DEAL

Alvear is the leading brand of Montilla. Reasonably priced ($20 to $23 for a half-bottle), these wines are vintage-dated, and widely available as finos or amontillados.

Italy: Marsala, Vin Santo, and the Gang

Italy has a number of interesting dessert and fortified wines, of which Marsala (named after a town in western Sicily) is the best-known. Marsala is a fortified wine made from local grape varieties. It comes in numerous styles, all of which are fortified after fermentation, like Sherry, and aged in a form of the solera system (see the earlier section "Communal aging" for details). You can find dry, semi-dry, or sweet versions and amber, gold, or red versions, but the best Marsalas have the word *Superiore* or — even better — *Vergine* or *Vergine Soleras* on the label. Marsala Vergine is unsweetened and uncolored and is aged longer than other styles.

WORTH THE SEARCH

Marco De Bartoli is the most acclaimed producer of dry-style Marsala. His 20-year-old Vecchio Samperi (about $80 to $95 for a 500-ml bottle) is an excellent example of a dry, apéritif Marsala. Pellegrino, Rallo, Donnafugata, and Florio are larger producers of note. (For more info on Marsala and all other Sicilian fortified or dessert wines, see our book *Italian Wine For Dummies,* published by Wiley.)

WORTH THE SEARCH

Two fascinating dessert wines are made on small islands near Sicily from dried grapes. One is Malvasia delle Lipari, from the estate of the late Carlo Hauner. This wine has a beautiful, orange-amber color and an incredible floral, apricot, and herb aroma ($33 for a half-bottle; $60, full bottle). The other is Pantelleria, a very delicious sweet wine. Until 2013, it was called Moscato di Pantelleria, and some producers still use that name; some others refer to it as Zibibbo di Pantelleria, using the Sicilian name of the Muscat of Alexandria grape variety. De Bartoli is one of the best producers; look for his Bukkuram Passito Pantelleria (about $100 to $135 for a 500-ml bottle). Donnafugata also makes a fine Passito Pantelleria, Ben Ryé ($40, half-bottle, $80, full bottle).

The region of Tuscany is rightfully proud of its Vin Santo (vin *sahn*-toh), a golden amber wine made from dried grapes, generally white Malvasia and Trebbiano, and barrel-aged for several years. Vin Santo can be dry, medium-dry, or sweet. We prefer the first two — the dry style as an apéritif and the medium-dry version as an accompaniment to the wonderful Italian almond cookies called *biscotti.*

TIP

Many Tuscan producers make a Vin Santo; four outstanding examples of Vin Santo (conveniently available in half-bottles as well as full bottles) are from Avignonesi (very expensive! over $200 a half-bottle), Badia a Coltibuono, Castello di Cacchiano, and San Giusto a Rentennano. The Badia a Coltibuono is the bargain of the group at $40 to $50 a half-bottle.

Greece's Santorini Island also makes a Vinsanto from Assyrtiko and Aidani grapes, which is similar to Italy's Vin Santo. Greek producers claim that this type of wine originated on Santorini, but Italians disagree. The leading producers of Santorini Assyrtiko, such as Argyros and Sigalas, also produce Vinsanto.

Port: The Glory of Portugal

Port is the world's greatest fortified red wine. The British invented Port thanks to one of their many wars with the French, when they were forced to buy Portuguese wine as an alternative to French wine. To ensure that the Portuguese wines were stable enough for shipment by sea, the British added a small amount of brandy to finished dry red wine, and early Port was the result. The English established their first Port house, Warre, in the city of Oporto in 1670, and several others followed.

Ironically, the French, who drove the British to Portugal, today drink three times as much Port as the British! But, of course, the French have the highest per capita consumption of wine of any major country in the world.

Home, home on the Douro

Port wine takes its name from the city of Oporto, situated where the northerly Douro River empties into the Atlantic Ocean. But its vineyards are far inland, in the hot, mountainous Douro Valley. Some of the most dramatically beautiful vineyards in the world are on the slopes of the upper Douro — still very much a rugged, unspoiled area. (In 1756, this wine region became one of the first in the world to be officially recognized by its government.)

Port wine is fermented and fortified in the Douro Valley, and then most of it travels downriver to the coast. Large shippers finish and mature the wine in the Port lodges of Vila Nova de Gaia, a suburb of Oporto, while most small producers mature their wine upriver. From Oporto, the wine is shipped all over the world.

TECHNICAL STUFF

To stop your wine-nerd friends in their tracks, ask them to name the authorized grape varieties for Port. (More than 80 exist!) In truth, most wine lovers — even Port lovers — can't name more than one variety. These grapes are mostly local and unknown outside of Portugal. For the record, the five most important varieties are *Touriga Nacional*, *Tinta Roriz* (Tempranillo), *Tinta Barroca*, *Tinto Cão*, and *Touriga Franca*.

MY REAL NAME IS PORTO

The term *Port* has been borrowed even more extensively around the world than *Sherry* has. Many countries outside the E.U. make sweet, red wine in the Port style and label it as Port. Some of it can be quite good, but it's never as fine as the genuine article that is made only in Portugal. The trick in identifying authentic Portuguese Port is to look for the word *Porto*, which always appears on the label.

Many Ports in a storm

Think Sherry is complicated? In some ways, Port is even trickier. Although all Port is sweet because it is fortified during fermentation, and almost all of it is red, a zillion styles exist. The styles vary according to the quality of the base wine (ranging from ordinary to exceptional), how long the wine is aged in wood before bottling (ranging from 2 to 40-plus years), and whether the wine is from a single year or blended from wines of several years.

TIP

Don't let all the complicated styles of Port deter you from picking up a bottle and trying it. If you've never had Port before, you're bound to love it — almost no matter which style you try. (Later, you can fine-tune your preference for one style or another.) Port is simply delicious!

The following sections feature brief descriptions of the main styles, from simplest to most complex.

White Port

This type of Port is an anomaly, because most Port wine is red. But white Port does exist. Made from white grapes, this gold-colored wine can be off-dry or sweet. We couldn't quite figure out why it existed — Sherries and Sercial Madeiras (discussed later in this chapter) are better as apéritifs and red Ports are far superior as sweet wines — until someone served us white Port with tonic and ice. Served this way, white Port can be a bracing warm-weather apéritif.

Non-vintage Ports

Most Port wine is not vintage-dated and is blended from wines of various years. The types of non-vintage Port that we describe in this list encompass the majority of Port wines that you can see in a wine shop:

>> **Ruby Port:** This young, non-vintage style is aged in wood for about three years before release. Fruity, simple, and inexpensive ($13 to $15 for major brands), it's the best-selling type of Port. If labeled *Reserve* or *Special Reserve,* the wine has usually aged about six years and costs a few dollars more. Ruby Port is a good introduction to the Port world.

>> **Vintage Character Port:** Despite its name, this wine is not single-vintage Port — it just tries to taste like one. Vintage Character Port is actually premium ruby blended from higher-quality wines of several vintages and matured in wood for about five years. A definite step-up from simple ruby Port. Full-bodied, rich, and ready to drink when released, these wines are a good value at about $17 to $21. But the labels don't always say Vintage Character; instead, they often bear proprietary names— as if the name Vintage Character wouldn't

have been confusing enough! Examples are Founder's Reserve (from Sandeman), Bin 27 (Fonseca), Six Grapes (Graham), First Estate (Taylor Fladgate), Warrior (Warre), and Distinction (Croft). Fonseca's Bin 27 is probably the most well-known Vintage Character Port.

» **Tawny Port:** Tawny is the most versatile Port style. The best tawnies are good-quality wines that have faded to a pale garnet or brownish red color during long wood aging. Their labels carry an indication of their average age (the average age of the wines from which they were blended) — 10, 20, 30, or over-40 years. Ten-year-old tawnies cost about $30 to $35; 20-year-olds sell for $50 to $55; 30-year-olds, $135 to $140 00; and over-40-year-old tawnies cost a lot more ($200+). We consider 10- and 20-year-old tawnies the best buys; the older ones, for us, aren't always worth the extra bucks. Tawny Ports have more finesse than other styles and are appropriate both as apéritifs and after dinner. Inexpensive tawnies that sell for about the same price as ruby Port are usually weak in flavor and not worth buying.

TIP

A serious tawny Port can be enjoyed in warm weather (even with a few ice cubes!) when a Vintage Port would be too heavy and tannic.

Vintage-dated Ports

Although the Port wines described in the preceding section can be excellent, the Ports made from grapes grown in a single year are generally of a higher caliber and are more expensive. These vintage–dated Ports include the following styles (only one of which is actually called Vintage Port):

» **Colheita Port:** Often confused with Vintage Port itself because it is vintage-dated, colheita is actually a tawny Port from a single vintage. In other words, it has aged (and softened and tawnied) in wood for many years. Unlike a typical aged tawny, though, it's the wine of a single year. Niepoort is one of the few Port houses that specializes in colheita Port. It can be very good, but older vintages are quite expensive ($50 to more than $100, depending on the vintage). Smith Woodhouse and Delaforce offer some colheita Portos for $48 to $62. Kopke is another Port house specializing in colheita Portos.

» **Late Bottled Vintage (LBV) Port:** This type is from a specific vintage, but usually not from a very top year. The wine ages four to six years in wood before bottling and is then ready to drink, unlike Vintage Port itself, which requires additional aging in bottle. Quite full-bodied but not as hefty as Vintage Port, it sells for about $20 to $23.

» **Vintage Port:** The pinnacle of Port production, Vintage Port is the wine of a single year blended from several of a house's best vineyards. It's bottled at about two years of age, before the wine has much chance to shed its tough

WARNING

tannins. It requires, therefore, an enormous amount of bottle aging to achieve the development that didn't occur in wood. Vintage Port is usually not mature (ready to drink) until at least 20 years after the vintage.

Because it's very rich and very tannic, this wine throws heavy sediment and *must* be decanted, preferably several hours before drinking (it needs the aeration). Vintage Port can live 70 or more years in top vintages.

Most good Vintage Ports sell for $100 to $120 -plus when they're first released (years away from drinkability). Mature Vintage Ports can cost well over $100. Producing a Vintage Port amounts to a *declaration of that vintage* (a term you hear in Port circles) on the part of an individual Port house.

» **Single Quinta Vintage Port:** These are Vintage Ports from a single estate *(quinta)* that is usually a producer's best property (such as Taylor's Vargellas and Graham's Malvedos). They're made in years that are good but not in the best vintages, because in the best years their grapes are needed for the Vintage Port blend. They have the advantage of being readier to drink than declared Vintage Ports — at less than half their price — and of usually being released when they're mature. You should decant and aerate them before serving, however. (Some Port houses, incidentally, are themselves single estates, such as Quinta do Noval, Quinta do Infantado, and Quinta do Vesuvio. When such a house makes a vintage-dated Port, it's a Vintage Port, as well as a single quinta Port. But that's splitting hairs.)

Storing and serving Port

Treat Vintage Ports like all other fine red wines: Store the bottles on their sides in a cool place. You can store other types of Ports either on their sides (if they have a cork rather than a plastic-topped cork stopper) or upright. All Ports, except white, ruby, and older Vintage Ports, keep well for a week or so after opening, with aged-stated tawny capable of keeping for several weeks.

TIP

You can find Vintage Ports and some Vintage Character Ports, such as Fonseca Bin 27, in half-bottles — a brilliant choice for Port lovers. Enjoying a bottle after dinner is far easier to justify when it's just a half-bottle. The wine evolves slightly more quickly in half-bottles, and, considering the wine's longevity, that may even be a bonus!

Serve Port at cool room temperature, 62 to 64 degrees Fahrenheit (17 to 18 degrees Celsius), although tawny Port can be an invigorating pick-me-up when served chilled during warm weather. The classic complements to Port are walnuts and strong cheeses, such as Stilton, Gorgonzola, Roquefort, Cheddar, and aged Gouda.

Recommended Port producers

In terms of quality, with the exception of a few clunker producers, Port is one of the most consistent of all wines. We've organized our favorite Port producers into two categories — outstanding and very good — in rough order of preference. As you might expect, wines in the first group tend to be a bit more expensive. Taylor–Fladgate and Dow are two Port producers who make their ports in a drier style than other Port producers. Our rating is based mainly on Vintage Port but can be generally applied to all the various Port styles of each house.

Outstanding	
Taylor-Fladgate	Dow
Fonseca	Smith-Woodhouse
Graham	Cockburn (coh-burn)
Quinta do Noval "Nacional" (made from ungrafted vineyards; see Chapter 3)	
Very Good	
Ramos Pinto	Ferreira
Warre	Cálem
Quinta do Noval	Churchill
Niepoort	Delaforce
Croft	Gould Campbell
Sandeman	Martinez
Quinta do Infantado	Osborne
Quinta do Vesuvio	Offley
Rozes	

ANOTHER PORTUGUESE CLASSIC

One of the great dessert wines made mainly from the white or pink Muscat grape is Setúbal (*shtoo*-bahl). Produced just south of Lisbon, Setúbal is made similarly to Port, with alcohol added to stop fermentation. Like Port, it's a rich, long-lasting wine. The most important producer is J. M. da Fonseca.

TIP

Recent good vintages of Vintage Porto to buy include 2013, 2012, 2009, 2007, 2000, 1994, 1992, and 1991. (For a complete list of Vintage Port vintages, see Appendix C.)

Long Live Madeira

The legendary wine called Madeira comes from the island of the same name, which sits in the Atlantic Ocean, nearer to Africa than Europe. Madeira is a subtropical island whose precarious hillside vineyards rise straight up from the ocean. The island is a province of Portugal, but the British have always run its wine trade. Historically, Madeira could even be considered something of an American wine, for this is the wine that American colonists drank.

Madeira can lay claim to being the world's longest-lived wine. A few years ago, we were fortunate enough to try a 1799 Vintage Madeira that was still perfectly fine. Only Hungary's Tokaji Aszú can rival Vintage Madeira in longevity, and that's true only of Tokaji Aszú's rarest examples, such as its Essencia.

Although Madeira's fortified wines were quite the rage 240 years ago, the island's vineyards were devastated at the end of the 19th century, first by mildew and then by the phylloxera louse. Most vineyards were replanted with lesser grapes. Madeira has spent a long time recovering from these setbacks. In the 19th century, more than 70 companies were shipping Madeira all over the world; now, only four companies of any size exist: Barbeito, H. M Borges, the Madeira Wine Company (the largest by far, a consolidation of four old companies — Blandy's, Cossart Gordon, Leacock's, and Miles — and only the Blandy family is still involved), and Pereira d'Oliveira.

The very best Madeira wines are still those from the old days, vintage-dated wines from 1920 back to 1795. Surprisingly, you can still find a few Madeiras from the 19th century. The prices aren't outrageous, either ($300 to $400 a bottle), considering what you'd pay for other wines that old, such as Bordeaux. (Refer to Chapter 17 for sources of old Madeira.)

Timeless, indestructible, tasty, and baked

The best Madeira comes in four styles, two fairly dry and two sweet. The sweeter Madeiras generally have their fermentation halted somewhat early by the addition of alcohol. Drier Madeiras have alcohol added after fermentation.

A curiosity of Madeira production is a baking process called the *estufagem* (es-too-*fah*-jem), which follows fermentation. The fact that Madeira improves with heat was discovered back in the 17th century. When trading ships crossed the equator with casks of Madeira as ballast in their holds, the wine actually improved! Today's practice of baking the wine at home on the island is a bit more practical than sending it around the world in a slow boat.

In the estufagem process, Madeira spends a minimum of three months, often longer, in heated tanks, in *estufas* (heating rooms). Any sugars in the wine become caramelized, and the wine becomes thoroughly *maderized* (oxidized through heating) without developing any unpleasant aroma or taste.

A more laborious and considerably more expensive way of heating Madeira is the *canteiro* method, in which barrels are left in warm lofts or exposed to the sun (the weather in Madeira stays warm year-round) for as long as three years. The same magical metamorphosis takes place in the wines. The *canteiro* method is best for Madeira because the wines retain their high acidity, color, and extract much better in the slow, natural three-year process; the finer Madeiras use this method of aging.

Endless finish

Technically, almost all the best Madeira starts as white wine, but the heating process and years of maturation give it an amber color. It has a tangy aroma and flavor that's unique, and as long a finish on the palate as you'll find on the planet. When Madeira is made from any of the island's five noble grapes (listed in the next section), the grape name indicates the style. When Madeira doesn't carry a grape name — and most younger Madeiras don't — the words *dry, medium-dry, medium-sweet,* and *sweet* indicate the style.

Vintage Madeira must spend at least 20 years in a cask, but in the old days, the aging was even longer. Some of the most memorable wines we've ever tasted were old Madeiras, and so we're afraid we might get carried away a bit, beginning any time now. Their aroma alone is divine, and you continue tasting the wine long after you've swallowed it. (Spitting is out of the question.) Words truly are inadequate to describe this wine.

If you can afford to buy an old bottle of vintage-dated Madeira (the producer's name is relatively unimportant), you'll understand our enthusiasm. And maybe some day when Madeira production gets back on its feet, every wine lover will be able to experience Vintage Madeira. In the meantime, for a less expensive Madeira experience, look for wines labeled *15 years old, 10 years old,* or *5 years old.* Don't bother with any other type, because it will be unremarkable, and then we'll look crazy.

Madeira styles and grape varieties

TIP

You never have to worry about Madeira getting too old. It's indestructible. The enemies of wine — heat and oxygen — have already had their way with Madeira during the winemaking and maturing process. Nothing you do after it's opened can make it blink.

TIP

If a Madeira is dated with the word *Solera* — for example, *Solera 1890* — it is *not* a Vintage Madeira but a blend of many younger vintages whose original barrel, or solera, dates back to the date indicated. Solera-dated Madeiras can be very fine and are generally not as expensive as Vintage Madeiras — nor as great. But Solera Madeiras are becoming obsolete today. In their place is a new style of Madeira, called *colheita* or Harvest. This style is modeled after *colheita* Porto (see the earlier section "Many Ports in a storm"), in that colheita Madeira is a single vintage-dated Madeira wine. Colheita Madeira doesn't have to spend a minimum of 20 years aging in cask, as does Vintage Madeira, but only five — or seven for the driest, Sercial. (For example, the 1994 colheita Madeira debuted in 2000 at only six years of age.) Colheita Madeira is much less expensive than Vintage Madeira. Most of the major Madeira shippers are now selling colheita; sales of vintage-dated Madeira have doubled since the introduction of this style.

Vintage, colheita, and solera-dated Madeiras are made from a single grape variety and are varietally labeled. The grapes include five noble white grape varieties and one less noble red variety. Each variety corresponds to a specific style of wine; we list them here from driest style to sweetest:

>> **Sercial:** The Sercial grape grows at the highest altitudes. Thus, the grapes are the least ripe and make the driest Madeira. The wine is high in acidity and very tangy. Sercial Madeira is an outstanding apéritif wine with almonds, olives, or light cheeses. Unfortunately, true Sercial is quite rare today.

>> **Verdelho:** The Verdelho grape makes a medium-dry style, with nutty, peachy flavors and a tang of acidity. It's good as an apéritif or with consommé.

>> **Bual (or Boal):** Darker amber in color, Bual is a rich, medium-sweet Madeira with spicy flavors of almonds and raisins and a long, tangy finish. Bual is best after dinner. Like Sercial, true Bual is rare today.

>> **Malmsey:** Made from Malvasia grapes, Malmsey is dark amber, sweet, and intensely concentrated with a very long finish. Drink it after dinner.

>> **Terrantez:** Medium-sweet, between Verdelho and Bual in style, this is a powerful, fragrant Madeira with lots of acidity. For some Madeira lovers, Terrantez is the greatest variety of all. Unfortunately, very little Terrantez is available today. Drink it after dinner.

The less-noble red Tinta Negra Mole variety is the dominant grape for today's Madeira production (used for more than 85 percent of Madeira wines), because it grows more prolifically than the five noble varieties (Sercial, Verdelho, Bual, Malmsey, and Terrantez) without the diseases to which they are prone. Also, it is less site-specific; it can grow anywhere on the island, unlike the noble varieties, which grow in vineyards close to the sea where the urban sprawl of Funchal, Madeira's capital city, impinges on them. Previously, the less-regarded Tinta Negra Mole wasn't identified as a variety on bottles of Madeira, but now the huge Madeira Wine Company is beginning to varietally label Tinta Negra Mole Madeiras.

A final grape that's traditional in Madeira is Bastardo, the only red grape of the noble varieties. Old Bastardos from the last century are mahogany-colored and rich, but not so rich as the Terrantez. Bastardo is no longer used for commercial production.

Sauternes and the Nobly-Rotted Wines

Warm, misty autumns encourage the growth of a fungus called *botrytis cinerea* in vineyards. (See "What's noble about rot?" In Chapter 12.) The best wines from botrytis-infected grapes are among the greatest dessert wines in the world, with intensely concentrated flavors and plenty of acidity to prevent the wine from tasting excessively sweet.

The greatest nobly rotted wines are made in the Sauternes district of Graves (Bordeaux) in France, in Germany (described in Chapter 12), and in the Tokaji district in Hungary, but they are also produced in Austria and California, among other places.

Sauternes: Liquid gold

Sauternes is a very labor-intensive wine. Grapes must be picked by hand; workers pass through the vineyard several times, sometimes over a period of weeks, each time selecting only the botrytis-infected grapes. Yields are low. Harvests sometimes linger until November, but now and then, bad weather in October dashes all hopes of making botrytis-infected wine. Often, only two to four vintages per decade make decent Sauternes. (The 1980s decade was exceptional, and the 2000s decade was phenomenal; see the vintage chart in Appendix C.)

Consequently, good Sauternes is expensive. Prices range from $50 a bottle up to over $400 (depending on the vintage) for Château d'Yquem (*d'ee-kem*). The greatest Sauternes, Yquem has always been prized by collectors (see Chapter 17). It was the only Sauternes given the status of *First Great Growth* in the 1855 Bordeaux Classification (see Chapter 10).

TIP

Sauternes is widely available in half-bottles, reducing the cost somewhat. A 375-ml bottle is a perfect size for after dinner, and you can buy a decent half-bottle of Sauternes or Barsac, a dessert wine similar to Sauternes, like Château Doisy-Védrines (*dwahs-ee-veh-dreen*) or Château Doisy-Daëne (*dwahs-ee-dah-en*) for $25.

Mining the gold

TIP

The Sauternes wine district includes five communes in the southernmost part of Graves (one of them named Sauternes). One of the five, Barsac, is entitled to its own appellation; Barsac wines are slightly lighter and less sweet than Sauternes. The Garonne River and the Ciron, an important tributary, produce the mists that encourage *botrytis cinerea* to form on the grapes.

The three authorized grape varieties are Sémillon, Sauvignon Blanc, and Muscadelle — although the latter is used by only a few châteaux, and even then in small quantities. Sémillon is the king of Sauternes. Most producers use at least 80 percent of Sémillon in their blend.

WARNING

Wine that is called *Sauterne* (no final *s*) is produced in California and other places. This semi-sweet, rather insipid wine is made from unremarkable grapes and usually sold in large bottles. It bears absolutely no resemblance to true, botrytis-infected Sauternes, from Sauternes, France. California does make late-harvest, botrytis-infected wines, mainly Rieslings, and while they are far better than California Sauterne (and even worth trying), they are very different wines from the botrytis wines of Sauternes or of Germany.

Recommended Sauternes

WORTH THE SEARCH

All the Sauternes in the following list range from outstanding to good. (Wines specifically from Barsac are labeled as such.) In Sauternes, vintages are just as important as in the rest of Bordeaux; check our vintage recommendations in Appendix C.

>> **Outstanding:**

- **Château d'Yquem:** Can last for 100 years or more ($400+)

- **Château de Fargues:** Owned by Yquem; almost as good as Yquem, at one-third the price ($140)

- **Château Climens (Barsac):** At $135, a value; near Yquem's level

- **Château Coutet (Barsac):** A great buy ($80)

» **Excellent:**

- **Château Suduiraut:** On the brink of greatness ($100)

- **Château Rieussec:** Rich, lush style ($88)

- **Château Raymond-Lafon:** Located next to Yquem (about $67)

» **Very Good:**

- **Château Lafaurie-Peyraguey**

- **Château Latour Blanche**

- **Château Guiraud**

- **Château Rabaud-Promis**

- **Château Sigalas-Rabaud**

- **Château Nairac (Barsac)**

- **Château Doisy-Védrines (Barsac)**

- **Château Doisy-Daëne (Barsac)**

- **Château Clos Haut-Peyraguey**

» **Good:**

- **Château Bastor-Lamontagne**

- **Château Rayne Vigneau**

- **Château d'Arche**

- **Château de Malle**

- **Château Lamothe-Guignard**

- **Château Romieu-Lacoste (Barsac)**

- **Château Doisy-Dubroca (Barsac)**

- **Château Filhot**

Letting baby grow

Sauternes has such balance of natural sweetness and acidity that it can age well (especially the better Sauternes mentioned here) for an extraordinarily long time. Unfortunately, because Sauternes is so delicious, people often drink it young, when it's very rich and sweet. But Sauternes is really at its best when it loses its baby fat and matures.

TIP

After about 10 to 15 years, Sauternes's color changes from light gold to an old gold-coin color, sometimes with orange or amber tones. The wine loses the perception of sweetness and develops flavors reminiscent of apricots, orange rind, honey, and toffee. This stage is the best time to drink Sauternes. The better the vintage, the longer Sauternes takes to reach this stage, but once there, it stays at this plateau for many years — sometimes decades — and very gradually turns dark amber or light brown in color. Even in these final stages, Sauternes retains some of its complex flavors.

In good vintages, Sauternes can age for 50 to 60 years or more. Château d'Yquem and Château Climens are particularly long-lived. (We recently had a half-bottle of 1893 Château d'Yquem that was glorious!)

TIP

Sauternes is best when served cold, but not ice cold, at about 52 to 53 degrees Fahrenheit (11 degrees Celsius). Mature Sauternes can be served a bit warmer. Because the wine is so rich and yet acidic, Sauternes is an ideal companion for *foie gras* — although, ordinarily, the wine is far more satisfying after dinner than as an apéritif. As for desserts, Sauternes is excellent with ripe fruits, lemon-flavored cakes, or pound cake.

Sauternes look-alikes

Many sweet, botrytis-infected wines similar to Sauternes exist in France; they sell for considerably less money than Sauternes or Barsacs. These wines are not as intense or as complex in flavor, but they are fine values at $20 to $30.

REAL DEAL

Directly north and adjacent to Barsac is the often overlooked Cérons wine region. You can probably convince many of your friends that a Cérons (about $34), served blind, is a Sauternes or Barsac. From the Entre-Deux-Mers district of Bordeaux, look for wines with the Cadillac, Loupiac, or Sainte-Croix-du-Mont appellations — all less expensive versions of Sauternes.

Hungary's Tokaji Aszú and Tokaji Eszencia

Hungary's most renowned wines are its sweet wines made from nobly rotted grapes in the Tokaj region, in the foothills of the Carpathian Mountains in northeastern Hungary, close to the Slovakian border. Producers there make both dry and sweet wines mainly from the Furmint grape variety, which also grows in Austria, Slovakia, and Slovenia. But Furmint is most famous as the primary grape variety in Tokaji Aszú botrytised wines, sometimes blended with two other varieties.

Aszú grapes (Aszú refers to botrytis-infected berries) are added to a dry base wine before, during or after fermentation, to bring sweetness to the wine while maintaining bracing acidity. The more Aszú berries added to the base wine, the more concentrated and sweet the wine is. The measure of sweetness is named *puttony*, a reference to harvest baskets used to collect the nobly-rotted grapes; the higher the number of puttonyos (traditionally, from three to six), the sweeter the wine.

You can find bottles of Tokaji Aszú labeled "3 Puttonyos" to "6 Puttonyos" but changes in wine regulations will mean that the lower levels of sweetness will no longer qualify as Tokaji Aszú and will be labeled otherwise. Tokaji Aszú is a sweet, intense dessert wine with high acidity and intense aromas of orange peel, apricots, and honey. A rare and exotic variation is Tokaji Eszencia, made only from the free-run juice of the aszú berries, without blending into dry wine.

Because of its scarcity, Eszencia is quite expensive (from $600 to $1,200, depending on the vintage). Due to its high residual sugar, Eszencia can take years to ferment, but the finished wine remains very low in alcohol — typically less than 5 percent. Eszencia is enormously concentrated, with very high acidity — so much so that it is often served by the spoonful rather than by the glass!

A few decades ago, we tasted an 1888 Eszencia from a half-bottle. It was still very aromatic and extremely delicious, with intense orange peel and apricot flavors, one of the greatest wines we have ever tasted. Tokaji Eszencia probably can age as long as Vintage Madeira, but we are not sure if there is anyone alive who can verify its longevity.

6

When You've Caught the Bug

Find out what you need to know about buying and collecting wine.

Discover the fun ways you can learn even more about wine, such as classes, wine publications, websites, and more.

Get the lowdown on how to taste wine more thoughtfully and then put your impressions into words — and how to use a numeric scale for rating wines.

IN THIS CHAPTER

» Playing hardball with hard-to-get-wines

» Keeping your own little black book of wine retailers

» Shopping virtually

» Collecting wine

» Helping your wine stay healthy

Chapter **17**

Buying and Collecting Wine

You probably have plenty of opportunities to buy wines for everyday drinking, and they are as near as your local supermarket or discount store. But sometimes you might want a special bottle, or even many very good bottles to begin a wine collection. Once upon a time your choices were limited to a few collectible wines that you could find in your local specialty wine shop, and price comparisons were out of the question. Fortunately, the world of serious wine buying now extends far beyond your local resources.

Two factors have changed the way that wine lovers buy fine wines, whether older vintages or current releases: the burgeoning opportunities on the Internet and the growth of wine auctions. When we're looking for that hard-to-find bottle, we're on the web, searching. Our geeky wine-collector friends haunt the wine auctions — both in person and on the Internet — looking for special older bottles. Getting what you want is mostly a question of knowing where to look.

In this chapter, we show you exactly where to find rare and collectible wines; in addition, we explain how to balance, organize, and store your collection.

Finding the Rare and Collectible Wines

There's a Catch-22 for wine lovers who have really caught the bug: The more desirable a wine is, the more difficult it is to get; and the harder a wine is to get, the more desirable it is.

This situation exists for several reasons. The main reason is that some of the best wines are made in ridiculously small quantities. We wouldn't say that quantity and quality are necessarily incompatible in winemaking, but at the very highest levels of quality, there usually isn't much quantity to go around.

Sometimes when we search for a fairly scarce wine (most recently it was a special Italian white), we discover that it's available in only one store on the other side of the country, and that store has only three bottles in stock.

Today, many small-production wines sell *on allocation*, which means that distributors restrict the quantity that any one store can purchase, sometimes limiting stores to as few as six bottles of a particular wine. Most stores, in turn, limit customers to just one or two bottles. Certain wines are allocated in such a way that they're available primarily at restaurants. It's often the wine producer's wish to sell his scarce wine mainly in restaurants, figuring that the wine will get more exposure that way.

A final factor limiting availability of some wines is that wineries usually sell each wine just once, when the wine is young. In the case of many fine wines, such as top Brunello di Montalcino wines, the wine isn't at its best yet. But most wine merchants can't afford to store the wine for selling years later, and so they sell it young. This means that aged wines are invariably hard to get.

REMEMBER

When the wine you want plays hard to get, you have to play hardball; you have to look beyond your normal sources of supply. Your allies in this game are the Internet, wine shops in other cities, wine auction houses, and, in the case of domestic wines, the wineries themselves.

Buying fine and collectible wines on the Internet

As we mention in Chapter 6, the Internet is now a standard venue for wine buying, along with your local wine specialty shops. For sourcing collectible wines, online channels are all the more important. Sometimes, the *only* way to buy certain wines is on the Internet, because sought-after, small quantity wines are usually available in only a few states.

Some of the online resources for finding and purchasing hard-to-find wines are the websites of actual brick-and-mortar wine shops, and we list many of them in the next section.

TIP

As a first step when you want to purchase wine online, check out Wine-Searcher (www.wine-searcher.com). This site is indispensable to us. It searches for wines that you name and then lists stores and prices for them. You can use Wine-Searcher to compare prices and to find the most suitable store for purchasing the wine you want. Depending on the criteria you input, the search results can include merchants outside the United States as well as auction sites that list specific wines (see the later section "Buying wines at auctions"). The site is free, but purchasing the Pro Version ($39 per year) enables you to see results beyond those merchants who are sponsors of the site; we find it a good investment.

CROSSING STATE LINES

Because wine contains alcohol, it doesn't move through commercial channels as freely as other products do. Each state decides whether wineries and stores outside its borders may ship wine to state residents and under which conditions. By requiring consumers to buy wine only from their in-state, licensed retail stores or wineries, a state government can be sure it's getting all the tax revenue it's entitled to on every wine transaction in its jurisdiction.

Most wine shops and wineries are sympathetic to out-of-state customers, but out-of-state deliveries can be risky for their businesses, depending on regulations in their own state and the destination state. The risk is mainly theirs, too; the store or winery can lose its license, while all the buyer loses is any wine that's confiscated by the authorities.

If you want to buy wine from an out-of-state winery or merchant, discuss the issue with the people there. If shipping to you isn't legal, they can sometimes find a solution for you, such as holding the wine for you to pick up personally, or shipping to a friend or relative — or even another wine store — in a legal state.

Buy all the wine you want when you visit a winery: Different rules apply, and wine drinkers may legally ship home wines that they purchase during visits to out-of-state wineries, or buy online from wineries in the U.S.

Another Internet site worth knowing is Vinfolio (www.vinfolio.com). This company bills itself as "the fine wine source" and specializes in fine and collectible wines, although its offerings include some less exalted wines as well. You can purchase wine from the site, either from its inventory or from its peer-to-peer marketplace, where individuals list wines that they want to sell, subject to inspection by the Vinfolio team. Thanks to this collector-sourced marketplace, you can actually find older vintages to buy. The site also offers wine-cellar management services; we discuss that aspect of wine collecting in the section "Organization is peace of mind," later in this chapter.

Some U.S. wine stores worth knowing

We can't possibly list *all* the leading wine stores that sell fine wine, but the following purveyors are some of the best. Most of them specialize in certain kinds of fine wine that can be difficult to obtain elsewhere. We name the stores alphabetically, with each store's main wine specialties here:

>> Astor Wines & Spirits, New York, NY; www.astorwines.com — French, Italian, Spanish

>> Brookline Liquor Mart, Allston, MA; www.blmwine.com — Italian, Burgundy, Rhône

>> Burgundy Wine Company, New York, NY; www.burgundywinecompany.com — Burgundy, Oregon, Rhône

>> Chambers Street Wines, New York, NY; www.chambersstwines.com — French, Italian, biodynamic/organic wines

>> Corti Brothers, Sacramento, CA; www.cortibros.biz — Italian, California, dessert wines

>> Crush Wine & Spirits, New York, NY; www.crushwineco.com — French, German, Champagne

>> Flatiron Wines & Spirits, New York, NY; www.flatiron-wines.com — French, Italian, Champagne

>> Flickinger Wines, Chicago, IL; www.flickingerwines.com — French, Italian, Rhône

>> Garnet Wines & Liquors, New York, NY; www.garnetwine.com — Bordeaux, Champagne

>> Hart Davis Hart Wine Co., Chicago, IL; www.hdhwine.com — Bordeaux, Burgundy, Champagne

>> Kermit Lynch Wine Merchant, Berkeley, CA; www.kermitlynch.com — French country wines, Burgundy, Rhône

>> K&L Wine Merchants, San Francisco, CA; www.klwines.com — French, California, Champagne

» MacArthur Beverages, Washington, D.C.; www.bassins.com — California, Burgundy, Bordeaux, Italian, Rhône, Alsace, Australian, German, Vintage Port

» McCarthy & Schiering Wine Merchants, Seattle, WA; www.mccarthyandschiering.com — Washington, Oregon

» The Rare Wine Co., Sonoma, CA; www.rarewineco.com — Italian, French, Port, Madeira

» Rosenthal Wine Merchant, New York, NY; www.madrose.com — Burgundy, Rhône, Loire, Italian

» Sherry-Lehmann Wine & Spirits, New York, NY; www.sherry-lehmann.com — Bordeaux, Burgundy, California

» Table & Vine, West Springfield, MA; www.tableandvine.com — French, California

» TwentyTwenty Wine Merchants, West Los Angeles, CA; www.2020wines.com — Bordeaux (especially rare, old), California, rare wines

» Wally's, Los Angeles, CA; www.wallywine.com — Italian, California, French, Champagne

» The Wine Club, Santa Ana, CA; San Francisco, CA; www.thewineclub.com — Bordeaux, California

» The Wine Library, Springfield, NJ; www.winelibrary.com — Bordeaux, California, Champagne

» Wine Warehouse, Los Angeles, CA; www.winewarehouse.com — California, French, Italian

» Zachys Wine & Liquor, Scarsdale, NY; www.zachys.com — Bordeaux, Burgundy

Buying wines at auctions

TIP

The clear advantage of buying wine through auction houses is the availability of older and rarer wines. In fact, auction houses are the principal source of mature wines — their specialty. (In general, you can obtain younger wines at better prices elsewhere.) At auctions, you can buy wines that are practically impossible to obtain any other way. Many of these wines have been off the market for years — sometimes decades!

The main disadvantage of buying wine at auction is that you don't always know the storage history, or *provenance*, of the wine you're considering buying. The wine may have been stored in somebody's warm apartment for years. And if the wine does come from a reputable wine collector's temperature-controlled cellar, and thus has impeccable credentials, it will sell for a very high price.

BUYING TIME: WINE FUTURES

Every so often, you may see an offer for *futures* of certain wines (usually Bordeaux, but sometimes California wines). The offers suggest that, to ensure getting a particular wine at the lowest price, you should buy it now for future delivery. In other words, "Give us your money now; you'll get the wine in due course, when the winery releases it."

Generally, we recommend that you *don't* buy futures. Often, the wine will be the same price, or only slightly higher, when it hits the market. To save little or nothing, you will have tied your money up for a year or more. You face the risk that the store could go bankrupt before delivering your wine. And during recessionary times in the past, some people who bought wine futures actually paid more for their wine than they would have paid if they had waited for the wine to arrive before purchasing it.

Futures are useful in only two situations: For wines that are made in such small quantity that you're pretty sure the wine will sell out before it reaches wine shops; and for a wine that receives an extraordinarily high rating in the wine press before its release, assuring that its price could double and even triple by the time the wine reaches the market.

Here's the bottom line: Buy futures only when you must have a particular wine, and buying futures might be the only way you can get it. For most wines, though, keep your wallet in your pocket until the wine is actually available.

Also, almost all auction houses charge you a buyer's premium, a tacked-on charge that's 10 or 15 percent of your bid. In general, prices of wine at auctions range from fair (you rarely ever find bargains) to exorbitant.

You can attend an auction personally or submit bids by phone or online. To plan your attack, you can obtain a catalog for the auction ahead of time, sometimes for a small fee. The catalog lists wines for sale by lots (usually groupings of 3, 6, or 12 bottles) with a suggested minimum bid per lot.

WARNING

If you're personally present at an auction, be careful not to catch auction fever. The desire to win can motivate you to pay more for a wine than it's worth. Carefully thought-out, judicious bidding is in order.

New York is currently one of the hottest wine auction markets in the United States. (You can either sell or buy wines at auction.) Four retail stores lead the crusade: Morrell & Company (www.morrellwineauctions.com), Zachys (www.zachys.com/auctions), Sotheby's Wine (www.sothebyswine.com), and Acker Merrall & Condit (www.ackerwines.com). Christie's Auction House (www.christies.com), along with Sotheby's, one of the grand auction houses based in the United Kingdom, is also a major player.

In Illinois, The Chicago Wine Company (www.tcwc.com) and Hart Davis Hart Wine Co. (www.hdhwine.com) are leading auction houses. In California, The Rare Wine Co. (www.rarewineco.com) is a leader.

IMPROVING YOUR ODDS OF GETTING A *GOOD*, OLD BOTTLE

Acquiring and drinking old wines requires you to be a bit of a gambler. But you *can* reduce the odds against buying a bottle well past its peak by following a few easy tips:

- Buy from reputable wine merchants and auction houses. They often know the history of their older wines and most likely acquired the wines from sources that they trust.

- Trade bottles with only wine-savvy friends who know the storage history of their wines.

- Stick to well-known wines with a proven track record of longevity.

- Inspect the wine if you can. Look at the *ullage* (the airspace between the wine and the cork). Ullage of an inch or more can be a danger sign indicating that evaporation has occurred, either from excessive heat or lack of humidity — both of which can spoil the wine. (On a very old wine, say 35 or more years old, an inch of ullage is quite acceptable, though.) Another sign of poor storage is leakage or stickiness at the top of the bottle, suggesting that wine has seeped out through the cork.

- Inspect the wine's color, if the bottle color permits. A white wine that is excessively dark or dull or a red wine that has become quite brown can be oxidized and too old. (Shine a small flashlight through the bottle to check the color of red wines.) But some red wines and Sauternes can show quite a bit of brown and still be very much alive. If you're not sure about the color, get advice from someone who knows about older wines before plunking down your money.

- If you buy at auction by telephone or online, ask the seller to inspect the bottle and describe its fill level and color.

- Be wary if the price of the bottle seems too low. Often, what appears to be a bargain is a damaged or over-the-hill wine.

- Ask wine knowledgeable friends or merchants about the particular wines you're considering buying. Frequently, someone will be familiar with them.

- Say a prayer, take out your corkscrew, and plunge in. Live dangerously!

Purely online wine auctions also exist. WineBid.com (www.winebid.com) conducts auctions at its website and is the most established such service. Other online wine auction houses include Cellar Bid (www.cellarbid.com) and Spectrum Wine Auctions (www.spectrumwine.com).

WARNING

Wine counterfeiting is an active scam these days, but mainly for the world's very rarest, priciest, most elite wines. This trend underscores the need to work only with reputable auction houses.

The Urge to Own: Wine Collecting

Most people consume wines very quickly after buying them. If this is your custom, you have plenty of company. But some people who enjoy wine operate a bit differently. Oh, sure, they buy wine because they intend to drink it; they're just not exactly sure *when* they'll drink it. And until they do drink it, they get pleasure out of knowing that the bottles are waiting for them. If you count yourself in this second group, you're probably a wine collector at heart. The chase, to you, is every bit as thrilling as the consummation.

If you're a closet wine collector, developing a strategy of wine buying (with the help of this section) can prevent a haphazard collection of uninteresting or worthless bottles from happening to you. (Even if you never intend to have a wine collection, it's worthwhile to put at least a little thought into your wine purchases.)

The first step in formulating a wine-buying strategy is to consider the following:

>> How much wine you drink

>> How much wine you want to own (and can store properly)

>> How much money you're prepared to spend on wine

>> What types of wine you enjoy drinking

Balancing your inventory

Unless your intention is to fill your cellar with wines that bring you the greatest return on investment when you later sell them — in other words, unless you aren't interested in actually drinking the wines you own — you should like a wine before buying it. (We're not talking about all those bottles you buy while you're playing the field and experimenting with new wines — just those that you're thinking of making a commitment to, such as Barolo or Burgundy, by buying in quantity.) Liking a wine before you buy it sounds like the plainest common sense, but you'd be surprised at how many people buy a wine merely because somebody gave it a high rating! Fortunately, we have noticed a decrease in interest in wine ratings among today's informed wine–buying populace.

A well–planned wine inventory features a range of wines. It can be heavy in one or two types of wine that you particularly enjoy, but it has other types of wine, too. If you like California Cabernet Sauvignons, for example, you may decide to make them your specialty. But consider that you may grow weary of them if you have nothing else to drink night after night. Boring! One of the greatest mistakes a novice collector can make is to buy mainly one type of table wine.

REMEMBER

Table wines, of course, are the bulk of most wine collections. But it's a good idea to have some apéritif wines, such as Champagne or dry Sherry, and dessert wines, such as Port or sweet white wines, so you're prepared when occasions arise. (If you're like us, you'll invent plenty of occasions to open a bottle of Champagne!)

TIP

Another hallmark of a balanced collection is a healthy selection of both inexpensive wines ($12 to $25 a bottle) that can be enjoyed on casual occasions and important wines that demand a special occasion. Purchasing only expensive wines is unrealistic.

You also want to purchase wines that are ready to drink and those that require additional aging. Check out the following sections for our recommendations.

Everyday wines

TIP

What you stock as everyday wines will depend on your personal taste. Our candidates for everyday white wines include the following:

>> Simple white Burgundies, such as Mâcon-Villages or St.-Véran

>> Sauvignon Blancs from France (Sancerre and Pouilly-Fumé); New Zealand; Friuli and Alto-Adige in Italy; and California

>> Pinot Gris/Pinot Grigio from Oregon, Alsace, and Italy

>> Italian Pinot Bianco

>> Flavorful Italian whites, such as Vermentino, Verdicchio, or Falanghina

>> Grüner Veltliner from Austria

>> Riesling from Germany, Austria, Alsace, Western Australia, Clare and Eden Valleys in Southeastern Australia

>> Moschofilero and Assyrtiko from Greece

>> Albariños from Spain

>> Chablis (AOC Village) and Muscadet from France

For everyday red wines, we especially like Italian reds, such as Barbera, Dolcetto, Nebbiolo, Montepulciano d'Abruzzo, Valpolicella, and simple (under $25) Chianti Classico. These red wines are enjoyable young, versatile enough to go well with the simple, flavorful foods many people eat every day, and sturdy enough to age for a couple of years if you don't get around to them (that is, they won't deteriorate quickly).

Everyday French red wines we recommend include Beaujolais, Côtes du Rhône, and lighter-bodied (under $20) Bordeaux. We also suggest inexpensive (under $15) Portuguese reds.

Age-worthy wines

The wines on this list are the types that we ourselves — and many other wine lovers — collect. They are capable of improving over the course of many years, if not decades. Age-worthy white wines we recommend include

>> Above all, Grand Cru and Premier Cru white Burgundies — such as Corton-Charlemagne, Bâtard- and Chevalier-Montrachets, Meursault, and Chablis Grand Crus (the latter is the best value)

>> Better (over $30) white Bordeaux

>> Great German and Austrian Rieslings

>> Alsace Rieslings and Gewurztraminers

See Chapters 10 and 12 for explanations of these wines.

Among the many long-lived red wines, some likely candidates for *cellaring* (the term for letting wines mature) are

>> Fine Bordeaux

>> Grand Cru and Premier Cru Burgundies

>> From the Rhône: Hermitage, Côte-Rôtie, and Cornas

>> Powerful Italian reds, such as Barolo, Barbaresco, Brunello di Montalcino, Chianti Classico Riserva, Taurasi, and Super-Tuscan blends

>> From Spain: Rioja, Ribera del Duero (especially Vega Sicilia Unico), and Priorato wines

>> Portugal's Barca Velha and other good Douro table wines

>> Australia's Grange (Penfolds), the Henschke Shiraz wines, such as Hill of Grace, and other super-premium Shirazes

>> From California: Better Cabernet Sauvignons (and Cabernet blends)

Parts 3 and 4 discuss these wines in more detail.

Other age-worthy wines include

>> Finer Champagnes (usually Vintage Champagnes and prestige cuvées; see Chapter 15)

>> The finest dessert wines, such as late-harvest German Rieslings (see Chapter 12), French Sauternes, sweet Vouvrays from the Loire Valley (see Chapter 10), Vintage Port, and Madeira. (See Chapter 16 for Sauternes, Port, and Madeira.)

THE CHARM OF AN AGED WINE

Aged wines are a thing apart from young wines. Some wines simply don't reach their full expression until they've aged. Try drinking a highly acclaimed young red Bordeaux, say a 2010 Château Lafite-Rothschild. You taste a mouthful of tannin, and although the wine has concentration, you probably wonder what all the fuss is about. Try it in 10 to 15 years; the assertive tannins have softened, a wonderful bouquet of cedar, tobacco, and black currants emerges from the glass, and a natural sweetness of flavor has developed.

As a fine wine matures in the bottle, a series of chemical and physical changes occur. These changes are poorly understood, but their effects are evident in the style of a mature red wine:

- The wine becomes paler in color.

- Its aroma evolves from the fruity aromas (and often oakiness) it had when young to a complex, non-fruity, leathery and earthy bouquet.

- Its tannic, harsh texture diminishes, and the wine becomes silky.

Mature wines seem to be easier to digest, and they go to your head less quickly. (Perhaps that's because we tend to drink them slowly, with reverence.) Besides visceral pleasure, they offer a special emotional satisfaction. Tasting an aged wine can be like traveling back in time, sharing a connection with people who have gone before in the great chain of humanity.

Organization is peace of mind

When you're not only a wine drinker but also a wine collector, you become aware that you need to keep track of all your wine so that

>> You can find a bottle quickly when you're looking for it.

>> You know what you own. (Many a bottle has gone over the hill because the owner forgot that he had it!)

>> You can show off your wine collection to your friends (something like showing your baby's pictures).

You can keep track of your wine in many different ways. At the very least, your wine inventory on paper, or on a computer database or spreadsheet, should include a list of the specific wines in your collection, the number of each, and their location.

Many years ago, when we decided to catalog our wine collection by computer, we created a FileMaker database into which we typed, for each wine we own, all the details that we imagined we'd ever want to search for or sort by — such as vintage, producer name, wine name, appellation, region, country, type (red, white, rosé, sparkling, apéritif, or dessert), quantity owned, price paid, and bottle size.

TIP

The world of wine cellar management has changed dramatically since then. Now, you can upload your inventory to the Internet so you can view it from any computer or even from a smartphone or tablet. Two excellent websites enable you to see lists of what you own, track your consumption, get current valuations of your collection, share tasting notes in a wine-community setting, and read expert tasting notes from major critics.

>> The original of these cellar-tracking sites is named (logically) CellarTracker (www.cellartracker.com). Today, more than 550,000 wine lovers participate in the CellarTracker community to keep records of their collections and share tasting notes.

>> Another way to manage your wine cellar online is to enter your inventory with VinCellar (www.vincellar.com), the cellar management application of Vinfolio, which we mention in the section "Buying fine and collectible wines on the Internet," earlier in this chapter. This site enables you to track your cellar by app or Internet. One of the key features of this site is its connection with Vinfolio, which enables you to buy wines online and seamlessly add them to your inventory, store wines at Vinfolio's warehouse, and sell wines from your collection via Vinfolio's store or peer-to-peer marketplace. The site also provides consulting services to collectors. VinCellar is free.

A Healthy Environment for Your Wines

WARNING

If you've decided to collect wine — or if you discover that a wine collection is happening to you — please take heed: Poorly stored wines make disappointment after disappointment inevitable.

If you plan to keep wines indefinitely, you really need a wine storage facility with controlled temperature and humidity (the following sections offer different options). This is especially important if you live where the temperature exceeds 70 degrees Fahrenheit (21 degrees Celsius) for any length of time. Without proper storage, you may be tempted to drink those fine wines long before they reach their best drinking period (known in wine circles as infanticide), or worse yet, the wines may die an untimely death in your closet, garage, or warm cellar.

TIP

If you plan to build a wine cellar or buy a wine cabinet, allow for expansion in your wine collection. Like most waistlines, wine cellars inevitably grow larger with the passing years.

The passive wine cellar

You may be fortunate enough to have conditions suitable for a passive wine cellar (if you live in the cool Northeastern United States or in Canada, if your cellar is below ground and not heated, or if you've recently inherited a castle in Scotland, for example).

If the place where you intend to store your wine is very cool year-round (below 60 degrees Fahrenheit, 15.5 degrees Celsius) and very damp (75 percent humidity or higher), you can be the lucky owner of a *passive cellar*. (It's called passive because you don't have to do anything to it, such as cool it or humidify it.) Usually, only deep cellars completely below ground level with thick stone walls or comparable insulation can be completely passive in temperate climates. Passive cellars are certainly the ideal way to store wines. And you can save a lot of money on their upkeep to boot.

TIP

If you don't have a space that's already ideal for a passive wine cellar, you might decide that you can dig one. For instructions on building your own passive wine cellar, see Richard M. Gold's authoritative book, *How and Why to Build a Wine Cellar* (Board and Bench Publishing).

If you can't be passive, be bullish

Most of us are neither lucky enough to have a passive wine cellar nor fortunate enough to be able to create one without extraordinary expense and trouble (bulldozers, wrecking crews, and so on). But second best — a mechanically cooled and/or humidified room — is far better than a laissez-faire approach.

The following are key features of a good wine storage area:

>> The temperature stays cool — ideally, in the 53 to 59 degrees Fahrenheit range (12 to 16 degrees Celsius).

>> The temperature is fairly constant; wide swings in temperature aren't good for the wine.

>> The area is damp or humid, with a minimum of 70 percent humidity and a maximum of 95 percent (mold sets in above 95 percent).

>> The area is free from vibrations, which can travel through the wine; heavy traffic and motors cycling on and off — such as in refrigerators — are detrimental to your wine.

>> The area is free from light, especially direct sunlight; the ultraviolet rays of the sun are especially harmful to wine.

>> The storage area is free from chemical odors, such as paints, paint remover, and so on.

We built a room in our basement for wine storage and installed a refrigeration device. Whatever area you use, your wine will keep well provided that the space has a climate control unit and is properly insulated (see the following sections).

Buy a hygrometer (an instrument that measures humidity) for your wine storage area. Our hygrometer gives us both the percentage of humidity and a digital reading of the temperature — information so valuable that we check it almost daily.

Avoid refrigerators for wine storage. Don't leave good wine or Champagne in the refrigerator for more than a week; not only is the refrigerator motor harmful, but the excessively cold temperature (as low as 35 degrees Fahrenheit, 1.6 degrees Celsius) tends to numb and flatten the flavors of the wine.

Climate control

You can find professional cooling devices advertised in wine accessory catalogs and wine magazines. These climate-control units humidify and cool the air of a room. They come in various capacities to suit rooms of different dimensions. Many require professional installation.

Depending on where you live, you may not need to run your cooling unit all year. When we lived in Long Island, New York, we kept our refrigeration unit running from about mid-May to October. The additional expense for electricity was well worth it when we considered the value of the wine we were protecting. During the winter months when the air got dry, we often ran a humidifier in our wine room.

THE ISSUE OF HUMIDITY

Some wine collectors aren't particularly concerned about the humidity level of their cellars. They argue that high humidity causes mold and disfigures labels. But dry air can dry the cork and allow the airtight seal to deteriorate. This in turn enables oxygen penetration or causes your wine to evaporate or leech out around the cork, resulting in excessive *ullage* (space between the wine and the cork). The greater the ullage, the greater the chance of your wine's becoming oxidized.

Warning: Because we recommend humidity between 70 and 95 percent, we believe that air conditioners, which dehumidify the air to about 50 percent, aren't suitable for wine storage areas.

Wine racks

Racking systems vary from elaborate redwood racks to simple metal or plastic racking. The choice of material and configuration really hinges on how much you want to spend and your own personal taste.

Large, diamond-shaped wooden (or synthetic composition) racks are popular because they efficiently store eight or more bottles per section and make maximum use of space. Such racks permit the easy removal of individual bottles.

A rack configuration that gives each wine its own cubbyhole is more expensive; if you're checking out such racks, consider whether any of your oversized bottles (such as bulbous sparkling wine bottles) may be too large to fit the cubbyholes. (And consider whether your half-bottles may be too small!)

TIP

Some collectors prefer to store their wine in the wines' original wooden crates. (Many classic wines, such as Bordeaux and Vintage Port, come in these crates; you can also usually pick up empty wooden crates in wine stores.) The crates are beneficial for storing wine because the wine remains in a dark environment inside the case, and the temperature changes very slowly thanks to the mass of wine bottles packed together in the closed case. Retrieving a bottle from the bottom row of the case can really be inconvenient, though.

WARNING

Cardboard boxes aren't suitable for wine storage. The chemicals used in the manufacture of the cardboard can eventually affect the wine. Also, the cardboard boxes become damaged, in time, from the moisture in the air, assuming that you're maintaining a proper humidity in your cellar.

Insulation

Far more important than your choice of racks is your choice of insulation.

WARNING

We definitely don't recommend fiberglass insulation because it absorbs the moisture created by your cooling unit. We've heard of cases in which the weight of the moisture inside the insulation actually caused parts of ceilings to come tumbling down, creating quite a mess.

The ideal insulation is a 3-inch-thick, thermoplastic resin called polyurethane. It's odorless, doesn't absorb moisture, and makes a fine seal. Even when a cooling unit isn't running, temperatures will change extremely slowly in most wine rooms with this kind of insulation.

Wine caves for apartment dwellers

If you live in a house that has either a cellar or a separate area for your wine, consider yourself fortunate. What if you have no space — for example, what if you live in an apartment?

As an apartment dweller, you have three choices:

>> Leave your wine in a friend's or relative's house (provided that he has adequate storage facilities — and that you trust him not to drink your wine!).

>> Rent storage space in a refrigerated public warehouse.

>> Buy a wine cave — also known as a wine cabinet — which is a self-contained, refrigerated unit that you plug into an electrical outlet.

We find the first two options barely acceptable because they don't give you immediate access to your wine. It's downright inconvenient to make a trip every time you want to get your hands on your own wine. And both of these options rob you of the pleasure of having your wines readily available in your home where you can look at them, fondle the bottles, or show them off to your friends.

In our apartment, we have a wine cave for several dozen bottles that we plan to drink in the short term. Many wine caves resemble attractive pieces of furniture, either vertical or horizontal credenzas. Many have glass doors, and all of them can be locked.

Wine caves range in size and capacity from a tiny unit that holds only 24 bottles to really large units that hold up to 2,800 bottles, with many sizes in between. Prices range from $400 to about $10,000. The two wine cave brands we recommend are Le Cache (www.lecachewinecabinets.com) and Vinothèque (www.vinotheque. com). You can buy less expensive brands, but they won't be of the same quality.

IN THIS CHAPTER

» School was never such fun

» Phys Ed for your palate

» The magical places behind the labels

» Wine publications to keep you current

» Surfing the wine web

Chapter **18**

Continuing Education for Wine Lovers

earning about wine is like space travel: Once you get going, there's no end in sight. Fortunately for those who choose to be educated wine drinkers, learning about wine is a fascinating experience, full of new flavors, new places, and new friends.

Although we teach others about wine, we are also avid students of wine. We can't imagine we'll ever reach the point where we say, "Now we know enough about wine; we can stop here." So off we go to another vineyard, to another wine tasting, or deep into the pages of another wine magazine or website. Every step brings not only more knowledge but also more appreciation of this amazing beverage. This chapter shows you how to educate yourself about wine with the help of classes, publications, and more.

Back to the Classroom

The best way to learn about wine and to improve your wine-tasting skills is to take a wine course. If you live in a medium-sized or large city, you're sure to find several wine courses offered by private wine schools, by universities as adult-education extension programs, or by local wine shops or restaurants. If you're out of reach of such courses, you can research wine online.

Most wine courses are *wine appreciation* courses — they don't teach you how to make wine, they don't provide you with professional credentials, and they're not accredited. But they do give authoritative instruction about wine in general or specific types of wine and — just as importantly — they provide immediate, expert feedback on your tasting impressions. (For information on professional wine credentials, see the sidebar "What do the initials MW mean?" later in this chapter.)

Introductory classes generally deal with wine grape varieties and how to taste wine, while more advanced classes discuss in depth the various wine regions of the world or the wines of a particular region. Instructors are usually experienced professionals who work in the wine trade or who write about wine; in the best cases, they have also had some training in the principles of adult learning.

WARNING

Brand promotion and education often enjoy too cozy a relationship in the wine field. Many wine instructors, such as distributor salespeople or winery reps, have a vested interest in the brands of wine that they offer as tasting samples in class. As long as the instructor has expertise beyond his or her own brands, you can certainly still benefit from the instruction. But you should request disclosure of any commercial affiliations at the first class.

One wine school in action

The following announcement is a shameless plug: We run a wine school in New York City called International Wine Center (www.internationalwinecenter. com). We offer the programs of the Wine & Spirit Education Trust (WSET), the world's leading wine education organization. The courses cover four levels of study (from beginner to very advanced) and range from 6 hours to two years in duration; each course has a textbook or similar informational content, self-study aides, and an examination. Students who pass the exam corresponding to their level of study earn a certificate attesting to the credential they have gained. The same programs are available in other wine schools across the United States and in 65 other countries.

Many other wine courses are less comprehensive or less formally structured — but most wine classes have a lot in common. A typical class usually lasts about two hours; students listen to a discussion of a particular topic and taste six to eight wines related to that topic. Maps of wine regions or slides punctuate the discussion and reiterate key facts or concepts. The instructor encourages questions and guides students in tasting and understanding the wines that she or he presents.

WHAT DO THE INITIALS MW MEAN?

You may have noticed that one of the co-authors of this book has *Master of Wine* (often shortened to MW) after her name. Wine professionals receive this title — which is the most respected wine credential in the world — by passing a grueling three-part exam. The Institute of Masters of Wine awards the credential; it offers preparatory programs and/or exams in Australia, the United States, the United Kingdom, and continental Europe. A high level of knowledge, several years of experience in the wine trade, and completion of any locally available wine courses (such as the WSET programs) are the normal prerequisites. As of this writing, there are 380 Masters of Wine in the world (54 in North America). For more information, visit the Institute online at www.masters-of-wine.org.

At most wine classes, each student sits before a place setting of wine glasses — ideally one glass per wine to be tasted. Water and crackers are available to help students clear their palates between tastes of wine. Next to each student is a large plastic cup so that students can spit out the wines rather than swallow them, and can dump their leftover wine. (If the idea of spitting wine discourages you, read the section "To spit or not to spit?" later in this chapter.) Each student should receive a printed list of the wines being tasted as well as other material about the subject of that particular class session.

Wine tastings of all shapes and sizes

Wine tastings are events designed to give enthusiasts the opportunity to sample a range of wines. The events can be very much like classes (seated, seminar-like events), or they can be more like parties (tasters milling around informally). Compared to a wine class, the participants at a wine tasting are more likely to have mixed levels of knowledge. Tastings don't come in beginner, intermediate, and advanced levels — one size fits all.

Wine tastings are useful because they override the limitations of sampling wine alone, at home. How many wines can you taste on your own (unless you don't mind giving away three-quarters of every bottle)? How many wines are you willing to buy on your own? And how much can you really learn, tasting wine in isolation — or with a friend whose expertise is no greater than yours?

At wine tastings, you can gain insight from your fellow tasters, as well as make new friends who share your interest in wine. Most important, you can taste wine in the company of some individuals who are more experienced than you, which is a real boon in training your palate.

We have led or attended literally thousands of wine tastings in our lives — so far. And it's fair to say that we've learned something about wine at almost all of them.

TIP

To find out about wine tastings in your area, contact your local wine merchant. Your local shop might sponsor wine-tasting events occasionally (apart from informal sampling opportunities in the store itself) and staff should also be aware of wine schools or other organizations that conduct wine tastings in your area. The website Local Wine Events (www.localwineevents.com) is also an excellent source of information about wine-tastings and a platform for registering for many of the events listed on the site.

Dinner with the winemaker

A popular type of wine event is the winemaker dinner, a multicourse dinner at which a winemaker or winery executive is the guest of honor. Wine drinkers pay a fixed price for the meal and taste various wines from the featured winery that are matched to each course.

As far as learning goes, winemaker dinners rank below seminar-style wine tastings but above many informal, reception-style tastings. These dinners offer the chance to taste wines under ideal circumstances — with food — but we find that most speakers disseminate very little information of any value and give you precious little opportunity to ask questions. In their potential for fun, however, winemaker dinners are right up there at the top of the list — even if you don't get to sit next to the winemaker.

Winery visits

TIP

One of the best — and most fun-filled — ways to find out about wine is to actually visit wineries and speak to the winemakers or other winery personnel about their wines. You get to immerse yourself in the region you visit — experiencing the climate firsthand, seeing the soil and the hills, touching the grapes, and so on. You can walk through the vineyards if you want, visit nearby towns or villages, eat the local food, and drink the wine of the region.

You discover that there's something special about the people who devote their lives to making wine. Maybe it's their commitment to bringing pleasure to the world through their labor. Whatever the reason, they are exceptional people. We have found some of our dearest friends in wine regions throughout the world.

TIP

When you do plan to visit a winery, you usually need to call or write ahead for an appointment if the winery is small, elite, or situated off the beaten track, in an area that does not have many tourists. This advice applies to most wineries outside the U.S.

BLIND MAN'S BLUFF

One of the favorite diversions of wine tasters is tasting wines blind. Before you conjure up thoughts of darkened rooms, blindfolded tasters, or other forms of hanky-panky, let us explain that the tasters aren't blind, the bottles are. Or anyway, the bottles have their faces covered.

In *blind tastings,* the tasters don't know the identities of the wines. The theory behind this exercise is that knowing the identities could prejudice the tasters to prefer (or dislike) a particular wine for its reputation rather than for "what's in the glass," as they say. Sometimes, extremely skilled tasters try to identify the wines that they taste blind, in an effort to sharpen their tasting skills even further.

If you don't know enough about wine to be prejudiced by the labels, there's little point in tasting blind. Nevertheless, there's something about blind tasting that really helps you focus your concentration on what you're tasting — and that's always a good practice.

Many wineries in the United States do have tasting rooms that are open every day during the busy tourism months and on weekends during the winter, and you don't need an appointment for the tasting room. (But do check the hours in advance.) You can sample wines (often for a small fee), learn about the wines from the tasting room staff, buy wine, and sometimes buy souvenirs, such as T-shirts imprinted with the logo of the winery, or wine paraphernalia.

If you visit wineries that are less geared toward tourism — which is the case in most of the rest of the wine world — you can simply sample the wines, talk to the winemaker or proprietor when he's available (you *have* made an appointment, right?), take an informal tour of the winery, and buy some wine if you want (an especially nice idea if the wine isn't available back home).

TIP

Don't let your limited (or nonexistent) ability to speak the local language prevent you from visiting wine regions. These days, English is the nearly universal language of the wine world. Even if the person you're visiting doesn't speak English, he invariably has someone available (his wife, his son, or his dog) who does. Besides, wine itself is a universal language. A smile and a handshake go a long way toward communicating!

When in Rome

In case you've never been to a wine tasting or wine class, we should warn you that a few matters of etiquette apply. Familiarizing yourself with the etiquette in the following sections will help you feel more comfortable. Otherwise, you're likely to be appalled by what you see or hear. Why are those people behaving like that?!

To spit or not to spit?

Professional wine tasters long ago discovered that if they swallow every wine they taste, they become far less thoughtful tasters by the time they reach the ninth or tenth wine. So spitting each wine after evaluating it became acceptable. In working wineries, professional tasters sometimes spit right onto the gravel floor or into the drains. In more elegant surroundings and in wine classes, tasters spit into a *spittoon,* usually a simple container like a large plastic cup (one per taster) or an empty ice bucket that two or three tasters share.

At first, some tasters are naturally loath to spit out wine. Not only have they been brought up to believe that spitting is uncouth, but they've also paid good money for the opportunity to taste the wines. Why waste them?

WARNING

Well, you can drink all your wine at a wine tasting, if you want — and some people do. But we don't advise it, for the following reasons:

>> Evaluating the later wines is difficult if you swallow the earlier ones. The alcohol you consume clouds your perceptions. (And the later wines are often better wines.)

>> Swallowing is not really necessary in order to taste the wine fully. If you leave the wine in your mouth for several seconds (see Chapter 2), you are able to taste it thoroughly — while minimizing the effects of the alcohol.

>> If you are driving to the tasting, you're taking a risk driving home afterward if you drink rather than spit. The stakes are high — your life and health, others' lives, and your driver's license. Why gamble?

The simple solution: Spit out the wine. Just about all experienced wine tasters do. Believe it or not, spitting will seem to be a very normal thing to do at wine tastings after a while. (And, in the meantime, it's one sure way to appear more experienced than you are!)

TIP

If you know that you can't bring yourself to spit, be sure to have something substantial to eat before going to a wine tasting. You absorb alcohol more slowly on a full stomach — and the simple crackers and bread at most wine tastings aren't sufficient to do the trick. And, of course, don't drive afterward.

HORIZONTAL OR VERTICAL?

Two of the goofiest expressions in the world of wine apply to wine tastings. Depending on the nature of the wines featured, wine-tasting events can be categorized as *vertical tastings* or as *horizontal tastings.* These categories have nothing to do with the position of the tasters themselves — they're usually seated, and they're never lying down (that went out of fashion after the Romans).

A vertical tasting is a wine tasting featuring several vintages of the same wine — Château Latour in various vintages from 2000 to 2010, for example. A horizontal tasting examines wines of a single vintage from several different wineries; usually the wines are of a similar type, such as 2012 Napa Valley Cabernet Sauvignons. There's no particular name for tastings with less disciplined themes, but we suggest *plaid.*

More fine points of wine etiquette

REMEMBER

Because smell is such an important aspect of wine tasting, courteous tasters try not to interfere with other tasters' ability to smell. This means

>> Smoking (anything) is a complete no-no at any wine tasting.

>> Using any scent (perfume, after-shave lotion, scented hair spray, and so on) is unacceptable. These extraneous odors can really interfere with your fellow tasters' ability to detect the wine's aroma.

REMEMBER

Courteous wine tasters also don't volunteer their opinions about a wine until other tasters have had a chance to taste the wine. Serious tasters like to form their opinions independently and are sure to throw dirty looks at anyone who interrupts their concentration.

Most of these wine–tasting etiquette guidelines apply to wine classes as well — and are also relevant when you visit wineries around the world.

Armchair Travel

Traveling around the world takes time and money. Alternatively, you can travel through the wine world from the comfort of your living room or your home office, letting the written word carry you to faraway wine regions. Apart from bookstores and online sellers, many retail wine stores sell wine books and magazines. And with every passing month, the number of websites and smartphone or tablet apps about wine increases.

Recommended books

TIP

The following books are some of *the* established tomes; they take you into great depth on particular aspects of wine.

General knowledge

Hugh Johnson and Jancis Robinson, MW, *World Atlas of Wine*, 7th Edition, Mitchell Beazley, 2013 (also available as a digital book). Johnson and Robinson, both English, are probably the world's most respected wine writers. Complete with detailed maps of all the world's wine regions, this book is essential for any serious wine lover's library. (*Hugh Johnson's Wine Companion* and *Hugh Johnson's Pocket Wine Book 2018*, both published by Mitchell Beazley, are two additional worthwhile books to check out.)

Jancis Robinson, MW and Juliet Harding MW, *The Oxford Companion to Wine*, 4th Edition, Oxford University Press, 2015. This encyclopedic reference book sets the standard in the wine field. It is a solid, trustworthy reference in all areas of the wine world, and particularly valuable for viticulture and vinification topics.

Jaime Goode, *The Science of Wine: From Vine to Glass*, University of California Press, 2014. The author is a highly respected expert in wine science who illuminates the behind-the-scenes processes in the vineyard and winery that make wines taste the way they do.

Bordeaux

Stephen Brook, *The Complete Bordeaux: The Wines, The Chateaux, The People*, 3rd Edition, Mitchell Beazley, 2017: Brook is an award-winning author whose works cover several parts of the wine world, but Bordeaux is a particular specialty. This book gives a thorough overview of the Bordeaux region and its districts, as well as detailed profiles of major producers.

Benjamin Lewin, MW, *What Price Bordeaux?* (Wine Appreciation Guild, 2009.) Lewin explores developments in Bordeaux with scientific rigor and explains how Bordeaux wine has reached astronomical prices. A provocative book.

David Peppercorn, MW, *Wines of Bordeaux*, Revised Edition, Mitchell Beazley, 2006. England's David Peppercorn is rightfully regarded as one of the great Bordeaux experts. In this succinctly written wine guide, he offers his own ratings of Bordeaux wines, when to drink them, and which ones are particularly good values.

Robert M. Parker, Jr., *Bordeaux: A Consumer's Guide to the World's Finest Wines*, 4th Edition, Simon & Schuster, 2003. Robert Parker is certainly America's most famous wine critic. He earned his reputation for his knowledge of Bordeaux; he was also the first writer to use the 100-point wine rating system. This fourth edition covers all major Bordeaux wines from 1961 to 2001, with info on wines dating back to 1945. Although now dated, it's an essential book for any Bordeaux lover.

Burgundy

Anthony Hanson, MW, *Burgundy,* Mitchell Beazley, 2006. A succinct, excellent work on this very complicated wine region by a recognized Burgundy wine expert.

Clive Coates, MW, *The Wines of Burgundy,* Revised Edition, University of California Press, 2008. This is the updated version of Coates's *Côte d'Or: A Celebration of the Great Wines of Burgundy.* Coates, another in the corps of fine British wine writers, covers all the major districts of Burgundy, reviews the producers, and provides detailed information on vintages, to make a thorough reference book. Coates's most recent work is *My Favorite Burgundies,* University of California Press, 2013 — an expert personal take on the author's favorite wine region.

Champagne

Peter Liem, *Champagne,* Ten Speed Press, 2017. Liem, one of the great Champagne experts in the world, has written an essential, comprehensive tome, with maps included separately. Brand new. Highly recommended.

Michael Edwards, *The Finest Wines of Champagne: A Guide to the Best Cuvées, Houses, and Growers,* University of California Press, 2009. A Champagne expert, Edwards explores 90 Champagne producers in depth. A Champagne lover's delight.

Ed McCarthy, *Champagne For Dummies,* Wiley, 1999. Your *Wine For Dummies* co-author, a Champagne specialist, has written this comprehensive guide to the world of Champagne, including a section on touring Champagne and a directory of Champagne houses.

Tom Stevenson, *Champagne, The Essential Guide,* Revised Edition, Barnes &Noble, 2017. England's Tom Stevenson knows more about Champagne than the Champenois themselves! A complete look at Champagne and all the major sparkling wines of the world.

Richard Juhlin, *4000 Champagnes,* Flammarion, 2005. Juhlin, an extremely knowledgeable Swedish lover of Champagne, gives his own personalized views of the Champagne houses. It's thorough and comprehensive. (Also check out Richard Juhlin's *Champagne Guide,* Wine Appreciation Guild, 2008.)

France

Benjamin Lewin, *Wines of Burgundy: Cote D'Or*, Vendange Press, 2017. A clever, insightful and prolific writer on the wines of France.

Andrew Jefford, *The New France: A Complete Guide to Contemporary French Wine*, Mitchell Beazley, 2006. A fresh look at the classic wine regions of France.

Ed McCarthy and Mary Ewing-Mulligan, MW, *French Wine For Dummies*, Wiley, 2001. Every French wine region is covered, with special emphasis on Bordeaux, Burgundy, and the Rhône Valley. Dare we say, "Eminently readable"?

James Turnbull, *Fine French Wines*, Flammarion, 2007. Turnbull selects and describes 220 of France's outstanding wines, covering just about every wine region. An excellent survey for the French wine connoisseur.

Italy

Kerin O'Keefe, *Barolo and Barbaresco*, University of California Press, 2014. The most comprehensive book written in English about these two important Italian wine regions. Also by O'Keefe, *Brunello di Montalcino: Understanding and Appreciating One of Italy's Greatest Wines*, University of California Press, 2012. *The* authoritative book on one of Italy's most important wines. O'Keefe does a thorough job that underscores her firsthand knowledge of the region.

Nicolas Belfrage, MW, *The Finest Wines of Tuscany and Central Italy: A Regional and Village Guide to the Best Wines and Their Producers*, University of California Press, 2009. Belfrage is one of the most knowledgeable writers on Italian wine today.

Mary Ewing-Mulligan, MW, and Ed McCarthy, *Italian Wine For Dummies*, Wiley, 2001. Every Italian wine region and every major Italian wine is covered, with special emphasis on Piedmont, Tuscany, northeastern Italy, and southern Italy.

Germany

Stuart Pigott, *The Best White Wine on Earth: The Riesling Story.* Published in 2014 by Stewart, Tabori & Chang. Although British, Pigott lives in Germany and is perhaps the world's leading expert on the intricacies of German wine. Pigott also wrote *The Wine Atlas of Germany*, Mitchell Beazley, 1996; an excellent reference for German wines.

California

Jon Bonné, *The New California Wine: A Guide to the Producers and Wines Behind a Revolution in Taste*, Ten Speed Press, 2013. Bonné is former wine editor of the

San Francisco Chronicle. His book provides insights into California's cutting-edge wineries, wine regions, and wine styles.

Stephen Brook, *The Finest Wines of California: A Regional Guide to the Best Producers and Their Wines,* University of California Press, 2011. A respected British writer gives us a refreshing look at California's wines in this easy-to-read guide.

Ed McCarthy and Mary Ewing-Mulligan, MW, *California Wine For Dummies,* Wiley, 2009. Ed and Mary (yes, yours truly) take the varietal approach in this book, devoting a chapter to each of California's major varieties and recommending wines in various price categories.

Washington

Paul Gregutt, *Washington Wines and Wineries: The Essential Guide,* 2nd Edition, University of California Press, 2010. Washington State local Paul Gregutt writes the definitive guide for Washington's wines.

Argentina

Laura Catena, *Vino Argentino: An Insider's Guide to the Wines and Wine Country of Argentina,* Chronicle Books, 2014. The multitalented Laura Catena of Bodega Catena Zapata Winery, emergency room doctor, and author, writes an authentic guide to the wines of her native Argentina.

Australia and New Zealand

James Halliday, *Australian Wine Companion,* 2012 Edition, Hardie Grant, 2011. This book is a compact but expert guide to the wine regions of Australia from the prolific James Halliday.

Michael Cooper, *Wine Atlas of New Zealand,* 2nd Edition, Hatchette, 2010. Cooper is arguably the world's leading authority on New Zealand's wines. This comprehensive tome is required reading for all New Zealand wine lovers.

Wine magazines and newsletters

Wine magazines and newsletters can provide more topical information about wine than books can. They keep you up-to-date on the current happenings in the wine world, give you timely tasting notes on newly released wines, profile the currently hot wines and winemakers, and so on. Also, the classified ads in the back of most wine magazines are a good way to hear about wine-related equipment for sale, wine tours, and other useful offers.

Magazines

TIP

Here, we name some wine magazines we recommend. Be sure to check out the websites of these magazines for even more timely information. (Some of them do require a digital subscription.)

» *Decanter* (www.decanter.com): One of the oldest and one of the best, this monthly magazine covers the world but is especially strong on French and Italian wines. *Decanter* also frequently issues supplements on major wine regions as part of your subscription.

» *Wine & Spirits* (www.wineandspiritsmagazine.com): This high-class magazine offers comprehensive, thoughtful coverage of wine and spirits. Extensive tasting notes are always included. It's published eight times a year.

» *Wine Enthusiast* (www.winemag.com): A colorful, newsy monthly that includes an extensive wine-buying guide.

» *Wine Spectator* (www.winespectator.com): Much of the current wine news is in the *Spectator,* but the magazine also includes rather extensive coverage of the world's major wine regions, with plenty of tasting notes. It's published 15 times a year.

» *World of Fine Wine* (www.finewinemag.com): The wine world's equivalent of a literary magazine, this truly fine quarterly published in the United Kingdom covers wine-related topics at the highest level of fine wine.

Newsletters online

Wine newsletters as a category have undergone the transition from printed periodicals to online platforms, and thus fall into a hybrid category that is part (online) wine magazine and part blog, with frequent video content. Most wine newsletters are intended for the intermediate to advanced wine buff. Here are the three we recommend:

» *Vinous* (www.vinousmedia.com): Antonio Galloni, who formerly wrote for Robert Parker, publishes *Vinous,* the most comprehensive, up-to-date newsletter on wine today. It now incorporates Steve Tanzer's *International Wine Cellar* newsletter, long regarded highly for its comprehensive wine reviews. Galloni's *Vinous* combines thoughtful articles, extensive tasting notes, and video features and interviews with leading wine people; it makes an intelligent guide for the advanced wine buff. $140 a year.

» *Peter Liem's ChampagneGuide.net* (www.champagneguide.net): American journalist Peter Liem has lived in the Champagne region and is expert in its wines. His authoritative comments on producers and Champagnes are incisive and clear, making him one of the best writers on Champagne today. The cost for this bimonthly online newsletter subscription is $89 a year.

>> *Burghound.com* (www.burghound.com): Allen Meadows's comprehensive, quarterly review of red and white Burgundies has become *the* most respected newsletter on Burgundy, covering what is perhaps the most challenging wines of all to evaluate. Each issue averages 150 pages. A "must read" for Burgundy lovers. Subscription for four quarterly issues is $145 per year, $260 for 2-year subscription, $375 for 3 years.

The blogosphere of wine

TIP

If you're thirsty for wine knowledge, you can spend hours and hours researching wine on Internet sites. Most wineries and wine importers have websites, as do the promotional boards of major wine-producing countries and wine regions, and those sites can be useful. But third-party websites and blogs provide more free-ranging information. Here are some of our favorite places to read about, or chat about, wine online. (Unless otherwise noted, the sites have free access.)

>> **Wine Review Online** (www.winereviewonline.com): Robert Whitley, a San Diego–based wine writer and radio wine show host, is publisher of this weekly newsletter, edited by writer Michael Franz. Contributors include a very experienced group of wine writers from all over the United States, including both authors of this book. The site's articles are free.

>> **Jancis Robinson.com** (www.jancisrobinson.com): This site features articles and commentary from England's leading wine journalist and regular contributing writers, as well as lively, active chat boards with international participation. Subscribers gain access to the site's Purple Pages, where they can even search Robinson's authoritative *Oxford Wine Companion*.

>> **Wine Anorak** (www.wineanorak.com): An online magazine from writer Jamie Goode with a distinctly British flavor. Strong in technical information about wine.

>> **Vinography** (www.vinography.com): Alder Yarrow's wine blog was one of the first to gain fame, and understandably so, because it's one of the best-written and authoritative blogs we have come across.

>> **Dr. Vino** (www.drvino.com): Tyler Coleman has established a reputation as the policeman of wine. He fearlessly goes after people in the wine business who make dubious claims. Not afraid to take on anybody, Coleman definitely has the pulse of the wine biz in his grasp.

>> **1WineDude** (www.1winedude.com): Joe Roberts, wine dude, has a humorous, hip, and knowledgeable blog with lots of entertaining scoops about the wine business. Particularly relevant for new and young wine lovers.

>> **The Feiring Line Natural Wine Newsletter** (www.thefeiringline.com): Alice Feiring is another wine journalist who will take on anybody or any topic in wine in her blog — no matter how controversial. She is also a major advocate of natural wine. $68, six issues annually.

Chapter **19**

Describing and Rating Wine

When we first got excited about wine, we tried to share our enthusiasm with a friend who appeared to have some interest in the subject (well, he drank a glass now and then). Each time we served a wine, we'd talk about it in great detail. But he wasn't interested. "I don't want to talk about wine — I just want to drink it!" he proclaimed.

On the fundamental level where wine is just a generic beverage, it's certainly possible to drink wine without talking about it. But if you're the kind of person who likes to talk about food, or if you've been bitten by the wine bug, you know that it's difficult (if not impossible) to enjoy wine without talking about it at least a little. Wine is a social pleasure that's enhanced by sharing your opinions with others.

Ironically, the experience of a wine is highly personal. If you and three other people taste the same wine at the same time, each of you will have your own impression of that wine based on personal likes and dislikes, physiology, and experience. Maybe some day, if humans learn how to link their minds through Bluetooth, someone else will be able to experience your experience of a wine — but until then, your taste is singular. The only way you can share your impressions with others is through conversation; the guidelines in this chapter will help you do that.

The Challenge of Putting Taste to Words

Language is our main vehicle for communicating our entire experience of life. Our vocabulary of taste is undeveloped, however. When we were young, we were taught a visual vocabulary: what green is, and what yellow, gold, and orange are — and for that matter, what pine green is, or jungle green, olive green, forest green, and sea green (thanks, Crayola!). But no one ever taught us the precise difference in the words *bitter*, *astringent*, and *tart*. Yet to talk about wine taste, we use these words as if we all agree on what they mean. That's one reason wine descriptions can sound like mumbo jumbo.

REMEMBER

Another reason wine descriptions are challenging is that a wine's taste is complicated. Wine is a complex beverage that gives us multiple taste sensations:

>> Aromatic sensations (all those flavors we perceive by smelling them in our mouths — as we discuss in Chapter 2)

>> Basic taste sensations (sweetness, sourness, and bitterness)

>> Tactile sensations (the bite of astringency, for example, as well as the prickliness, roughness, smoothness, richness, or other textural impressions of a wine in our mouths)

>> Sensations on the holistic level, a synthesis of all the wine's characteristics taken together

For example, say we just tasted an oaked Sauvignon Blanc from California. We may perceive the wine as intense in herbaceous and fruity, melonlike flavors with some smokiness (aromatic impressions), very slightly sweet, yet with firm acidity (basic taste impressions), smooth and rich (tactile impressions), a vibrant wine with personality to spare (holistic impression). That description risks sounding like some insufferable wine snob showing off, when it's actually just a wine lover trying his best to report the taste data the wine is sending him.

You've probably gotten many a laugh from wine descriptions you've read. At face value, they sound preposterous: Unctuous, with butter and vanilla flavors that coat the sides of your mouth. Supple and smooth, showing some fatness in the mouth, and a long finish. (Wait! They forgot to say wet and "liquidy.") Imperfect medium that language is, however, it's the only way we have of communicating the taste of wine.

Reading wine descriptions (or *tasting notes*, as they're often called) in wine newsletters or magazines can be as difficult as writing them. We must admit that our eyes often glaze over when we try to read tasting notes. And we're not alone. The late Frank Prial, long-time wine columnist of *The New York Times*, once wrote that "a stranger's tasting notes, to me anyway, are about as meaningful as a Beijing bus schedule."

When It's Your Turn to Speak

Describing your experience or impression of a wine involves two steps: First, you have to form the impression; second, you have to communicate it.

When you drink wine with friends purely for enjoyment and appreciation — over dinner, for example — simple impressions and silly comments are perfectly appropriate. If a wine strikes you as exotic, full and voluptuous, why *not* say that it's like Kim Kardashian? If a wine seems tight and unyielding, go ahead and call it Ebenezer Scrooge. Everyone will know exactly what you mean.

In other circumstances, though, such as when you're attending a wine-tasting event, you probably want to form more considered impressions of each wine in order to participate in the discussion and gain the most from the event. To form a considered impression, you need to taste thoughtfully. The guidelines in the following sections will help.

Organizing your thoughts

The language you use to describe a wine starts with your own thoughts as you taste the wine. Thus, the process of tasting a wine and the process of describing it are intertwined.

Although wine tasting involves examining wine visually and smelling it as well as tasting it, those first two steps are a breeze compared to the third. When the wine is in your mouth, the multiple taste sensations — flavors, texture, body, sweetness or dryness, acidity, tannin, balance, length — occur practically all at once. In order to make sense of the information you receive from the wine, you have to impose some order on those impressions. (Turn to Chapter 2 for information on the steps involved in examining, smelling, and tasting wine.)

TIP

One way of organizing the impressions a wine sends you is to classify those impressions according to the nature of the "taste":

>> The wine's *aromatics* (all the flavors you smell in your mouth)

>> The wine's *structure* (its alcohol/sweetness/acid/tannin makeup, that is, its basic tastes — the wine's bricks and mortar, so to speak)

>> The wine's *texture* (the tactile data, how the wine feels in your mouth; texture is a function of the wine's structural components — a high acid, dry, low-alcohol white wine may feel thin or sharp, for example, whereas a high-alcohol red wine with moderate tannin may feel soft and silky)

TIP

Another way of organizing the impressions a wine sends you is by the sequence of your impressions, as we describe in Chapter 2. The words that tasters use to describe the sequence are

>> **Attack:** The first impression of the wine, which may involve sweetness, dryness, richness or thinness of texture, or even fruitiness (although most of the wine's flavors register a few moments later).

>> **Evolution:** The development of the wine in your mouth. You can think of this stage in two parts:

- The *mid-palate impression,* a phase when you tend to notice the wine's acidity, perhaps get a first impression of its tannin (in red wines), and notice its flavors and their intensity

- The *rear-palate impression,* which involves persistence that the wine's flavors have (or don't have) across the length of your mouth, the amount and nature of the wine's tannins, and any indication of a burning sensation from overly high alcohol

>> **Finish or aftertaste:** Flavors or impressions that register after the wine has been spat or swallowed. Both the duration of the aftertaste and its nature are noteworthy. (A long finish is commendable, for example, and a bitter one is not.) A suggestion of concentrated fruit character on the finish often can indicate that a wine is age-worthy.

TO TASTE, PERCHANCE TO DRINK

In wine circles, tasting and drinking are two different activities. Tasting involves thoughtful evaluation of a wine's quality, flavors, texture, aging potential, and so on; if more than a couple of wines are being tasted comparatively, usually tasters spit the wine out (as we mention in Chapter 18) in order to keep their thinking clear. Drinking, on the other hand, involves consumption and sheer appreciation, without any particular analysis of the wine other than the judgment that you like it. (If you don't like it, you don't drink it.)

Unless you're a wine professional, you don't ever have to taste a wine seriously; you can just drink it. However, many wine drinkers have discovered that wine tasting can be a fun way to discover more about wine.

Describing a wine

Some people have a special ability to remember tastes. But other people need to take notes in order to remember what wine they tasted, and what they thought of it.

TIP

If you have the slightest difficulty remembering wine names, jot down the names of wines you try and like, or take a picture of the label; doing so will enable you to find and enjoy those wines — or similar wines — again. It's a good idea to write comments about the wines, too. Even if you're one of those lucky few who can remember everything you taste, we recommend that you write tasting notes now and then because the exercise of taking notes helps discipline your tasting methods.

TIP

When we take notes on wines, we automatically write the letters

>> *C* (for color and appearance in general)

>> *N* (for nose)

>> *T* (for taste, or mouth impressions)

We put one below the other, under the name of each wine on our tasting sheet, leaving space to record our impressions.

When we taste, we take each wine as it comes: If a wine is very aromatic, we write lots of things next to *N*, but if the aroma is understated, we can just write *subtle* or even *not much*. When the wine is in our mouths, we approach it sequentially, noting its attack and evolution; we hold the wine long enough to note its balance and texture, too. Then (having spat), we sometimes taste the wine again to determine what else it may be saying. At that point, we could arrive at a summary description of the wine, like *a huge wine packed with fruitiness that's ready to drink now,* or *a lean, austere wine that will taste better with food than alone.* Our tasting notes are a combination of fragmented observation — *high acid, very crisp* — and summary description.

At first, your own notes will be brief. Just a few comments, like *soft fruity* or *tannic austere* are fine to remind you later what the wine was like. And as an evaluation of overall quality, there's absolutely nothing wrong with *yummy!*

REMEMBER

Just keep in mind that the taste of a wine is more than just aromas and flavors. Instead of searching for ever more fruit or flower descriptors, move on to consider the dryness or sweetness, the body, or the texture. As we mention in Chapter 9, these characteristics are more important in pairing wine with food than the wine's actual flavors are.

THE DIGITAL OPTION

Today it is easier than ever to remember the wines you taste and record your comments about them, thanks to the many apps designed for wine drinkers. All you need to do is take a picture of the label with your smartphone and enter your impressions. As a bonus, you can read about the wine, view comments about it from other people, and even find out where to buy it, depending on which app you use. (These apps are also very useful when you're considering whether to buy a wine or not.) The two most highly regarded such apps are Delectable and Vivino.

Sometimes, if a wine is really a great wine, tasters stumble into the most controversial realm of wine description: poetry. We never *try* to come up with picturesque metaphorical descriptions for wines, but sometimes a wine just puts the words in our mouths. One memorable wine in our early days of tasting was a 1970 Brunello di Montalcino that we described as a rainbow in the mouth, its flavors so perfectly blended that each one was barely perceptible individually. A friend of ours described a glass of great but too-young Vintage Port as "like rubbing a cat in the wrong direction."

If a wine inspires you to such fanciful description, by all means go with it. The experience of that wine will become memorable through the personal words you use to name it. When you do lapse into metaphor over a wine, though, don't expect others to necessarily understand what you mean.

Beware of anyone who is moved to poetry over every wine, however. The vast majority of wines are prosaic, and their descriptions should be, too.

REMEMBER

In the end, the experience of wine is so personal that the best any of us can do is to *try* to describe the experience to others. Your descriptions will be meaningful to people who share your approach and your language, especially if they're tasting the wine along with you. But someone else picking up your notes could find them incomprehensible. Likewise, you'll find some wine descriptions you read incomprehensible. Such is the nature of the exercise.

Rating Wine Quality

When a wine critic writes a tasting note, he usually accompanies it with a point score, which is a judgment of the wine's quality on a scale of 20 or 100. You see these numbers plastered all over the shelves in your wine shop, in wine advertisements, and in wine blogs.

Because words are such a difficult medium for describing wine, the popularity of number ratings is almost universal. Many wine lovers don't bother to read the descriptions in a critic's wine reviews — they just run out to buy the wines with the highest scores. (Hey, they're the best wines, right?) Wines that receive high scores from the best-known critics sell out almost overnight as the result of the demand generated by their scores.

WARNING

Numbers do provide convenient shorthand for communicating a critic's opinion of a wine's quality. But number ratings are problematic, for several of reasons:

>> The sheer precision of a score suggests that the score is objective, when in fact it represents either the subjective opinion of an individual critic or the combined subjective opinions of a panel of critics.

>> Different critics can apply the same scale differently. For example, some may assign 95 points only to wines that are truly great compared to all wines of all types, while others could assign the same score to a wine that's great among wines of its own type.

>> The score probably reflects an evaluation of a wine under different circumstances than those in which you'll taste it. Most critics rate wines by tasting them without food, for example, while most wine drinkers drink wine with food. Also, the wine glass the critic uses can be different from what you use, and even this detail can seriously affect the way the wine presents itself.

>> Number scores tell you absolutely nothing about how the wine tastes.

REMEMBER

This last point, for us, is the most important. You may hate a wine that's rated highly — and not only that, but you may end up feeling like a hopeless fool who can't recognize quality when it's staring him in the face. Save your money and your pride by deciding what kinds of wine you like and then trying to figure out from the words whether a particular wine is your style — *regardless of the number rating.*

TIP

Despite the pitfalls of number ratings, you might be inclined to score wines yourself — and we encourage you to do that. Numbers *can* be meaningful to the person assigning them. Here are some basic steps to follow:

1. **To start, decide which scale you'll use.**

We suggest a scale with 100 as the highest score, because it's more intuitive than a scale ending at 20, which some British writers use. (Most 100-point scales are actually only 50-point scales, with 50 points, not 0, representing the poorest conceivable quality. And in practice, they are 20-point scales, because few wines score below 80.)

2. **After deciding your scale, create several groupings of points, and write down the quality level that each group represents.**

It can be something like this:

- 95–100: Absolutely outstanding; one of the finest wines ever
- 90–94: Exceptional quality; excellent wine
- 85–89: Very good quality
- 80–84: Above-average quality; good
- 75–79: Average commercial quality (a "C" student)
- 70–74: Below average quality
- Below 70: Poor quality

Then assign a number to a wine after you have tasted it thoughtfully. At first, you could give each wine a range rather than a precise score, such as 80 to 84 (good) or 85 to 89 (very good). As you gain experience in tasting wine and rating wine quality, you become more opinionated and your scores will naturally become more precise.

Just remember that like every other critic, you have your own taste preferences that inevitably influence your scores, no matter how objective you try to be. Don't fall into the trap of thinking that all your wine friends should agree with you.

7
The Part of Tens

Chapter **20**

Answers to Ten Common Questions about Wine

n our years of teaching about wine and helping customers in wine shops, we've noticed that the same questions about wine pop up again and again. Here are our answers.

What's the Best Wine?

This is probably the question customers ask most frequently in wine shops. They want to know, in other words, "Which wine should I buy?" The retailer usually responds with a barrage of questions, such as

>> "Do you prefer red wines or white wines?"

>> "How much do you want to spend for a bottle?"

>> "Are you planning to serve the wine with any particular dish?"

As all these questions suggest, the "best wine" depends on your taste and circumstances. There's no single "best wine" for everyone.

Hundreds of very good wines can be found in most wine shops. These days, winemaking and grape-growing know-how has progressed to the point that there are now few poor wines.

REMEMBER

You won't necessarily like every one of those good wines, however. There's simply no getting around the fact that taste is personal. If you want to drink a good wine that's right for you, you have to decide what the characteristics of that wine could be. And then get advice from a knowledgeable retailer.

Which Vintage Should I Buy?

This question assumes that you have a choice among several vintages of the same wine. Most of the time, however, you don't. Nearly every wine is available in only one vintage, which is referred to as the *current* vintage.

For white wines, the current vintage represents grapes that were harvested as recently as nine months ago or as long as three years ago, depending on the type of wine; for red wines, the current vintage is a date one to four years ago. Sparkling wines often have no vintage date at all (they are usually blends of several vintages) but when they do, the date is generally three to eight years ago — or more, for the most elite Champagnes.

Classified-growth red Bordeaux wines (see Chapter 10) are a notable exception: Most wine shops feature several vintages of these wines. A few other fine wines — such as Burgundies, Barolos, or Rhône wines — could also be available in multiple vintages, but often they're not because the quantities produced are small and the wines sell out.

A red Rioja or a Chianti Classico could appear to be available in multiple vintages, but if you read the label carefully, you see that one vintage of the Rioja could be a *crianza* (aged two years before release), another may be a *reserva* (aged three years), and another may be a *gran reserva* (aged five years) — so they are each actually different wines, not multiple vintages of the same wine. Likewise, a Chianti or Chianti Classico could be available in an aged *riserva* version in one vintage, as well as a non-riserva style in a younger vintage.

What Grape Variety Made This Wine?

Most non-European wines tell you what grape variety they're made from right on the front label — it's often the very name of the wine. Traditional European wines blended from several grape varieties usually don't give you that information a) because the winemakers consider the name of the place more important than the grapes, anyway, and b) because often the grapes they use are local varieties whose names few people would recognize.

If you really want to know what grape varieties make a Valpolicella, Châteauneuf-du-Pape, Rioja, Côtes du Rhône, or other blended European wines, you'll generally have to look it up. (See our charts in Chapters 11, 12, and 14.) If you want to know more about those varieties — and even the grape varieties that make varietal wines — turn to Chapter 3.

How Do I Know if a Wine Is Flawed?

The great majority of the wines you taste will not exhibit any flaws.

When a wine is flawed, your sense of smell will generally alert you. The most common flaw in a wine is *cork taint,* which is caused by a faulty cork. In serious cases of *cork taint,* the wine has an offensive, moldy odor, like damp cardboard. In fact, this so-called *corkiness* gets worse when the wine is exposed to air. Cork taint is a major reason why screw caps have become more popular as closures for wine.

When a wine is just slightly corky, it doesn't have a rank odor — it just seems lifeless, as if its aromas and flavors have been neutralized. If you are not someone who is very familiar with that wine, you might not realize that this is not the normal style of that wine, but comparing the wine against another bottle of the same wine will clarify the situation. This problem occurs more frequently than the flagrantly corky wines, which are obvious to everyone.

If a wine smells flat or dull, and its fruit aromas seem cooked, it has probably suffered from exposure to oxygen, usually because of overly warm storage or an ill-fitting cork. If you detect a vinegary note in a wine's smell, that wine has deteriorated with age or poor storage, combined with winemaking issues. (See our description of various wine flaws in Chapter 2 for more information.)

If you don't like the taste of a wine — for example, it is too tannic for you, or too acidic; too tart or too sweet; unbalanced — the wine is not necessarily flawed. It's just not for you!

Are There Any Wines without Sulfites?

Sulfur dioxide exists naturally in wine as a result of fermentation. It also exists naturally in other fermented foods, such as bread, cookies, and beer, and various sulfur derivatives are regularly added as preservatives in packaged foods.

Winemakers use sulfur dioxide at various stages of the winemaking process because it stabilizes the wine (preventing it from turning to vinegar or from deteriorating from oxygen exposure) and safeguards the wine's flavor.

Very few winemakers refrain from using sulfur dioxide, but some do. Winemakers who produce what they call *natural wines* generally do not add sulfites during winemaking; however, the wines are generally vulnerable to deterioration, in our experience.

If a wine does not carry the phrase Contains Sulfites on its label, the sulfite content must be less than 10 parts per million according to U.S. regulations, and sulfites were probably not added during winemaking. U.S. wines that are labeled as organic wines (not to be confused with the category of wines produced from organic grapes) cannot have sulfites added. (Refer to the following section for more information on organic wines.)

If you wish to limit your consumption of sulfites, dry red wines should be your first choice, followed by dry white wines. Sweet wines contain the most sulfur dioxide. For more info, turn to Chapter 1.

What Are Organic Wines?

The standards of organic agriculture established by the U.S. Department of Agriculture in 2002 contain two categories for wine:

>> **Wine made from organically grown grapes:** These are wines whose grapes come from certified organic vineyards.

>> **Organic wine:** These wines come from organically grown grapes and are also produced organically, that is, without the addition of chemical additives such as sulfur dioxide during winemaking. (Current E.U. regulations, however, do allow organic wines to contain added sulfur.)

Many more domestic wines, by far, fall into the first category than the second, because most winemakers do use sulfur dioxide in making their wines. (See the previous section for the reasons.)

But not all wines from organically grown grapes are labeled as such. Some winemakers whose vineyards are certified organic prefer to promote and sell their wines based on the wines' quality, not the incidental feature of their organic farming. For them, organic farming is a means to an end — better grapes, and therefore better wine — rather than a marketing tool.

Still other winemakers who are deeply committed to organic farming have chosen not to have their vineyards certified as organic. For some of them, the certification represents unwanted bureaucracy and extra paperwork. Therefore, their vineyards are not organic, technically speaking, even if their farming practices are.

We have the impression that organic grape growing is more prevalent than ever, whether the "O" word appears on wine labels or not. But we expect the number of wines in the more rigid *Organic wine* category to remain small, because of the sulfur dioxide restriction.

Should I Join a Wine Club?

Hardly a week goes by that we don't receive a solicitation of some sort to join a wine club that's affiliated with the magazines we admire or organizations that we support. For a low fee, the club will deliver several bottles of "expertly selected" wine to us each month. Easy as pie and sounds like a good deal.

Because we believe that experimentation is key in finding wines that you like, especially if your wine experience so far is limited, a wine club like this is not a bad idea, at least for a short period of time. But knowing a little bit about the way these clubs operate will help you manage your expectations for the experience.

First of all, most of these clubs are managed not by the magazine or newspaper or organization that they are named for, but by a company that manages wine clubs for several such businesses. That means that whether you choose one wine club or the other, it's essentially the same organization that selects the wines and ships them to you.

The wines are, in fact, generally selected by people who are expert in wine — that's one of the assurances that the sponsoring entity needs to protect its reputation with its readers or members. And they probably represent decent value, especially considering the convenience. The wines are different in each club, of course — that's necessary if the various clubs are to coexist. But the wines might appear to be different more than they really are different: They generally are private-label versions of similar wines. The brand of Côte du Rhône red that you receive, for example, does not exist elsewhere — it's an exclusive just for that wine club. But of course that unidentified producer in France makes more of the same wine, which he sells under other labels, maybe as an exclusive to your local wine shop chain, or maybe to that same management company for a competitive wine club.

Go ahead and join a wine club if it appeals to you, but realize that in the outside world you will not be able to find that same label of Côte du Rhône again. If you like the wine, you can explore other brands of Côte du Rhône from your wine shop, but you can't duplicate that precise experience. What you receive from the club is decent wine, thoughtfully selected to appeal to many people, but nothing even remotely "famous name."

Another type of wine club is the club run by a winery. Membership enables you to purchase special bottlings that are available only to members, and entitles you to VIP status for some winery events. When you find a winery that you like enough to become, in effect, a member of the family, joining its wine club will let you do that.

How Should I Store My Wine?

Most wines are ready to drink when you buy them and don't require any particular aging to make them taste best. If you have a few bottles that you are waiting to drink, store them in the coolest place available to you. This might be your basement or it might be a closet in the interior of your apartment. Ideally, the temperature will be fairly constant over the seasons and the air will not be very dry (as can occur through air conditioning). Do not store them in the refrigerator; it's too cold. Refrigerate a bottle to cool it down no more than a few hours before opening it.

If you own special, ageworthy wines, then you need to take your storage conditions more seriously, because your wine will be resting in storage longer. Refer to "A Healthy Environment for Your Wines" in Chapter 17 for details.

Are Wine Experts Sommeliers?

Because we are wine experts, people constantly assume, incorrectly, that we are sommeliers. Actually, a sommelier is a wine steward. It is a job title for individuals who run the beverage operation of a restaurant, from selecting the wines and spirits that the restaurant purchases and maintaining the inventory through to advising diners on their beverage choices and serving the wines.

A successful sommelier needs to have not only expert knowledge of wine but also training and experience in restaurant operations and a keen understanding of food-and-wine matching.

The Court of Master Sommeliers conducts a series of examinations through which individuals can prove their knowledge of wine and spirits and their service skills. Those who succeed at the highest tier become Master Sommeliers, a highly respected category. Other sommelier training programs also exist in the U.S., Canada, and various other countries.

Many people who have studied and successfully completed testing in sommelier skills identify themselves as sommeliers whether they are actively working in a restaurant or not. For that reason, the term *sommelier* has become a synonym for *wine expert* in the minds of the general public. But while most sommeliers are indeed wine experts, most wine experts are not necessarily sommeliers.

How Do I Know When to Drink the Special Older Wines I've Been Keeping?

Unfortunately, no precise answer to this question exists because all wines age at a different pace. The aging curve of a wine is highly dependent on storage conditions. And even two bottles of the same wine that are stored under the same conditions can age differently.

When you have a specific wine in mind, you can get advice about its readiness to drink in several different ways:

>> Consult the comments of critics like Antonio Galloni, Robert Parker, or Steve Tanzer, who almost always list a suggested drinking period for wines they review in their newsletters and books (listed in Chapter 18); their educated guesses are usually quite reliable.

>> Contact the winery; in the case of fine, older vintages, the winemaker and his staff are usually happy to give you their opinion on the best time to drink their wine — and they typically have more experience with the wine than anyone else.

>> If you have several bottles of the same wine, try one from time to time to see how the wine is developing. Your own taste is really the best guide — you may enjoy the wine younger, or older, than the experts.

Chapter **21**

Ten Wine Myths Demystified

As you leaf through the pages of this chapter, you'll probably recognize several of the myths we mention. They all represent common thinking — and common misinformation — about wine. We set the record straight.

The Best Wines Are Varietal Wines

One advantage of varietal wines — wines that are named after a grape variety, such as Chardonnay or Merlot — is that you supposedly know what you're getting. (Actually, for most American wines, only 75 percent of the wine has to come from the named variety, and for most other wines, only 85 percent — so you don't know *exactly* what you're getting. But anyway. . .). The presence of a grape variety name on the label, however, even a top-quality variety such as Cabernet Sauvignon, tells you nothing about the quality of the wine.

Varietal wines range in quality from ordinary to excellent. Wines named in other ways (for their region of production or with a fantasy name) also range in quality from ordinary to excellent. Varietal wines in general are no better and no worse than other wines.

A More Expensive Wine Is a Wiser Choice

For wine, as for many other products, a high price often indicates high quality. Purchasing a high-priced wine shows others that you can afford "the very best" and presumably that you have good taste.

REMEMBER

But high quality alone is not the best criterion for choosing a wine, for the following reasons:

>> Your taste is personal, and you may not like a wine that critics consider very high in quality.

>> Not all situations call for a very high quality wine.

We certainly can enjoy even a $10 to $12 wine in many circumstances. At large family gatherings, on picnics, at the beach, and so on, an expensive, top-quality wine can be out-of-place — too serious and important.

Likewise, the very finest wines are seldom the best choices in restaurants — considering typical restaurant prices. Instead, we look for the best value on the wine list (keeping in mind what we are eating) or we experiment with some moderately priced wine that we haven't tried before. (There will *always* be some wines that you haven't tried.)

REMEMBER

Quality isn't the only consideration in choosing a wine. Often, the best wine of all for your taste or for a certain situation will be inexpensive.

The Palest Rosé Wines Are the Best

This is a new myth that has emerged since rosé wines have become very popular. It might be based on the fact that rosé wines from southern France, such as those from the Provence region, are generally pale. These wines are riding high in sales and also have a great image as a chic choice among rosé wines. But actually, the color of a rosé wine tells you almost nothing about its quality or its taste.

Pale rosé wines generally come from red grapes that have less pigmentation in their skins, such as Grenache, Cinsault, Clairette, or Pinot Noir, and also they are made in a way to minimize color transfer from the grapes into the wine. Other red grape varieties can make rosé wines with deeper or different hues, a true pink rather than an orangey hue, for example. And all winemakers can control the amount of color (and flavor) transfer from the grapes into the wine. The options in making rosé wines are so many that the final wines represent a whole range of styles, including body, sweetness, or dryness levels, intensity of flavor, and specific aromas and flavors. The only way to know what's best for you is experimentation.

One detail that you might want to notice in looking at a bottle of rosé wine is its alcohol level, because that number can sometimes be a guide to the dryness or sweetness of the wine. A low number such as 10 percent alcohol might indicate that some grape sugar was retained in the wine without being fermented, and that wine will taste sweeter.

A Screw-Cap Closure Indicates a Lower-Quality Wine

This is an outdated belief. True, screw-off caps are still the closure on large "jug" bottles of those old-fashioned, really inexpensive domestic wines, but that type of wine is a dying breed. Meanwhile, screw caps have reinvented themselves as the closure of choice on many bottles of fine wine, especially white wines, from all over the world.

Winemakers know that using a metal cap to close their bottles can eliminate the risk of wine spoilage from blighted corks. Research has also proven that screw-cap closures don't prevent wines from aging and developing just as wines in cork-sealed bottles don't. Today's screw-cap closures are attractive, they are easy for wine drinkers to use, and they protect the wine from cork taint: all good reasons to embrace them.

Screw-cap closures are not universal, and they probably won't be anytime soon. (Traditions die hard.) You will find screw-cap closures especially on wines from New Zealand and Australia but also wines from other non-European countries, on bottles of white wines (even high quality whites) from many other countries, and on inexpensive and mid-priced bottles of red wines. You won't find screw caps on bottles of many red wines from classic European wine regions because, in some cases, the local regulations haven't caught up with scientific progress. And of course many of the world's most elite wine producers continue to favor the traditional closure, cork.

When you encounter a wine with a screw cap, know that you have a wine from a conscientious producer who wants to protect his wine from off-flavors that could derive from a cork.

Red Wines Are More Sophisticated than White Wines

We know: There's something about red wine that just says "serious." Maybe that's because many people enjoy white wines when they start drinking wine and then with experience they progress to red wine. And good for them, if that's what they enjoy. But we can assure you from personal experience that, after years of drinking more red wine than white, many serious wine lovers, including us, rediscover the unique virtues of white wines, such as their compatibility with light meals and their easier drinkability. And some white wines can be serious indeed!

A corollary of this myth is, "The darker the red wine the better." Many red wines today are extremely deep in color, almost to the point of being black rather than red. An opaque appearance in a red wine suggests that the wine's aromas and flavors are as concentrated as its color is, and for that reason, some people have begun to equate deep color with high quality.

While it's true that some very great red wines have deep color, other great red wines do not. Wines made from lightly pigmented grape varieties such as Pinot Noir, Nebbiolo, and Sangiovese, for example, will never be naturally opaque in color, and yet they can certainly be great.

Winemakers today have additives for artificially deepening the color of red wines, and therefore even cheap, everyday wines can be deep in color if the winemaker wants to make them that way. Don't be fooled into thinking that dark equals high quality.

REMEMBER

Whether you're deciding between red wine versus white, or judging the appearance of a particular red wine, a dark red color is no indication of quality and no measure of your good taste. Drink what you like.

White Wine with Fish, Red with Meat

As guidelines go, this isn't a bad one. But we said *guideline*, not rule. Anyone who slavishly adheres to this generalization deserves the boredom of eating and drinking exactly the same thing every day of his life!

Do you want a glass of white wine with your burger? Go ahead, order it. You're the one who's doing the eating and drinking, not your friend and not the server who's taking your order.

Even if you're a perfectionist who's always looking for the ideal food and wine combination, you'll find yourself wandering from the guideline. The best wine for a grilled salmon steak is probably red — like a Pinot Noir or a Bardolino — and not white at all. Veal and pork do equally well with red or white wines, depending on how the dish is prepared. And what can be better with hot dogs on the grill than a cold glass of rosé?

REMEMBER

No one is going to arrest you if you have white wine with everything, or red wine with everything, or even Champagne with everything! There are no rules. (We offer a few additional suggestions for possible wine–food pairings in Chapter 9.)

Number Ratings Don't Lie

This one might be the silliest myth of all.

It's natural to turn to critics for advice. We do it all the time when we're trying to decide which movie to see, when we're choosing a new restaurant to try, or when we want to know what someone else thinks of a particular book.

In most cases, we weigh the critics' opinions against our own experience and tastes. Say a steakhouse just got three stars and a fabulous review from the dining critic. Do we rush to the telephone to make a reservation? Not if we don't like red meat! When the movie critics give two thumbs up, do we automatically assume that we'll like the movie — or do we listen to their commentary and decide whether the movie may be too violent, silly, or serious for us? You know the answer to that.

TIP

Yet many wine drinkers, when they hear that a wine just got more than 90 points, go out of their way to get that wine. The curiosity to try a wine that scores well is understandable. But the rigid belief that such a wine a) is necessarily a great wine, and b) is a wine you will like, is simply misguided.

REMEMBER

The critics' scores are nothing more than the critics' professional opinion — and opinion, like taste, is *always* personal. (Chapter 19 tells you more about scoring wine.)

The Quality of a Wine Is Objectively Measurable

As wine critics, we constantly judge the quality of individual wines. Besides scribbling positive or negative comments about the wine's concentration or finesse or whatever, we quantify the quality by giving the wine a score. Usually, we are pretty much in agreement with each other and our scores are fairly close, which reinforces the notion that we have properly pegged the quality of the wine. What we have actually pegged, however, is our individual and collective *impression* of the wine's quality.

If human beings were machines, then maybe a person could taste a wine and ascribe a quality ranking to that wine with repeated and reproducible accuracy. As it is, however, the equipment we have to work with (our noses, mouths, and brains) is personal and varies in performance from one individual to the next. The experience of wine is *always subjective* and the quality statement given to a wine is therefore always subjective.

Everything about the wine-tasting experience influences our subjective impression of a wine's taste. Weather, your mood, and the ambiance of the situation all affect your reaction to a wine, for example. Not only that: One bottle of a wine can be subtly different from another bottle of the same wine, and the same wine in a different glass can taste different. Not even the world's greatest experts can objectively measure the quality of a wine.

Very Old Wines Are Good Wines

The idea of rare old bottles of wine being auctioned off for tens of thousands of dollars apiece, like fine art, is fascinating enough to capture anyone's imagination. But valuable old bottles of wine are even rarer than valuable old coins because, unlike coins, wine is perishable.

TIP

The huge majority of the world's wines don't have what it takes to age for decades. Most wines are meant to be enjoyed in the first one to five years of their lives. Even those wines that have the potential to develop slowly over many years will achieve their potential only if they are properly stored. (See Chapter 17 for information on storing wines.)

REMEMBER

The purpose of wine is to be enjoyed — usually, sooner rather than later.

Champagnes Don't Age

We don't know who started this myth; to the contrary, Champagne *does* age well! Depending on the particular year, Vintage Champagne can age especially well. We have enjoyed two outstanding 1928 Vintage Champagnes, Krug and Moët & Chandon's Dom Pérignon, neither of which showed any sign of decline. The oldest Champagne that we've ever tasted, a 1900 Pol Roger, was also in fine shape.

WARNING

But Champagne demands excellent storage. If kept in a cool, dark, humid place, many Champagnes can age for decades, especially in the great vintages. They lose some effervescence but take on a complexity of flavor somewhat similar to fine white Burgundy. Champagnes in magnum bottles (1.5 l) generally age better than those in regular size (750 ml) bottles.

TIP

If you want to try some very fine, reliable, older bottles of Vintage Champagne, look for either Krug or Salon in the 1964, 1969, 1973, or 1976 vintage. If stored well, they will be magnificent. Dom Pérignon is also reliable — the 1961 and 1969 DPs are legendary.

The following houses produce Champagnes known to age well:

>> **Krug:** All of their Champagnes are remarkably long lived.

>> **Pol Roger:** Especially Cuvée Sir Winston Churchill.

>> **Moët & Chandon:** Cuvée Dom Pérignon, ageless when well stored.

>> **Louis Roederer:** Cristal, Cristal Rosé, and Vintage Brut all age well.

>> **Paul Bara:** Special Club and Special Club Rosé.

>> **Bollinger:** All their Champagnes, especially the Grande Année.

>> **Gosset:** Grand Millésime and Célébris.

>> **Salon:** Remarkable Blanc de Blancs; needs at least 15 years of aging.

>> **Veuve Clicquot:** La Grande Dame and the Vintage Brut.

>> **Taittinger:** Their Blanc de Blancs (Comtes de Champagne).

>> **Billecart-Salmon:** The Vintage Blanc de Blancs.

>> **Pommery:** Cuvée Louise.

>> **Laurent-Perrier:** Cuvée Grand Siècle.

>> **Philipponnat:** Clos des Goisses.

Recent great, age-worthy vintages for Champagne are 2012, 2008, 2002, 1996, and 1988.

8

Appendixes

IN THIS PART . . .

Find out how to pronounce different wines and wine terminology correctly.

Use the glossary of wine terms to look up a wine-related word you hear that's unfamiliar.

Check out our vintage chart to find out how good the vintage is before you buy a wine. (But remember, a vintage chart is just a general guide.)

Appendix A

Pronunciation Guide to Wine Terms

Nothing will set a wine snob on your case more quickly than a mispronounced name of a famous wine or wine region. In order not to give snobs their smug satisfaction, we provide pronunciations of dozens of words here, for easy reference. This list is not exhaustive, however; the pronunciations of other, less common names and terms appear throughout this book. We place accented syllables, if any, in italics.

Name or term = Pronunciation
Agiorghitiko = eye-your-*yee*-tee-koe
Aglianico del Vulture = ah-lee-*ahn*-ee-coh del *vul*-toor-ay
Albariño = ahl-bah-*ree*-nyoh
Aligoté = ah-lee-go-tay
Aloxe-Corton = ah-luss-cor-tohn
Alsace = al-zass
(Alto)-Adige = *ah*-dee-jhae
amontillado = ah-moan-tee-*yah*-doh
Anjou = ahn-jhew
Arneis = ahr-*nase*
Assyrtiko = ah-*seer*-tee-koe
Au Bon Climat = oh bone klee-maht
Auslese = *ouse*-lay-seh
Auxerrois = aus-ser-whah
Auxey-Duresses = awk-see-duh-ress
Barbaresco = bar-bah-*res*-co

Name or term = Pronunciation

Barbera = bar-*bear*-ah

Barolo = bah-*ro*-lo

Batard-Montrachet = bah-tar-mon-rah-shay

Beaujolais = boh-jhoe-lay

Beaulieu (Vineyards) = bo-l'youh

Bianco di Custoza = bee-*ahn*-coh dee cus-*toez*-ah

Blanchot = blahn-shoh

botrytis = boh-*try*-tis

Bougros = boo-groh

Bourgogne = boor-guh-nyuh

Bourgueil = boor-guh'y

Brouilly = broo-yee

Brunello di Montalcino = brew-*nel*-lo dee mon-tahl-*chee*-no

brut = brute

Cabernet Sauvignon = cab-er-nay saw-vee-nyon

Canaiolo = cahn-eye-*oh*-loh

Carmignano = car-mee-*nyah*-no

Chablis = shah-blee

Chardonnay = shar-dohn-nay

Chassagne-Montrachet = shah-sah-nyuh-mon-rah-shay

(Château de) Fieuzal = fee-oo-zahl

(Château) Grillet = gree-yay

(Château) Haut-Brion = oh-bree-ohn

(Château) Lafite-Rothschild = lah-feet-roth-sheeld

(Château) Margaux = mahr-go

(Château) Mouton-Rothschild = moo-tohn-roth-sheeld

(Château) Petrus = peh-troos

(Château) Trotanoy = trot-ahn-wah

Name or term = Pronunciation

Châteauneuf-du-Pape = shah-toe-nuf-doo-pahp

Chénas = shay-nahs

Chenin Blanc = shen-in blahnk

Chevalier-Montrachet = sheh-vah-lyay-mon-rah-shay

Chianti = key-*ahn*-tee

(Chianti) Rufina = *roo*-fee-nah

Chinon = she-nohn

Chiroubles = sheh-roob-leh

Clos du Val = clo dew val

Colheita = col-*yay*-tah

Condrieu = cohn-dree-uh

Corton-Charlemagne = cor-tawn-shahr-luh-mahn

Côte de Beaune = coat deh bone

Côte Chalonnaise = coat shal-oh-naze

Côte d'Or = coat dor

Côte de Nuits = coat deh nwee

Côte de Nuits-Villages = coat deh nwee-vee-lahj

Côte-Rôtie = coat-roe-tee

Côtes du Ventoux = coat due vahn-too

cuvée = coo-vay

Dolcetto = dohl-*chet*-oh

(Domaine) Leroy = leh-wah

Eisele Vineyard = *eye*-seh-lee

Entre-Deux-Mers = ahn-truh-duh-mair

Fleurie = flehr-ee

Fourchaume = for-shahm

Friulano = free-ou-*lah*-noh

Friuli-Venezla Giulia = free-*oo*-lee-veh-*netz*-ee-ah *joo*-lee-ah

Name or term = Pronunciation

Galicia = gah-*leeth*-ee-ah

Garrafeira = gar-ah-*fay*-ah

Gattinara = gah-tee-*nah*-rah

Gavi = *gah*-vee

Genevrières = jen-ev-ree-aire

Gewürztraminer = geh-*vairtz*-trah-mee-ner

Gigondas = jhee-gohn-dahs

Givry = gee-vree

Grands Crus Classés = grahn crew clas-say

Graves = grahv

Grenouilles = greh-n'wee

Grüner Veltliner = *grew*-ner *velt*-lee-ner

halbtrocken = *hahlb*-tro-ken

Haut-Médoc = oh-may-doc

Hermitage = er-mee-tahj

Juliénas = jhool-yay-nahs

Languedoc-Roussillon = lahn-gweh-doc-roo-see-yohn

Les Clos = lay cloh

Les Forêts = lay for-ay

Les Preuses = lay preuhz

Liebfraumilch = *leeb*-frow-milsh

Listrac = lee-strahk

Loire = l'wahr

Mâcon-Villages = mah-cawn-vee-lahj

Malvasia = mal-va-*see*-ah

Margaux = mahr-go

Médoc = meh-doc

Menetou-Salon = meh-neh-too-sah-lohn

Name or term = Pronunciation

Mercurey = mer-cure-ay

Merlot = mer-loh

Meursault = muhr-so

Moët = moh-ett

Mont de Milieu = mon deh meh-lyew

Montagny = mon-tah-nyee

Montepulciano d'Abruzzo = mon-tae-pul-chee-*ah*-noh dah-*brute*-zoh

Monthélie = mohn-teh-lee

Montlouis = mon-loo-wee

Montmains = mon-man

Montrachet = mon-rah-shay

Moschofilero = mos-cho-*feel*-eh-roe

Mosel = *moh*-zel

Moulin-à-Vent = moo-lahn-ah-vahn

Moulis = moo-lees

Müller-Thurgau = *mool*-lair-*toor*-gow

Muscadet = moos-cah-day

Muscat = moos-caht

Nahe = *nah*-heh

Nantais = nahn-tay

Nebbiolo = neb-bee-*oh*-lo

Niebaum-Coppola = *nee*-baum-*cope*-poh-lah

Niederosterreich = nee-der-*oz*-ter-ryke

Nuits-St.-Georges = nwee-san-johrj

Orvieto = or-vee-*ae*-toh

Pauillac = poy-yac

Pays d'Oc = pay-ee doc

Penedés = pen-eh-*dais*

Name or term = Pronunciation

Pernand-Vergelesses = per-nahn-ver-jeh-less

Perrier-Jouët = per-ree-yay-joo-ett

Pessac-Léognan = pay-sac-lay-oh-nyahn

Pfalz = fallz

Pinot Bianco = pee-noh bee-*ahn*-coh

Pinot Blanc = pee-noh blahnk

Pinot Grigio = pee-noh *gree*-joe

Pinot Gris = pee-noh gree

Pinot Noir = pee-noh nwahr

Pinotage = pee-noh *tahj*

Pouilly-Fuissé = pwee-fwee-say

Pouilly-Fumé = pwee-foo-may

Premier Cru = prem-yay crew

Priorato = pree-oh-*rah*-to

Puligny-Montrachet = poo-lee-nyee-mon-rah-shay

Qualitätswein = *kal*-ee-tates-vine

Quincy = can-see

Quinta = *keen*-ta

Régnié = ray-nyay

Reuilly = reuh-yee

Rheingau = *ryne*-gow

Rheinhessen = *ryne*-hess-ehn

Rías Baixas = *ree*-ahse *byche*-ahse

Ribera del Duero = ree-*bear*-ah del *dwair*-oh

Ribolla Gialla = ree-*bohl*-lah *jahl*-lah

Riesling = *reese*-ling

Rioja = ree-*oh*-hah

Rueda = roo-*ae*-dah

Name or term = Pronunciation

Rully = rouh-yee

Saint-Amour = sant-ah-more

St.-Aubin = sant-oh-ban

St.-Nicolas-de-Bourgueil = san-nee-co-lah-deh-boor-guh'y

St.-Romain = san-roh-man

St.-Véran = san-veh-rahn

Sancerre = sahn-sair

Sangiovese = san-joe-*vae*-sae

Saumur = soh-muhr

Sauvignon Blanc = saw-vee-nyon blahnk

Savennières = sah-ven-nyair

Savigny-lès-Beaune = sah-vee-nyee-lay-bone

Scheurebe = *shoy*-reb-beh

Semillon = *sem*-eh-lon (Australian)

Sémillon = seh-mee-yohn (French)

Sèvre-et-Maine = sev'r-et-mehn

Soave = so-*ah*-vay

Spanna = *spah*-nah

Spätlese = *shpate*-lay-seh

spumante = spoo-*mahn*-tay

St.-Emilion = sant-ay-meal-yon

St.-Estèphe = sant-eh-steff

St.-Julien = san-jhoo-lee-ehn

Steiermark = *sty*-er-mark

Tempranillo = tem-prah-*nee*-yoh

Tinto = *teen*-toe

Tokaj-Hegyalja = toe-*kye*-heh-*jah*-yah

Torgiano = tor-gee-*ah*-no

Name or term = Pronunciation

Tre Venezie = trae veh-*netz*-ee-ae

Trebbiano = treb-bee-*ah*-noh

trocken = *troh*-ken

Vacqueyras = vah-keh-rahs

Vaillons = vye-yon

Valmur = vahl-moor

Valpolicella = val-po-lee-*chel*-lah

Vaudésir = voh-deh-zeer

Vendange Tardive = vahn-dahnj tahr-deev

Veneto = *ven*-eh-toh

Verdejo = ver-*day*-ho

Verdicchio = ver-*dee*-key-oh

Vernaccia di San Gimignano = ver-*nah*-cha dee san gee-mee-*nyah*-noh

Vinho = *veen*-yo

Vinho Verde = *veen*-yo *vaird*

(Vino) Nobile di Montepulciano = *no*-be-lay dee mon-tay-pul-chee-*ah*-no

Viognier = vee-oh-nyay

Vosne-Romanée = vone-roh-mah-nay

Vouvray = voo-vray

Wachau = va-*cow*

Weissburgunder = *vice*-boor-gun-der

Wien = vee-*en*

Willamette (Valley) = wil-*lam*-et

Xinomavro = ksee-*no*-mav-roe

Appendix B

Glossary of Wine Terms

Here, for handy reference, are definitions of dozens of the most common wine terms and wine-tasting terms.

acidity: A component of wine, generally consisting of tartaric acid (a natural acid in grapes) and comprising approximately 0.5 to 0.7 percent of the wine by volume.

aerate: To expose wine to air in preparation for drinking it, usually with the intention of softening the harshness of a younger wine or allowing the most attractive aromas to reveal themselves in an older wine.

alcohol level: The percentage of alcohol by volume that a wine has; most white wines have an alcohol level between 9 and 14 percent, and most red wines have an alcohol level between 12 and 15 percent.

American oak: Oak wood from a U.S. forest, of the species *quercus alba,* and the barrels made from such wood; some winemakers in certain wine regions (such as some in Spain and Australia) favor American oak for aging their wines.

ample: A descriptor for wines that give the impression of being full and expansive in your mouth.

AOC: Abbreviation for *Appellation d'Origine Contrôlée,* sometimes shortened to *Appellation Contrôlée* and abbreviated as AC; translates to "protected place-name"; France's original official category for its highest-ranking types of wine, whose name, origin, grape varieties, and other defining factors are regulated by law.

AOP: Abbreviation for *Appellation d'Origine Protégée*, the term that is equivalent to AOC in the European Union's new Designation of Origin system.

appellation: Name; often used to mean the official geographic origin of a wine, which is part of a wine's official name.

aroma: The smell of a wine. Some purists use the term *aroma* only for the straightforward, youthful smells of a wine, and use the term *bouquet* for the more complex smells of an aged wine. But we use *aroma* as a general term for all wine smells.

aromatic: A descriptor for a wine that has a pronounced smell, used particularly in reference to fruity and floral smells. Some white grape varieties are also dubbed *aromatic* because they are strong in aroma compounds.

aromatic compounds: Those substances in wine — derived from the grapes, from winemaking, or from aging — that are responsible for a wine's aromas and flavors.

astringent: A descriptor for the mouth-puckering, pore-tightening tactile character of some wines, caused by tannin, acid, or the combination of both. Generally not a positive trait.

attack: The first impression a wine gives you when you taste it. A wine's attack is related to sensations in the front of your mouth.

balance: The interrelationship of a wine's alcohol, residual sugar (if any), acid, and tannin; when no one component stands out obtrusively in your mouth, a wine is said to be well balanced; wines can also have balance between their aromas/flavors and their structure.

barrel: A relatively small wooden container for fermenting and/or aging wine, generally 60 gallons in size and generally made of oak.

barrel-aged: A term that applies to wines that are fermented in containers of inert material, such as stainless steel, and subsequently placed into wooden barrels for a period of maturation; the term also applies to the maturation period of wines that also fermented in the barrel.

barrel-fermented: A term that applies to white wines that are fermented in oak barrels; the oaky character of such wines is generally more subtle than that of wines that have been merely barrel-aged.

big: A general descriptor for wines that are either very full or very intense.

black fruits: A general term for wine aromas and flavors that suggest blackberries, blueberries, black cherries, black currants, or other black fruits.

black grapes: Wine grapes that have a reddish or blue pigmentation in their skins; used to make red wine.

blend: To mix together two or more individual lots of wine, usually wines from different grape varieties (but also applies to wines from different vineyards, different regions, or different vintages); a wine derived from the juice of different grape varieties is called a blend.

bodega: A winery in Spain; also the Spanish word for a building where wine is stored.

body: The impression of a wine's weight in your mouth. A wine's body is generally described as light, medium, or full.

bottle-age: Maturation of a wine after it has been bottled; most wines undergo a short period of bottle-age at the winery before release; fine wines could require additional bottle-age from the consumer.

bouquet: An evolved, complex, mature aroma.

bright: Indicates a wine whose characteristics are perceived as vivid by the senses. A wine can be visually bright, or it can have bright aromas and flavors; in both cases, the opposite is dull.

cask: A relatively large wooden container for making or storing wine.

castello: Italian for *castle;* refers to a wine estate.

cedary: Having aromas or flavors that resemble the smell of cedar wood.

character: An anthropomorphic descriptor for wines that give the impression of having substance and integrity.

charry: Having aromas or flavors that suggest burnt wood or charred wood.

château: A French name for a grand winery estate, commonly used in the Bordeaux region as well as other regions.

classico: An Italian term applicable to certain DOC/DOCG (or PDO) wines whose vineyards are situated in the original, classic part of the territory for that particular type of wine.

clone: A subset of a grape variety; a vine, or set of genetically identical vines, that exhibits characteristics specific to it as compared to other vines of the same variety.

colheita: Vintage, in Portuguese.

commune: A village and its surrounding vineyard territory.

compact: A descriptor for wines that give the impression of being tight and concentrated, but not full.

complex: Having a multiplicity of aromas and flavors.

concentrated: A descriptor for wines with aromas and flavors that are dense rather than dilute.

concentration: A characteristic of wines whose flavors are tightly knit as opposed to being dilute or watery.

cosecha: Vintage, in Spanish.

crisp: A wine that feels clean and slightly brittle in your mouth; the opposite of *soft.* Crispness is usually the result of high acidity, and crisp wines, therefore, are usually relatively light in body and go well with food.

decant: To transfer wine from a bottle to another container, either for the purpose of aerating the wine or to separate a red wine from its sediment.

depth: A characteristic of fine wines that give the impression of having many layers of taste, rather than being flat and one-dimensional; a positive trait.

dilute: A descriptor for wines whose aromas and flavors are thin and watery, as opposed to concentrated; a negative characteristic.

district: A geographic entity more specific than a region and less specific than a commune.

DO: Abbreviation for *Denominación de Origen,* which translates to "place-name"; Spain's original, official category for wines whose name, origin, grape varieties, and other defining factors are regulated by law.

DOC: Abbreviation for *Denominazione di Origine Controllata,* which translates to "controlled place-name"; Italy's original, official category for wines whose name, origin, grape varieties, and other defining factors are regulated by law. Also an abbreviation for *Denominacão de Origem Controlada,* Portugal's similar phrase.

DOCa: Abbreviation for *Denominación de Origen Calificada*, which is Spain's original category for wine regions of the highest status.

DOCG: Abbreviation for *Denominazione di Origine Controllata e Garantita,* which translates to "controlled and guaranteed place-name"; Italy's official category for its highest-ranking wines.

domaine: A French term for wine estate, commonly used in the Burgundy region.

DOP: Abbreviation for *Denominazione di Origine Protetta*, Italy's category in the new E.U. system of designating wine origin that encompasses DOC and DOCG wines; in Spanish, an abbreviation for *Denominación de Origen Protegida,* which is, in the new E.U. framework, Spain's category encompassing DO and DOCa wines; and in Portuguese, abbreviation for *Denominação de Origem Protegida*, Portugal's similar phrase.

dry: A wine that is not sweet. The word *dry* can also describe the texture of a wine that feels rough in your mouth, as in *dry texture* or *dry mouthfeel.* But when used alone, it refers specifically to lack of sweetness.

dull: A wine whose expression is muddled and unclear. This term can apply to a wine's appearance, to its aromas and flavors, or to its general style. It is a negative characteristic.

earthy: Having pleasant aromas and flavors that suggest earth, such as wet soil, dry earth, certain minerally aromas, and so forth. This term is sometimes used as a euphemism for wines that are rustic and lack refinement.

elegance: A somewhat overused descriptor for wines that express themselves in a fine or delicate manner as opposed to an intense or forceful way — considered a positive trait.

estate: A property that grows grapes and produces wines from its own vineyards; wines labeled *estate-bottled* are made from vineyards owned by (or in some cases, under the direct control of) the same entity that owns the winery and makes the wine; use of the term is regulated by law in most areas.

extraction: The absorbtion of substances from the grapes, such as color and tannin, that occurs when the skins co-mingle with the juice or wine during the winemaking process.

fermentation: The natural process by which the sugar in grape juice is transformed into alcohol (and the juice is, thus, transformed into wine) through the action of yeasts.

finish: The final impressions a wine gives in the rear of your mouth after you have swallowed it or spat it out; aftertaste.

firm: A descriptor for wines that are not soft but are not harsh and tough; generally relates to the tannic content of a red wine or the acidity of a white wine.

flabby: A pejorative term used to describe wines that taste too soft, generally due to a lack of acidity or tannin.

flavor intensity: The degree to which a wine's flavors are pronounced and easily perceived.

flavors: Aromatic constituents of a wine that are perceived in the mouth.

fleshy: A descriptor for a rich textural or tactile impression of some wines.

fortified wine: A wine that has had alcohol added to it.

French oak: Oak wood from the forests of France, of the species *quercus robur,* considered the finest type of oak for aging most white wines and many red wines; the barrels made from such wood.

fruit character: Those characteristics of a wine that derive from the grapes, such as a wine's aromas and flavors.

fruity: Having aromas and flavors suggestive of fruit. This is a broad descriptor; in some cases, the fruity aroma or flavor of a wine can be described more precisely as suggestive of fresh fruit, dried fruit, or cooked fruit, or even more precisely as a specific fresh, dried, or cooked fruit, such as fresh apples, dried figs, or strawberry jam.

full: A descriptor for wines that give the impression of being large and weighty in your mouth. A wine's fullness can derive from high alcohol or from other aspects of the wine. A wine can be pleasantly full or too full, depending on one's taste preferences.

garrafeira: A Portuguese term for a reserva wine with specific aging requirements — for red wines, at least three years of aging in oak and bottle before release.

generous: A descriptor for wines whose characteristics are expressive and easy to perceive; usually describes fuller, rounder styles.

gran reserva: On Spanish red wines, a term indicating a wine that has aged at least five years before release, at least two of which were in oak.

grape tannin: Those tannins in a red wine that come from the grapes from which the wine was made, from the grapes' skins and seeds but sometimes from stems.

grape variety: A distinct type of grape within a species.

harmonious: A flattering descriptor for wines that are well balanced and also express themselves in a particularly graceful manner.

herbal: Having aromas and flavors that suggest herbs, such as fresh herbs, dried herbs, or specific herbs (rosemary, thyme, tarragon, and so forth).

IGP: Abbreviation for the French, Italian, and Spanish phrases that mean "protected geographic indication," the E.U.'s secondary and looser category of place-name classification.

IGT: Abbreviation for the phrase that indicates Italy's original, lower tier of protected appellations for wine; translates as "typical geographic indication."

intense: Usually used in reference to a wine's aromas and flavors, to describe the volume of those aromas or flavors — how pronounced the smell of lemon is in the wine, for example, or how flavorful the wine is.

lees: Grape solids and dead yeast cells that precipitate to the bottom of a wine vessel after fermentation.

length: A characteristic of fine wines that give a sustained sensory impression across the length of the tongue.

maceration: The process of soaking the skins of red grapes in their grape juice to leach the skins' color, tannin, and other substances into the juice. Can also be used to create an unusual style of white wine.

malolactic fermentation: A natural conversion of harsh malic acid into milder lactic acid, which weakens the total acidity of a wine; an optional process in white wine production.

maturation: The aging period at the winery during which a wine evolves to a state of readiness for bottling or for shipping; the process of development and evolution that fine wines undergo after they are bottled.

medium-dry: A term to indicate the perceived sweetness of wines that are somewhat sweet but close to dry.

medium-sweet: A term to indicate the perceived sweetness level of wines that are sweeter than medium-dry, but not fully sweet.

minerally: Having aromas or flavors that suggest minerals (as opposed to organic substances, such as plants or animals). This is a broad descriptor; in some cases, the minerally aroma or flavor of a wine can be described more precisely as suggestive of chalk, iron, steel, and so forth.

new oak: Oak barrels that are used for the first time in making a particular wine; sometimes called *"first use" oak.*

New World: Collective term for those winemaking countries of the world that are situated outside of Europe.

nutty: Having aromas or flavors that suggest nuts. This is a broad descriptor; in some cases, the nutty aroma or flavor of a wine can be described more precisely as suggestive of roasted nuts, toasted nuts, nut butter, or cashews, almonds, hazelnuts, and so forth.

oaky: Having characteristics that derive from oak, such as toastiness, smokiness, a charry smell or flavor, vanilla aroma, or a higher tannin level than the wine might otherwise have. Usually, these oaky characteristics occur as the wine ages in oak barrels, but in very inexpensive wines, they may have been added as an actual flavoring.

off-dry: A generalized term for wines that are dryish but not truly dry.

old oak: Oak barrels or casks that are old enough to have lost most of their oaky character, generally 3 years old and older. Sometimes called *neutral* oak.

old vines: An unregulated term for grape vines whose fruit quality presumably is quite good due to the fact the vines are old — generally 40 years old or older — and therefore produce a very small crop of concentrated grapes.

Old World: Collective term for the winemaking countries of Europe.

palate: A term used by wine tasters as a synonym for "mouth," or to refer to the characteristics of a wine that manifest in the taster's mouth.

PDO: Abbreviation for *Protected Denomination of Origin,* the E.U.'s higher category for wines with protected place-names.

petrol: Having aromas or flavors that suggest diesel fuel; can be a positive trait.

PGI: Abbreviation for *Protected Geographic Indication,* the E.U.'s lower category for wines from officially recognized regions.

phylloxera: A parasite louse that feeds on the roots of Vitis vinifera grape vines, resulting in the vines' premature death.

plummy: Having aromas or flavors that suggest ripe plums.

powerful: An anthropomorphic descriptor for wines that convey an impression of strength and intensity.

pretty: An anthropomorphic descriptor for wines that are attractive for their delicacy and finesse.

primary aromas: Fresh aromas in a wine that derive from the grapes used to make that wine.

region: A geographical entity less specific than a district but more specific than a country; for Italian wines, the term *region* applies to the political entity as well as to the wine zones within that area.

reserva: On a Spanish wine, a term indicating that the wine has aged longer at the winery (usually some specified combination of oak aging and bottle aging) than a non-reserva version of the same type; red reserva wines must age at least three years (with a year in oak) before release. On a Portuguese wine, a wine of superior quality from a single vintage. In South America, a common but unregulated term.

reserve: A designation for wines that are presumably finer than the non-reserve (normal) version of the same wine; use of the term is unregulated in the United States and in France.

residual sugar: Sugar remaining in the wine after fermentation.

rich: A descriptor of wines that offer an abundance of flavor, texture, or other sensory perceptions.

riserva: Italian word for *reserve,* indicating a wine that has aged longer before release from the winery than a non-reserve version of the same type of wine, and suggesting higher quality; whether a wine may use this term and the conditions of use are defined by individual DOC regulations.

round: A descriptor for wines that are perceived in the mouth to be neither flat nor angular. Roundness relates to the wine's structure — that is, its particular makeup of acid, tannin, sweetness, and alcohol, which dictates texture and mouthfeel.

second-label wine: A less-expensive, second wine (or a second brand of wine) made by a winery from grapes or wine not considered worthy of the winery's primary label.

Secondary aromas: Aromas and flavors that derive from winemaking, such as oak-derived notes or a buttery note from malolactic fermentation.

sediment: The residue in a bottle of red wine that forms as the wine matures.

serious: A metaphorical descriptor for a wine that is of high quality, as opposed to a popularly styled, mass-market wine.

silky: Having a supple, smooth texture suggestive of silk.

single-vineyard wine: A wine that is made from the grapes of a single (presumably exceptionally good) plot of land and that usually carries the name of the vineyard on its label; the term is unregulated, in that *vineyard* is not defined as to size or ownership.

skin contact: The process during which the juice of grapes rests in contact with the grape skins; in red wine, the process by which the wines absorb color, tannin, and other substances; not normally used in white wine production, but occasionally used to enhance the aromatic character of the wine.

smoky: Having aromas or flavors that suggest smoke or smoked wood.

smooth: Descriptor for a wine whose texture is not rough or harsh.

soft: Textural descriptor for a wine whose alcohol and sugar (if any) dominate its acidity and tannin, resulting in a lack of hardness or roughness.

stemmy: Descriptor for red wines that give the impression of having dry, raspy, woody tannins, as if from the stems of grape bunches.

stems: The woody part of a grape bunch, which are high in tannin; usually the stems are removed and discarded prior to fermentation.

stony: Having minerally aromas or flavors that suggest stones. In some cases, the stony aroma or flavor of a wine can be described more precisely as suggestive of wet stones.

structural components: Principally, a wine's alcohol, acid, tannin, and sugar (if any).

structure: That part of a wine's taste that derives from perception of the wine's structural elements.

style: The set of characteristics through which a wine manifests itself.

supple: A descriptor for wines that seem fluid in texture in the mouth, without roughness or sharpness; a positive trait especially for red wines.

süssreserve: German for *sweet reserve;* unfermented grape juice that is added to a white wine to increase the wine's residual sugar and sweetness.

sweetness: The impression of sugary taste in a wine, which can be due to the presence of residual sugar or to other sweet-tasting substances in the wine, such as alcohol.

tannic: A word used to describe wines that seem to be high in tannin.

tannin: A substance in the skins, stems, and seeds of grapes; a principal component of red wines, which — unlike most white wines — are made by using the grape skins. Tannin also is a component of oak barrels.

tarry: Having aromas or flavors that suggest fresh tar.

tart: A descriptor for aromas or flavors of under-ripe fruit. This term can also apply to a wine that is too high in acid.

taste: A general term for the totality of impressions a wine gives in the mouth; more specifically, the primary tastes found in wine: sweetness, sourness, and bitterness.

terroir: A French word that is the collective term for the growing conditions in a vineyard, such as climate, soil, drainage, slope, altitude, topography, and so on.

Tertiary aromas: Aromas and flavors that derive from aging of the wine, such as notes of mushroom, leather, dried fruit, and other aromas.

texture: A wine's consistency or feel in the mouth.

thin: A word used to describe wines that are lacking in substance or meager in texture.

tight: A descriptor for wines that seem to be inexpressive at the moment. This term can apply to a wine's aromas and flavors or to its structure.

underbrush: Aromas or flavors that suggest wet leaves, dampness, and slight decay; a welcome note in many older reds.

varietal: A wine named for the sole or the principal grape variety from which it was made.

varietal character: The characteristics of a wine that are attributable to the grape variety from which it was made.

vegetal: Having aromas or flavors that suggest vegetables, such as green peppers or asparagus; these can be pleasant or not, depending on the taster.

vin de pays: French phrase for *country wine;* in France's original regional classification system, a category that holds lower status than AOC wines.

vinification: The activity of making grape juice into wine.

vintage: The year in which a wine's grapes grew and were harvested; sometimes used as a synonym for the grape harvest.

viticulture: The activity of growing grapes.

Vitis vinifera: The species to which most of the world's wine grapes belong.

weight: The impression of a wine's volume in the mouth.

wood tannin: Those tannins in a wine that are attributable to the barrels in which the wine aged, as opposed to the grapes.

yeasts: One-cell microorganisms responsible for transforming grape juice into wine.

Appendix C

Vintage Wine Chart: 1996-2015

Any vintage wine chart must be regarded as a rough guide — a general, average rating of the vintage year in a particular wine region. Remember that many wines will always be exceptions to the vintage's rating. For example, some wine producers will manage to find a way to make a decent — even fine — wine in a so-called poor vintage.

Wine Region	1996	1997	1998	1999	2000	2001	2002	2006	2007
Bordeaux									
Médoc, Graves	90b	85c	85b	85b	90b	85b	85b	85b	80c
Pomerol St.-Emil	85b	85c	95b	85b	90b	85b	85b	85b	85c
Sauternes/Barsac	85b	85c	85b	85a	85b	95a	90a	85b	90b
Burgundy									
Côte de Nuits	90b	85c	80c	90c	85c	80c	90b	85b	85b
Côte de Beaune	90c	85c	80c	90c	75c	75c	90b	80c	75c
Burgundy, White	90c	85d	80c	85c	85c	85c	90c	85b	80c
Rhône Valley									
Northern Rhône	85c	90c	90b	95b	85c	90b	75c	90b	85b
Southern Rhône	80d	80d	95c	90c	90c	95b	55d	85b	95b
Other Wine Regions									
Alsace	85c	85c	90c	85c	85c	90c	85c	75c	85c
Champagne	100b	80c	85c	85c	80c	NV	95b	90b	80b
Germany	90b	85c	90b	85c	70d	95b	90b	95a	85b
Rioja	85c	85c	80d	85c	85c	95b	70d	80b	85b
Vintage Port	NV	90a	95a	NV	95a	NV	NV	NV	90a

Wine Region	1996	1997	1998	1999	2000	2001	2002	2006	2007
Italy									
Piedmont	95a	85c	90b	90b	85c	95b	75c	90a	85b
Tuscany	75c	90c	85c	85c	85c	95b	75d	90a	85b
California North Coast									
Cab. Sauvignon	90b	90c	85c	85b	75c	90b	85b	85b	95b

Wine Region	2008	2009	2010	2011	2012	2013	2014	2015
Bordeaux								
Médoc, Graves	85b	90b	95a	85a	85a	75c	85a	90a
Pomerol, St.-Emil	85b	90b	95a	85a	90a	80c	95a	90a
Sauternes/Barsac	90a	95a	95a	90a	85a	90b	95a	95a
Burgundy								
Côte de Nuits	90a	95a	95a	90a	90a	90c	90b	95b
Côte de Beaune	90a	95a	95a	90a	90a	90c	90b	95b
Burgundy, White	90b	85b	90a	90a	90a	85c	95b	90c
Rhône Valley								
Northern Rhône	75b	95a	95a	85a	90c	90b	85b	95a
Southern Rhône	80b	90a	95a	85c	90c	85c	85b	90a
Other Wine Regions								
Alsace	90b	80c	85b	80c	90c	90b	90c	85a
Champagne	95a	85c	80b	75c	95a	80c	90a	90c
Germany	90b	95b	85a	95b	90a	80c	75c	95b
Rioja	90b	95a	95a	85a	90a	80c	85c	95b
Vintage Port	90a	95a	85a	95a	85c	75c	70c	90a

Wine Region	2008	2009	2010	2011	2012	2013	2014	2015
Italy								
Piedmont	90a	85a	95a	90a	85b	90b	75b	90a
Tuscany	85b	85a	95a	85b	90a	95a	85a	85c
California North Coast								
Cab. Sauvignon	90a	90a	95a	80b	95a	95a	85b	90a

Early reports suggest that 2016 will be a great vintage for Bordeaux, also for white Burgundy, especially Chablis.

Key:

100 = Outstanding	50–60 = Very Poor
95 = Excellent	a = Too young to drink
90 = Very Good	b = Can be consumed now, but will improve with time
85 = Good	
80 = Fairly Good	c = Ready to drink
75 = Average	d = May be too old
70 = Below Average	NV = Non-vintage year
65 = Poor	? = Too soon; not rated yet

Wine Region	Recent Past Great Vintages (prior to 1991)
Bordeaux	
Médoc, Graves	1959, 1961, 1966, 1982, 1986, 1989
Pomerol, St.-Emilion	1961, 1964, 1970, 1975, 1982, 1989
Sauternes	1959, 1962, 1967, 1975, 1983, 1986, 1988, 1990
Burgundy	
Côte de Nuits, Red	1959, 1964, 1969, 1978, 1990
Côte de Beaune, Red	1959, 1969, 1990
Burgundy, White	1962, 1966, 1969, 1973, 1978, 1989

Wine Region	Recent Past Great Vintages (prior to 1991)
Rhône Valley	
Northern Rhône	1959, 1961, 1966, 1969, 1970, 1972 (Hermitage), 1978, 1989, 1990
Southern Rhône	1961, 1967, 1978, 1988, 1990
Other Wine Regions	
Alsace	1959, 1961, 1967, 1983, 1989, 1990
Champagne	1961, 1964, 1969, 1971, 1979, 1982, 1985, 1988
Germany	1959, 1971, 1976, 1988, 1989, 1990
Rioja (Spain)	1964, 1970, 1981, 1982, 1989
Vintage Port	1963, 1966, 1970, 1977, 1983
Italy	
Piedmont	1958, 1964, 1971, 1978, 1982, 1989
Tuscany	1967, 1970 (Brunello di Montalcino), 1971, 1985, 1988
California North Coast	
Cabernet Sauvignon	1951, 1958, 1968, 1970, 1974, 1978

Index

A

N

O

P

supertasters, 30

super-Tuscan wines, 190

süssreserve (sweet reserve) method, 214

Swartland district, South Africa, 279

sweet reserve method, 214

sweetness. *See also* dessert wines

    Champagne and sparkling wine, 285–286, 295–296

    food pairings, 127–128

    general discussion, 26, 30

    of German wines, 214

swirling wine in glasses, 20, 21

Syrah/Shiraz

    from Australia, 262–263

    from Chile, 274

    general discussion, 45–46

    from South Africa, 280

T

table wines, 16

tank fermentation, 287–288, 289–290

tannic wines, 127

tannin

    versus acidity, 28

    balance of wine, 30

    general discussion, 27

    overview, 12

    serving temperature, effect on, 13

    soft, 73

tartaric acid, 26

Tasmania, Australia, 267

tasting notes, 362–364

tasting wine

    aged wines, 341

    appearance, observing, 20

    aromas associated with wine, 24–25

    atmospheric pressure, effect on, 122

    describing taste, 25–29

    describing wines, 25–29

    overview, 19

    personal opinions, 30

    procedure for, 22–23

    quality of wine, 29–33

red Burgundy, 151

    in restaurants, 101

    rules of, 20

    smelling, 21–22

    subjective impressions, 384

    textural impressions, 23–24

    white Burgundy, 156

Taurasi, 196–197

Tavel wines, 164

tawny Port, 318

tears of wine, 20

Technical Stuff icon, 3

temperature control in fermentation, 72–73

temperature of wine, 11, 13, 119–120

Tempranillo, 47

Terrantez grape, 323

terroir

    in Australia, 262

    in Burgundy region, France, 149

    in England, 305

    in France, 134–136

    general discussion, 55, 65

    overview, 39

    in United States, 230, 239

textural impressions, 27, 364

Tignanello, 190

Timorasso, 183

Tinta Negra Mole grape, 324

Tip icon, 3

Tokaji Aszú, 224, 327–328

Tokaji Eszencia, 327–328

Toro region, Spain, 201, 207

Torres, 205

Torrontes, 275

traditional method for sparkling wine, 288–289

Trapiche, 277

Tre Venezie regions, Italy, 191–195

Trebbiano, 48

Trentino-Alto-Adige region, Italy, 193

trocken, 213

True Sonoma Coast, 239

trumpet glass, 116, 117

tulip glass, 116

About the Authors

Ed McCarthy and **Mary Ewing-Mulligan** are two wine lovers who met at an Italian wine tasting in New York City's Chinatown and subsequently merged their wine cellars and libraries when they married. They have coauthored 12 wine books in the *Wine For Dummies* series (including two of their favorites, *French Wine For Dummies* and *Italian Wine For Dummies*) as well as *Wine Style: Using Your Senses to Explore and Enjoy Wine* (Wiley); taught hundreds of wine classes together; visited nearly every wine region in the world; run five marathons; and raised 12 cats. Along the way, they have amassed well more than half a century of professional wine experience between them.

Mary is president of International Wine Center, a New York City wine school for wine professionals and serious wine lovers. She is also a wine journalist, having been the wine columnist of the *NY Daily News* for more than a decade, and having written for numerous periodicals. Mary's most impressive credential is that she became the first female Master of Wine (MW) in the United States, and is one of currently only 50 MWs resident in the U.S. and 380 worldwide.

Ed, a New Yorker, graduated from City University of New York with a master's degree in psychology. He taught high school English in another life, while working part-time in wine shops to satisfy his passion for wine and subsidize his growing wine cellar. That cellar is especially heavy in his favorite wines — Bordeaux, Barolo, and Champagne. Besides coauthoring 12 wine books with Mary, Ed went solo as author of *Champagne For Dummies*, a topic on which he's especially expert.

Ed also writes for *Beverage Media*, a trade publication. Both Ed and Mary are columnists for the online wine magazine *WineReviewOnline.com*, and both are accredited as Certified Wine Educators (CWE).

When they aren't writing, teaching, or visiting wine regions, Mary and Ed maintain a busy schedule of speaking, judging at professional wine competitions, and tasting as many new wines as possible. They admit to leading thoroughly unbalanced lives in which their only non-wine pursuits are hiking in the Berkshires and the Italian Alps. At home, they wind down to the tunes of U2, k.d. lang, Bob Dylan, and Neil Young, in the company of their feline roommates, Ponzi and Juliénas.

Dedication

We dedicate this book to all who have the courage to buy a book called *Wine For Dummies*. You are intelligent, not dummies, because you have the wisdom to realize that in the complex world of wine, everyone has something more to learn.

Authors' Acknowledgments

The wine world is dynamic — it's constantly changing. Because three years have passed since the sixth edition of *Wine For Dummies*, we are excited to revise and update the book. We especially felt an obligation to write this seventh edition because of all the readers who have personally told us how valuable *Wine For Dummies* has been to them over the years. We are grateful to have the opportunity to contribute to your knowledge of wine.

But this book would not have been possible without the team at Wiley. We sincerely thank Senior Acquisitions Editor Tracy Boggier, who engaged us to write the 7th edition of *Wine For Dummies*. Really special thanks goes to Chrissy Guthrie, our development editor and editorial project manager.

We thank our technical reviewer, Brian Freedman, for his expertise and his thoroughness in combing through our manuscript.

Special thanks to Steve Ettlinger, our agent and friend, who brought us to the *For Dummies* series in the first place and who is always there for us.

We thank all our friends in the wine business for your information and kind suggestions for our book; the reviewers, whose criticism has been so generous; and our readers, who have encouraged us with your enthusiasm for our previous books in this series.

Thanks also to Elise McCarthy, E.J. and Kim McCarthy, and Cindy McCarthy Tomarchio and her husband, David, for their encouragement and support.

Publisher's Acknowledgments

Senior Acquisitions Editor: Tracy Boggier

Editorial Project Editor and Development Editor:
Christina N. Guthrie

Technical Editor: Brian Freedman

Production Editor: Mohammed Zafar Ali

Illustrator: Lisa S. Reed

Cover Photos: © ansonmiao/iStockphoto